# You may be reading the wrong way!

In keeping with the original Japanese comic format, this book reads from right to left—so action, sound effects and word balloons are completely reversed. This preserves the orientation of the original artwork—plus, it's fun!

Check out the diagram shown here to get the hang of things, and then turn to the other side of the book to get started!

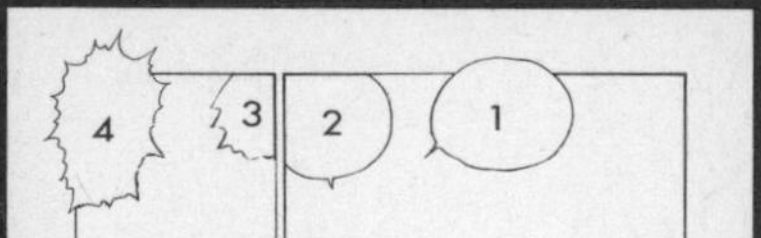
1
2
1
3
4
2
5
6
3
7
8
4
9
5
142

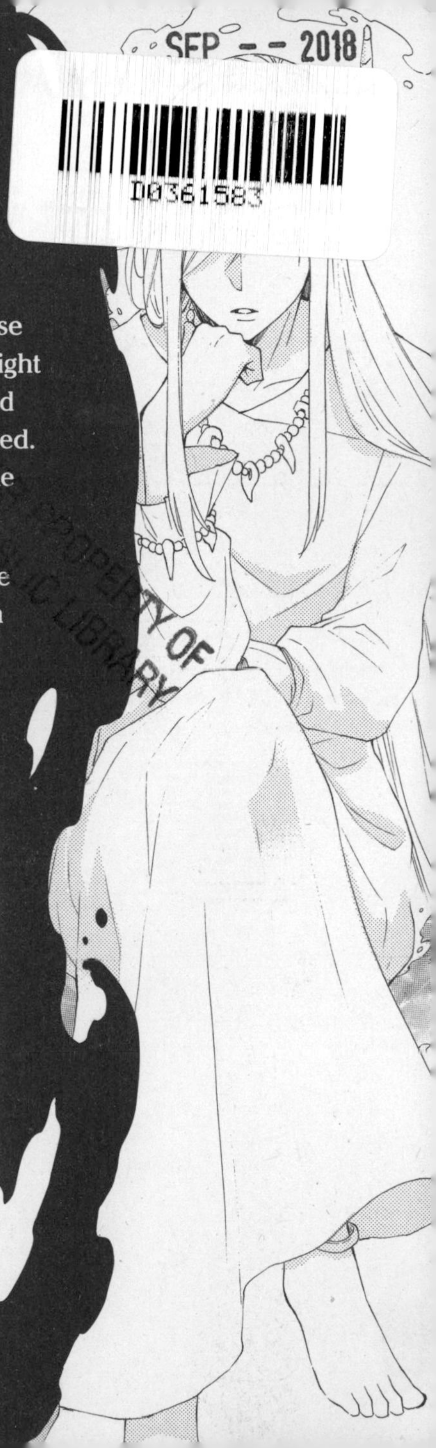

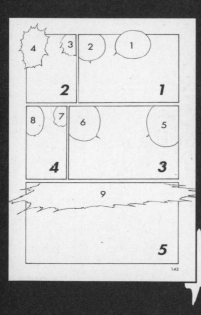

# QQ sweeper

Story & Art by
**Kyousuke Motomi**

## By the creator of *Dengeki Daisy* and *Beast Master*!

One day, Kyutaro Horikita, the tall,
dark and handsome cleaning expert
of Kurokado High, comes across a
sleeping maiden named Fumi Nishioka
at school… Unfortunately, their meeting
is anything but a fairy-tale encounter!
It turns out Kyutaro is a "Sweeper" who
cleans away negative energy from
people's hearts—and Fumi is about to
become his apprentice!

# The Water Dragon's Bride
## VOL. 6
Shojo Beat Edition

Story and Art by
# Rei Toma

SUIJIN NO HANAYOME Vol.6
by Rei TOMA
© 2015 Rei TOMA
All rights reserved.
Original Japanese edition published by SHOGAKUKAN.
English translation rights in the United States of America,
Canada, the United Kingdom, Ireland, Australia and New
Zealand arranged with SHOGAKUKAN.

ORIGINAL COVER DESIGN/Hibiki CHIKADA (fireworks.vc)

English Translation & Adaptation **Abby Lehrke**
Touch-Up Art & Lettering **Monaliza de Asis**
Design **Alice Lewis**
Editor **Amy Yu**

Printed in Canada

Published by VIZ Media, LLC
P.O. Box 77010
San Francisco, CA 94107

10 9 8 7 6 5 4 3 2 1
First printing, July 2018

viz.com

shojobeat.com

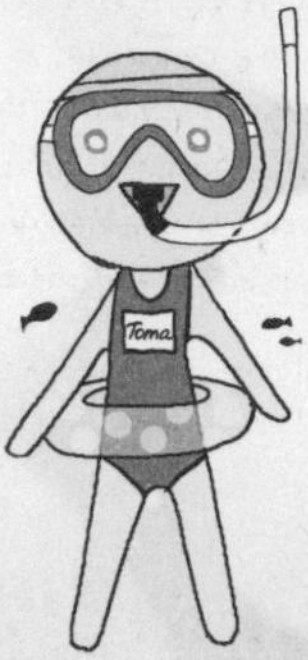
Toma

**This might seem somewhat random, but I've really gotten into shark movies lately. Sharks are so cute!**

– REI TOMA

Rei Toma has been drawing since childhood, and she created her first complete manga for a graduation project in design school. When she drew the short story manga "Help Me, Dentist," it attracted a publisher's attention and she made her debut right away. After she found success as a manga artist, acclaim in other art fields started to follow as she did illustrations for novels and video game character designs. She is also the creator of *Dawn of the Arcana*, available in North America from VIZ Media.

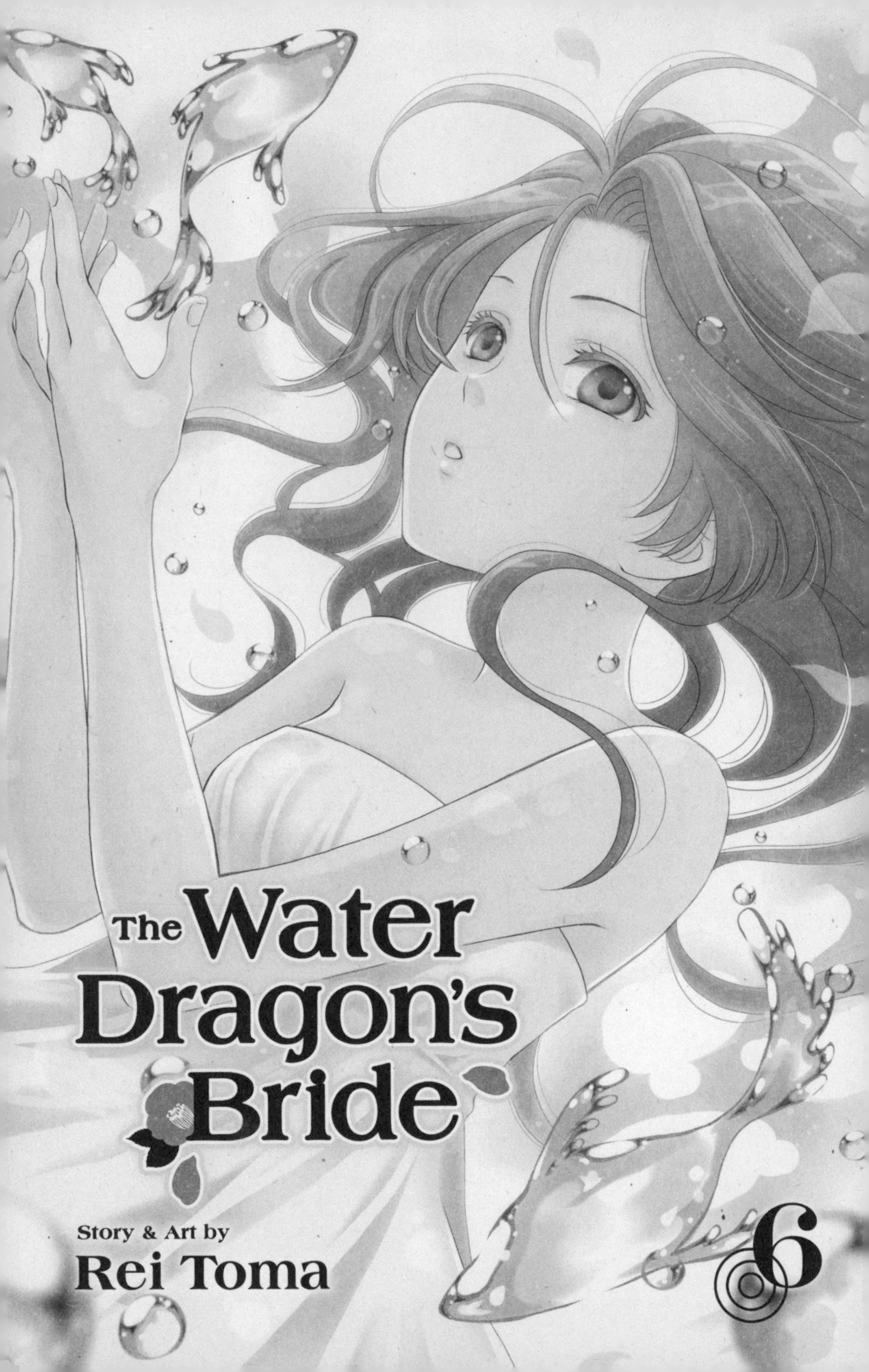
The Water Dragon's Bride
Story & Art by
Rei Toma
6

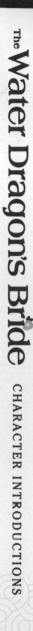

# The Water Dragon's Bride

## CHARACTER INTRODUCTIONS

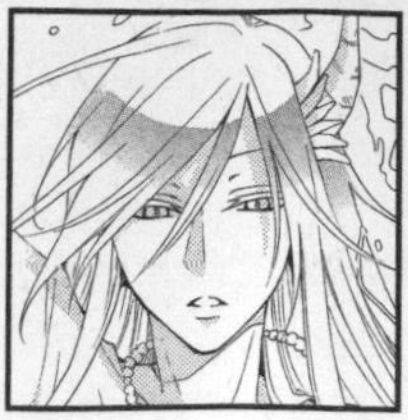

## The Water Dragon God

The god who rules over the waters. Though he hates humans, he seems to be intrigued by Asahi and feels compassion for her.

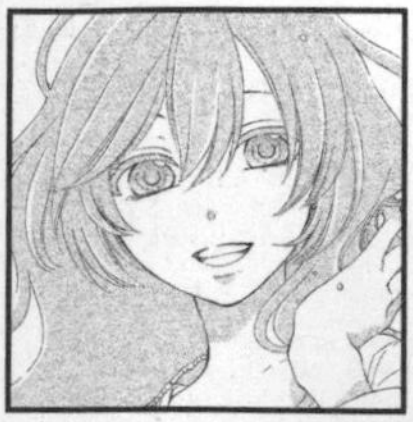

## Asahi

She was transported to another world when she was young. Subaru's mother sacrificed her to the water dragon god.

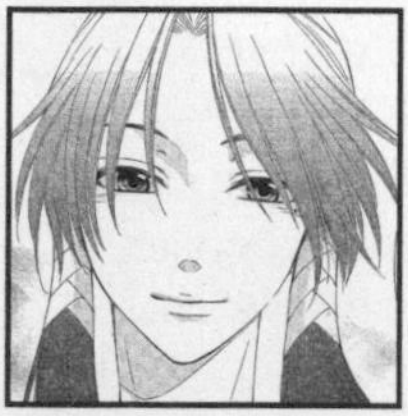

## Subaru

He is drawn to Asahi and has resolved to protect her.

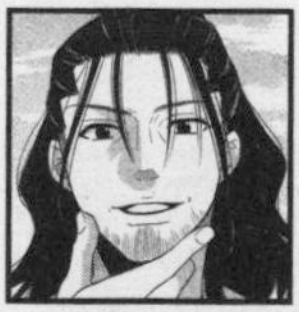

### Matori

The captain of the Imperial Defense Force. Subaru's instructor.

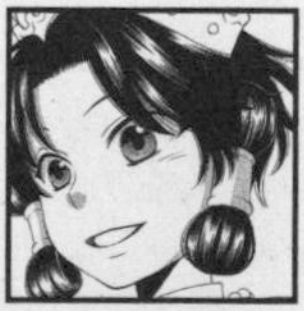

### The Emperor

A young boy, the emperor of the country of Naga.

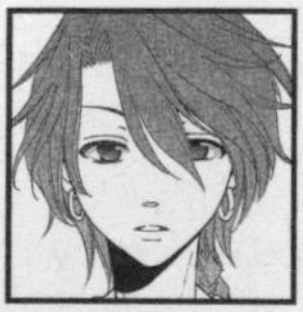

### Tsukihiko

Asahi's caretaker. He has the ability to sense people's thoughts and emotions.

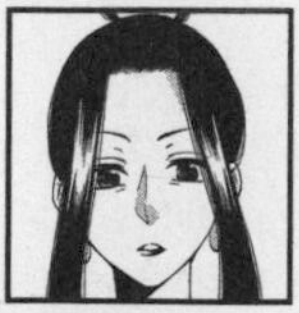

### Subaru's Mother

She despises Asahi.

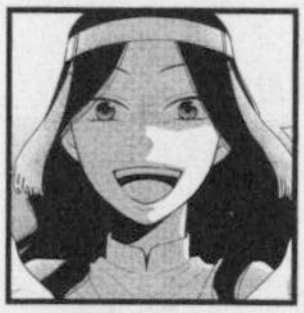

### Priestess

A priestess of Naga. She's scheming to gain the power of the water dragon god.

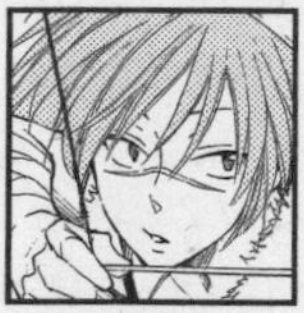

### Kogahiko

He's seeking the water dragon god's power by targeting Asahi.

# STORY THUS FAR

◎ Asahi is living a normal, sheltered life when she suddenly gets
pulled into a pond and is transported to a strange new world.
She gets sacrificed to a water dragon god, and he takes her voice
from her. Because of her connection to the water dragon god's
mysterious powers, Asahi is elevated to the position of priestess
in her village. She is unable to find a way to return home, and time
passes. As Asahi and the water dragon god spend time together,
their relationship begins to change.

◎ A man named Kogahiko starts a war against the village because
he wants to obtain Asahi's power. The water dragon god sees
that Asahi is miserable that a war has been started over her, so he
returns her voice and stops the war. He asks Asahi to marry him,
but she says the two of them don't have special feelings for one
another. In response, the water dragon god appears in human guise
and tells her he will live with her in the human world.

◎ The priestess of a village in Naga discovers the true nature of
the water dragon god and informs her country's emperor. The
emperor of Naga then approaches Asahi and orders her to lend
him the power of the water dragon god. Asahi's persuasive ability
allows her to escape without issue, but Kogahiko tries to kidnap
her again. The water dragon god and Asahi's friends rescue her,
and Tsukihiko, whose mother was in the same situation as Asahi
before, attempts to trade his life for Asahi's freedom.

◎ Asahi discovers Tsukihiko's secret and comes to understand his
feelings, but she doesn't want anyone to sacrifice themselves for her.
Accompanied by Subaru and the water dragon god, Asahi decides
to go live with the emperor of Naga. But unexpectedly, the emperor
asks Asahi to be his bride! At first, the water dragon god is indifferent,
but are feelings of jealousy starting to emerge inside of him?

# The Water Dragon's Bride

# CONTENTS

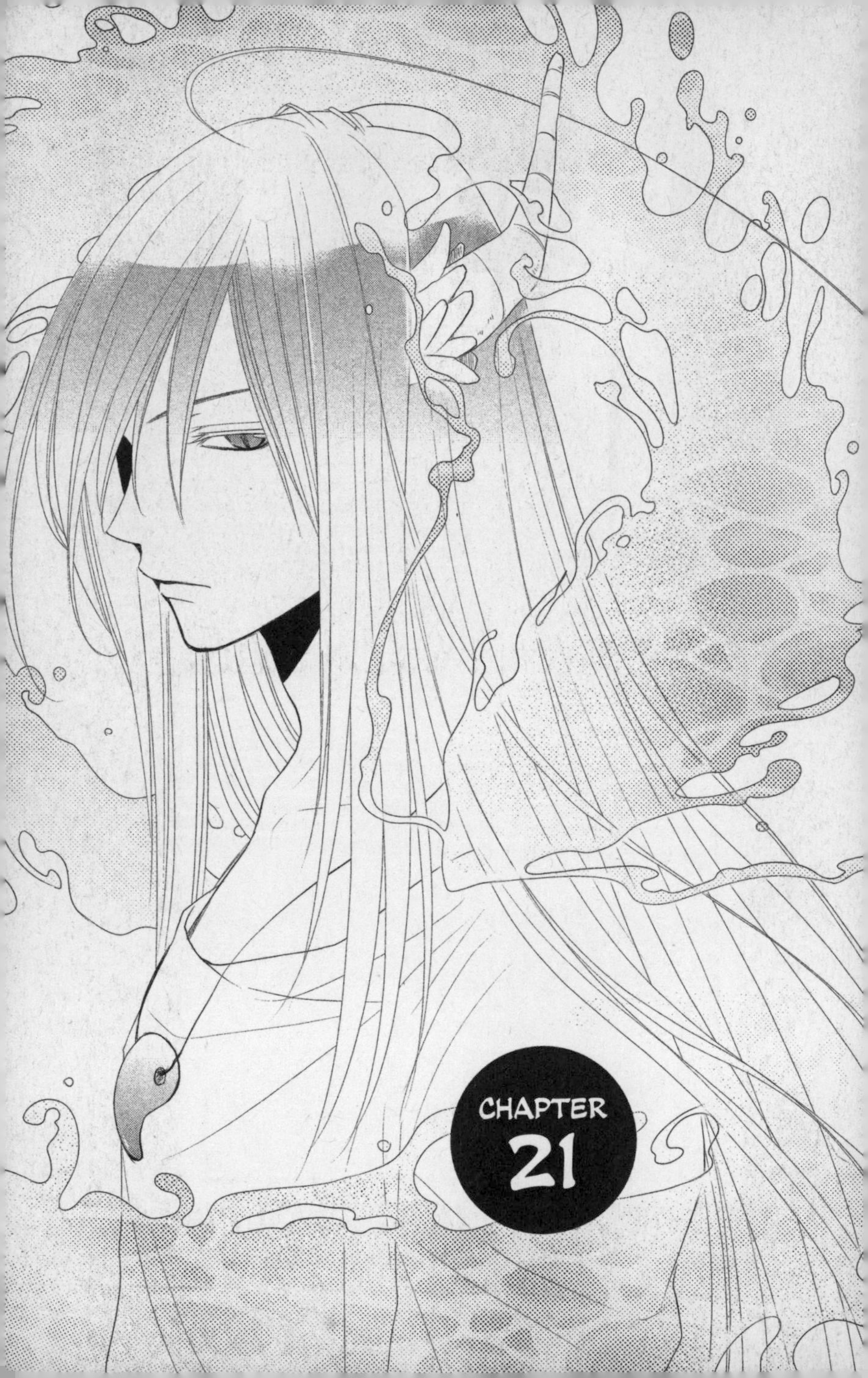
CHAPTER
21

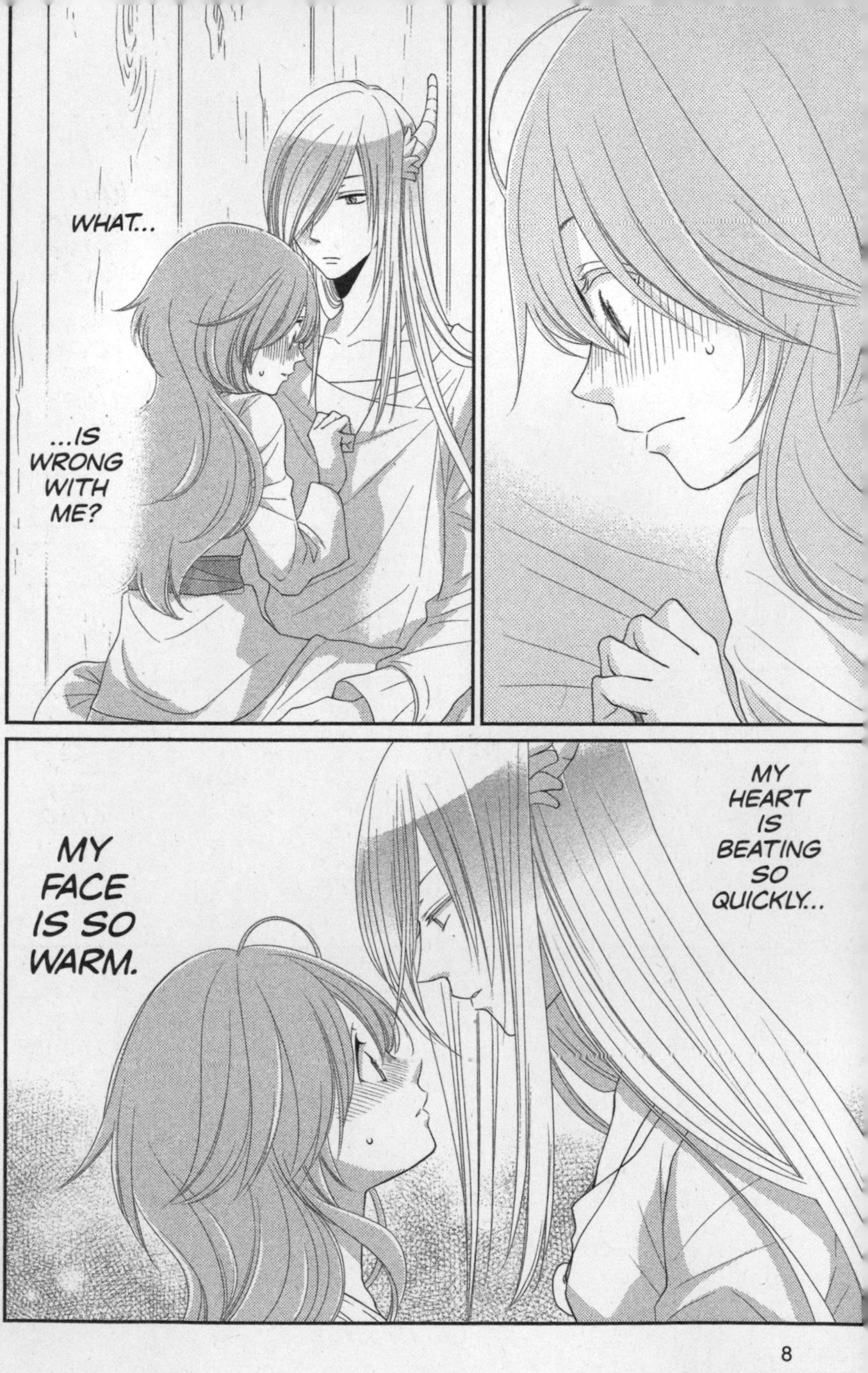
WHAT...
...IS WRONG WITH ME?
MY HEART IS BEATING SO QUICKLY...
MY FACE IS SO WARM.

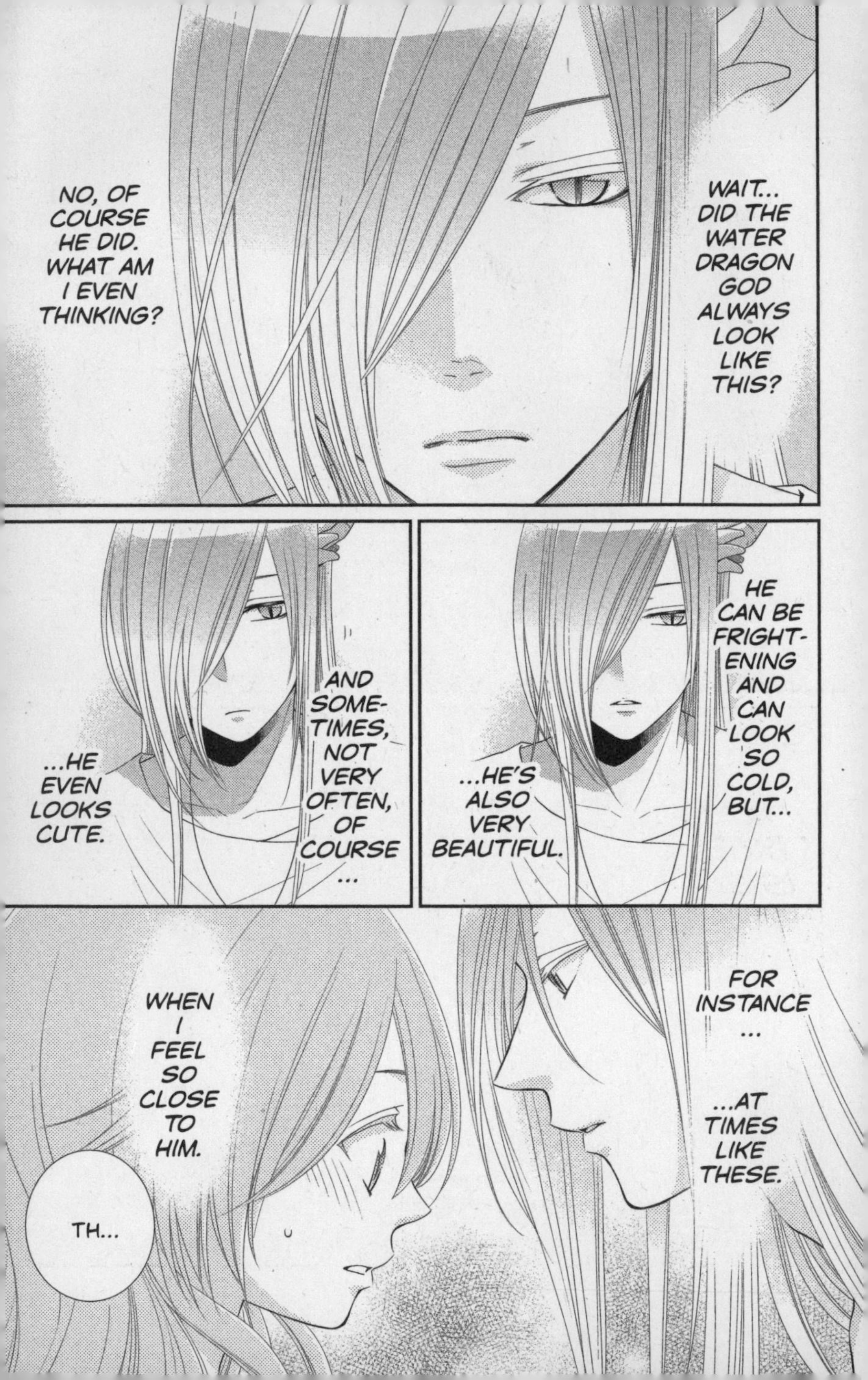
WAIT... DID THE WATER DRAGON GOD ALWAYS LOOK LIKE THIS?
NO, OF COURSE HE DID. WHAT AM I EVEN THINKING?
HE CAN BE FRIGHT-ENING AND CAN LOOK SO COLD, BUT...
...HE'S ALSO VERY BEAUTIFUL.
AND SOME-TIMES, NOT VERY OFTEN, OF COURSE...
...HE EVEN LOOKS CUTE.
FOR INSTANCE...
...AT TIMES LIKE THESE.
WHEN I FEEL SO CLOSE TO HIM.
TH...

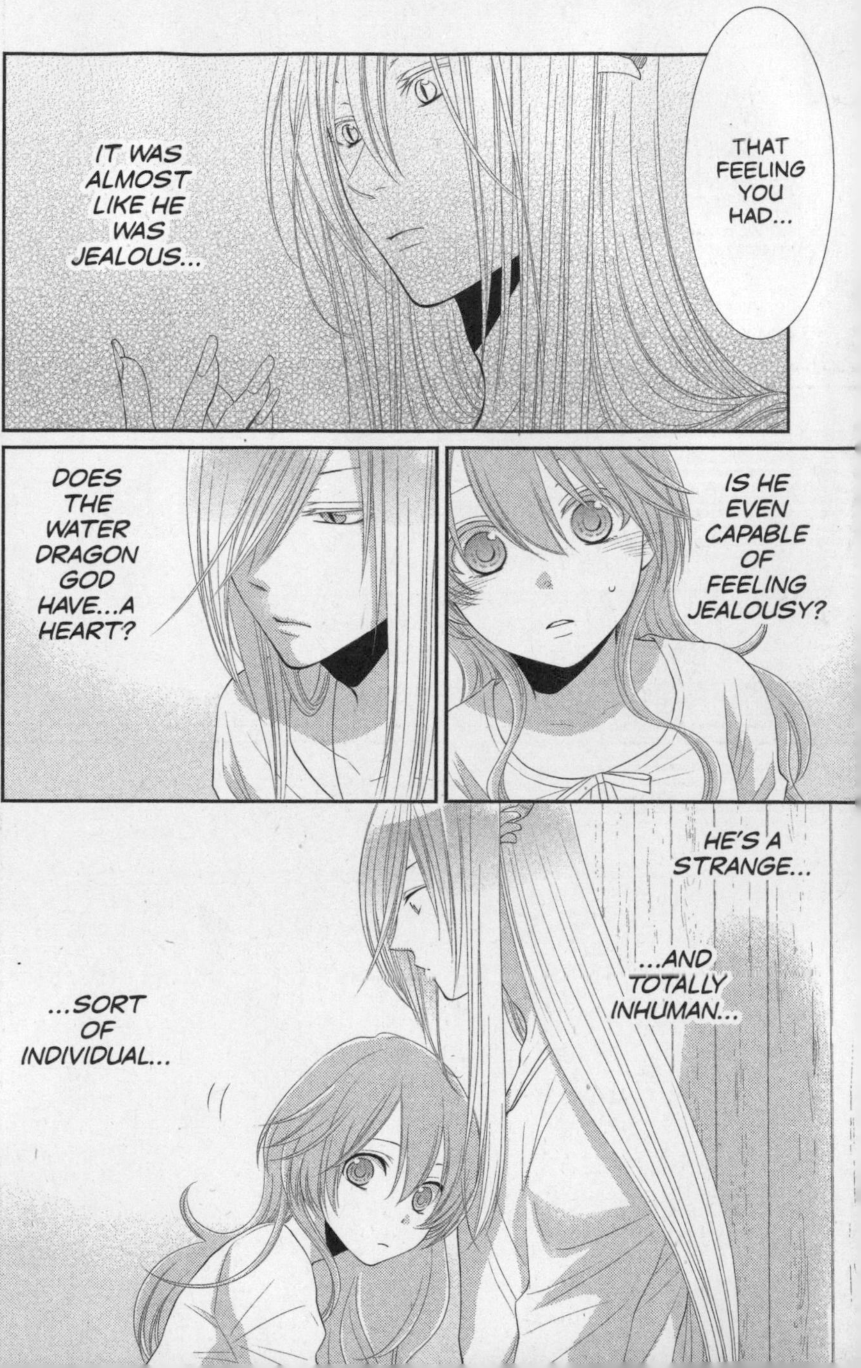
THAT FEELING YOU HAD...
IT WAS ALMOST LIKE HE WAS JEALOUS...
IS HE EVEN CAPABLE OF FEELING JEALOUSY?
DOES THE WATER DRAGON GOD HAVE...A HEART?
HE'S A STRANGE...
...AND TOTALLY INHUMAN...
...SORT OF INDIVIDUAL...

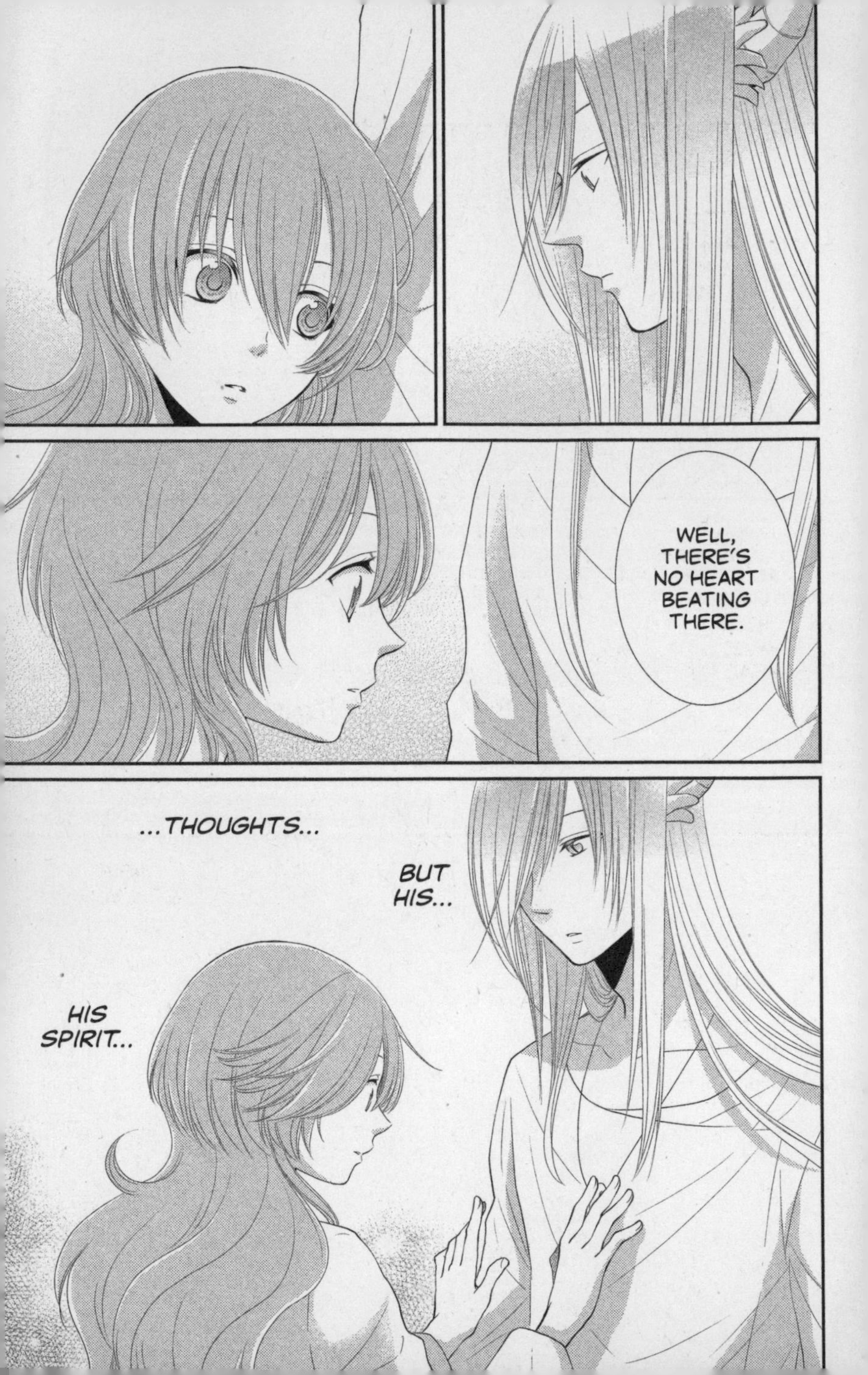
WELL, THERE'S NO HEART BEATING THERE.
BUT HIS...
...THOUGHTS...
HIS SPIRIT...

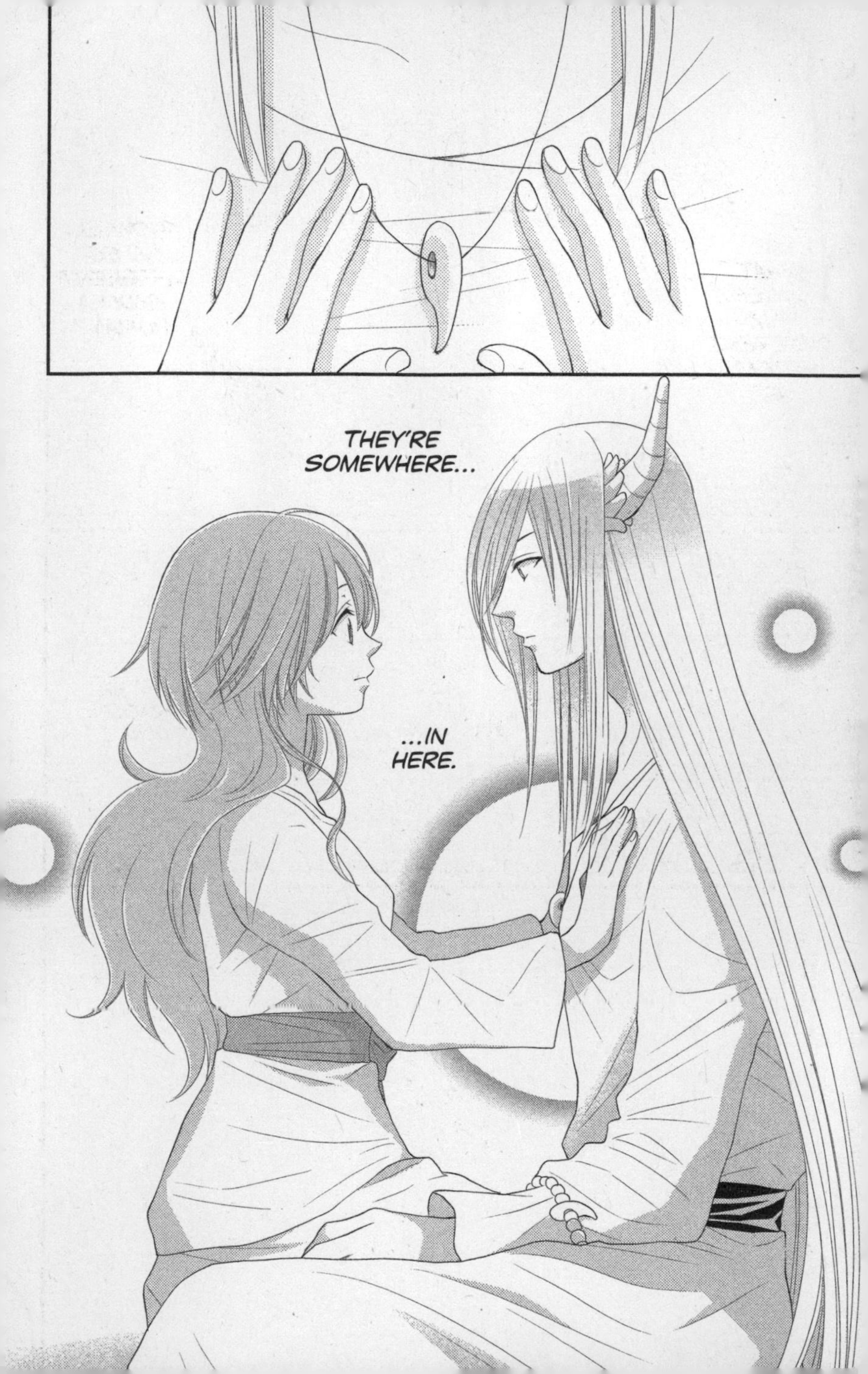
THEY'RE SOMEWHERE...
...IN HERE.

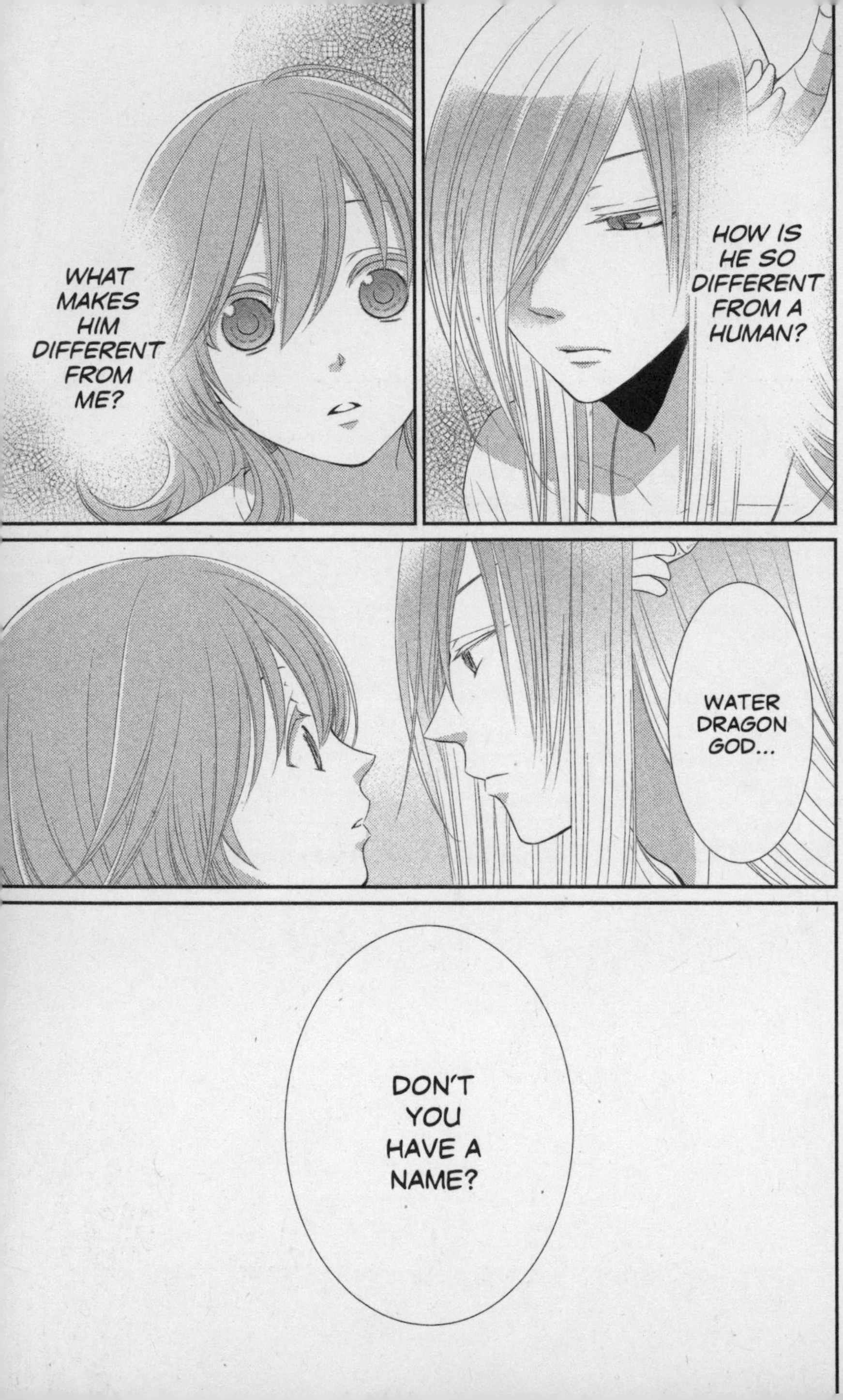
HOW IS HE SO DIFFERENT FROM A HUMAN?
WHAT MAKES HIM DIFFERENT FROM ME?
WATER DRAGON GOD...
DON'T YOU HAVE A NAME?

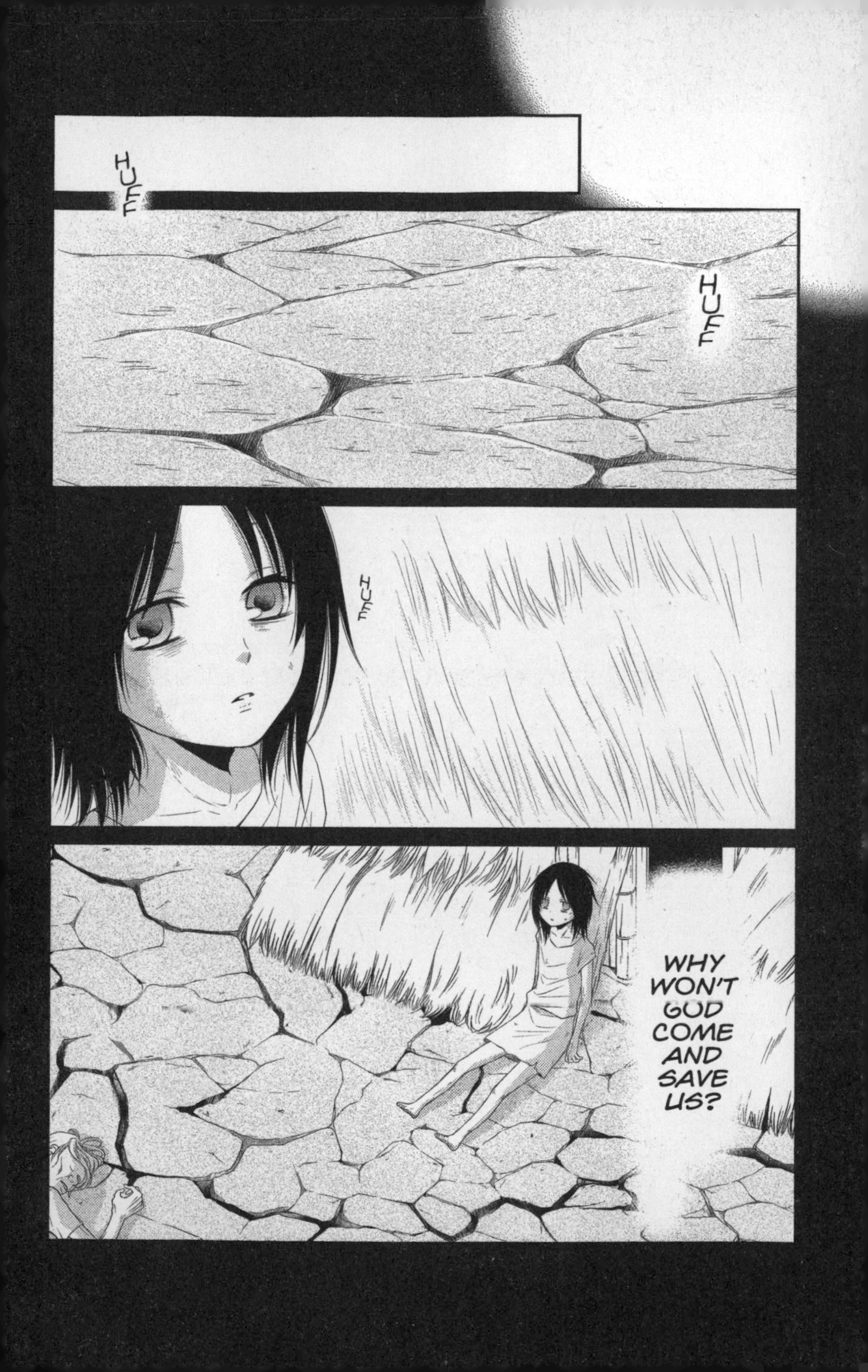
HUFF
HUFF
HUFF
WHY WON'T GOD COME AND SAVE US?

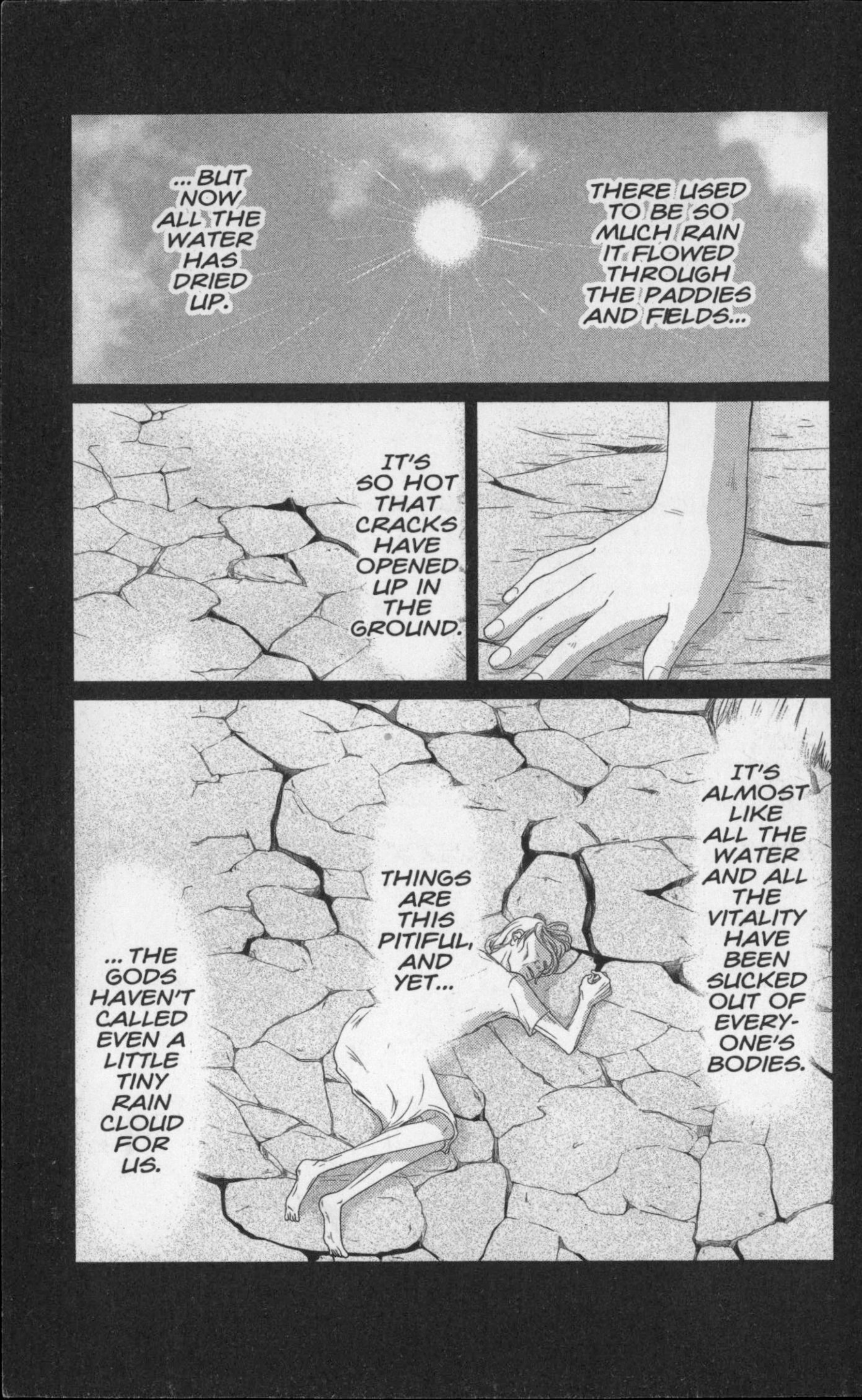
THERE USED TO BE SO MUCH RAIN IT FLOWED THROUGH THE PADDIES AND FIELDS...
...BUT NOW ALL THE WATER HAS DRIED UP.
IT'S SO HOT THAT CRACKS HAVE OPENED UP IN THE GROUND.
IT'S ALMOST LIKE ALL THE WATER AND ALL THE VITALITY HAVE BEEN SUCKED OUT OF EVERY-ONE'S BODIES.
THINGS ARE THIS PITIFUL, AND YET...
...THE GODS HAVEN'T CALLED EVEN A LITTLE TINY RAIN CLOUD FOR US.

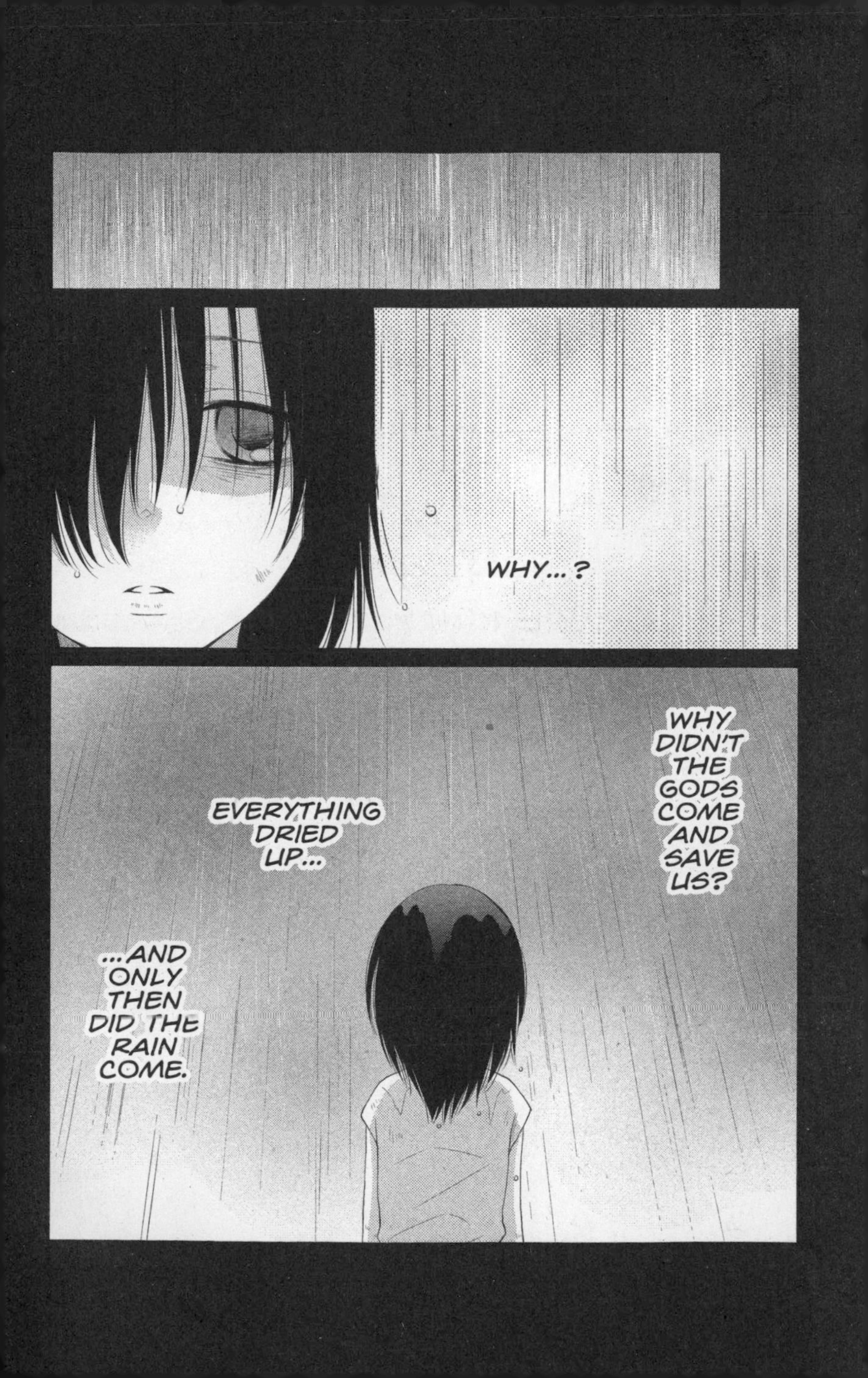
WHY...?
WHY DIDN'T THE GODS COME AND SAVE US?
EVERYTHING DRIED UP...
...AND ONLY THEN DID THE RAIN COME.

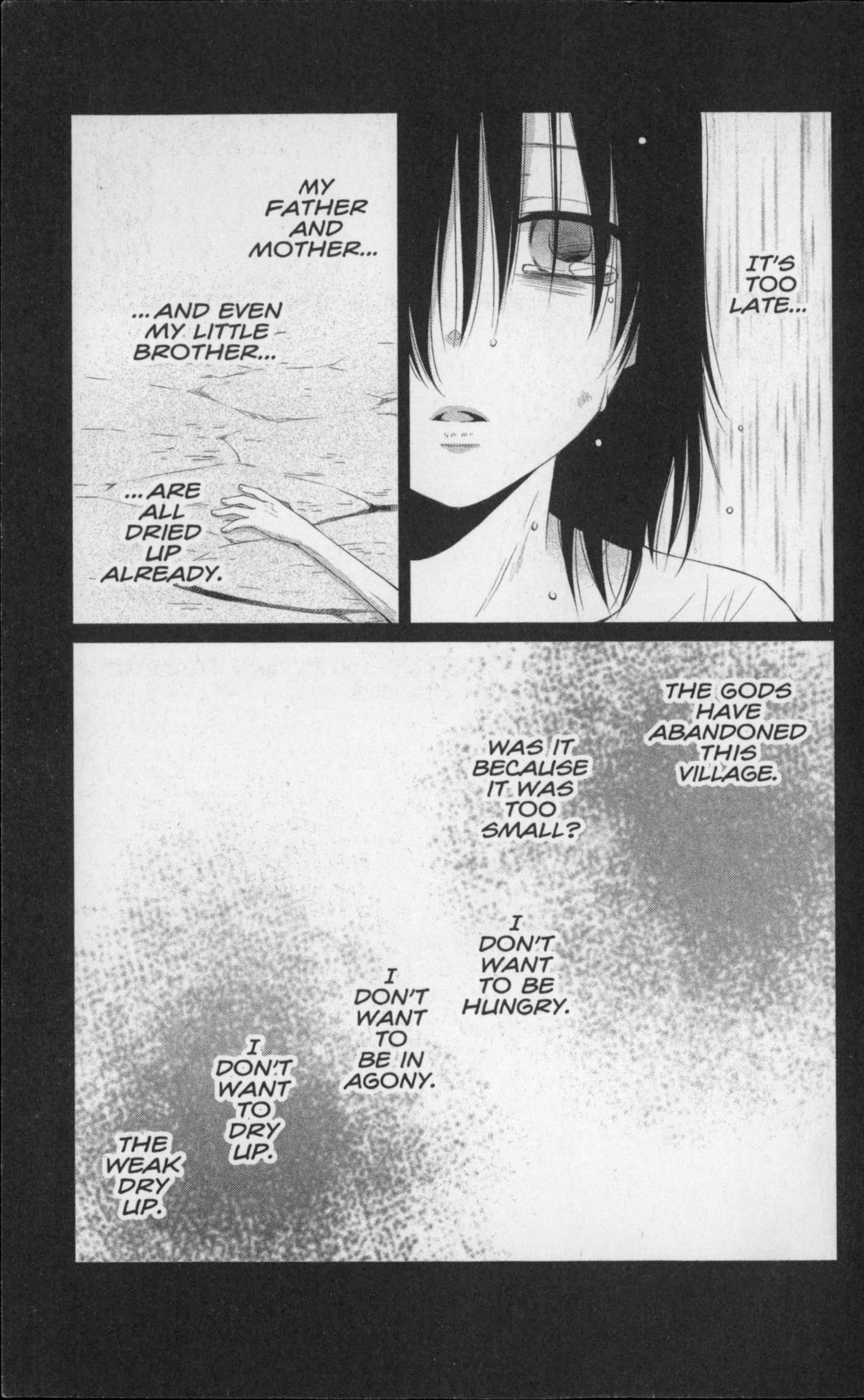
IT'S TOO LATE...
MY FATHER AND MOTHER...
...AND EVEN MY LITTLE BROTHER...
...ARE ALL DRIED UP ALREADY.
THE GODS HAVE ABANDONED THIS VILLAGE.
WAS IT BECAUSE IT WAS TOO SMALL?
I DON'T WANT TO BE HUNGRY.
I DON'T WANT TO BE IN AGONY.
I DON'T WANT TO DRY UP.
THE WEAK DRY UP.

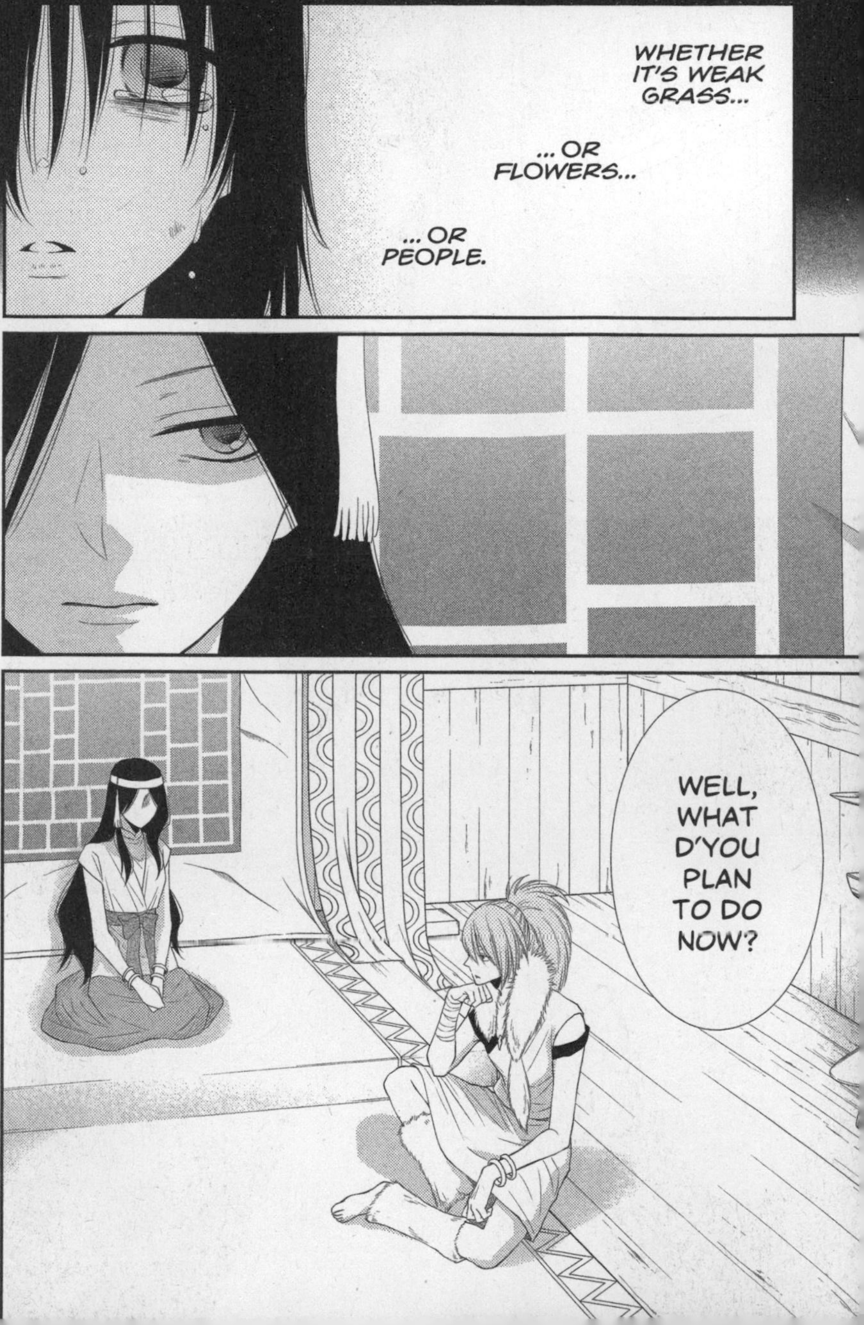
WHETHER IT'S WEAK GRASS...
...OR FLOWERS...
...OR PEOPLE.
WELL, WHAT D'YOU PLAN TO DO NOW?

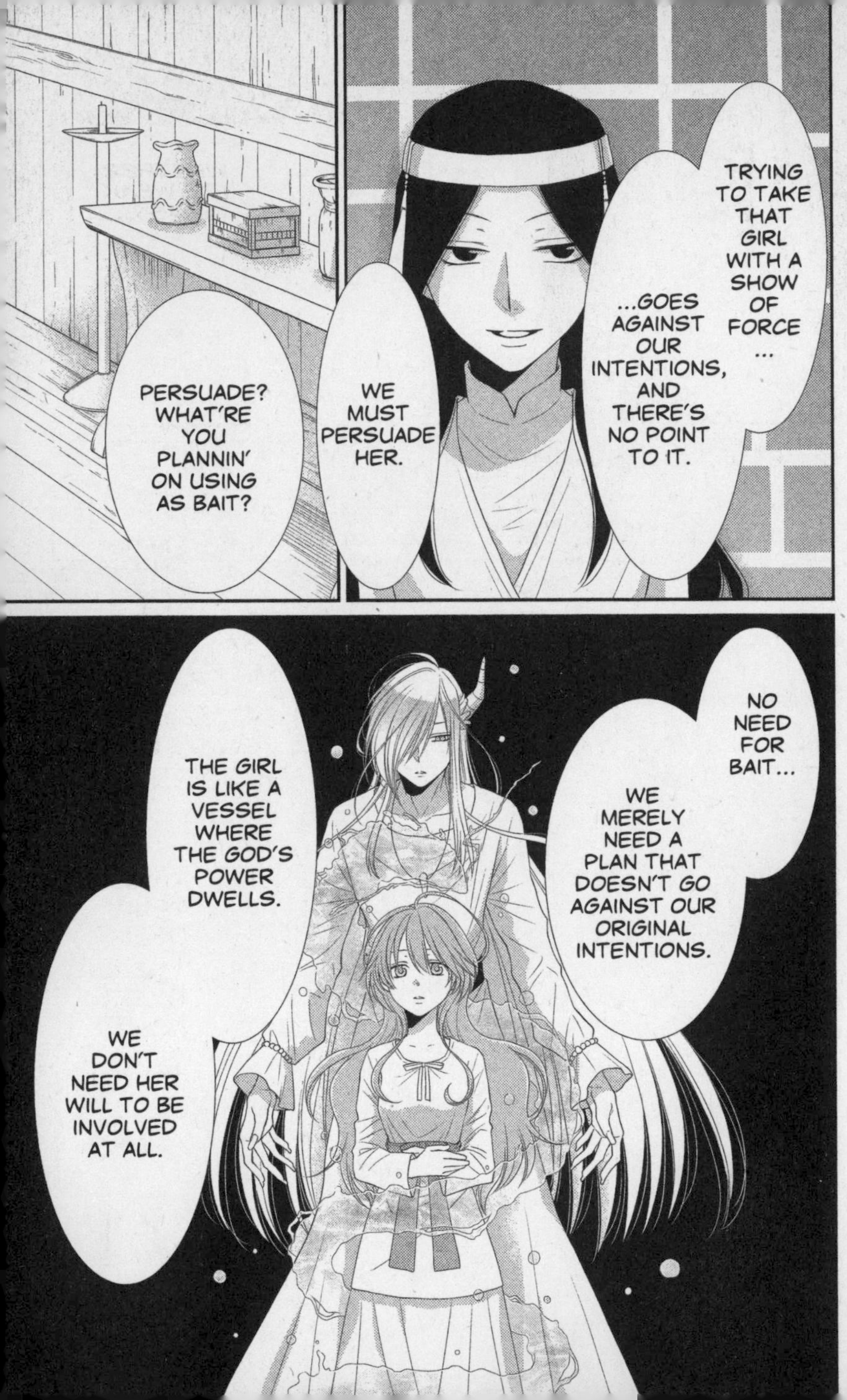
TRYING TO TAKE THAT GIRL WITH A SHOW OF FORCE...
...GOES AGAINST OUR INTENTIONS, AND THERE'S NO POINT TO IT.
WE MUST PERSUADE HER.
PERSUADE? WHAT'RE YOU PLANNIN' ON USING AS BAIT?
NO NEED FOR BAIT...
WE MERELY NEED A PLAN THAT DOESN'T GO AGAINST OUR ORIGINAL INTENTIONS.
THE GIRL IS LIKE A VESSEL WHERE THE GOD'S POWER DWELLS.
WE DON'T NEED HER WILL TO BE INVOLVED AT ALL.

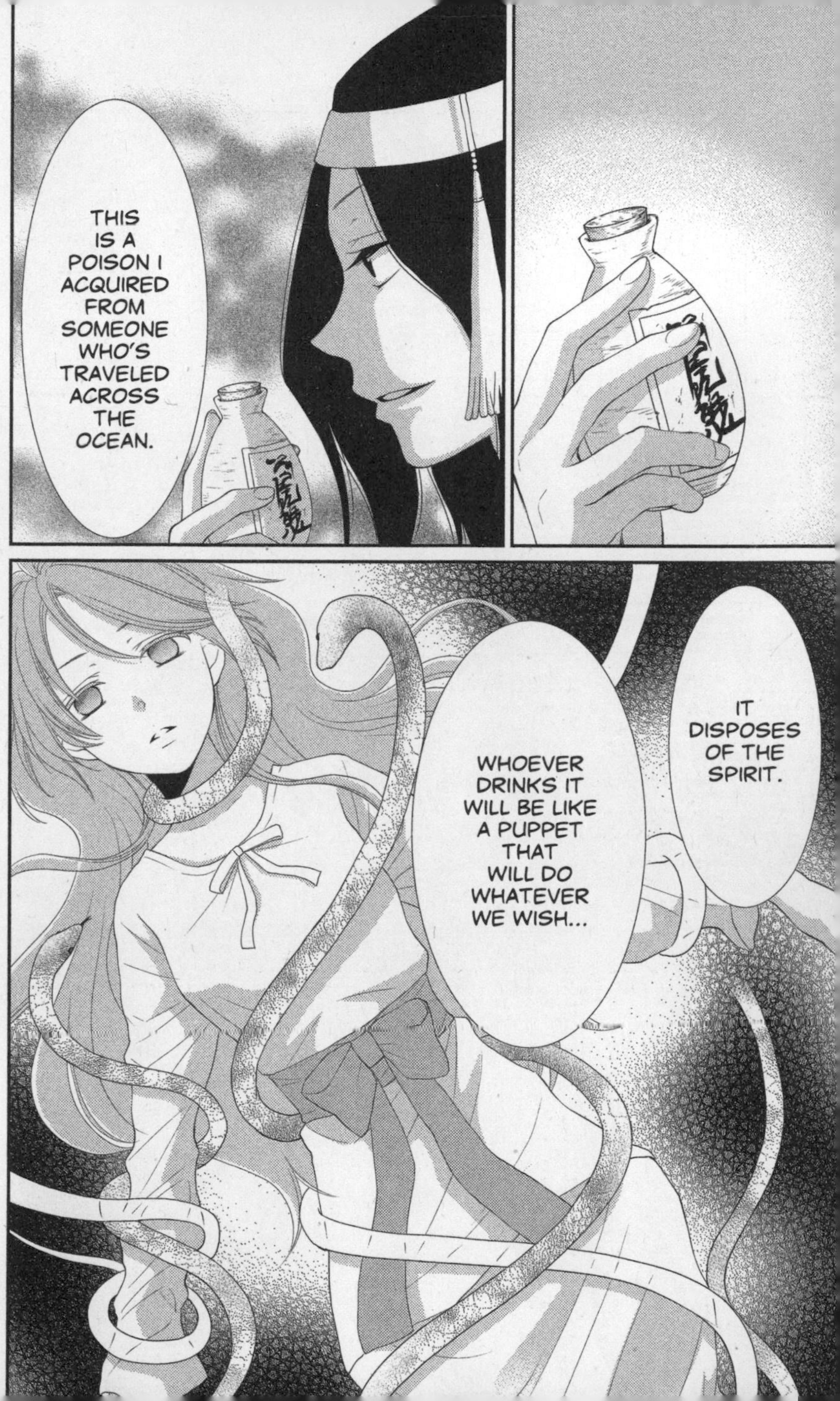
THIS IS A POISON I ACQUIRED FROM SOMEONE WHO'S TRAVELED ACROSS THE OCEAN.
IT DISPOSES OF THE SPIRIT.
WHOEVER DRINKS IT WILL BE LIKE A PUPPET THAT WILL DO WHATEVER WE WISH...

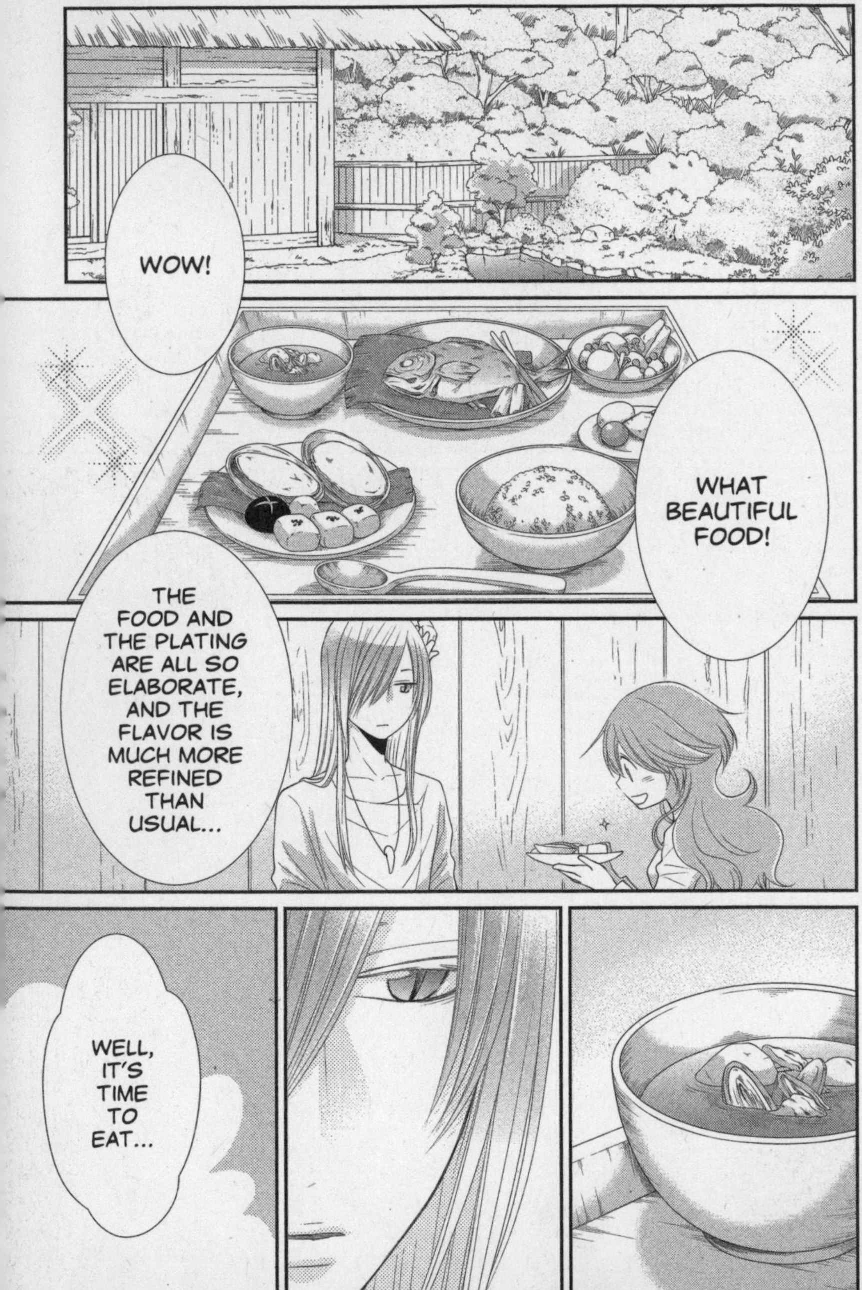
WOW!
WHAT BEAUTIFUL FOOD!
THE FOOD AND THE PLATING ARE ALL SO ELABORATE, AND THE FLAVOR IS MUCH MORE REFINED THAN USUAL...
WELL, IT'S TIME TO EAT...

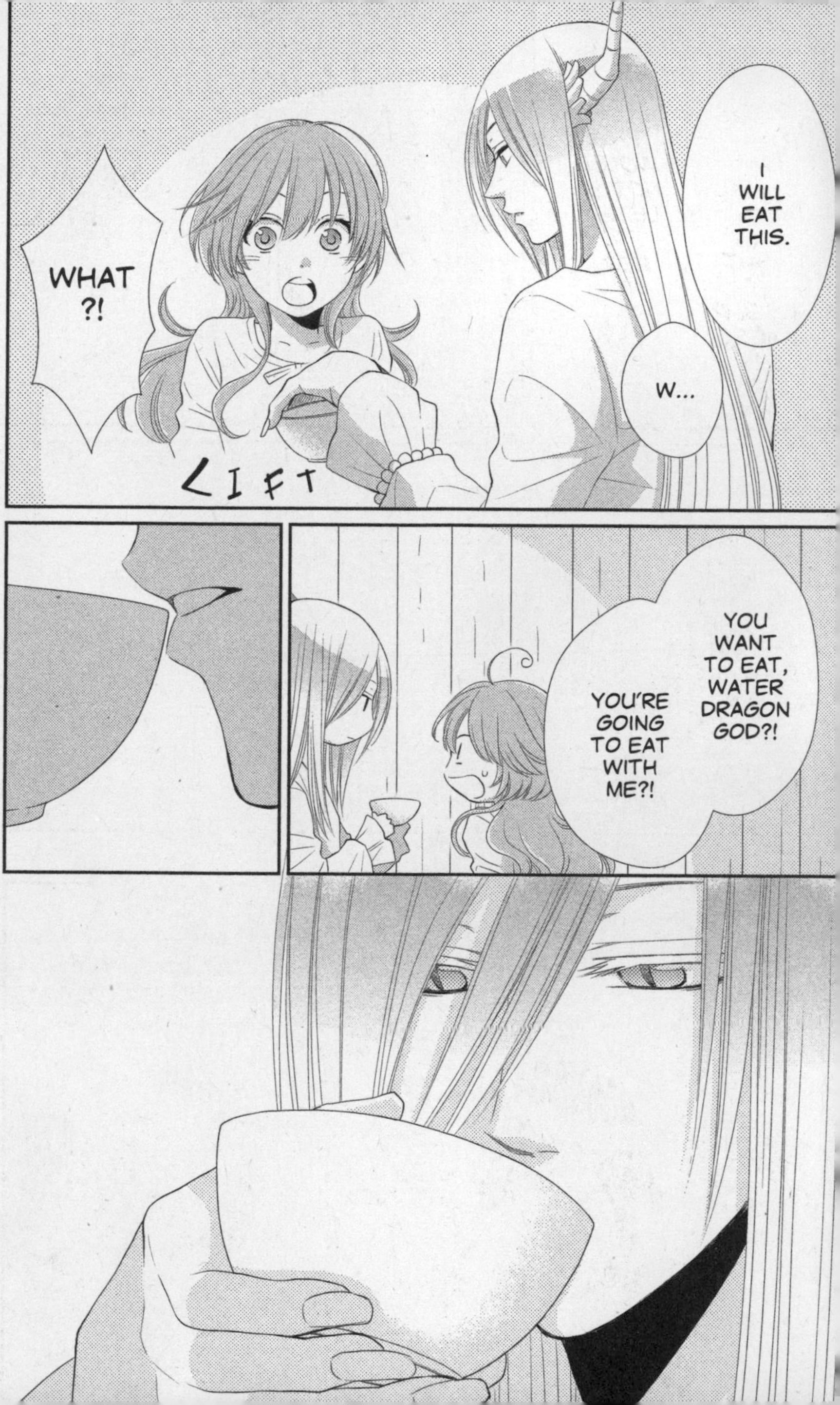
I WILL EAT THIS.
W...
WHAT?!
LIFT
YOU WANT TO EAT, WATER DRAGON GOD?!
YOU'RE GOING TO EAT WITH ME?!

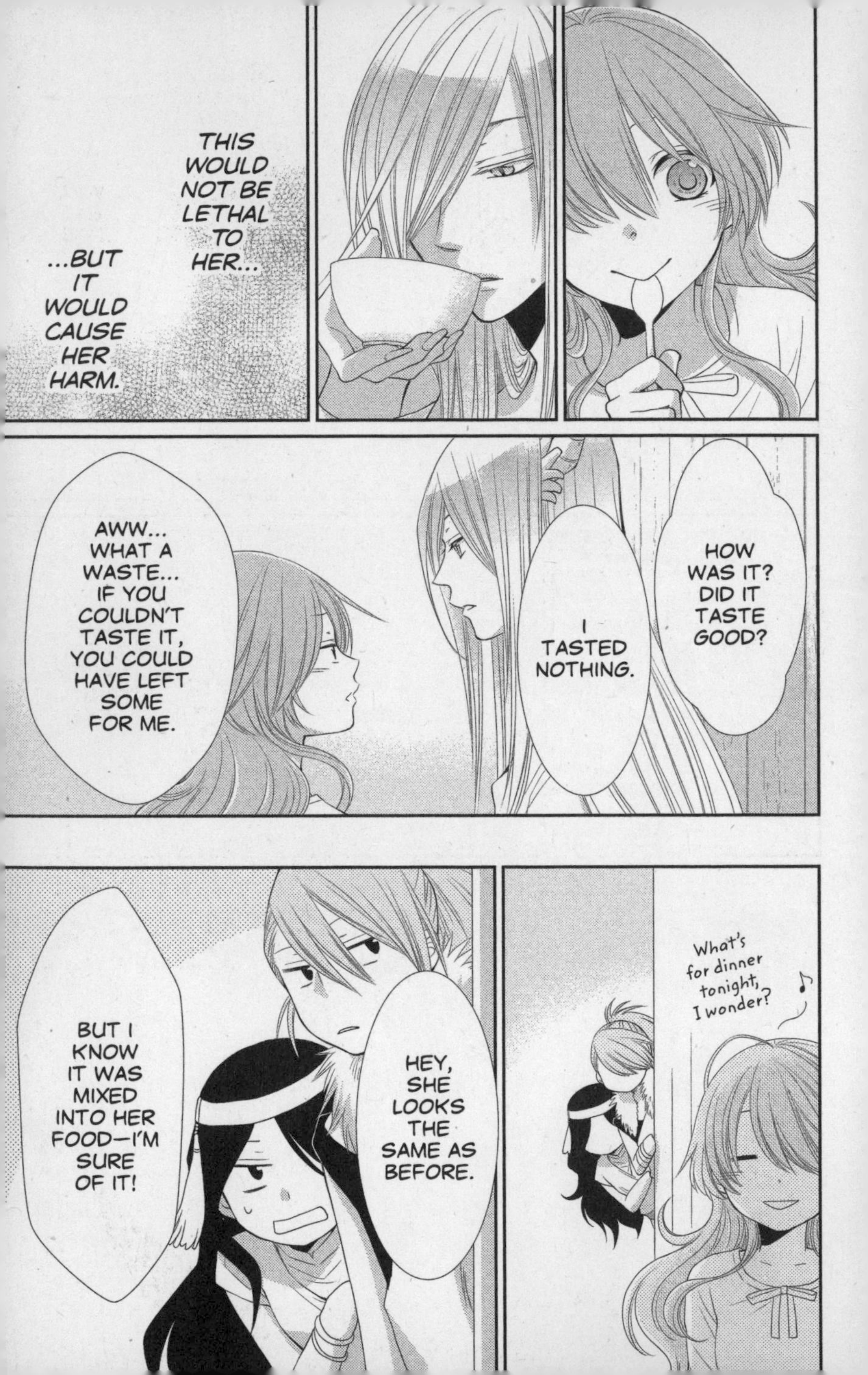
THIS WOULD NOT BE LETHAL TO HER...
...BUT IT WOULD CAUSE HER HARM.
HOW WAS IT? DID IT TASTE GOOD?
I TASTED NOTHING.
AWW... WHAT A WASTE... IF YOU COULDN'T TASTE IT, YOU COULD HAVE LEFT SOME FOR ME.
What's for dinner tonight, I wonder? ♪
HEY, SHE LOOKS THE SAME AS BEFORE.
BUT I KNOW IT WAS MIXED INTO HER FOOD—I'M SURE OF IT!

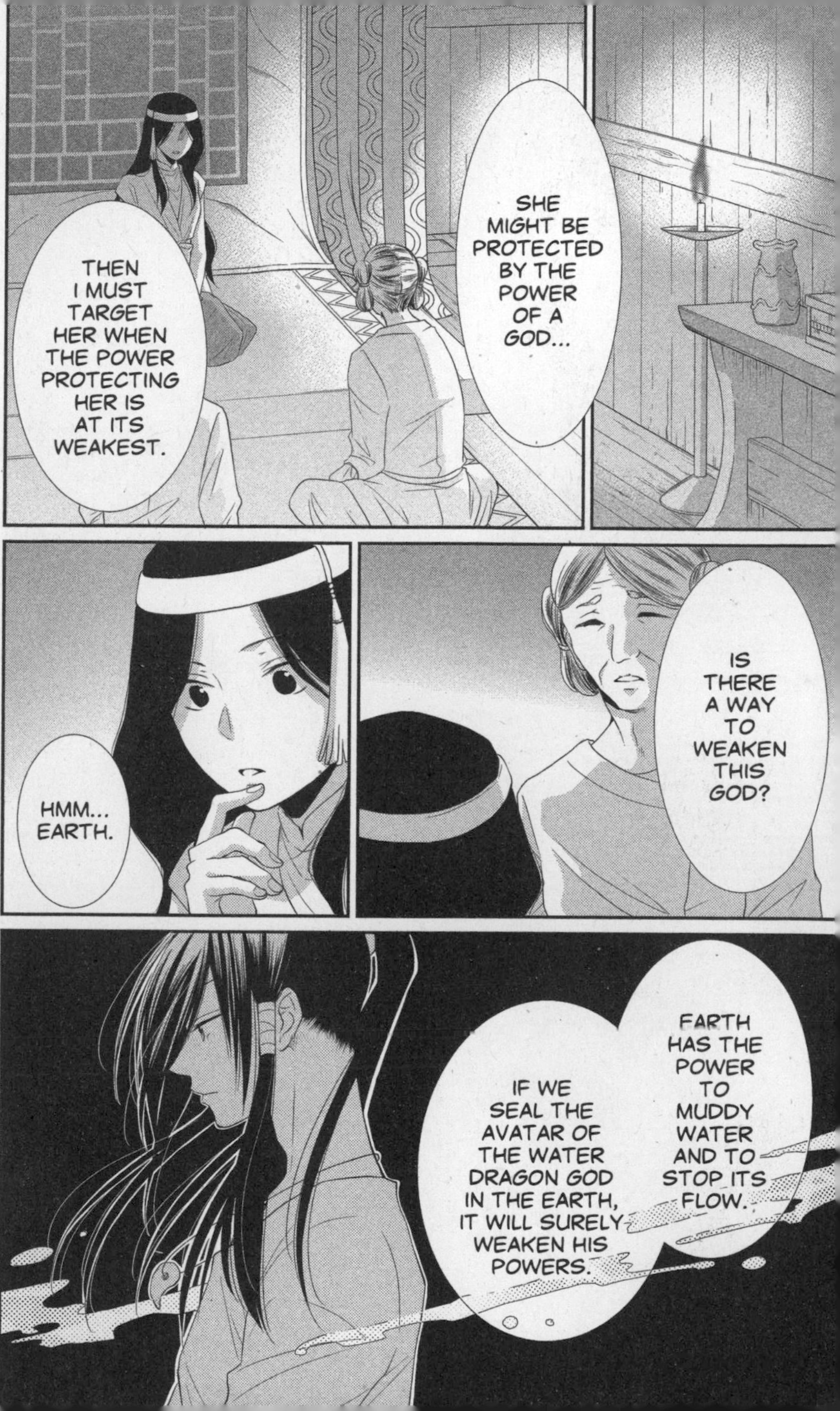
SHE MIGHT BE PROTECTED BY THE POWER OF A GOD...
THEN I MUST TARGET HER WHEN THE POWER PROTECTING HER IS AT ITS WEAKEST.
IS THERE A WAY TO WEAKEN THIS GOD?
HMM... EARTH.
EARTH HAS THE POWER TO MUDDY WATER AND TO STOP ITS FLOW.
IF WE SEAL THE AVATAR OF THE WATER DRAGON GOD IN THE EARTH, IT WILL SURELY WEAKEN HIS POWERS.

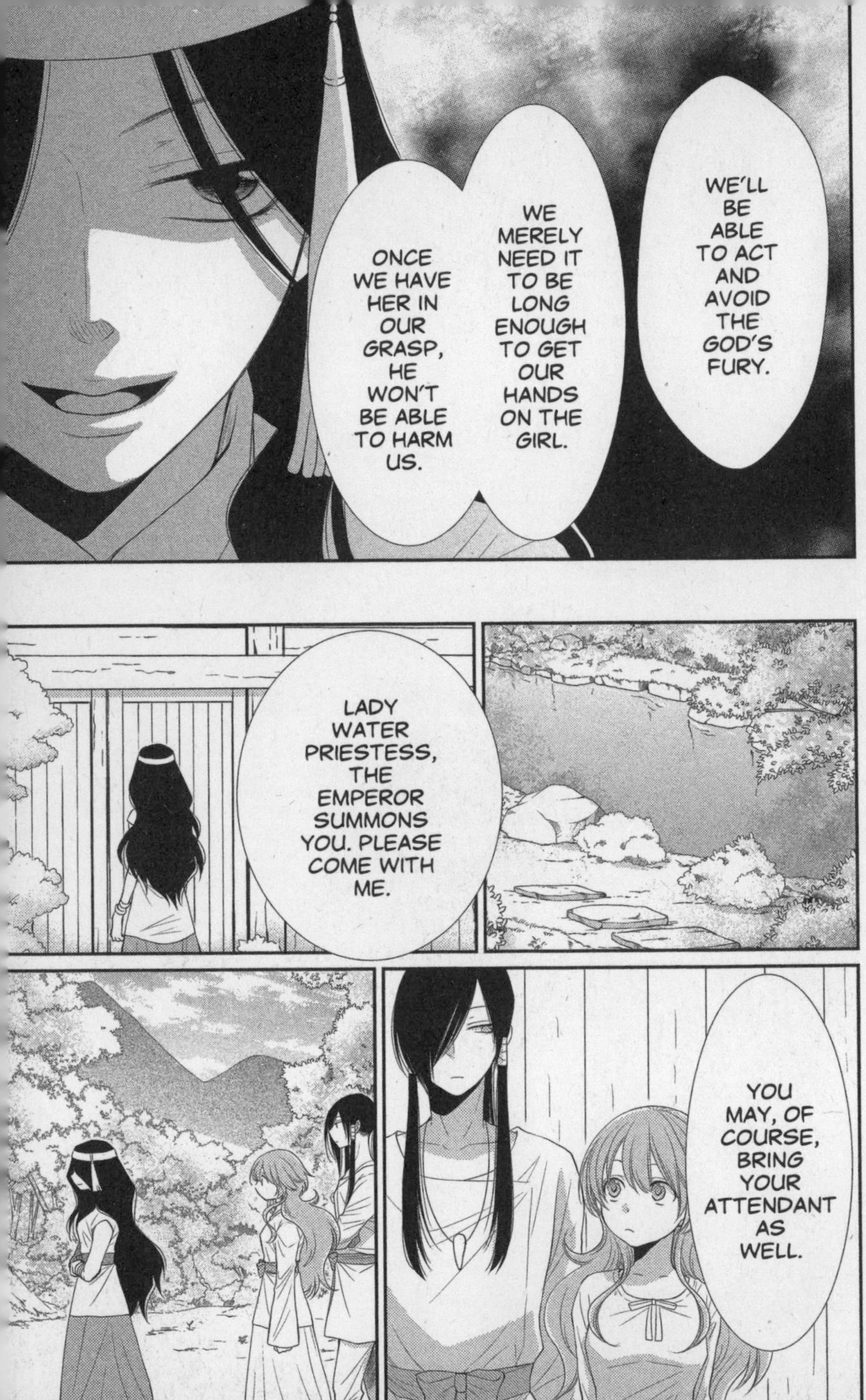
WE'LL BE ABLE TO ACT AND AVOID THE GOD'S FURY.
WE MERELY NEED IT TO BE LONG ENOUGH TO GET OUR HANDS ON THE GIRL.
ONCE WE HAVE HER IN OUR GRASP, HE WON'T BE ABLE TO HARM US.
LADY WATER PRIESTESS, THE EMPEROR SUMMONS YOU. PLEASE COME WITH ME.
YOU MAY, OF COURSE, BRING YOUR ATTENDANT AS WELL.

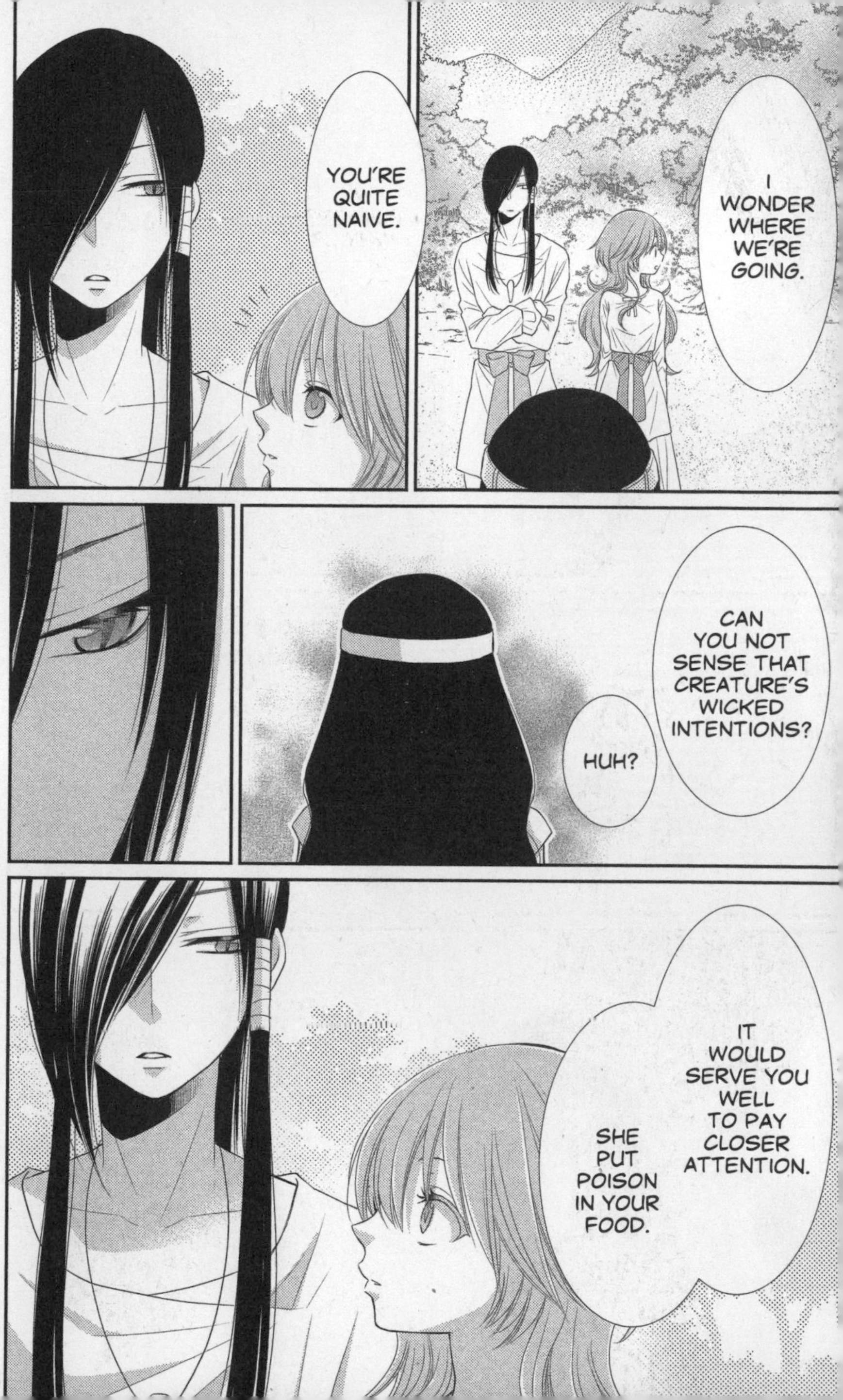
I WONDER WHERE WE'RE GOING.
YOU'RE QUITE NAIVE.
CAN YOU NOT SENSE THAT CREATURE'S WICKED INTENTIONS?
HUH?
IT WOULD SERVE YOU WELL TO PAY CLOSER ATTENTION.
SHE PUT POISON IN YOUR FOOD.

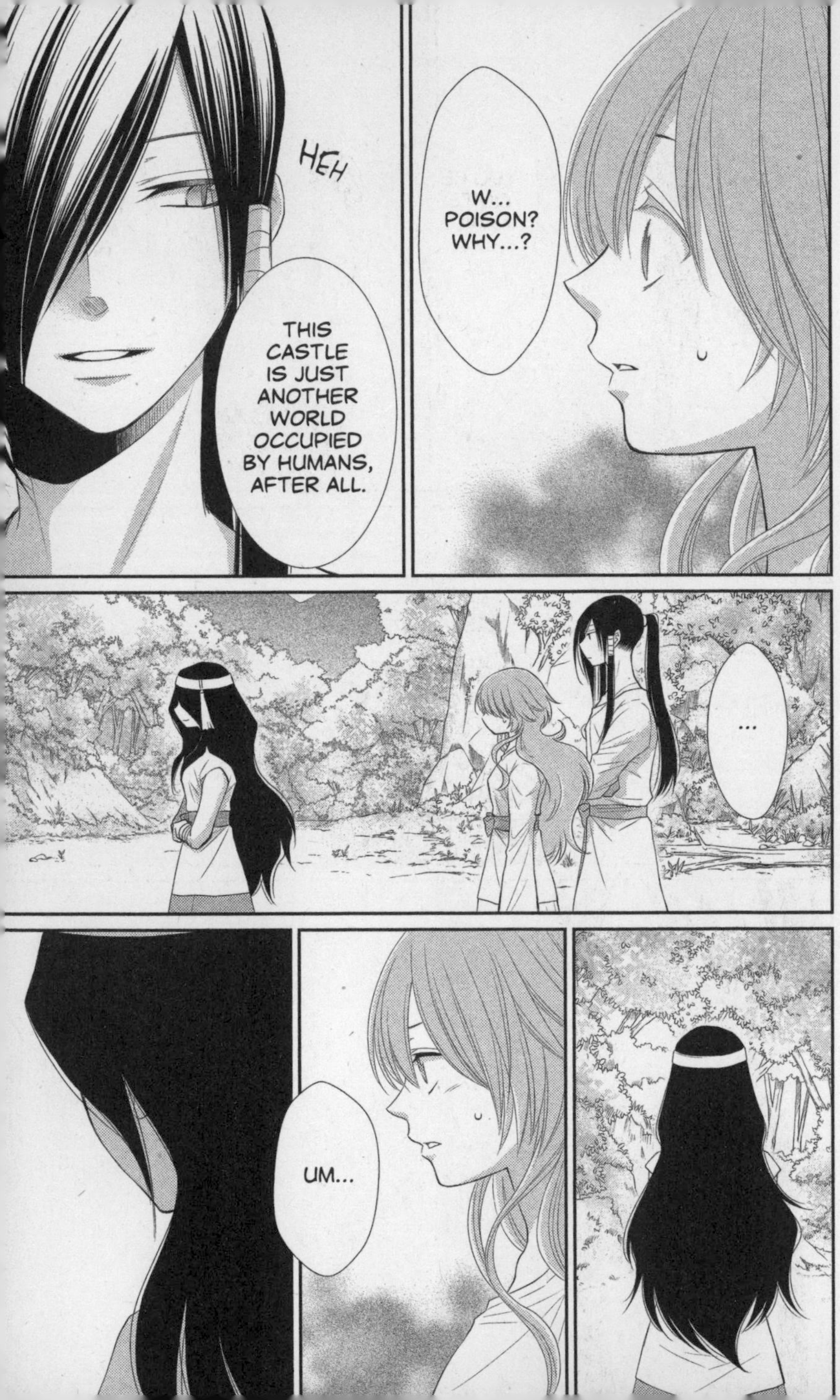
W... POISON? WHY...?
HEH
THIS CASTLE IS JUST ANOTHER WORLD OCCUPIED BY HUMANS, AFTER ALL.
...
UM...

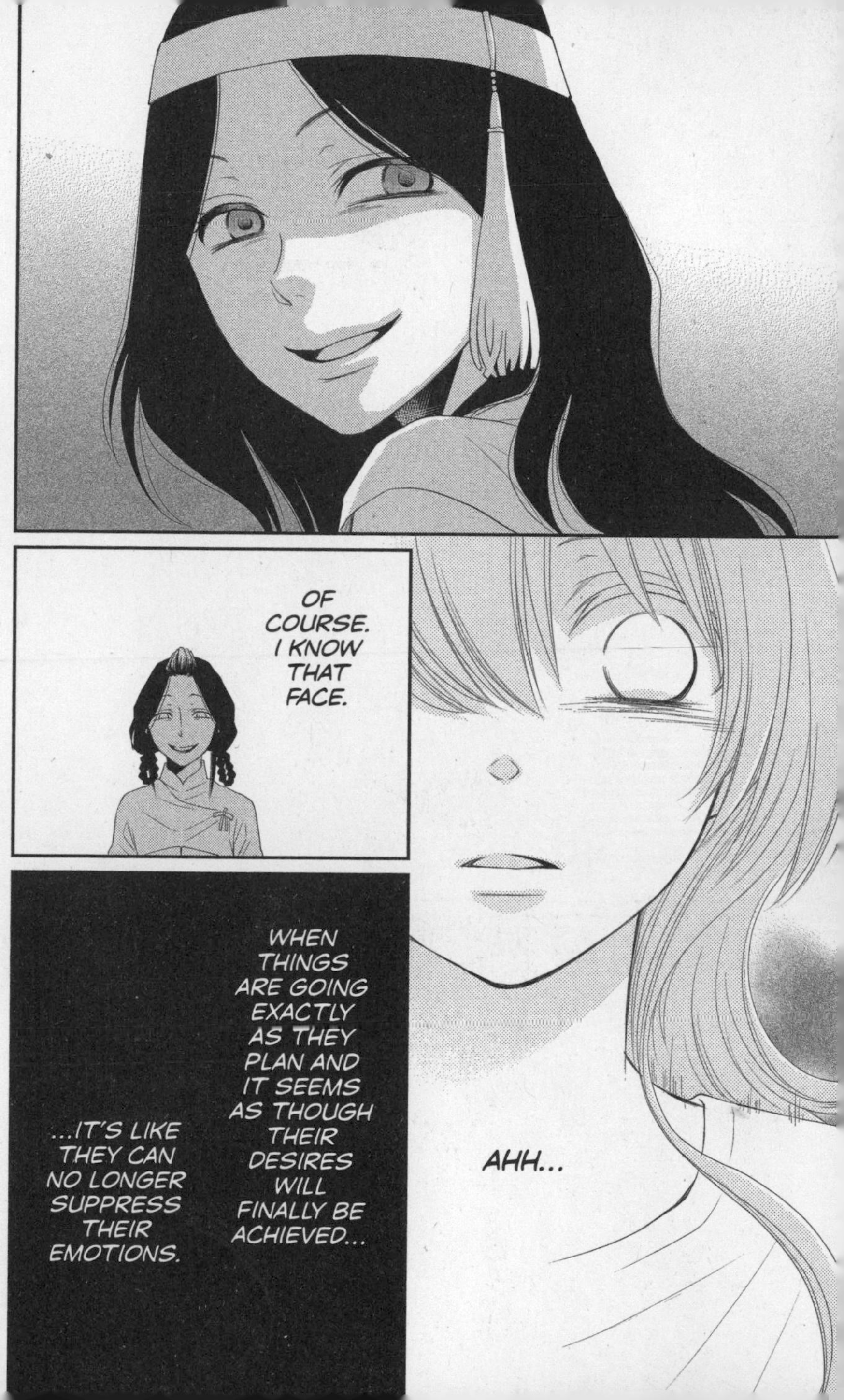
AHH...
OF COURSE. I KNOW THAT FACE.
WHEN THINGS ARE GOING EXACTLY AS THEY PLAN AND IT SEEMS AS THOUGH THEIR DESIRES WILL FINALLY BE ACHIEVED...
...IT'S LIKE THEY CAN NO LONGER SUPPRESS THEIR EMOTIONS.

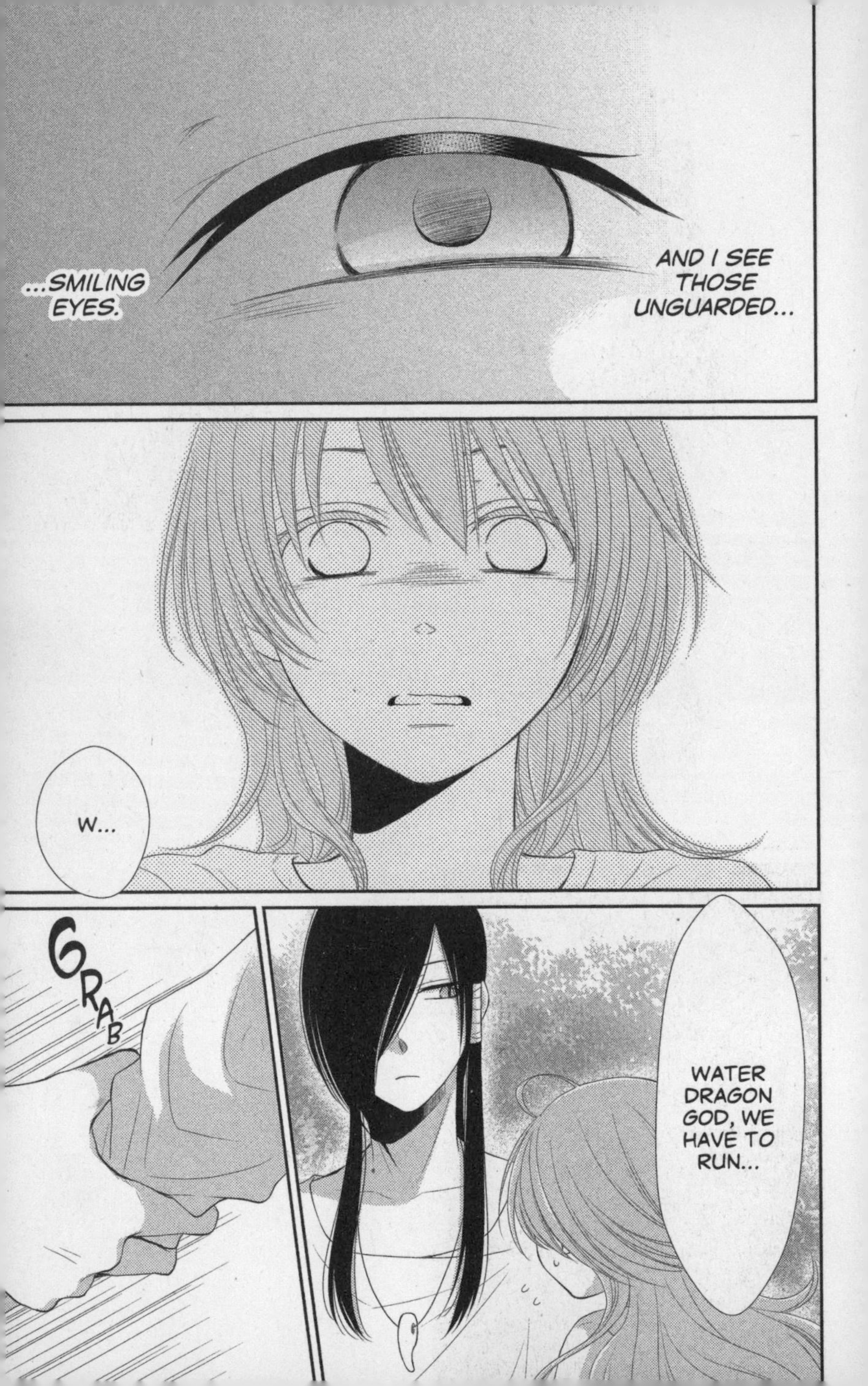
AND I SEE THOSE UNGUARDED...
...SMILING EYES.
W...
WATER DRAGON GOD, WE HAVE TO RUN...
GRAB

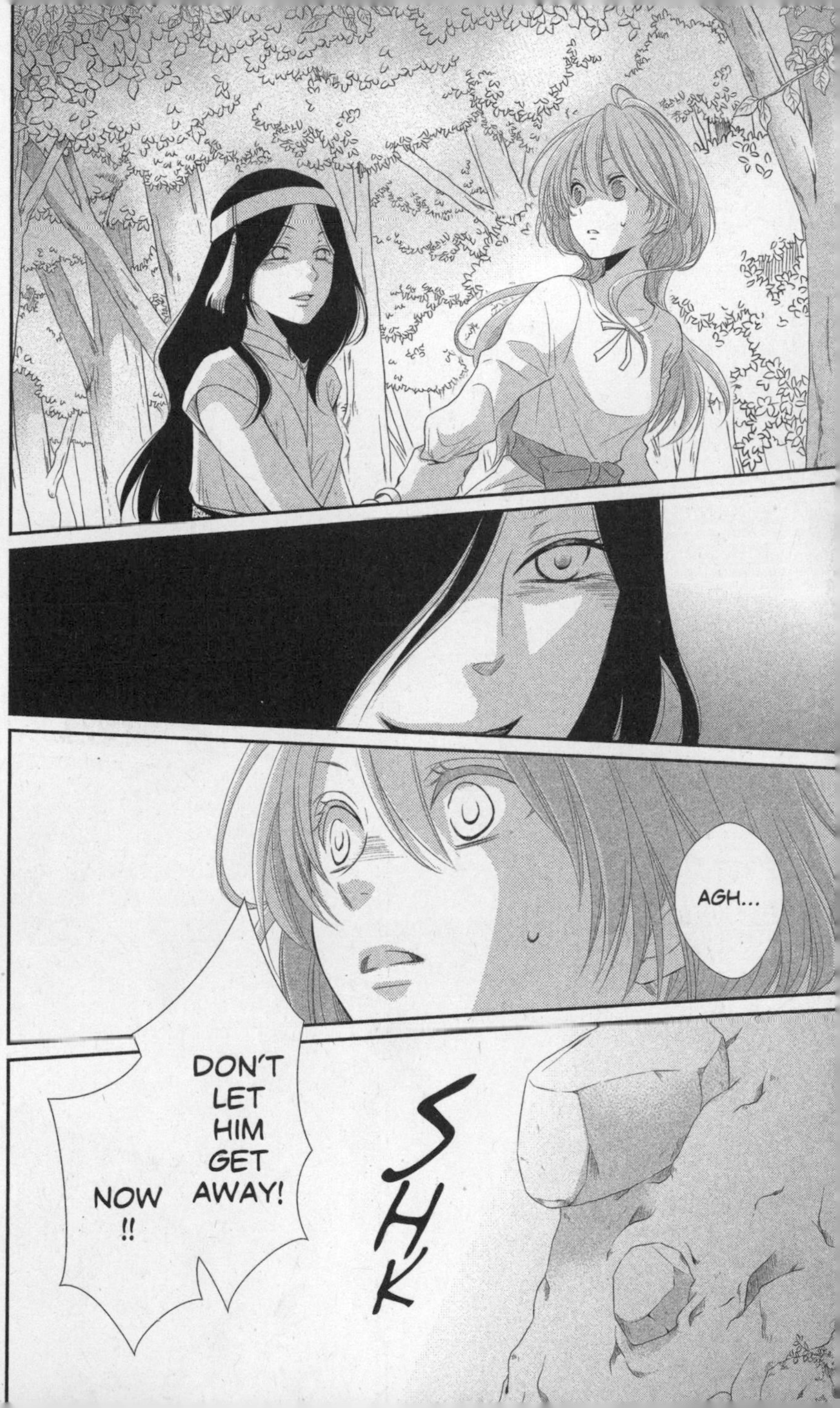
AGH...
DON'T LET HIM GET AWAY!
NOW !!
SHK

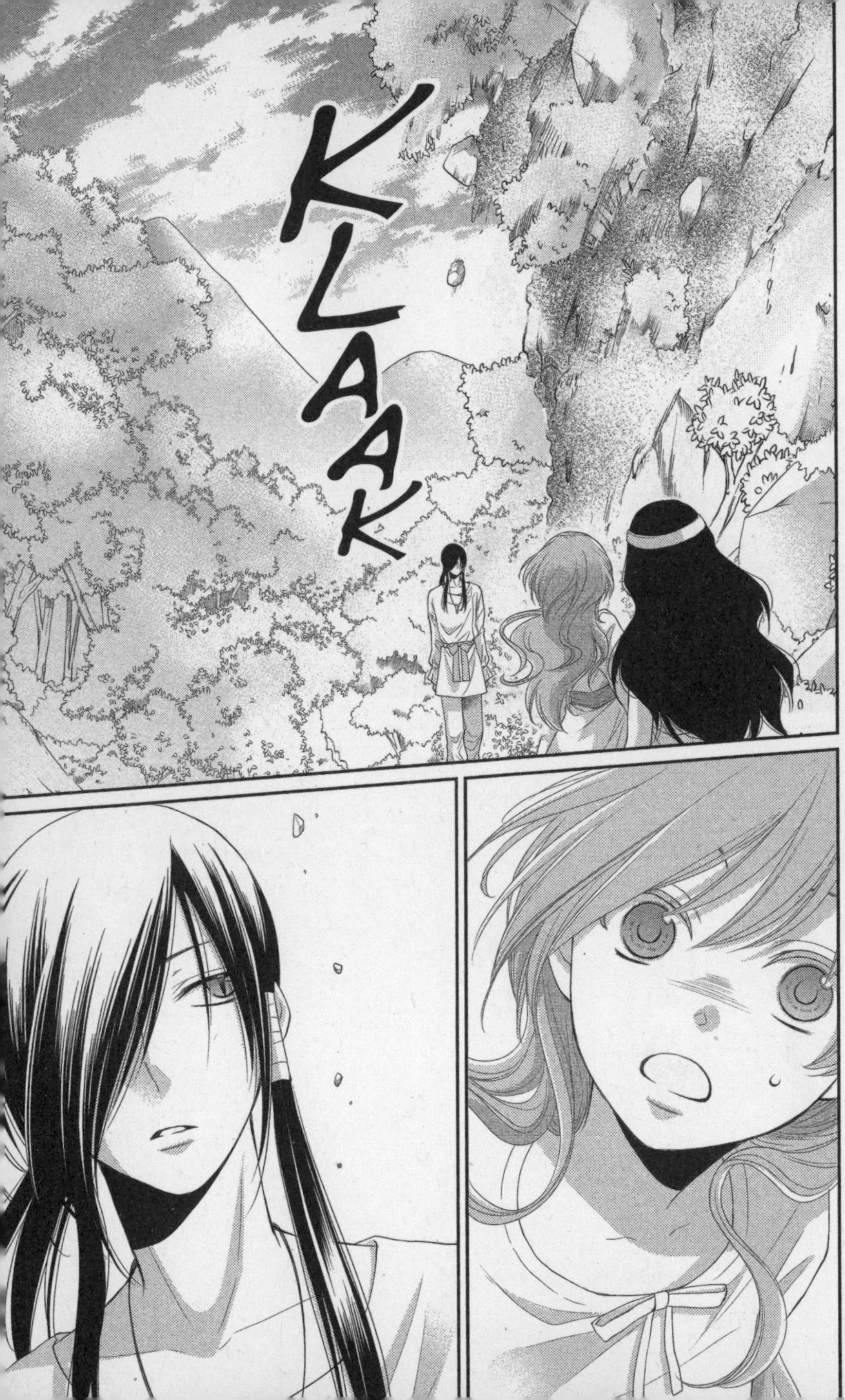
KLAAK

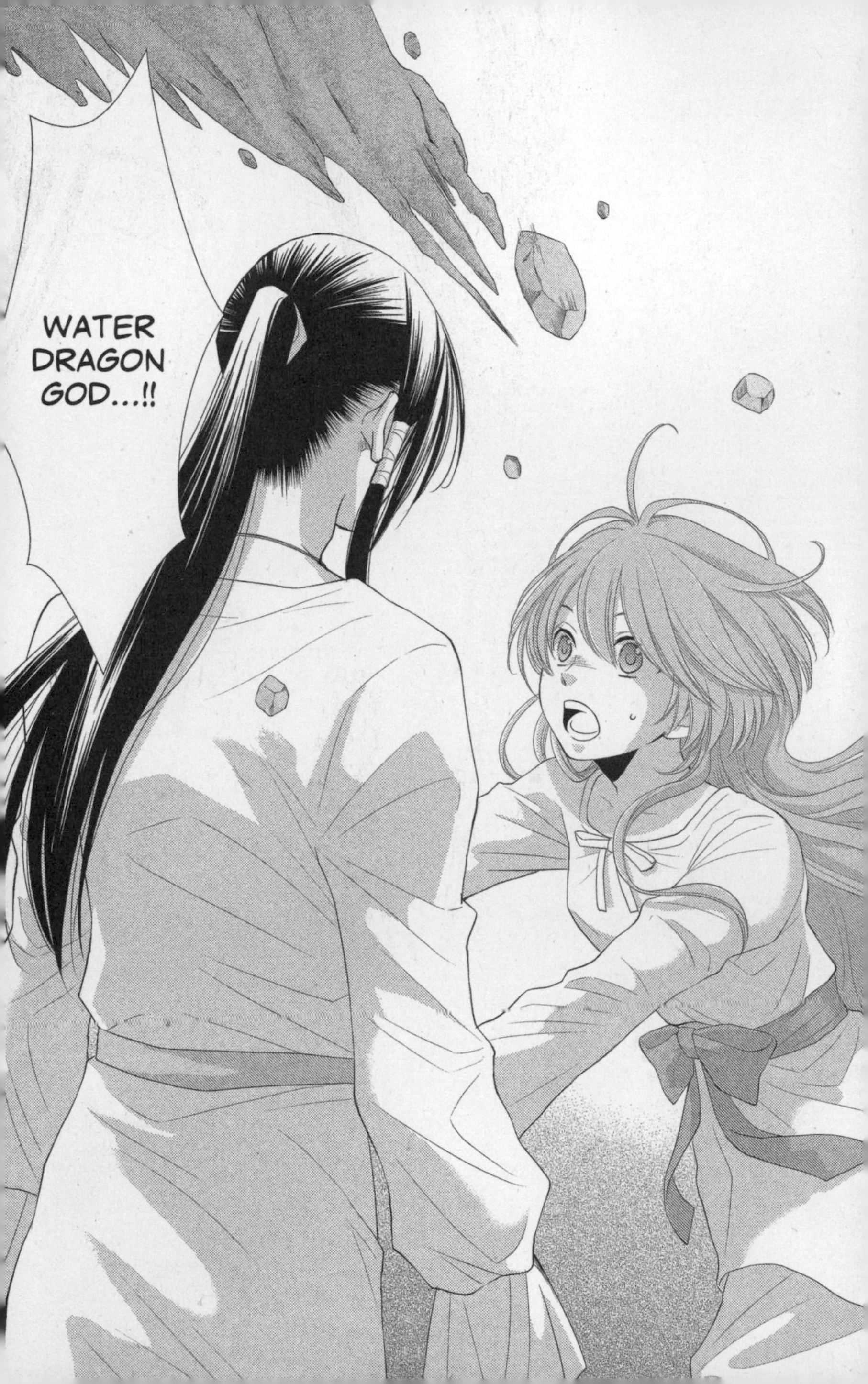
WATER DRAGON GOD...!!

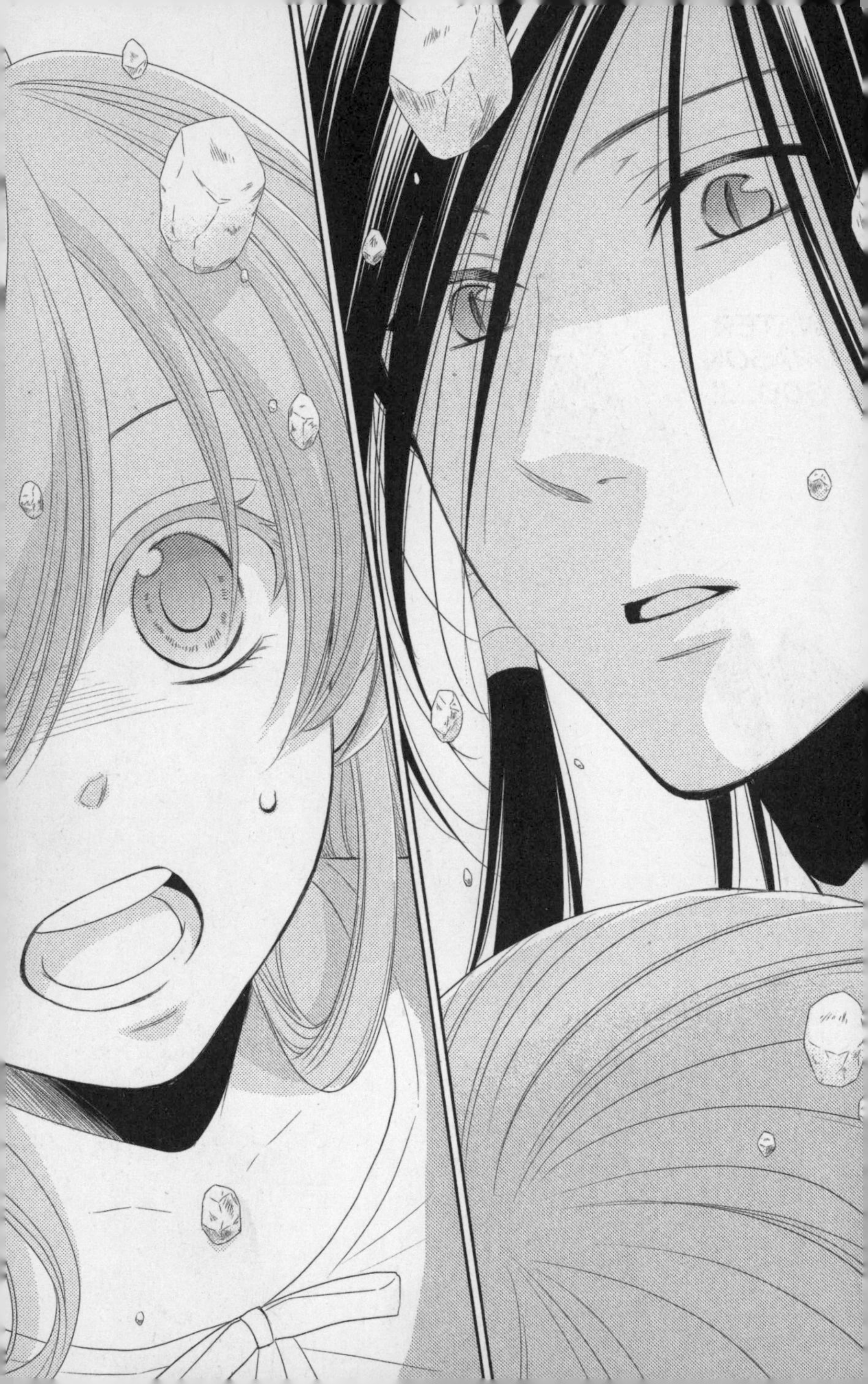

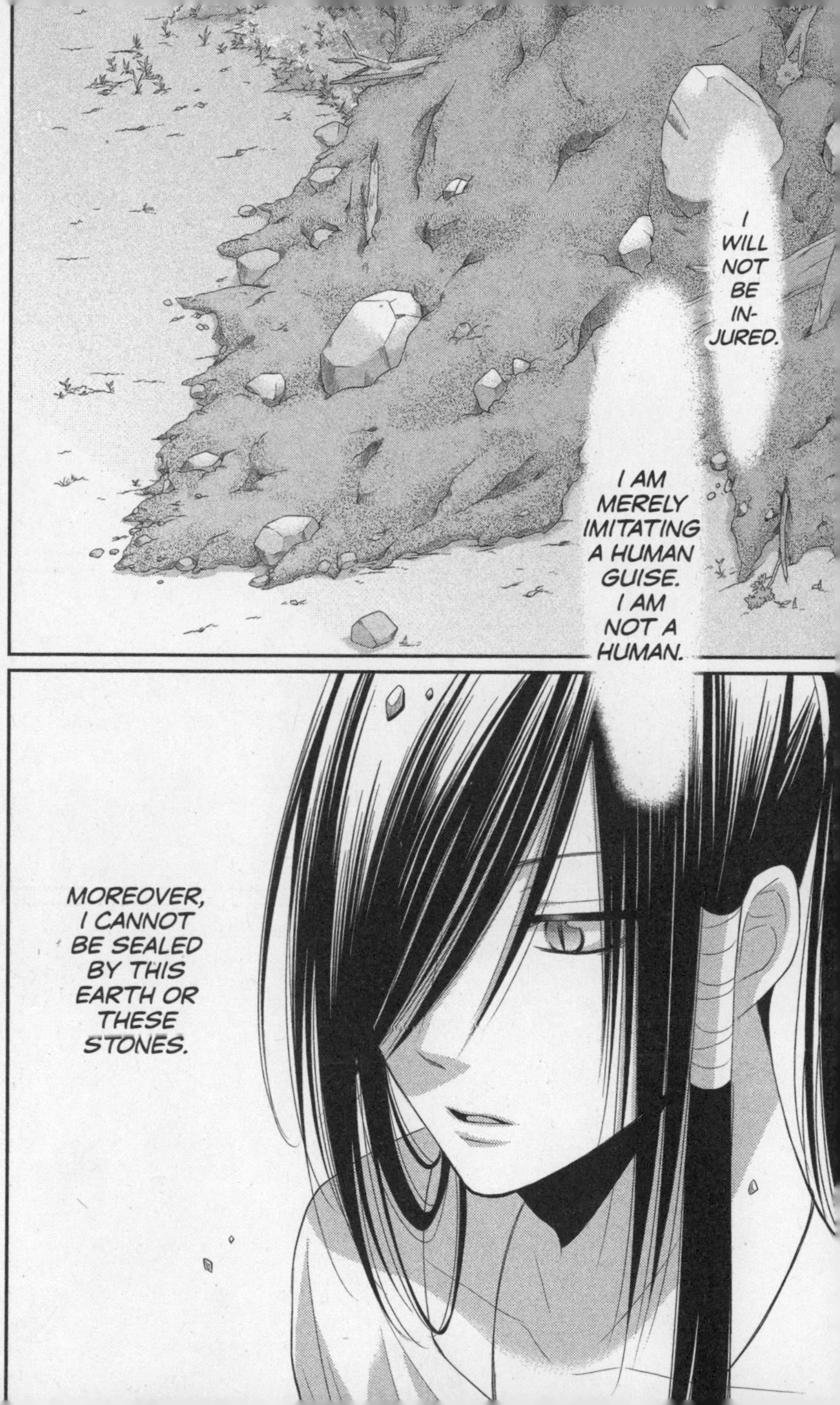
I WILL NOT BE IN-JURED.
I AM MERELY IMITATING A HUMAN GUISE. I AM NOT A HUMAN.
MOREOVER, I CANNOT BE SEALED BY THIS EARTH OR THESE STONES.

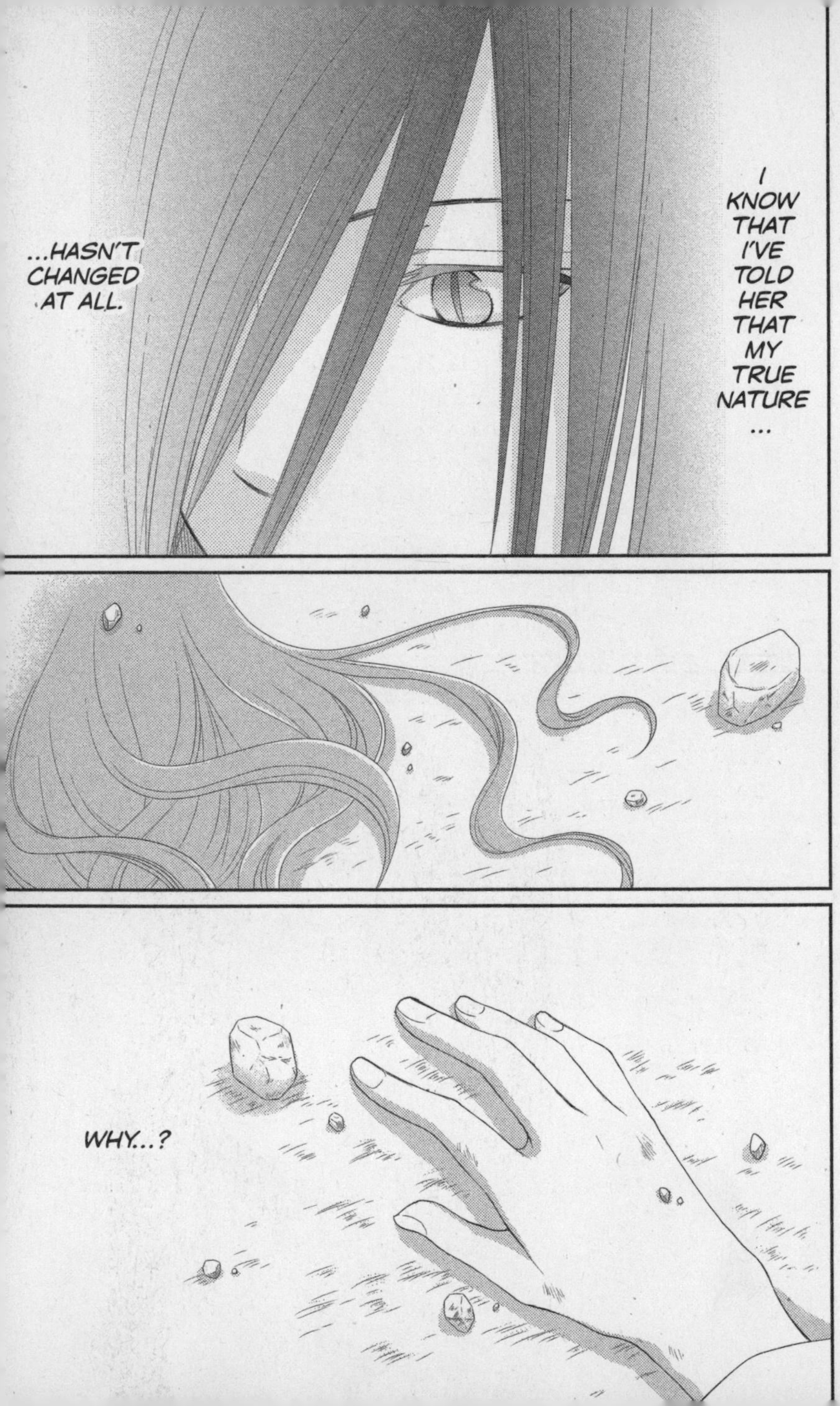
I KNOW THAT I'VE TOLD HER THAT MY TRUE NATURE...
...HASN'T CHANGED AT ALL.
WHY...?

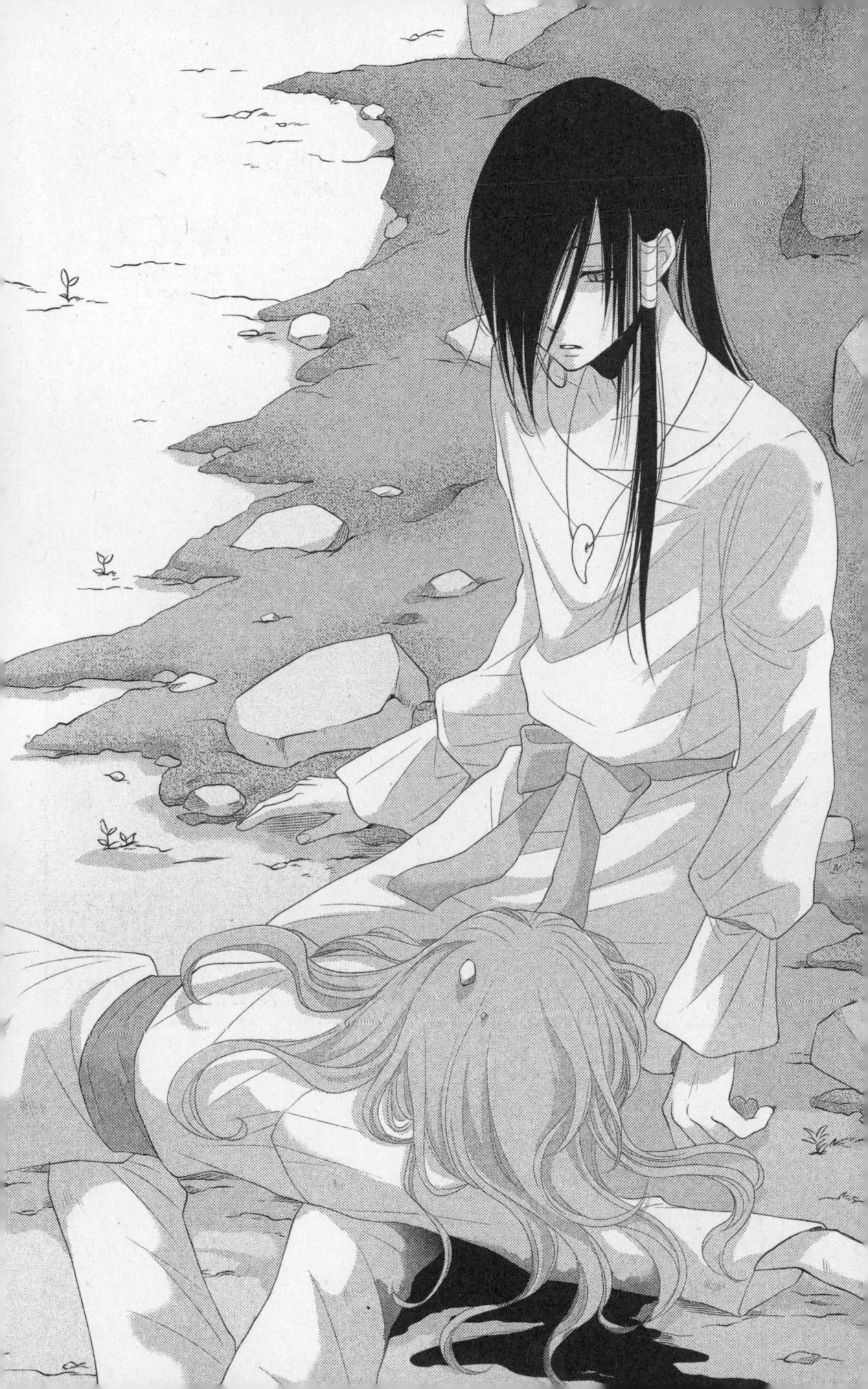

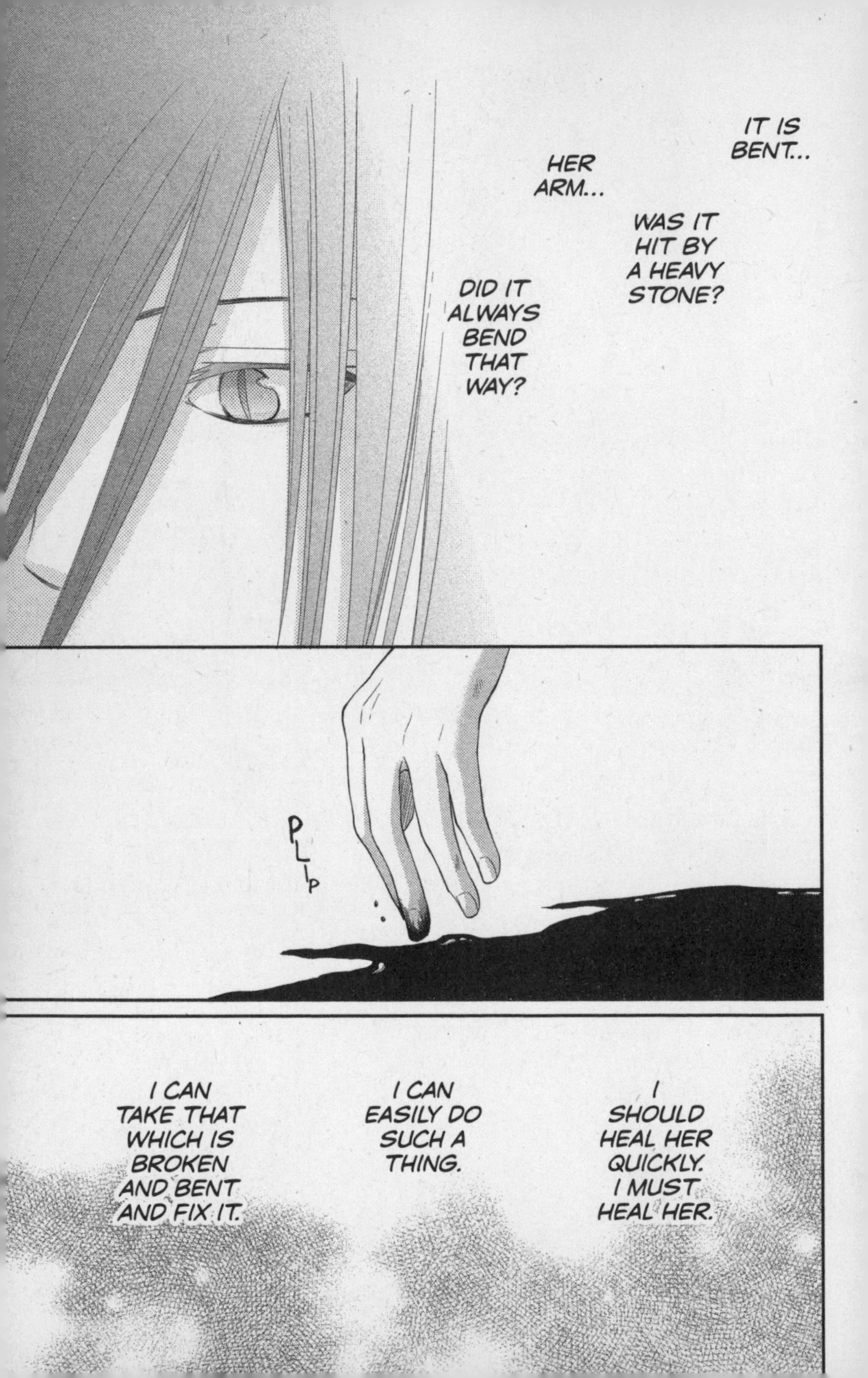
IT IS BENT...
HER ARM...
WAS IT HIT BY A HEAVY STONE?
DID IT ALWAYS BEND THAT WAY?
PLIP
I SHOULD HEAL HER QUICKLY. I MUST HEAL HER.
I CAN EASILY DO SUCH A THING.
I CAN TAKE THAT WHICH IS BROKEN AND BENT AND FIX IT.

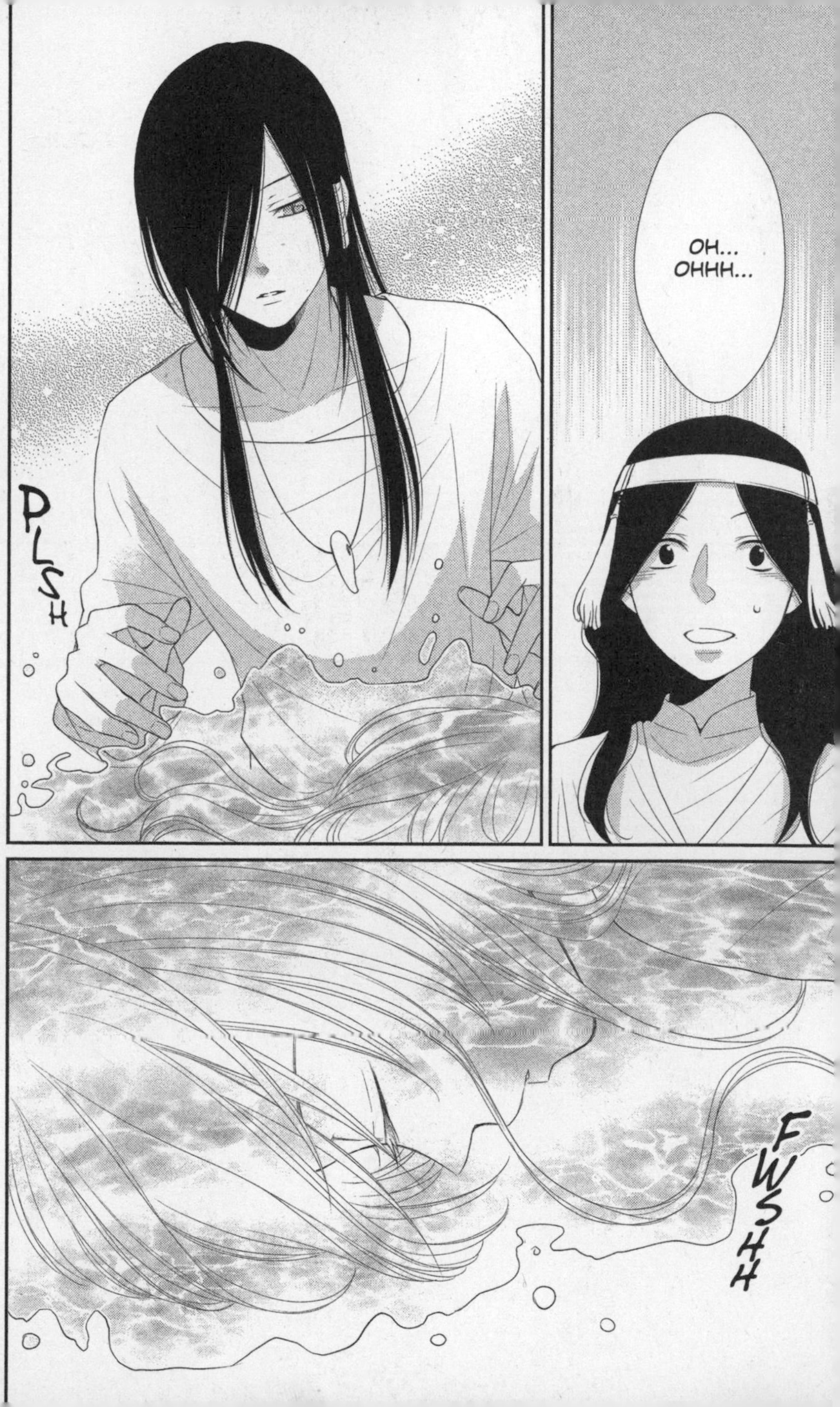
OH...
OHHH...
PLSH
FWSHH

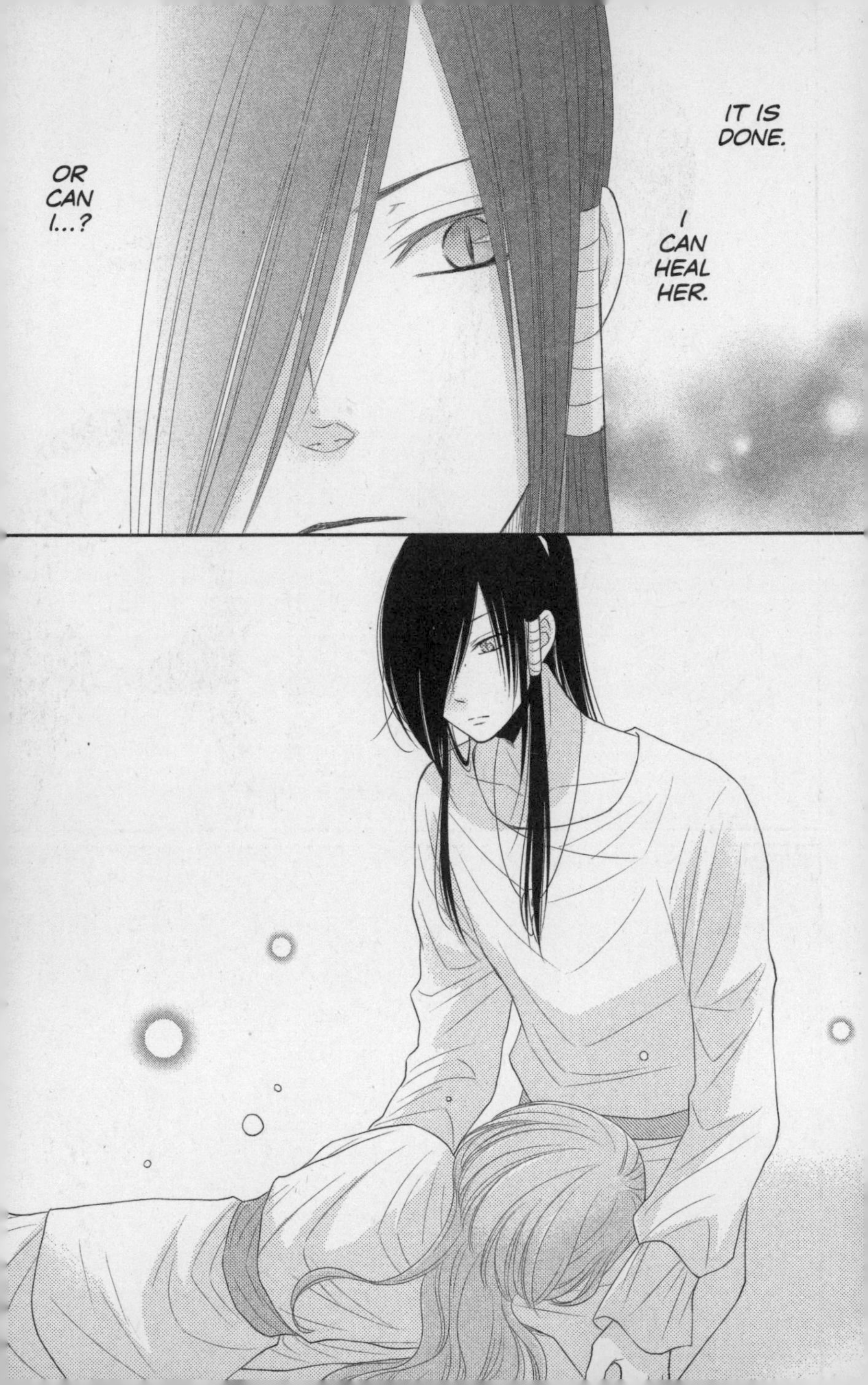
IT IS DONE.
I CAN HEAL HER.
OR CAN I...?

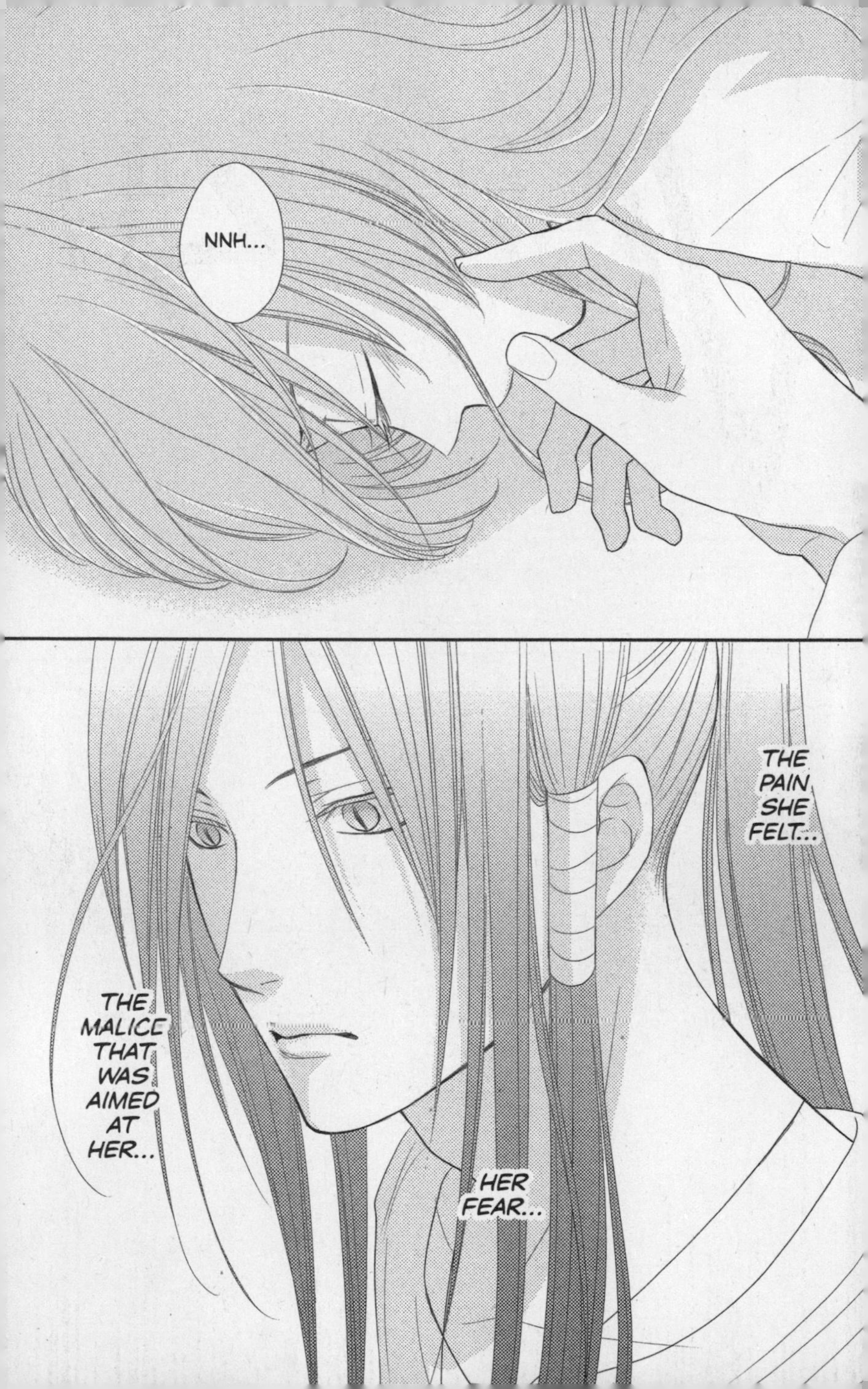
NNH...
THE PAIN SHE FELT...
THE MALICE THAT WAS AIMED AT HER...
HER FEAR...

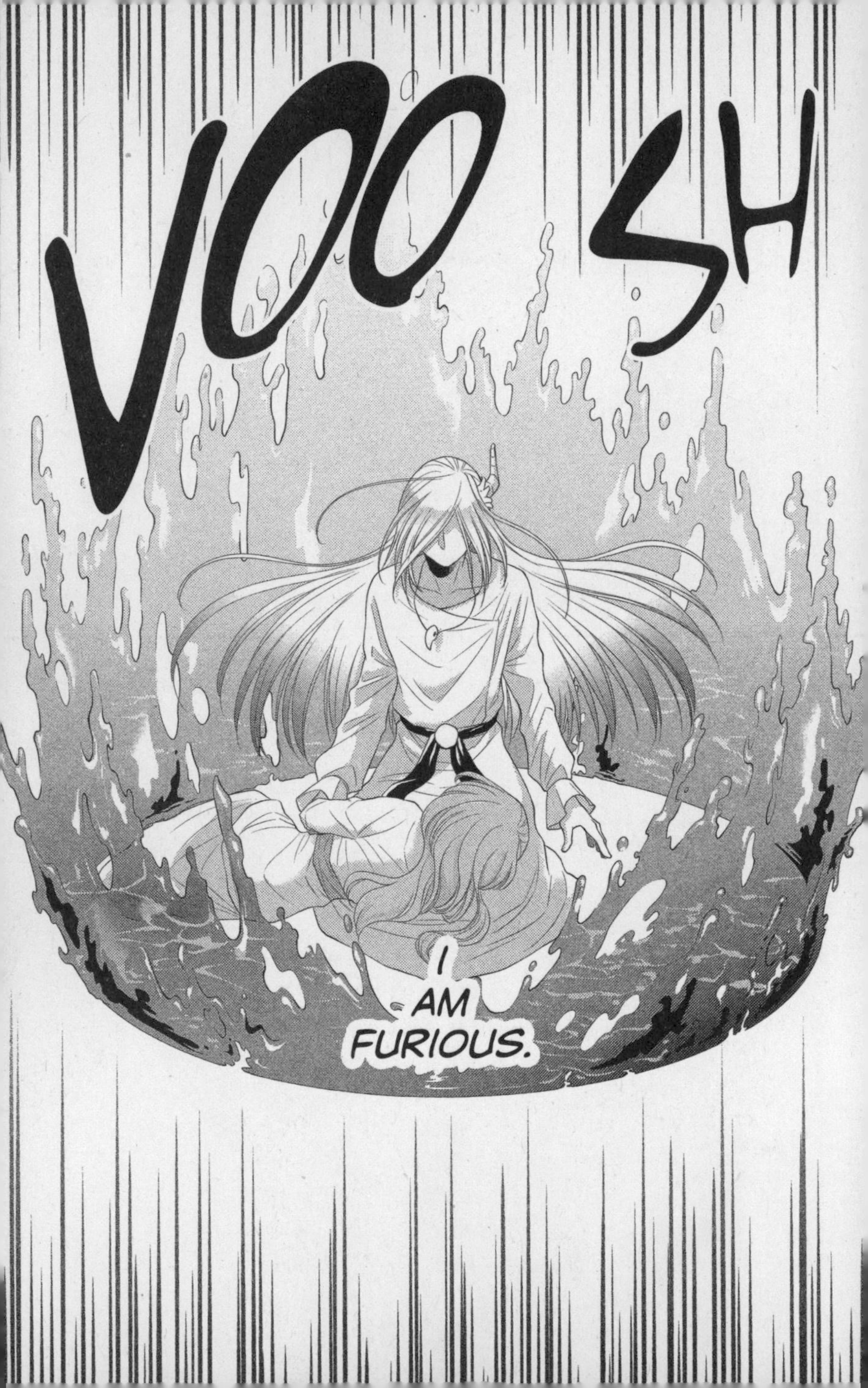
VOOSH
I AM FURIOUS.

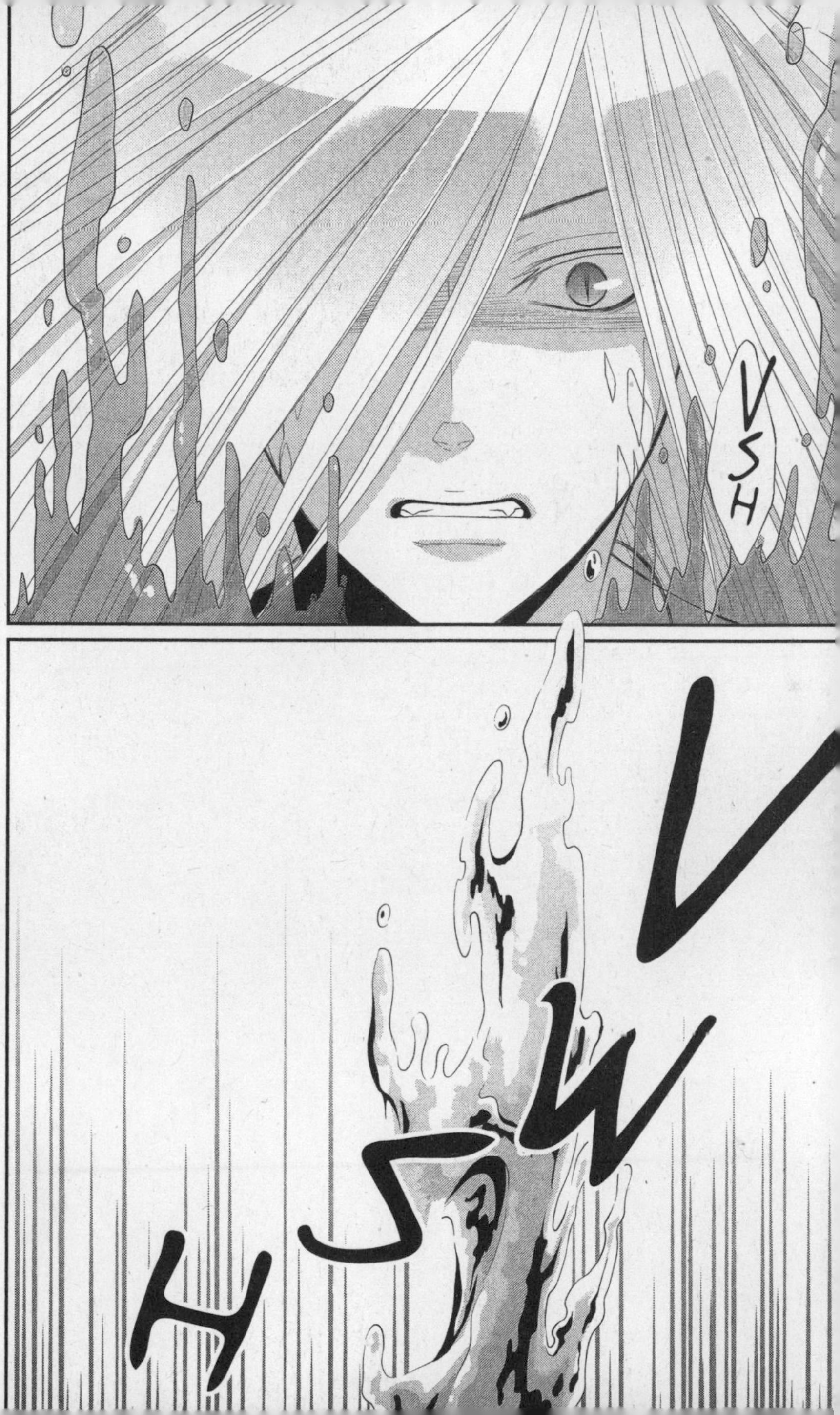
VSH
VSWSH

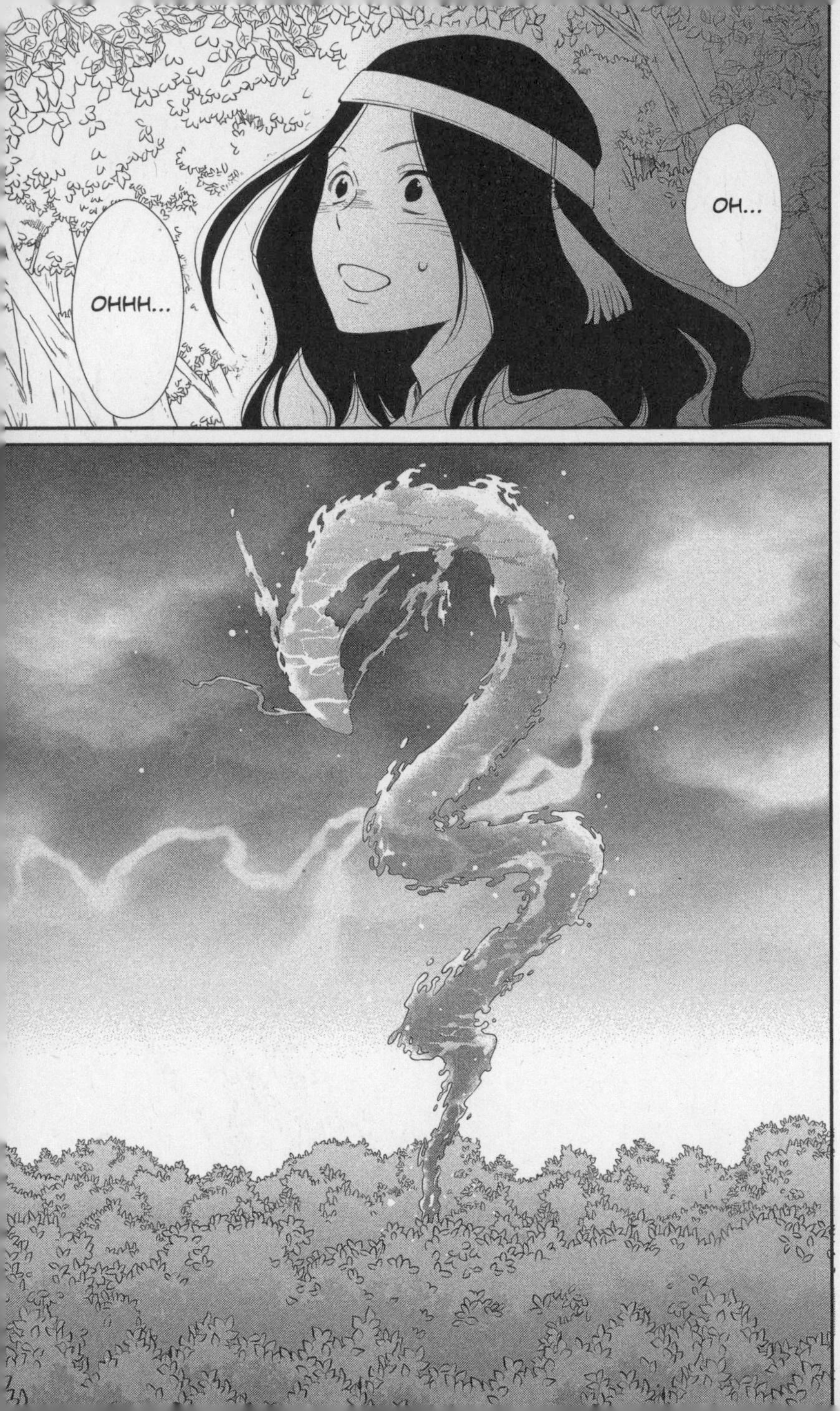
OH...
OHHH...

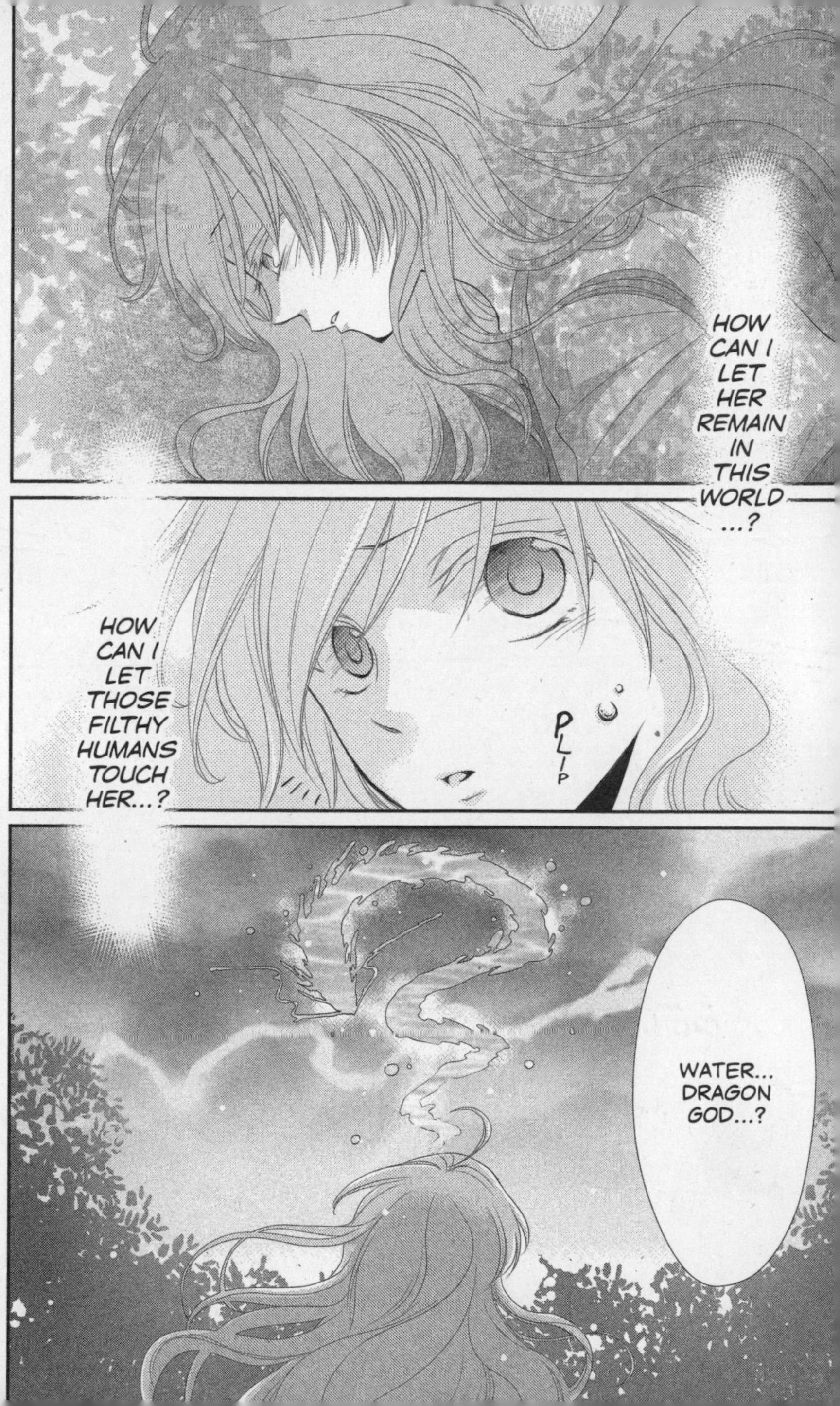
HOW CAN I LET HER REMAIN IN THIS WORLD ...?
HOW CAN I LET THOSE FILTHY HUMANS TOUCH HER...?
PLIP
WATER... DRAGON GOD...?

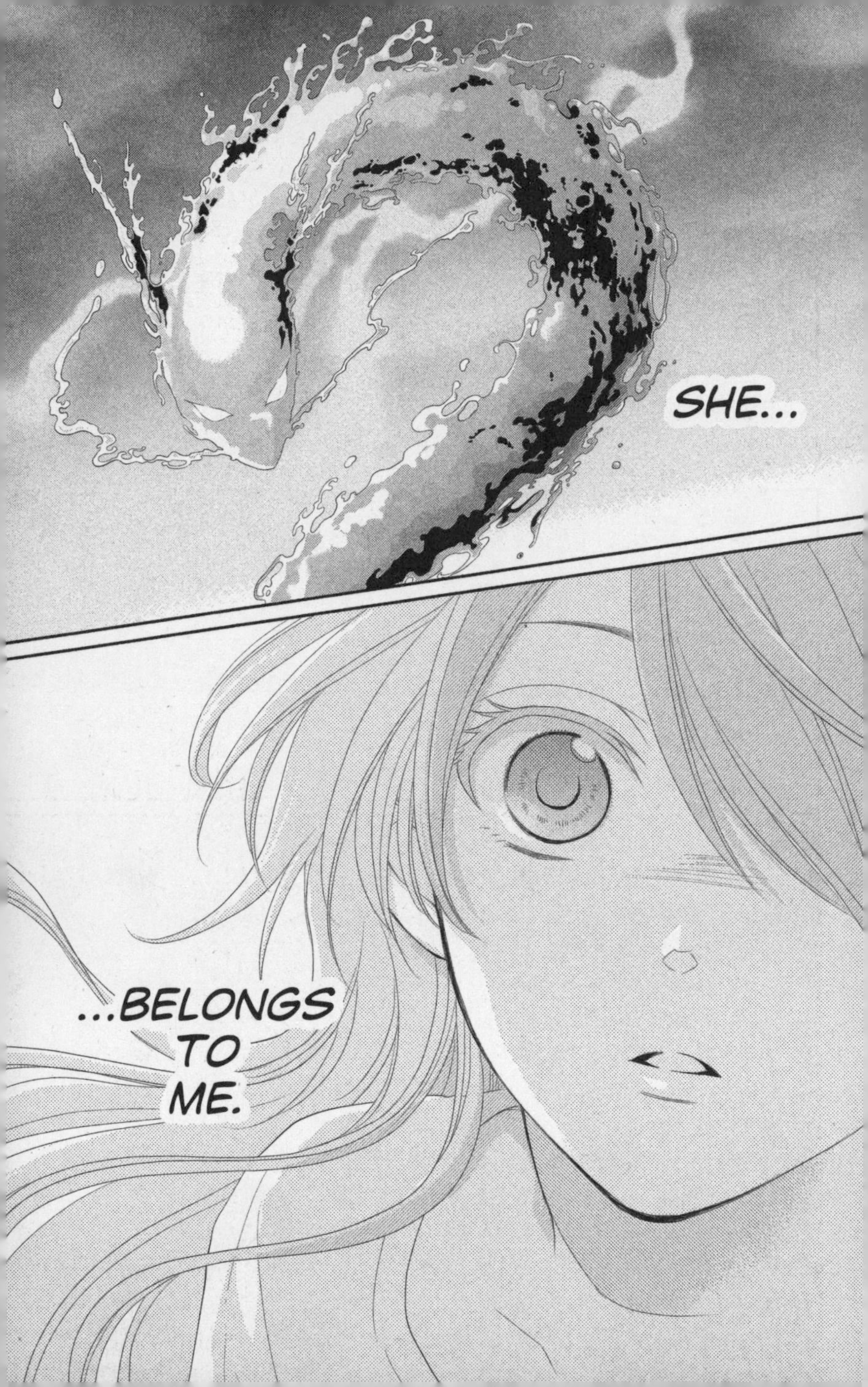
SHE...
...BELONGS TO ME.

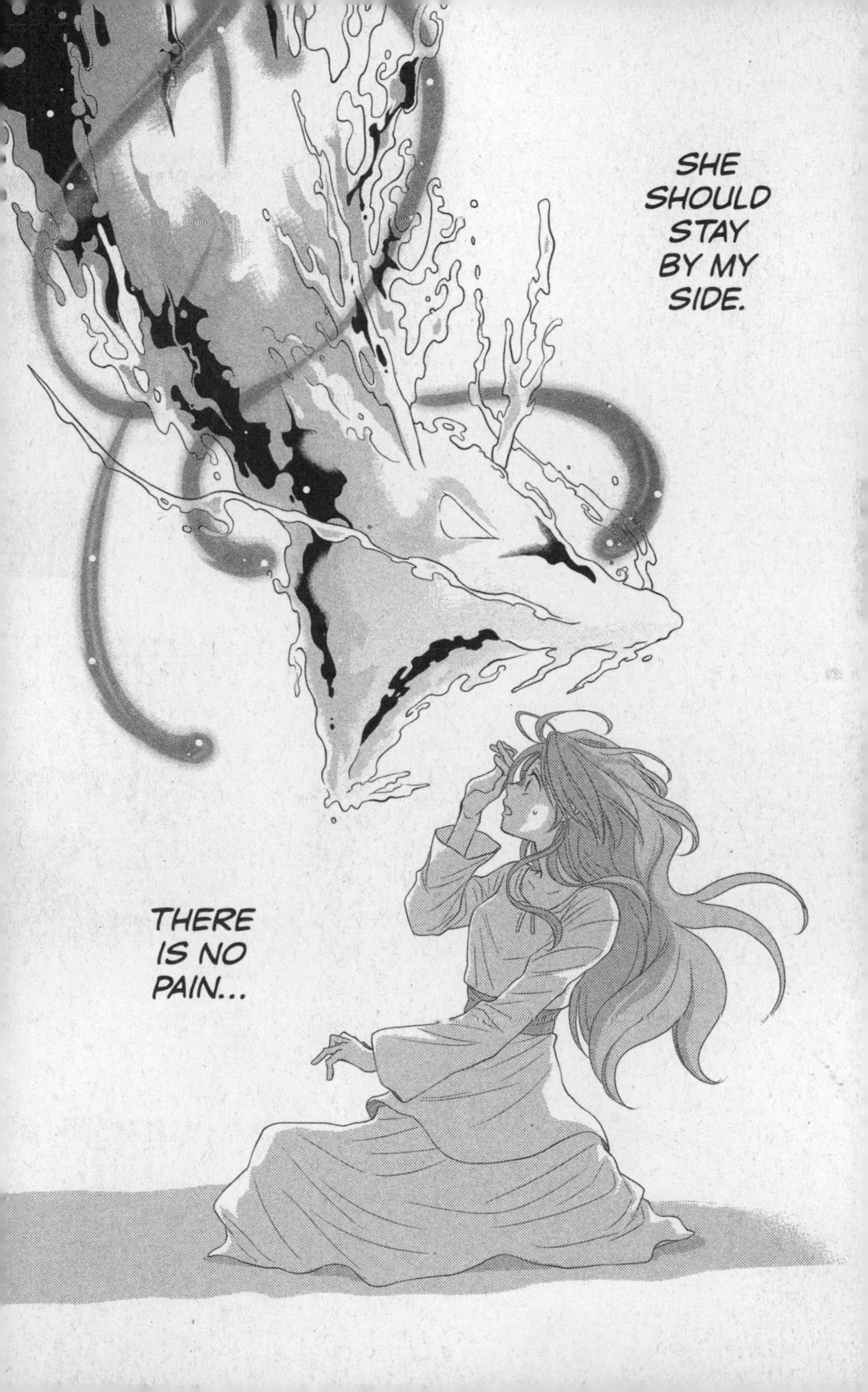
SHE SHOULD STAY BY MY SIDE.
THERE IS NO PAIN...

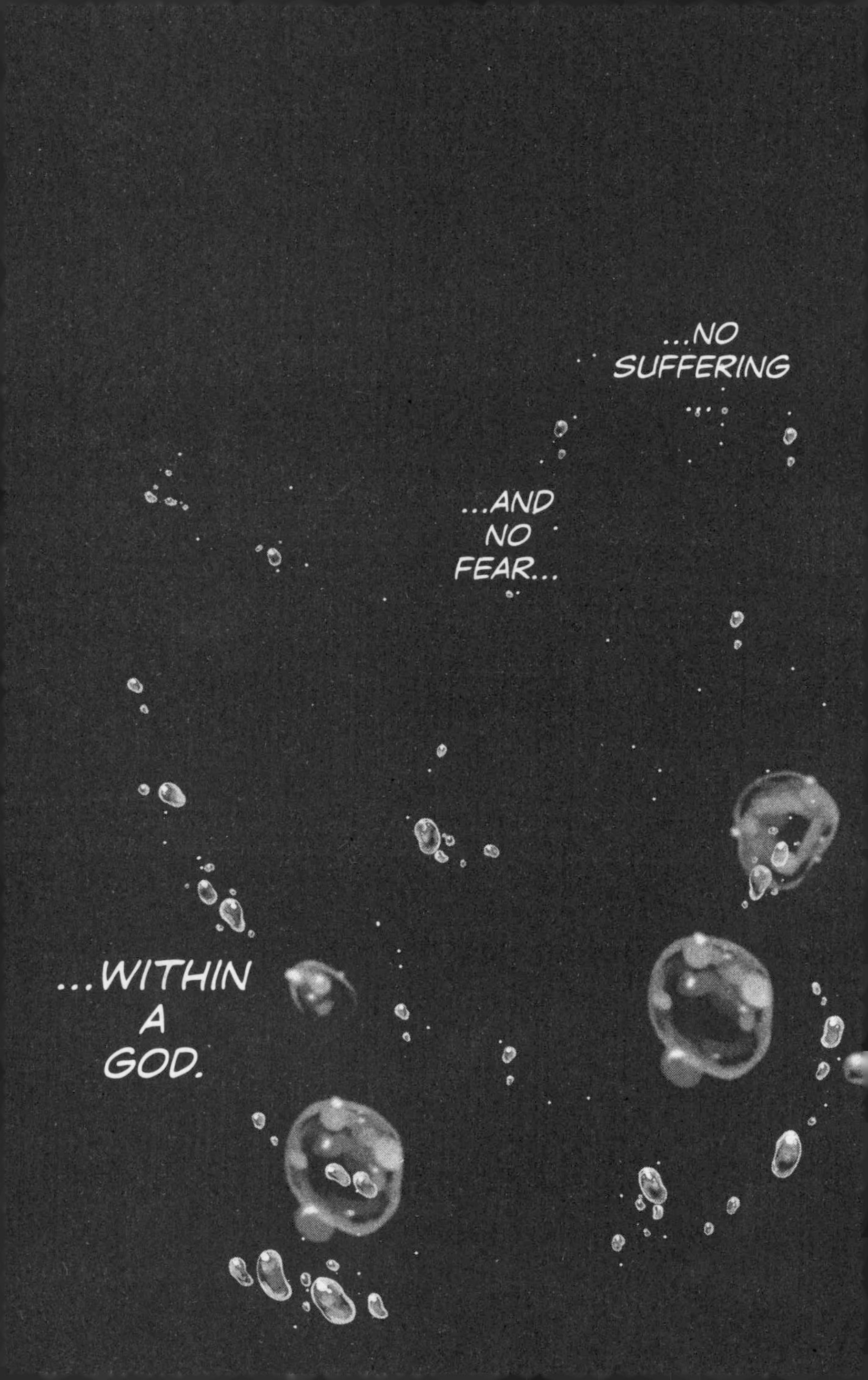
...NO SUFFERING
...AND NO FEAR...
...WITHIN A GOD.

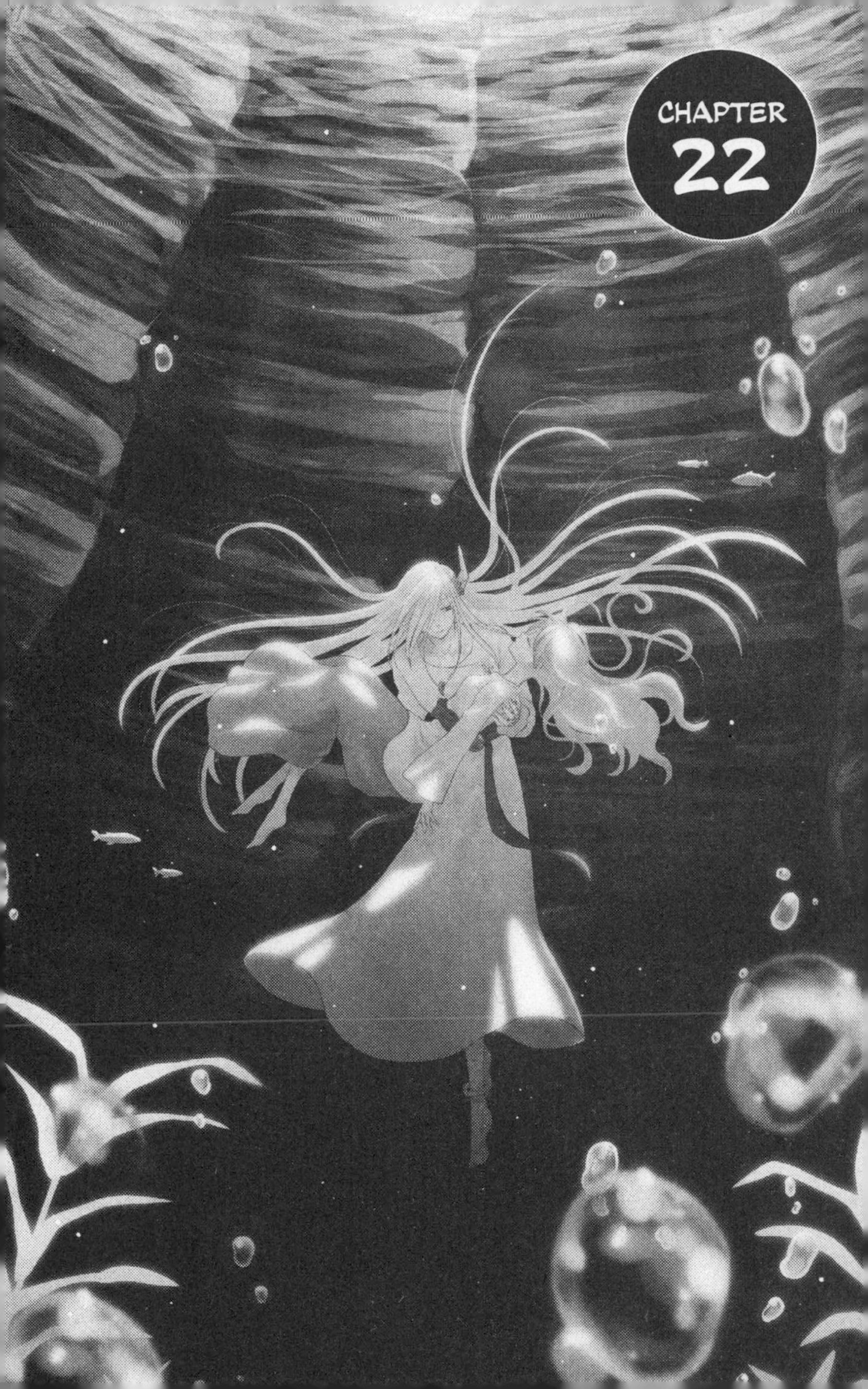
CHAPTER
22

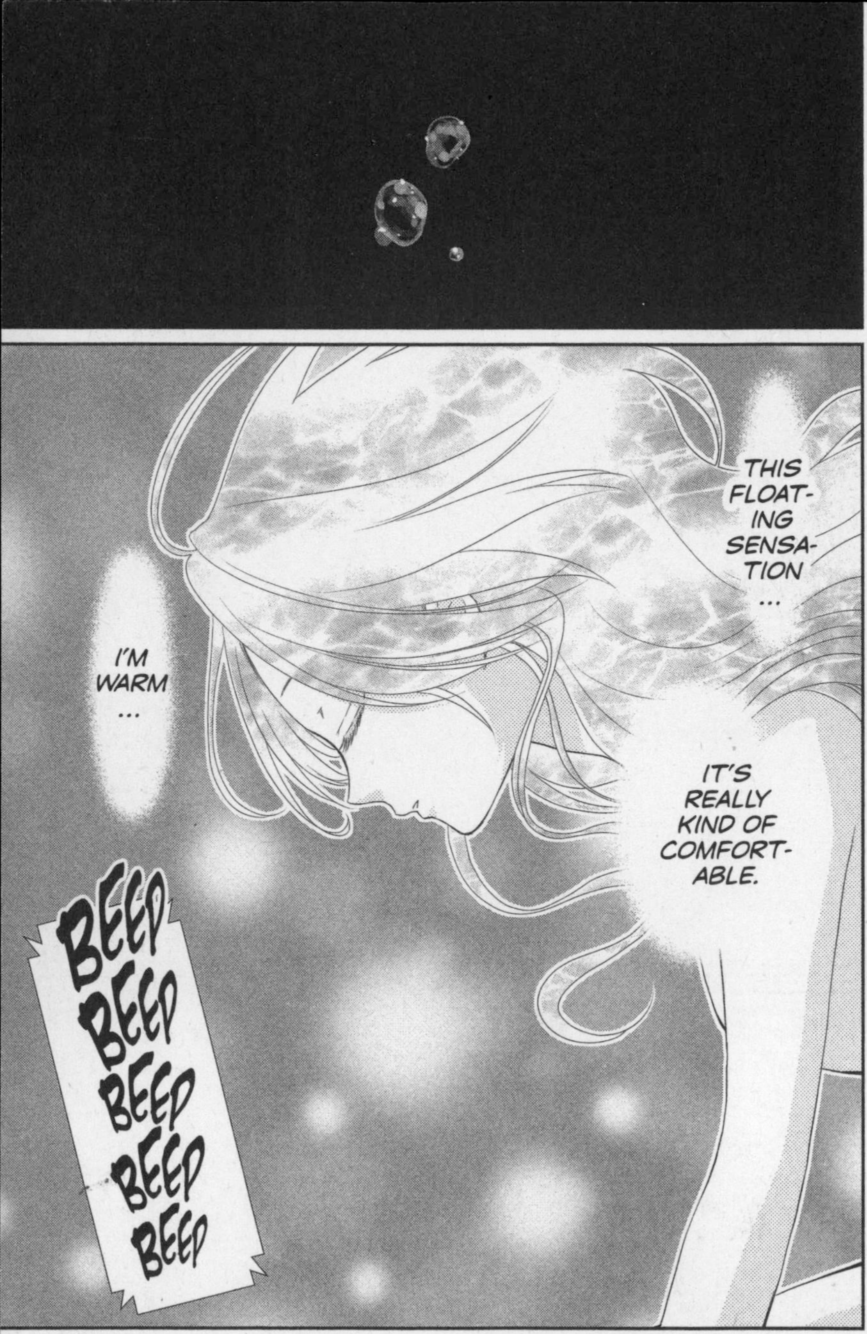
THIS FLOAT-ING SENSA-TION...
I'M WARM...
IT'S REALLY KIND OF COMFORT-ABLE.
BEEP BEEP BEEP BEEP BEEP

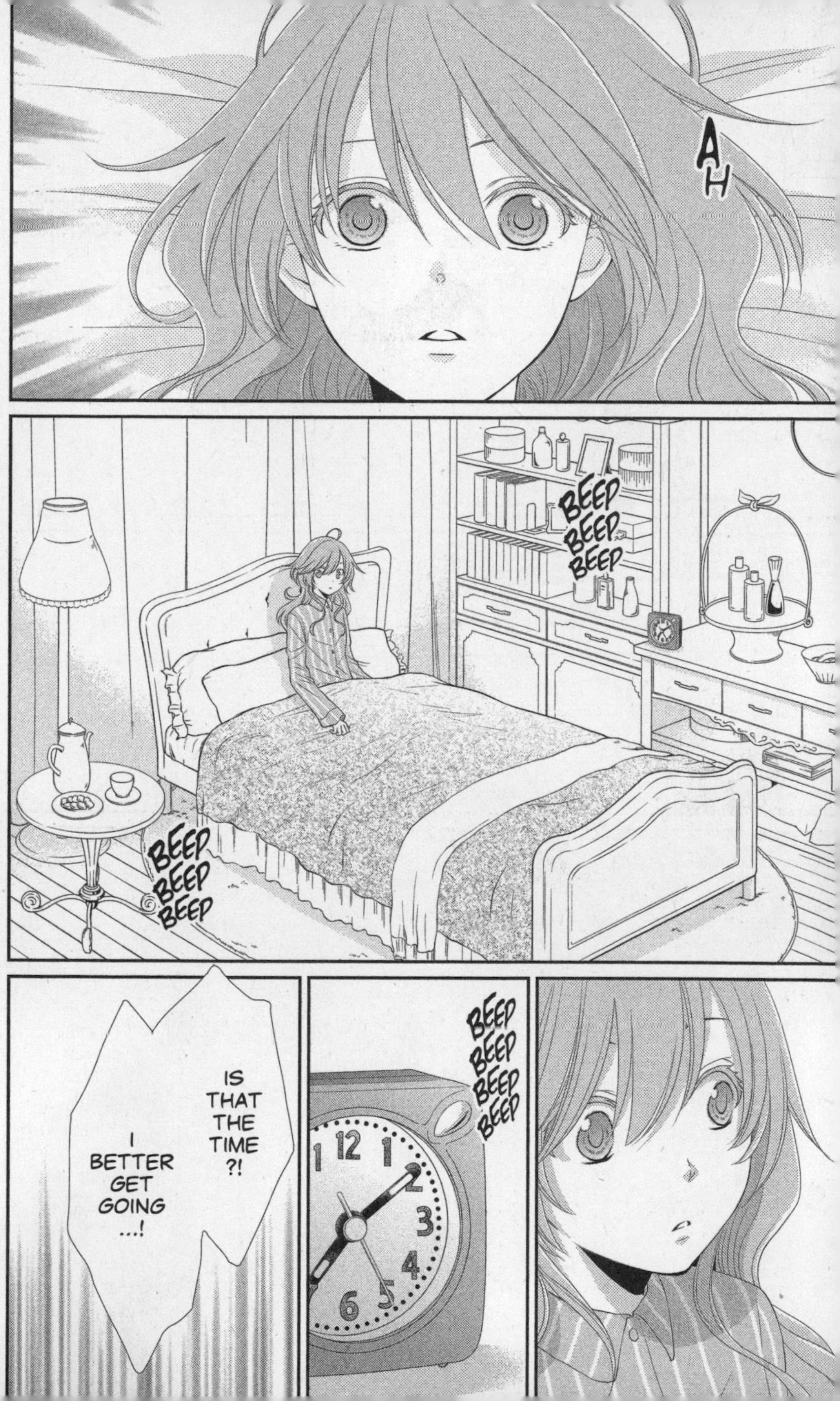
AH
BEEP BEEP BEEP
BEEP BEEP BEEP
BEEP BEEP BEEP BEEP
IS THAT THE TIME?!
I BETTER GET GOING...!

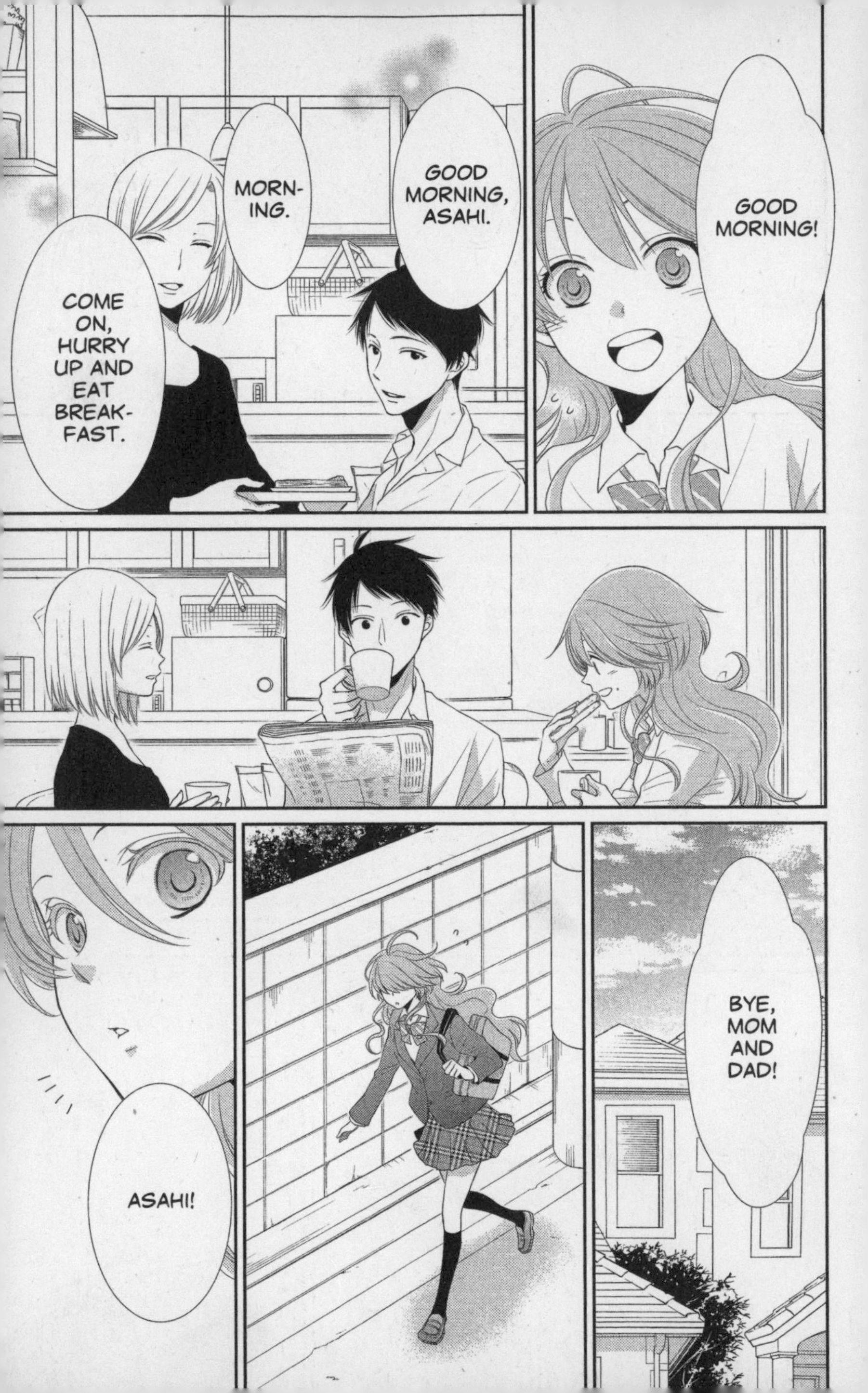
GOOD MORNING!
GOOD MORNING, ASAHI.
MORN-ING.
COME ON, HURRY UP AND EAT BREAK-FAST.
BYE, MOM AND DAD!
ASAHI!

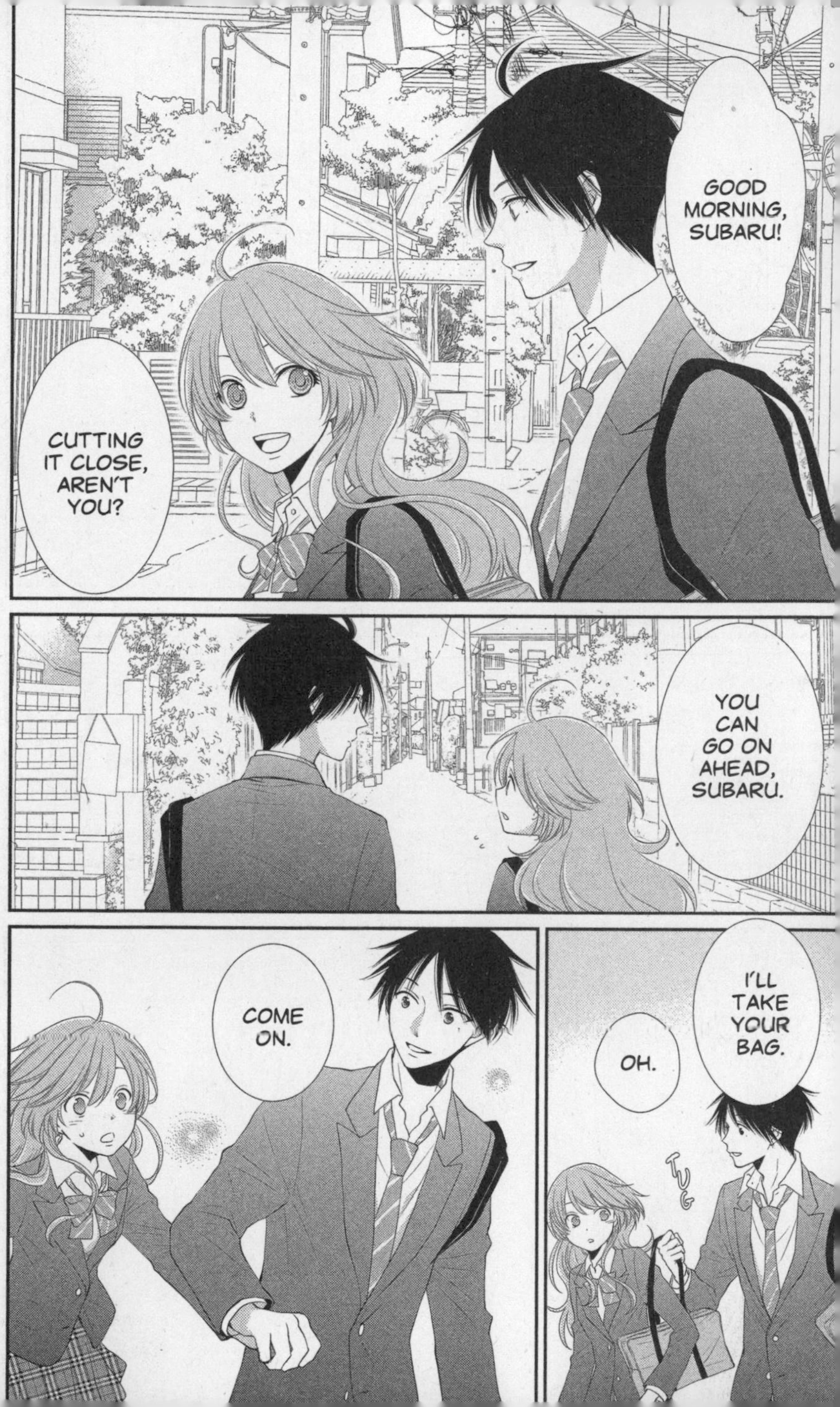
GOOD MORNING, SUBARU!
CUTTING IT CLOSE, AREN'T YOU?
YOU CAN GO ON AHEAD, SUBARU.
I'LL TAKE YOUR BAG.
OH.
TUG
COME ON.

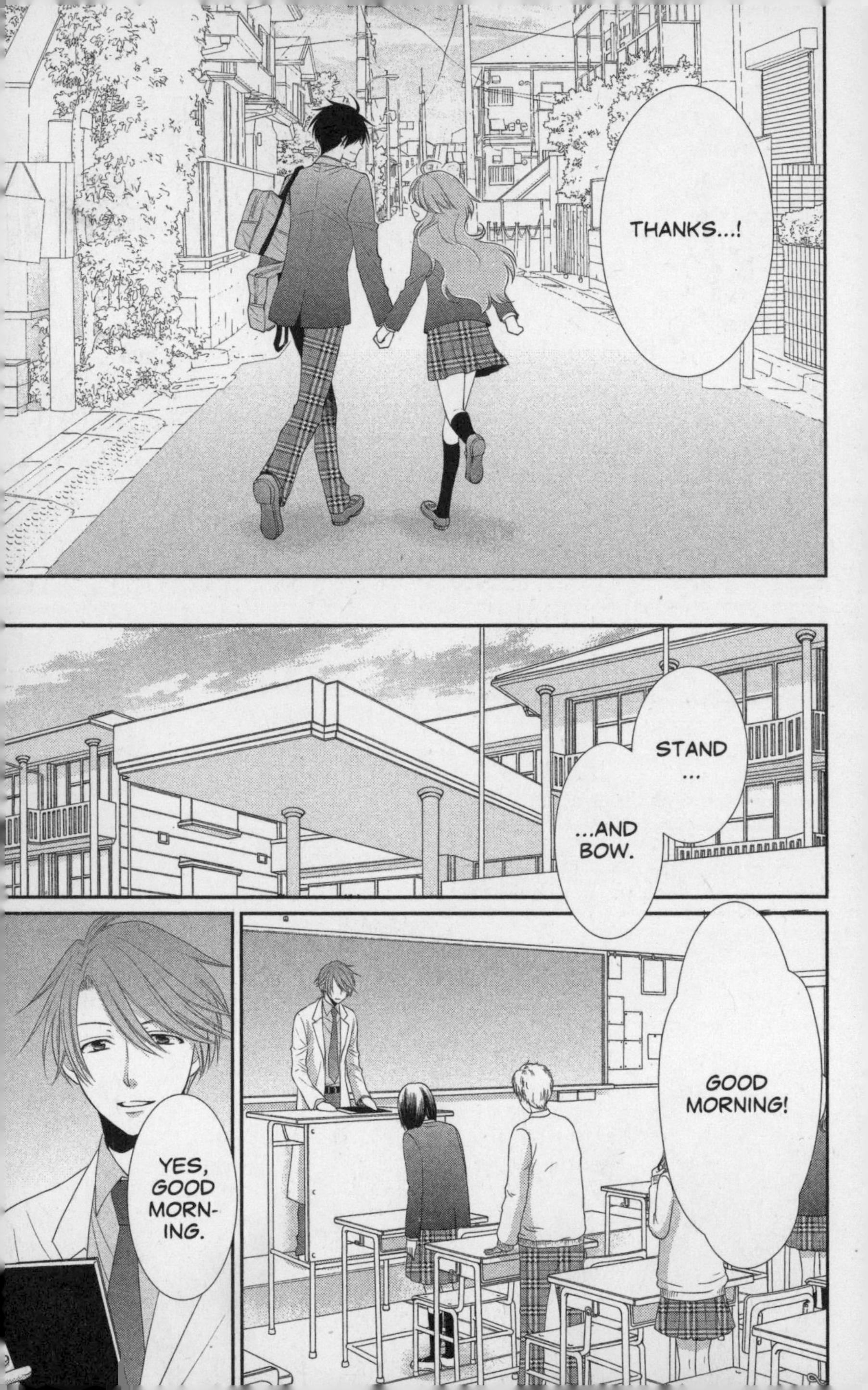
THANKS...!
STAND ...
...AND BOW.
GOOD MORNING!
YES, GOOD MORN-ING.

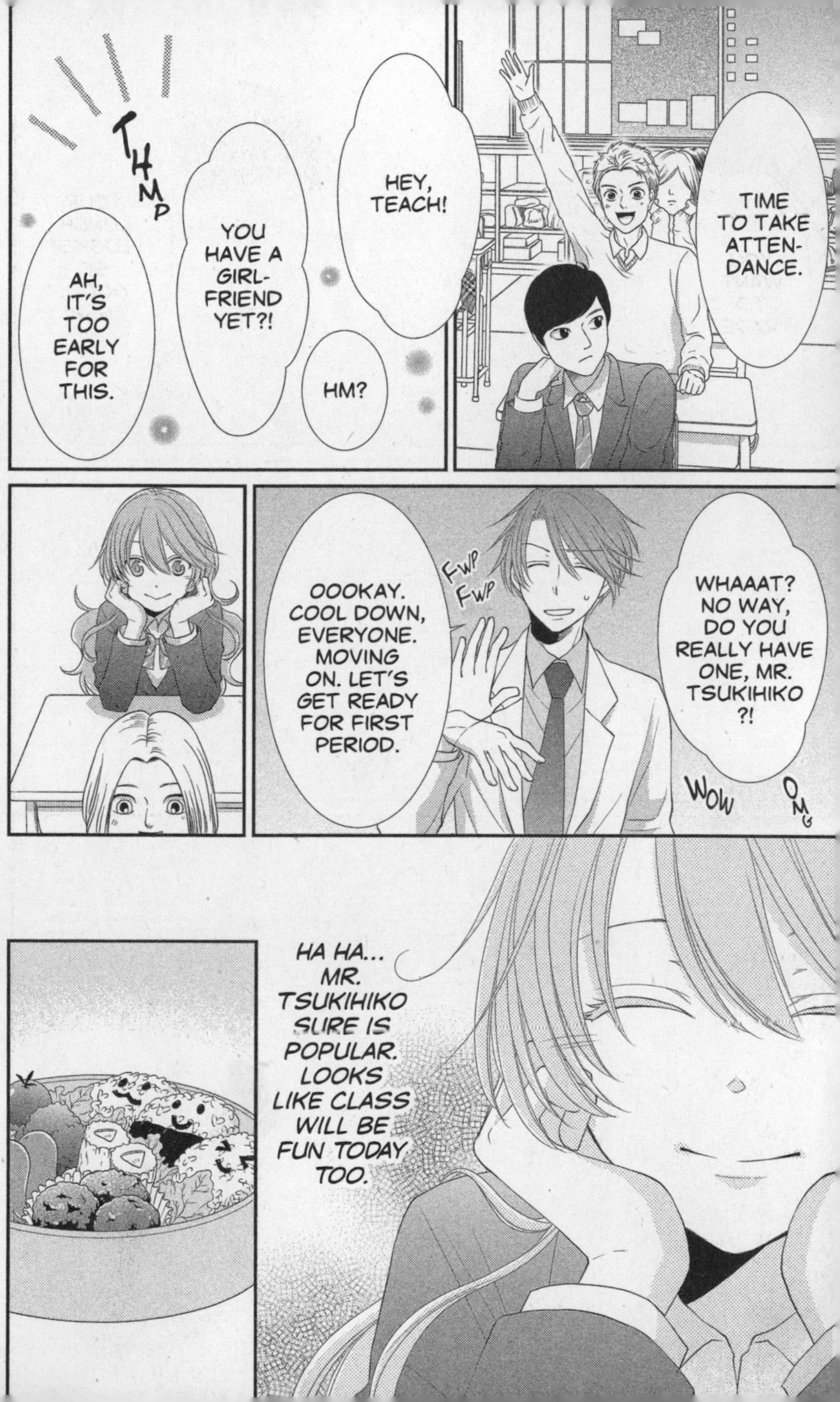
TIME TO TAKE ATTEN-DANCE.
HEY, TEACH!
HM?
YOU HAVE A GIRL-FRIEND YET?!
THMP
AH, IT'S TOO EARLY FOR THIS.
WHAAAT? NO WAY, DO YOU REALLY HAVE ONE, MR. TSUKIHIKO ?!
WOW
OMG
FWP FWP
OOOKAY. COOL DOWN, EVERYONE. MOVING ON. LET'S GET READY FOR FIRST PERIOD.
HA HA... MR. TSUKIHIKO SURE IS POPULAR. LOOKS LIKE CLASS WILL BE FUN TODAY TOO.

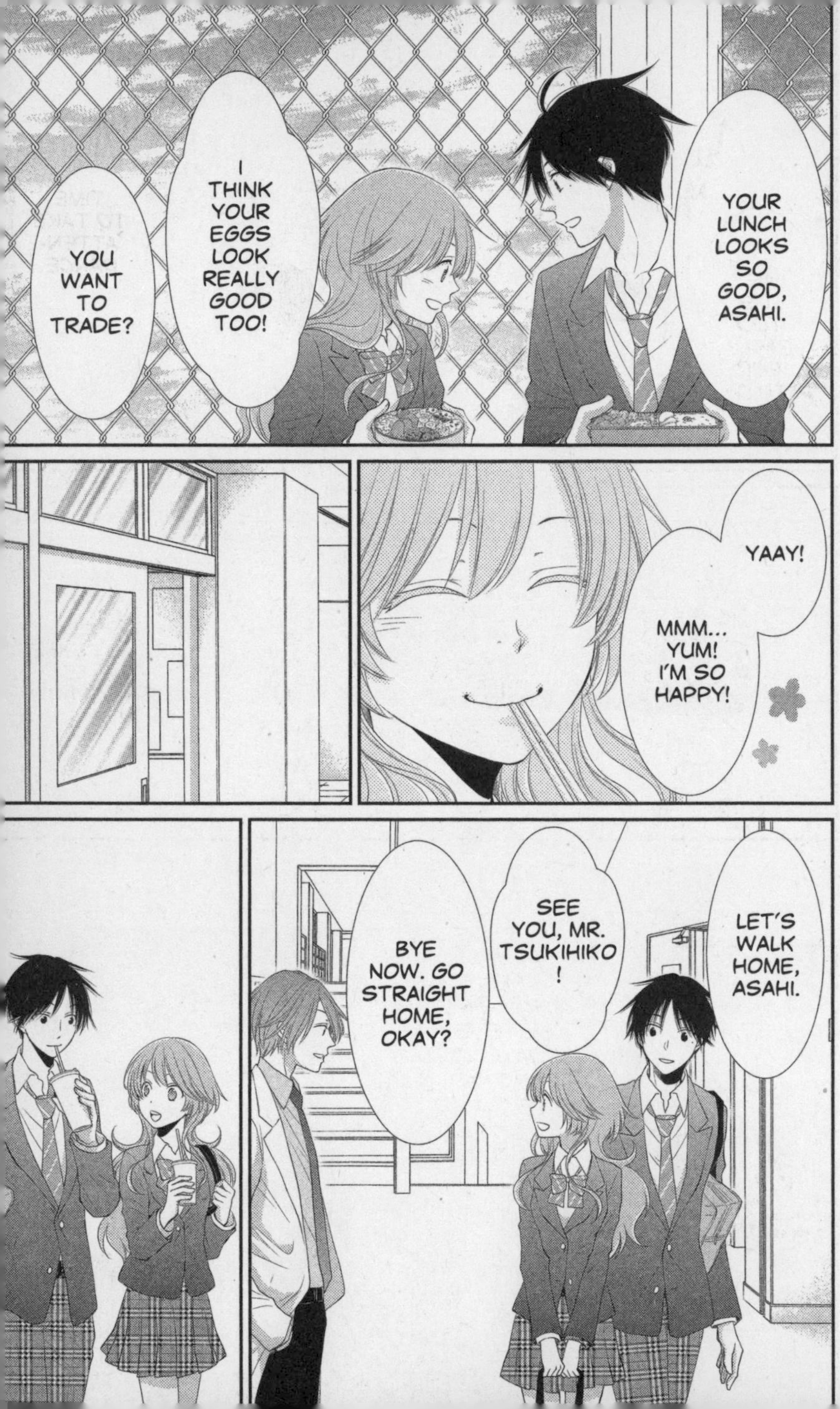
YOUR LUNCH LOOKS SO GOOD, ASAHI.
I THINK YOUR EGGS LOOK REALLY GOOD TOO!
YOU WANT TO TRADE?
YAAY!
MMM... YUM! I'M SO HAPPY!
LET'S WALK HOME, ASAHI.
SEE YOU, MR. TSUKIHIKO!
BYE NOW. GO STRAIGHT HOME, OKAY?

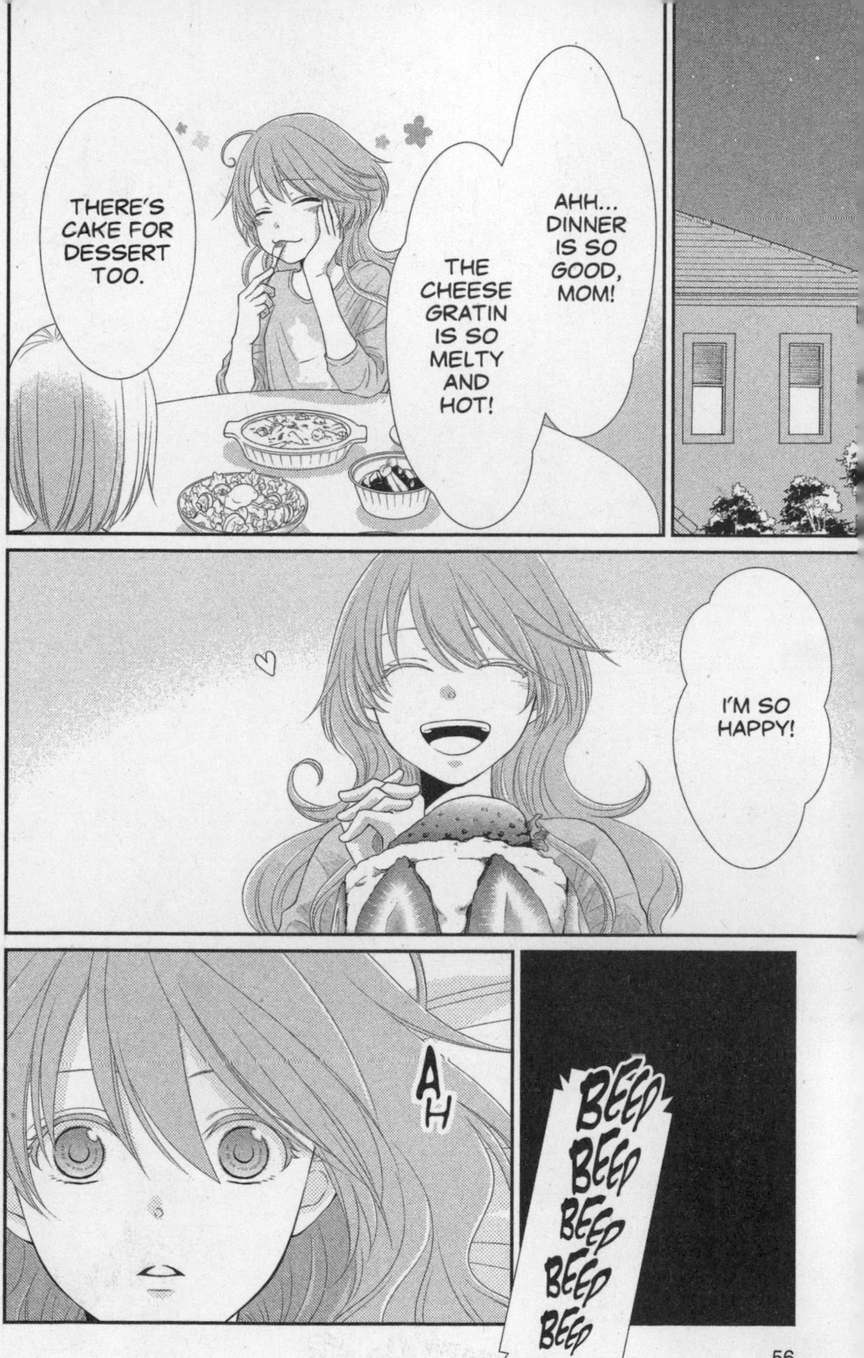
AHH... DINNER IS SO GOOD, MOM!
THE CHEESE GRATIN IS SO MELTY AND HOT!
THERE'S CAKE FOR DESSERT TOO.
I'M SO HAPPY!
BEEP BEEP BEEP BEEP BEEP
AH

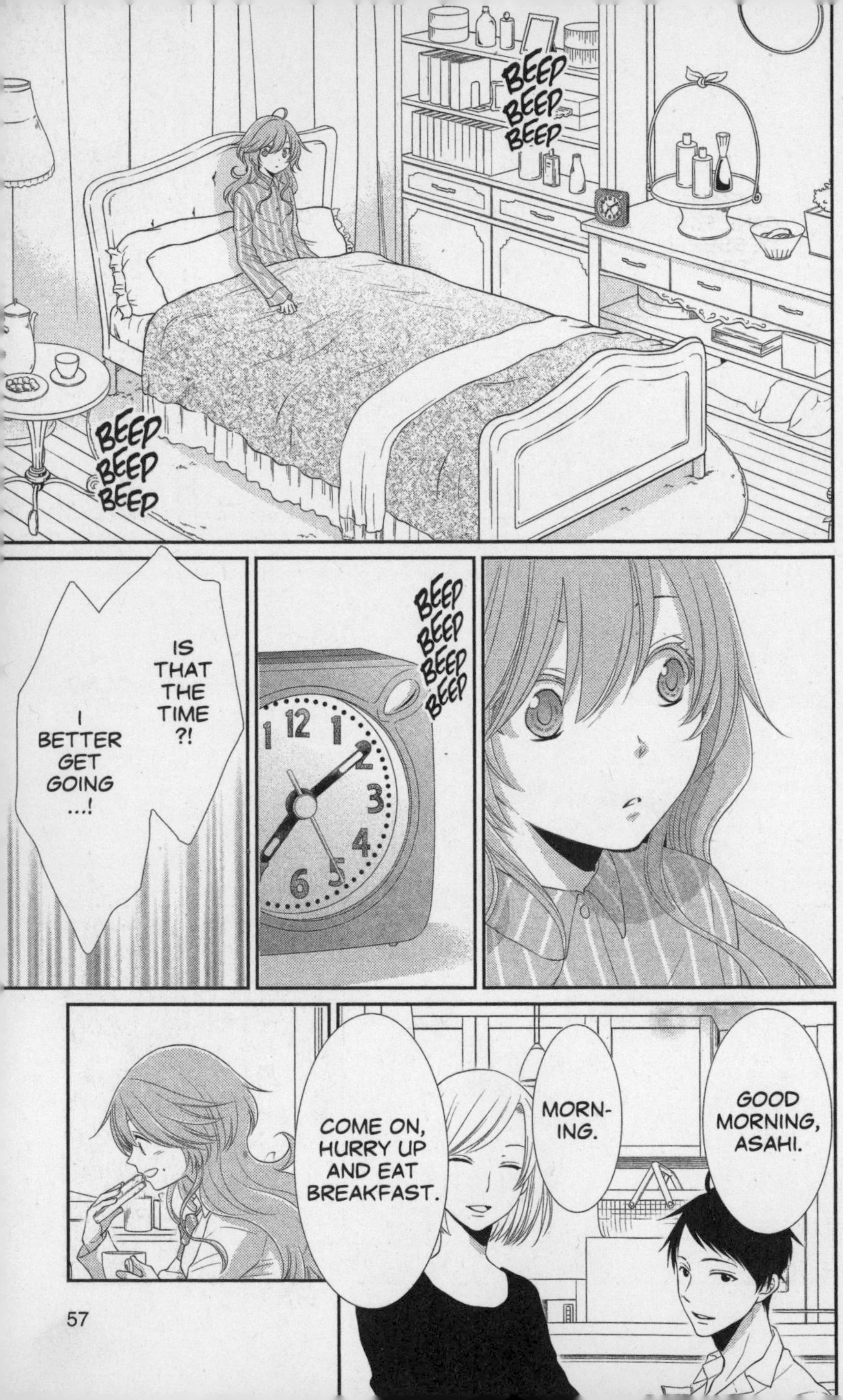
BEEP BEEP BEEP
BEEP BEEP BEEP
BEEP BEEP BEEP BEEP
IS THAT THE TIME?!
I BETTER GET GOING...!
GOOD MORNING, ASAHI.
MORN-ING.
COME ON, HURRY UP AND EAT BREAKFAST.

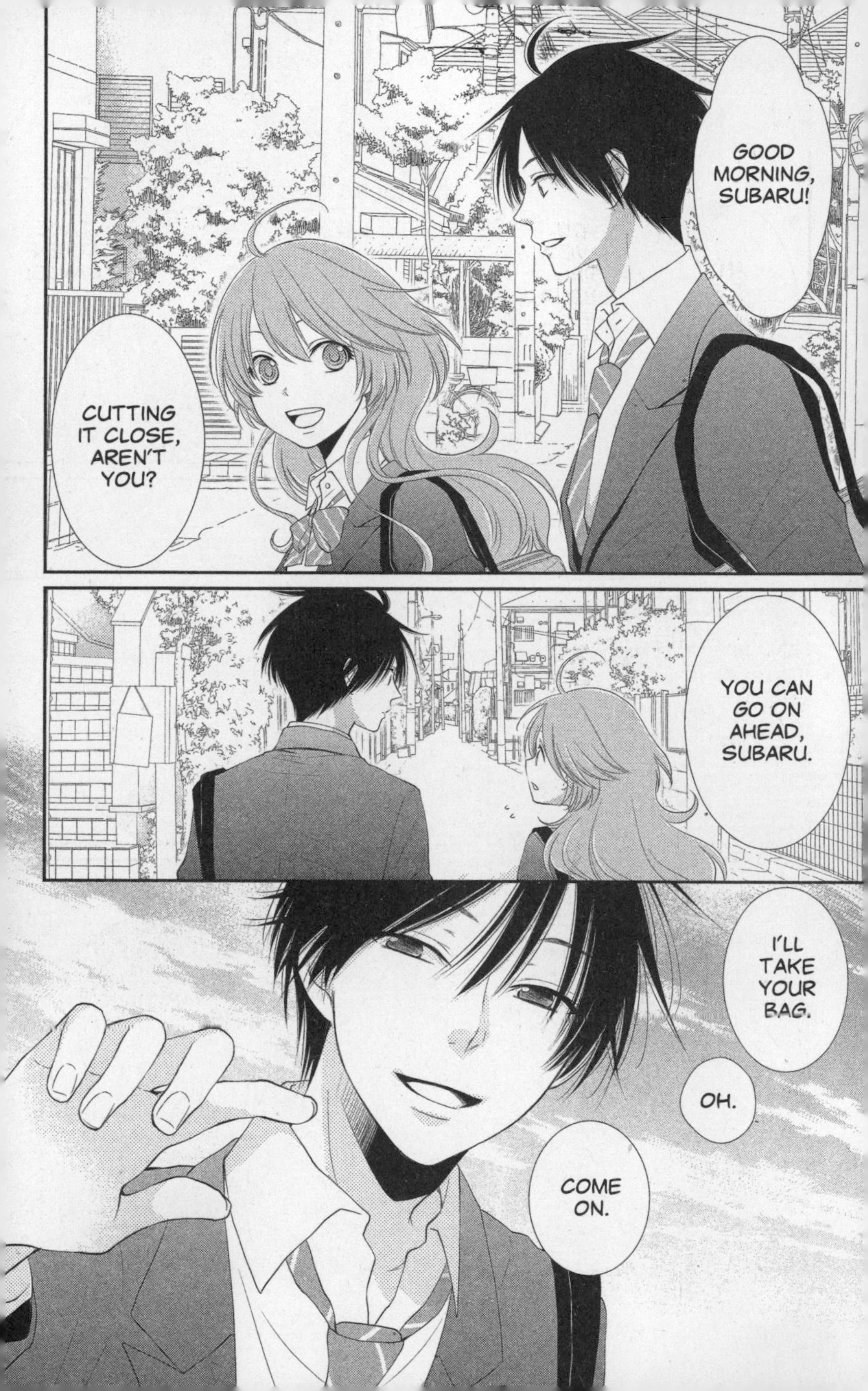
GOOD MORNING, SUBARU!
CUTTING IT CLOSE, AREN'T YOU?
YOU CAN GO ON AHEAD, SUBARU.
I'LL TAKE YOUR BAG.
OH.
COME ON.

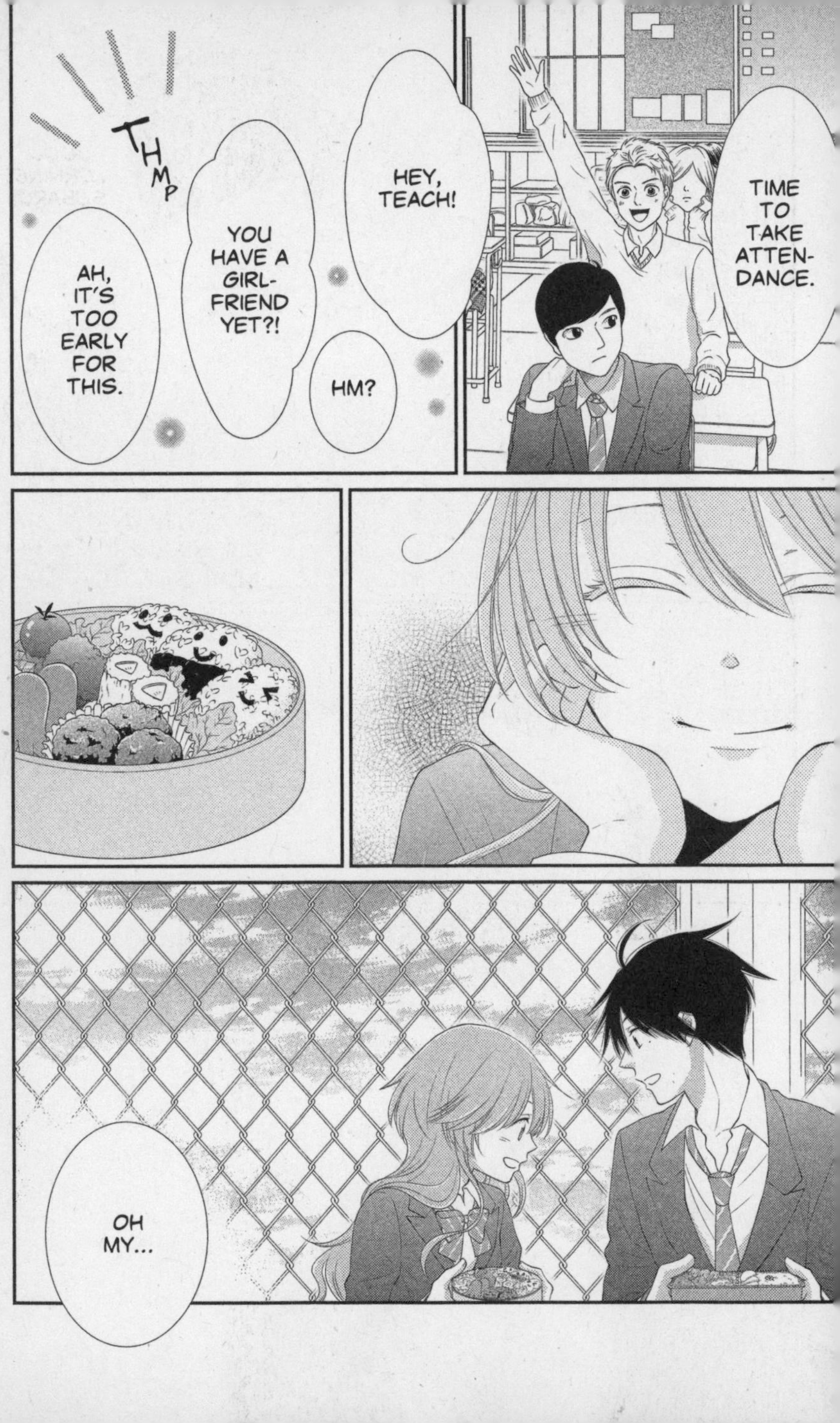
TIME TO TAKE ATTENDANCE.
HEY, TEACH!
YOU HAVE A GIRLFRIEND YET?!
HM?
THMP
AH, IT'S TOO EARLY FOR THIS.
OH MY...

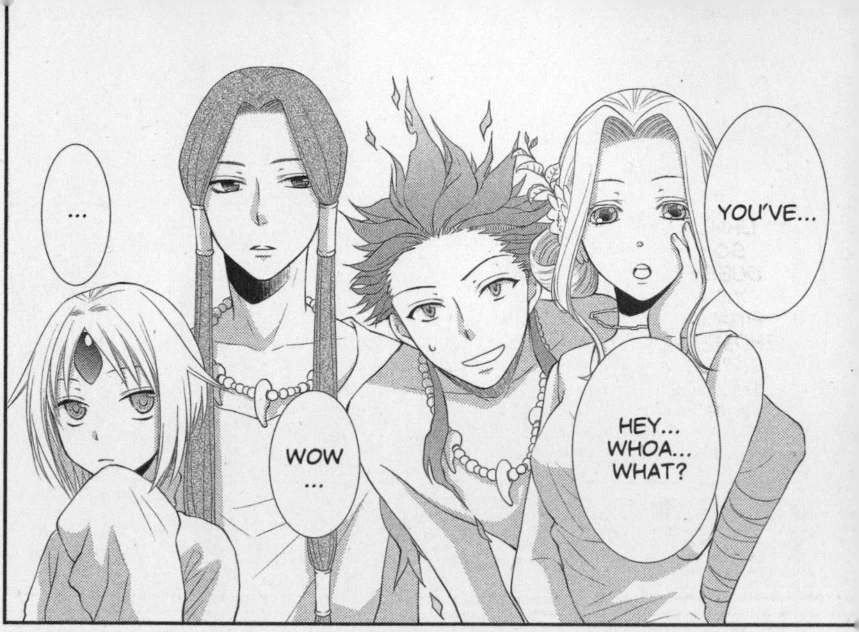
YOU'VE...
HEY... WHOA... WHAT?
WOW...
...

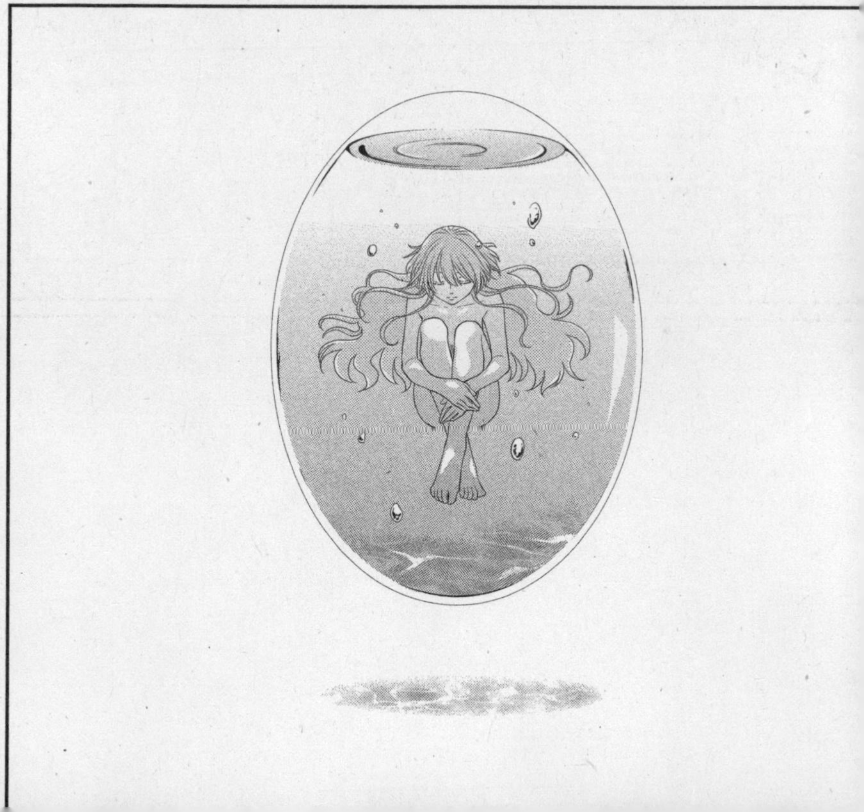

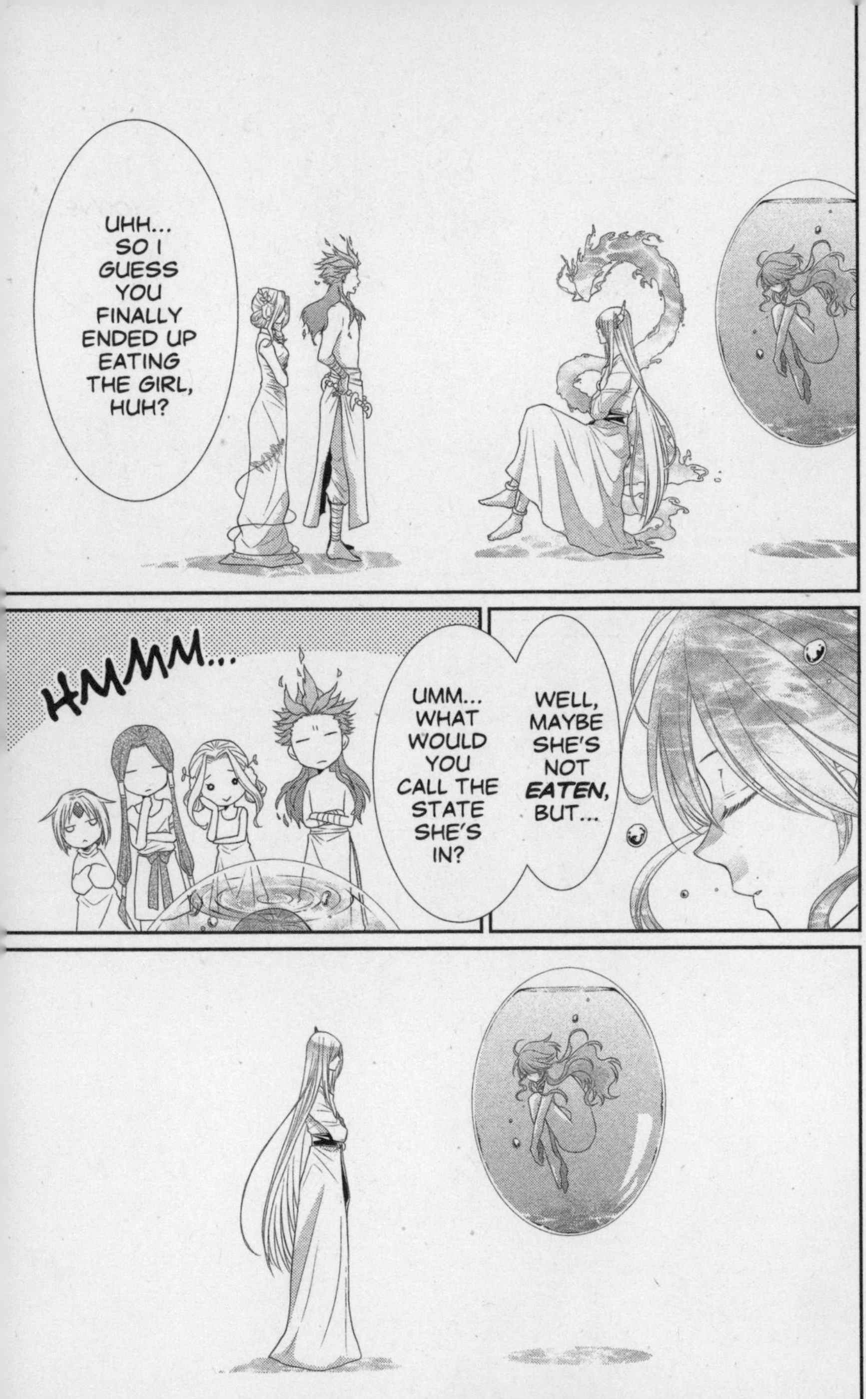
UHH... SO I GUESS YOU FINALLY ENDED UP EATING THE GIRL, HUH?
WELL, MAYBE SHE'S NOT *EATEN*, BUT...
UMM... WHAT WOULD YOU CALL THE STATE SHE'S IN?
HMMM...

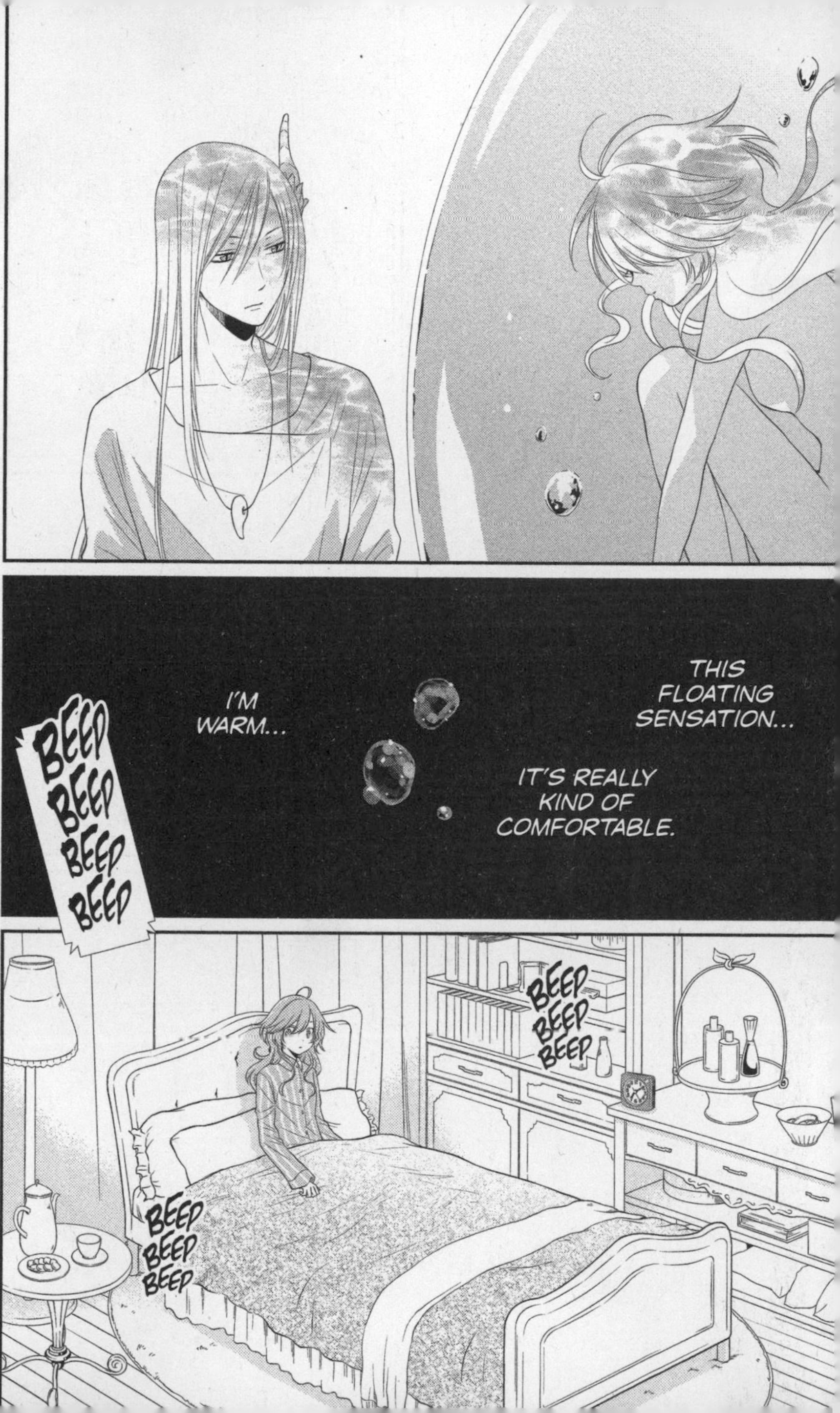
THIS FLOATING SENSATION...
IT'S REALLY KIND OF COMFORTABLE.
I'M WARM...
BEEP BEEP BEEP BEEP
BEEP BEEP BEEP
BEEP BEEP BEEP

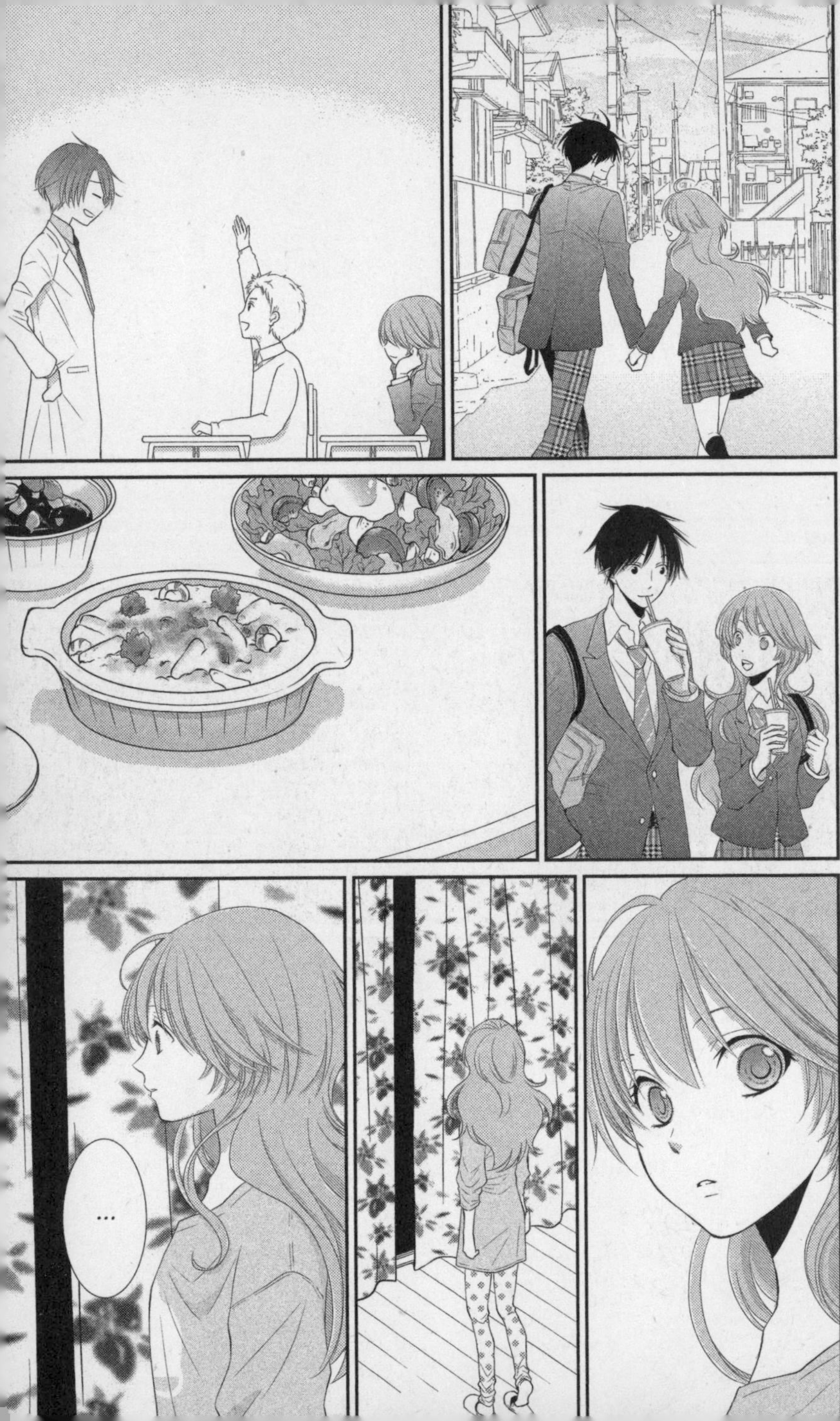
...

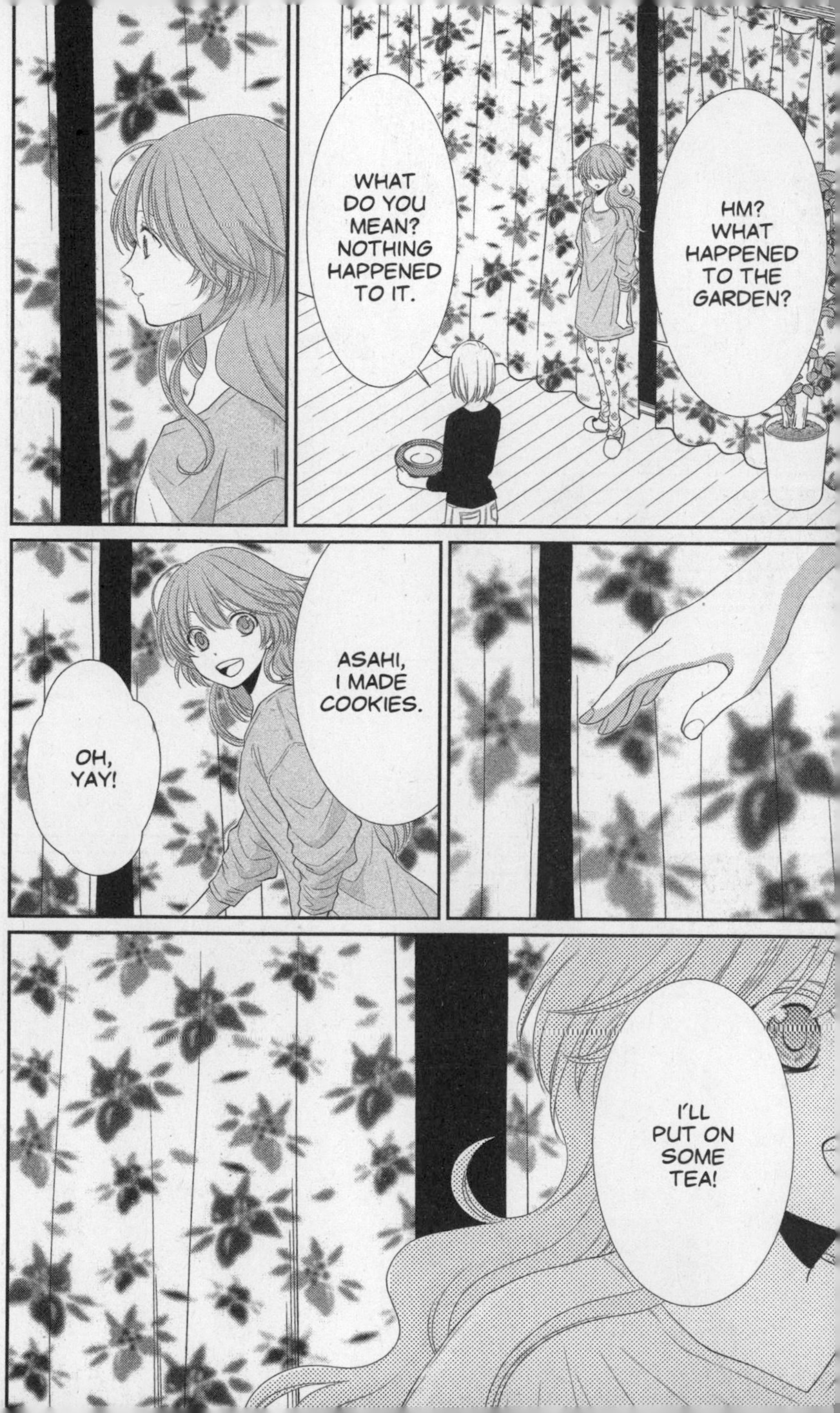
HM? WHAT HAPPENED TO THE GARDEN?
WHAT DO YOU MEAN? NOTHING HAPPENED TO IT.
ASAHI, I MADE COOKIES.
OH, YAY!
I'LL PUT ON SOME TEA!

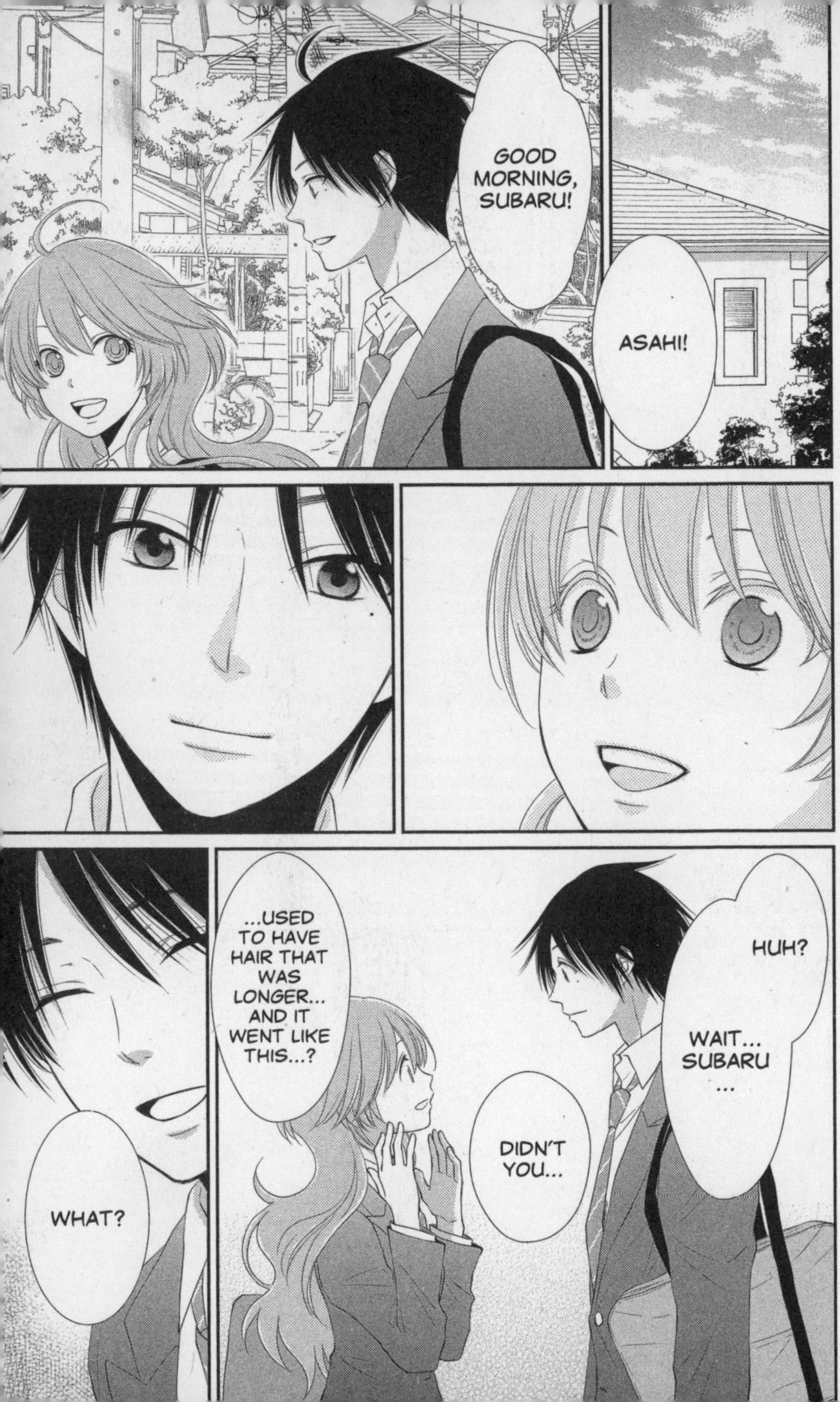
ASAHI!
GOOD MORNING, SUBARU!
HUH?
WAIT... SUBARU ...
DIDN'T YOU...
...USED TO HAVE HAIR THAT WAS LONGER... AND IT WENT LIKE THIS...?
WHAT?

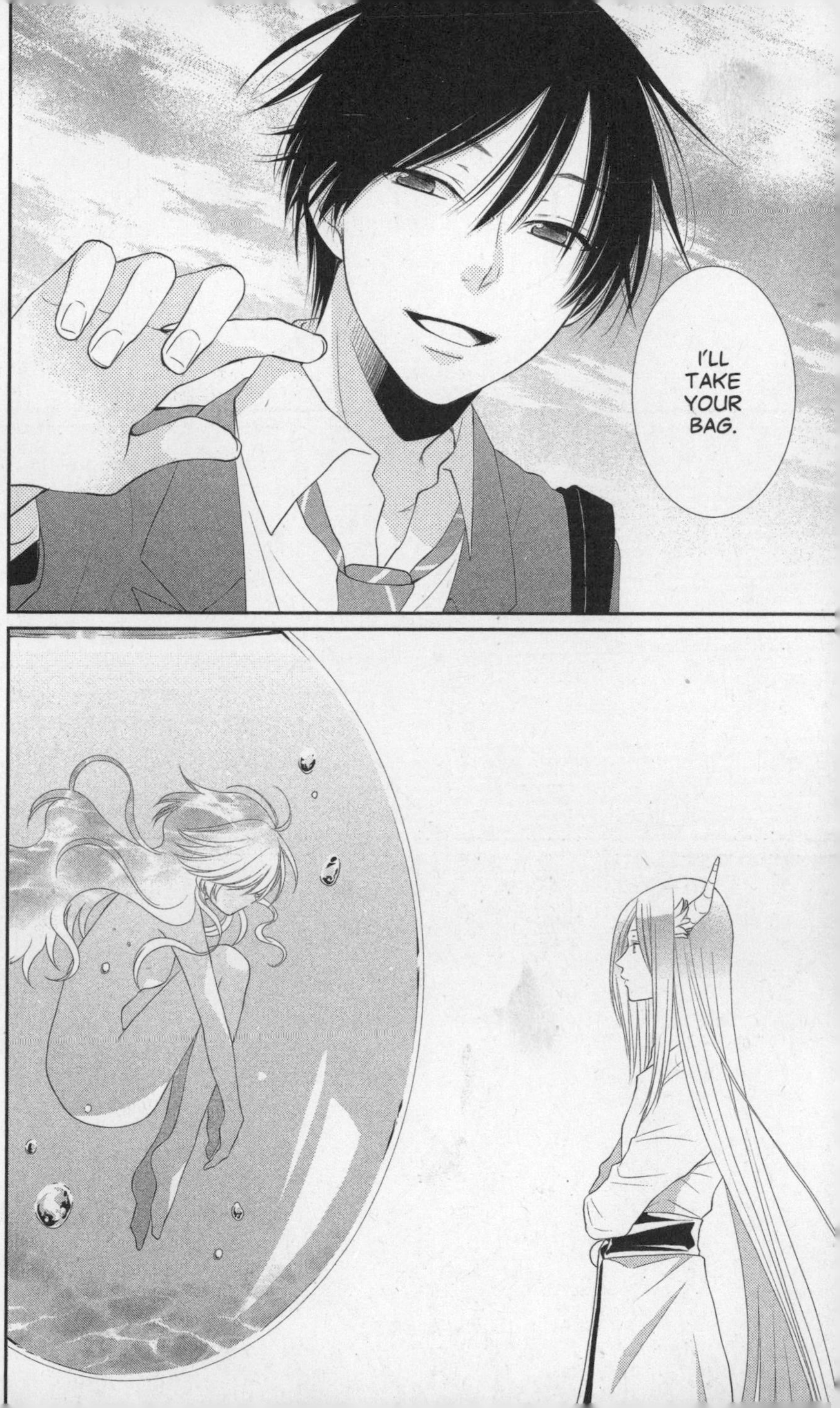
I'LL TAKE YOUR BAG.

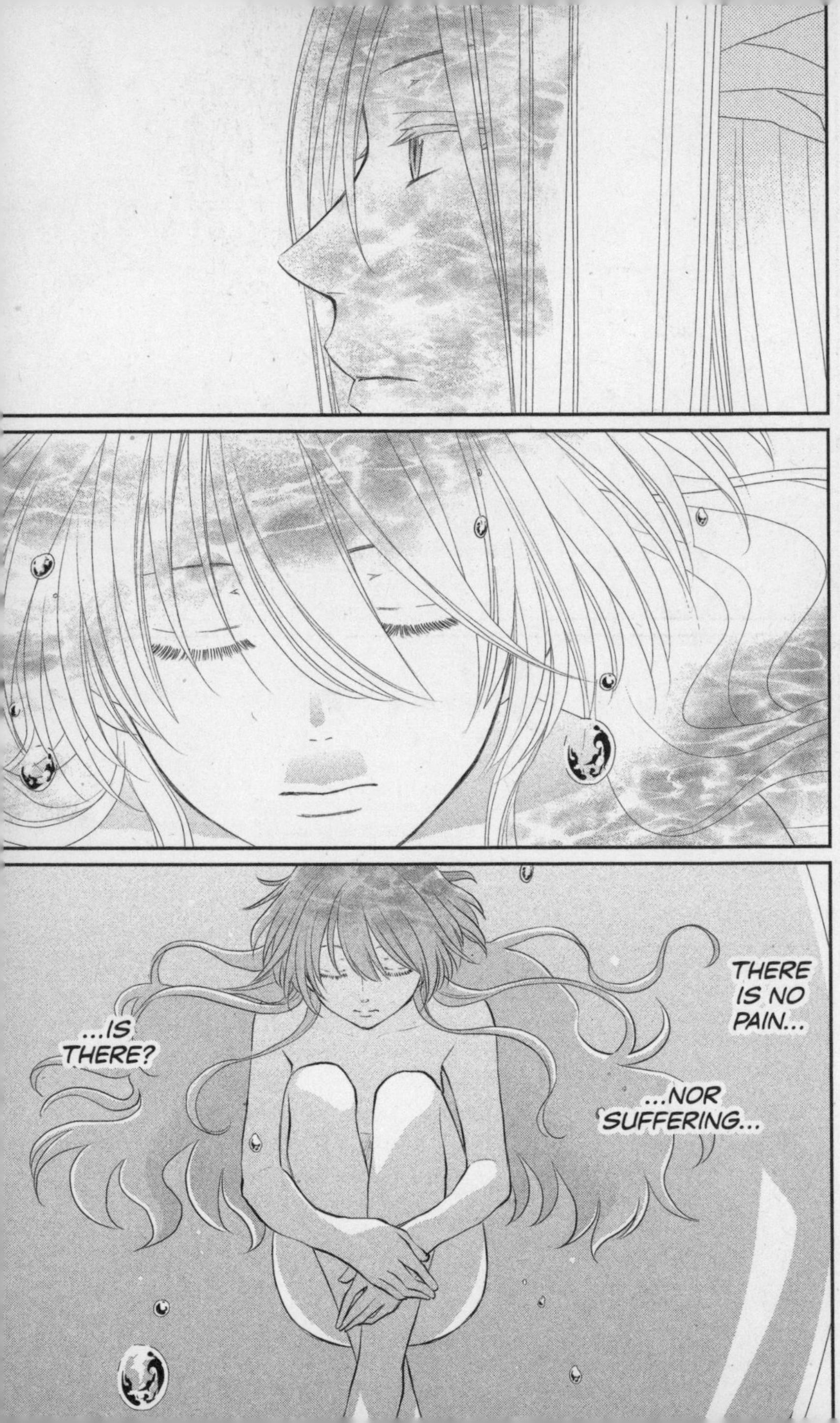
THERE IS NO PAIN...
...NOR SUFFERING...
...IS THERE?

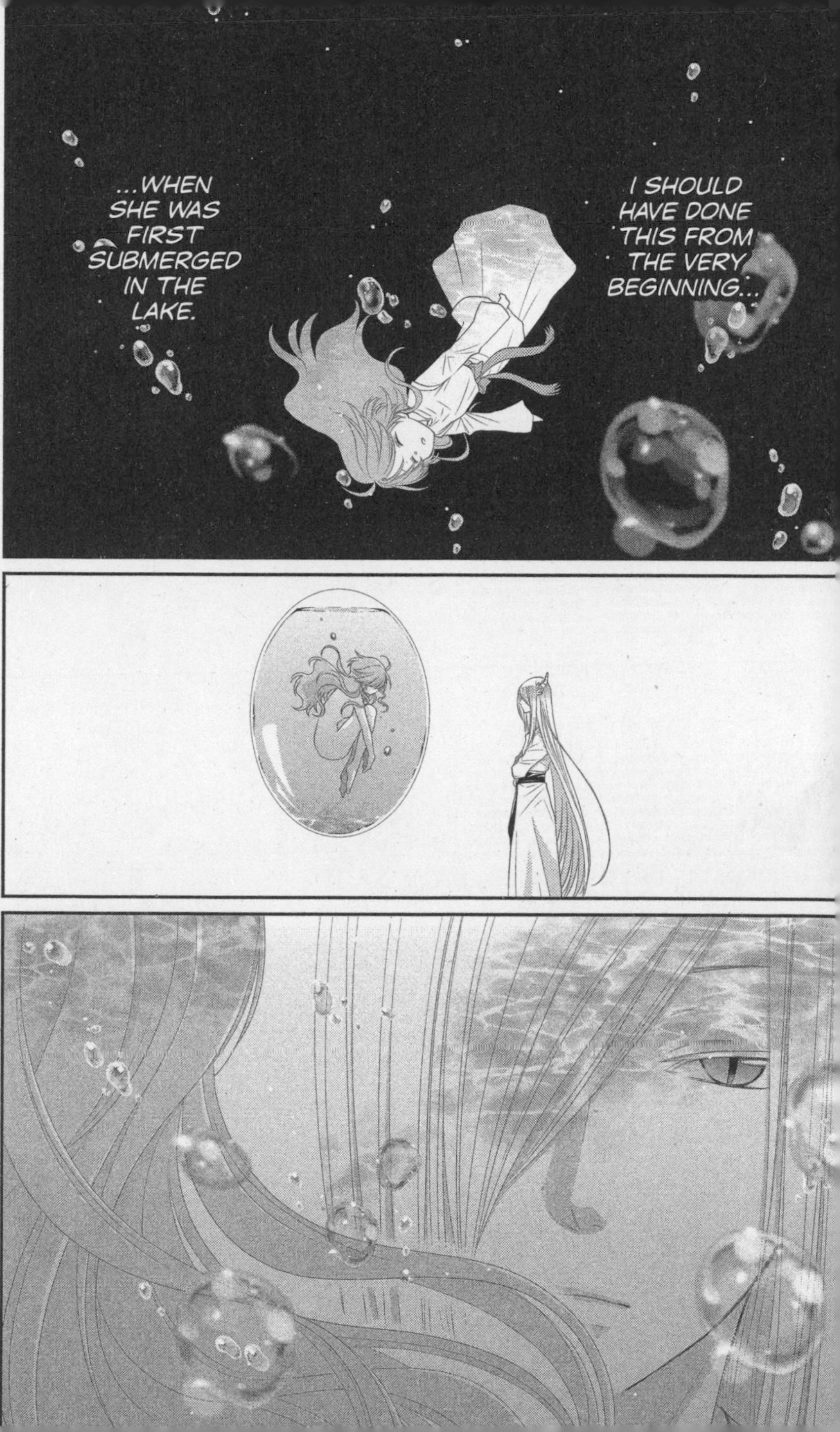
I SHOULD HAVE DONE THIS FROM THE VERY BEGINNING...
...WHEN SHE WAS FIRST SUBMERGED IN THE LAKE.

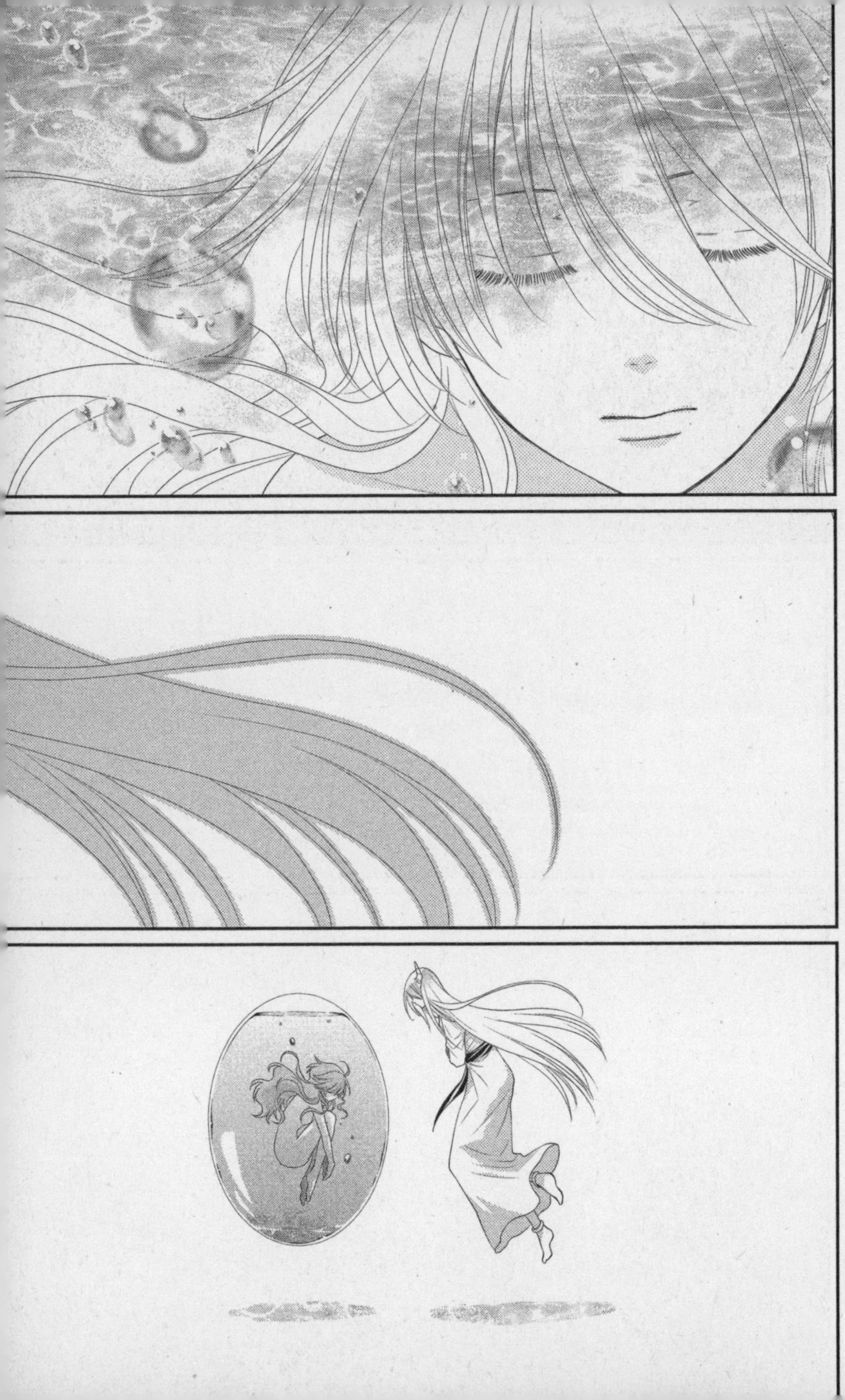

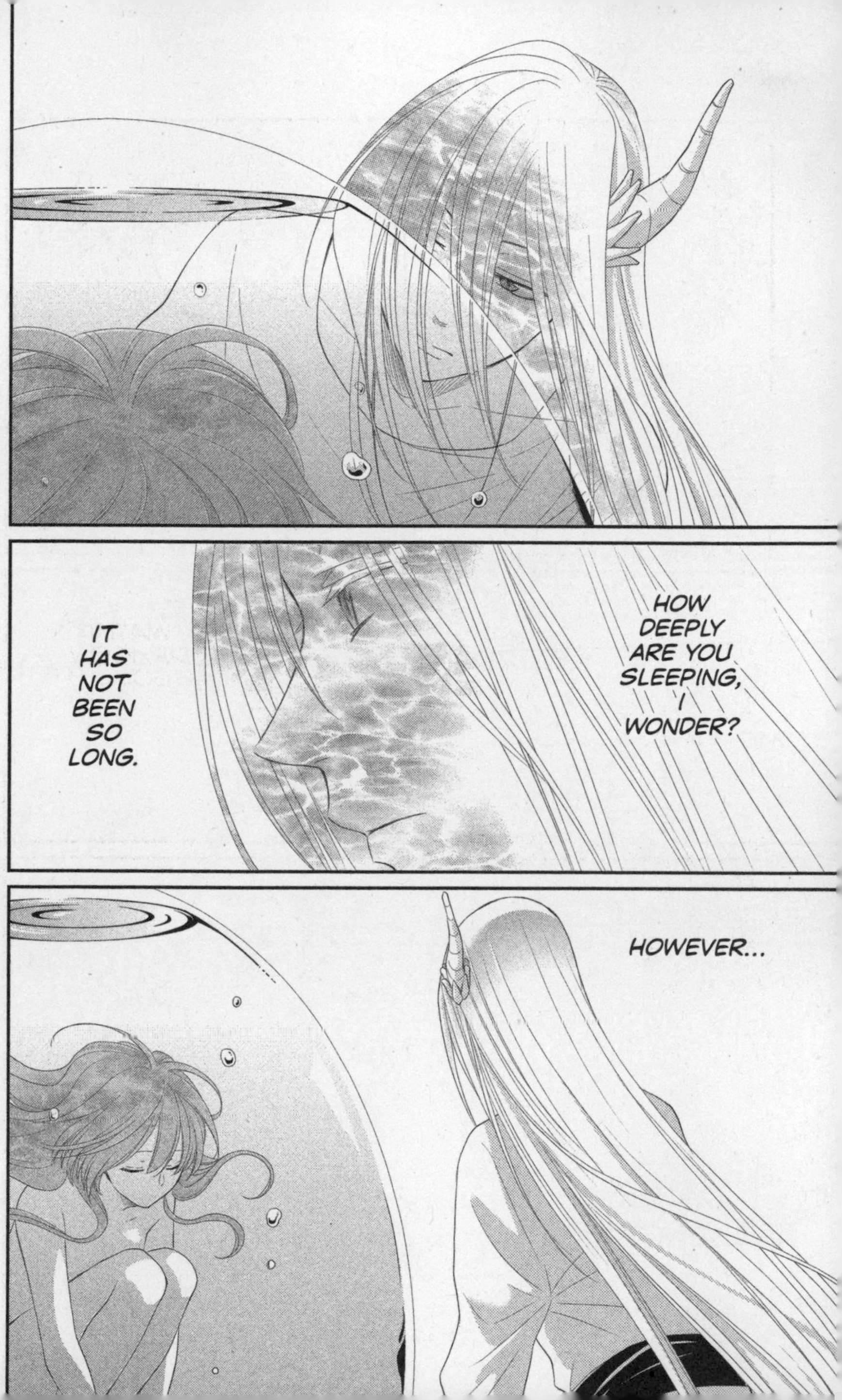
HOW DEEPLY ARE YOU SLEEPING, I WONDER?
IT HAS NOT BEEN SO LONG.
HOWEVER...

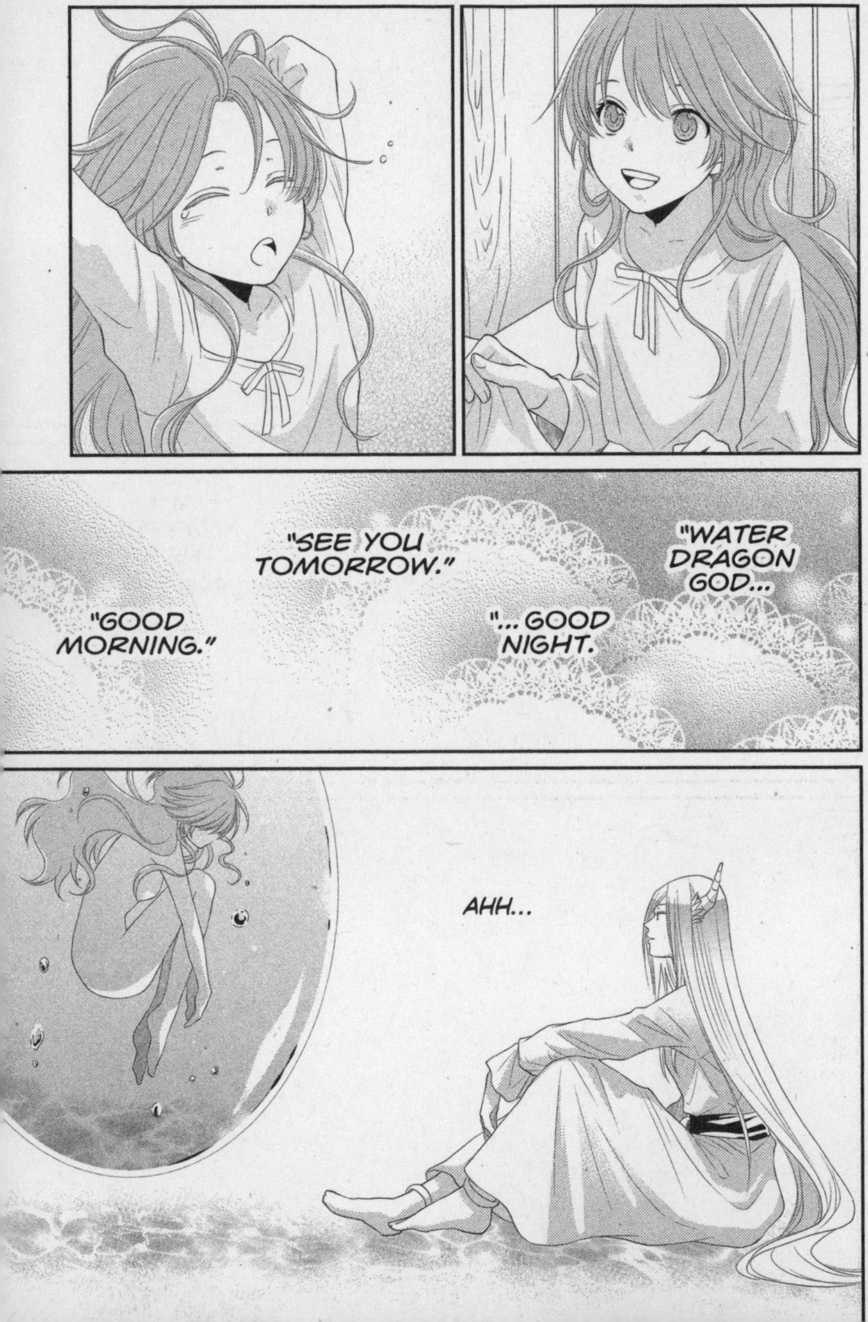
"WATER DRAGON GOD...
"... GOOD NIGHT.
"SEE YOU TOMORROW."
"GOOD MORNING."
AHH...

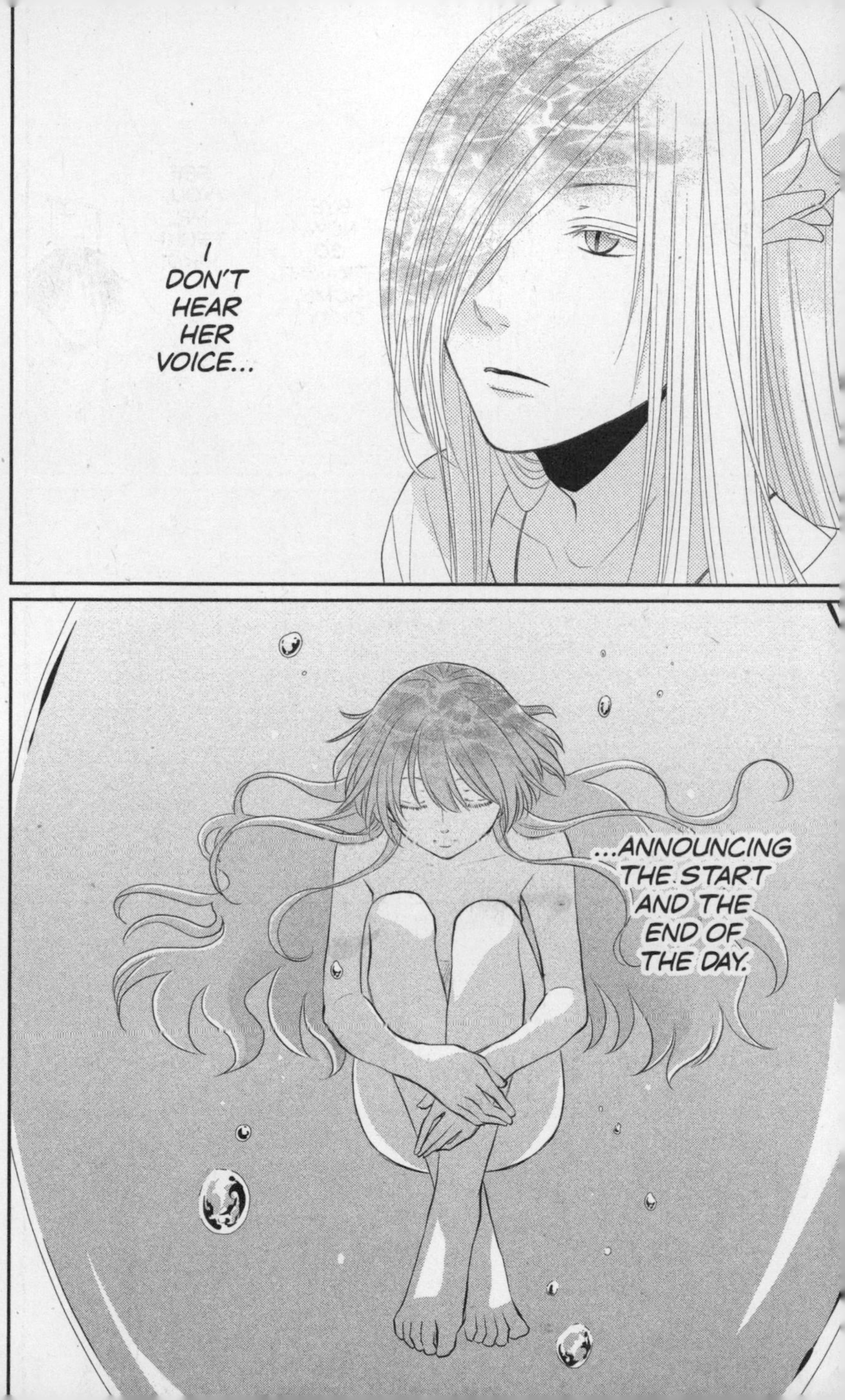
I DON'T HEAR HER VOICE...
...ANNOUNCING THE START AND THE END OF THE DAY.

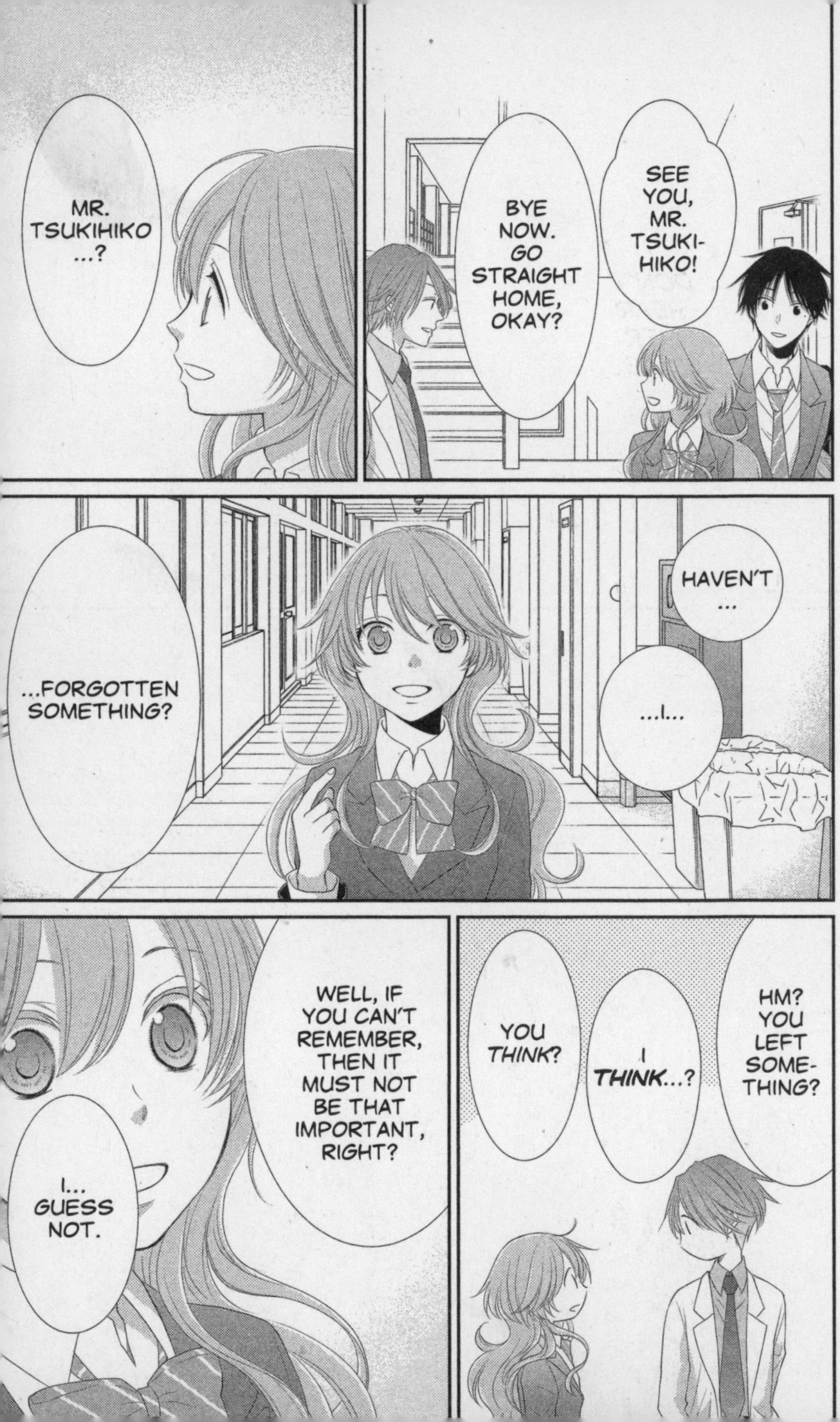
SEE YOU, MR. TSUKIHIKO!
BYE NOW. GO STRAIGHT HOME, OKAY?
MR. TSUKIHIKO ...?
HAVEN'T ...
...I...
...FORGOTTEN SOMETHING?
HM? YOU LEFT SOMETHING?
I *THINK*...?
YOU *THINK*?
WELL, IF YOU CAN'T REMEMBER, THEN IT MUST NOT BE THAT IMPORTANT, RIGHT?
I... GUESS NOT.

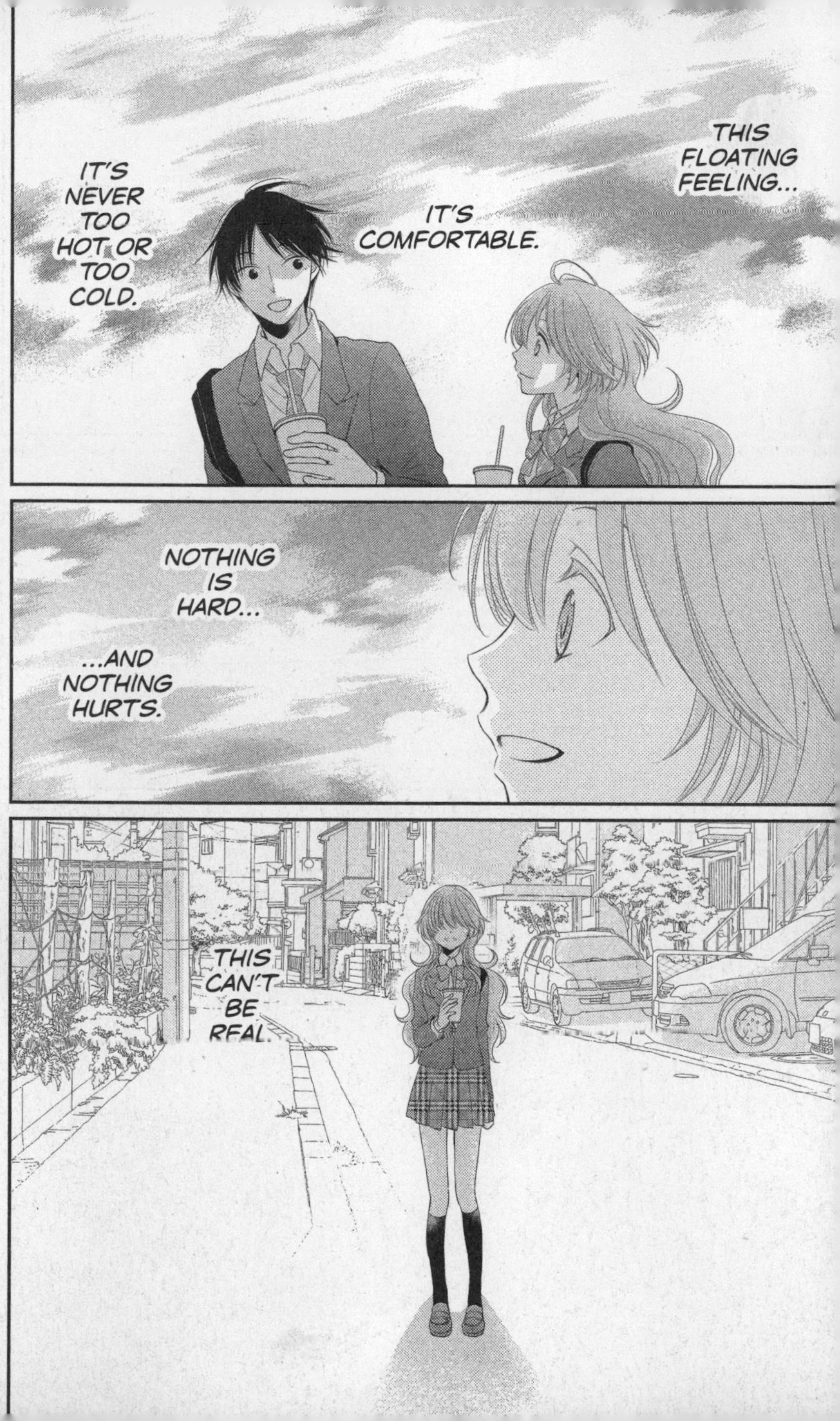
THIS FLOATING FEELING...
IT'S COMFORTABLE.
IT'S NEVER TOO HOT OR TOO COLD.
NOTHING IS HARD...
...AND NOTHING HURTS.
THIS CAN'T BE REAL

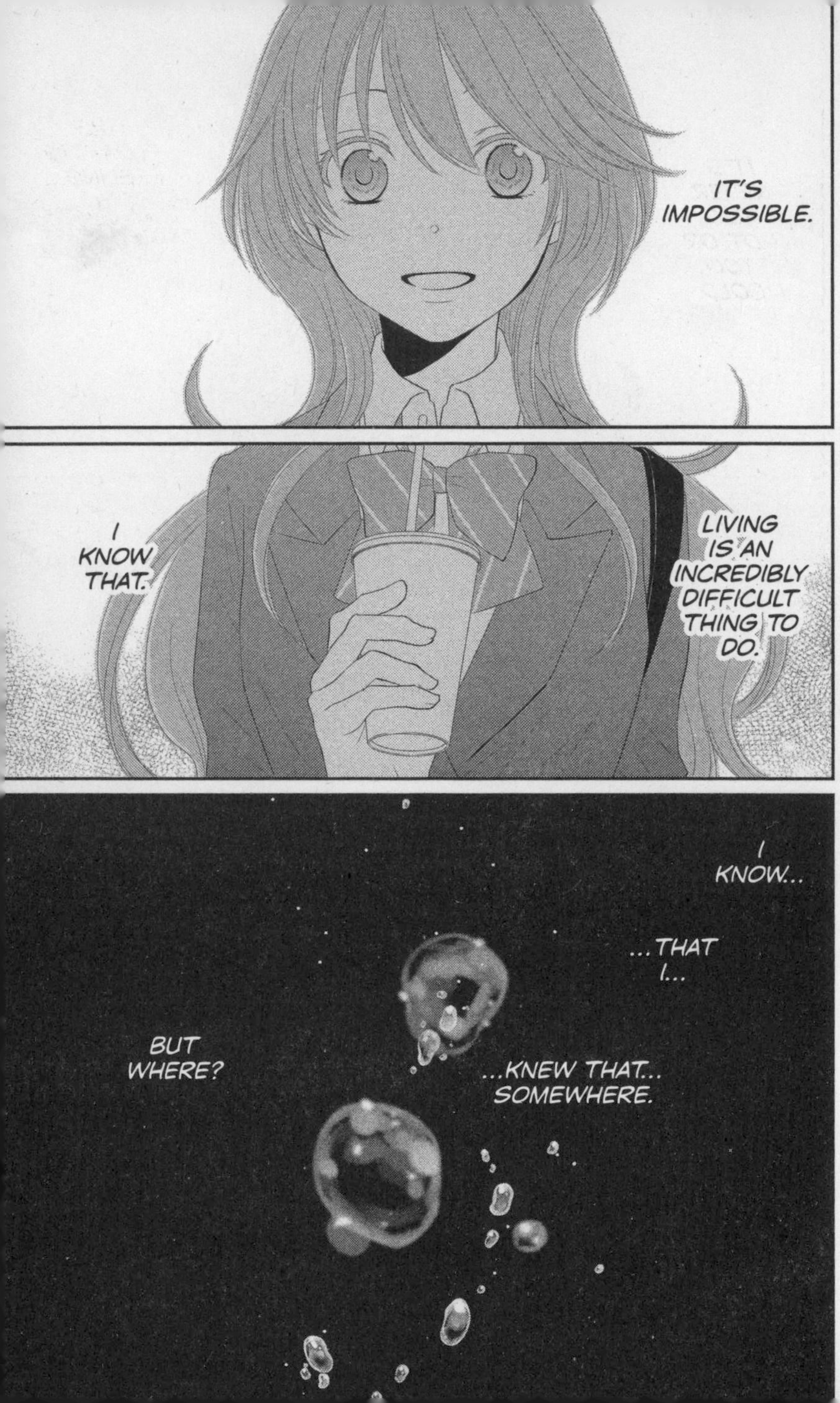
IT'S IMPOSSIBLE.
LIVING IS AN INCREDIBLY DIFFICULT THING TO DO.
I KNOW THAT.
I KNOW...
...THAT I...
...KNEW THAT... SOMEWHERE.
BUT WHERE?

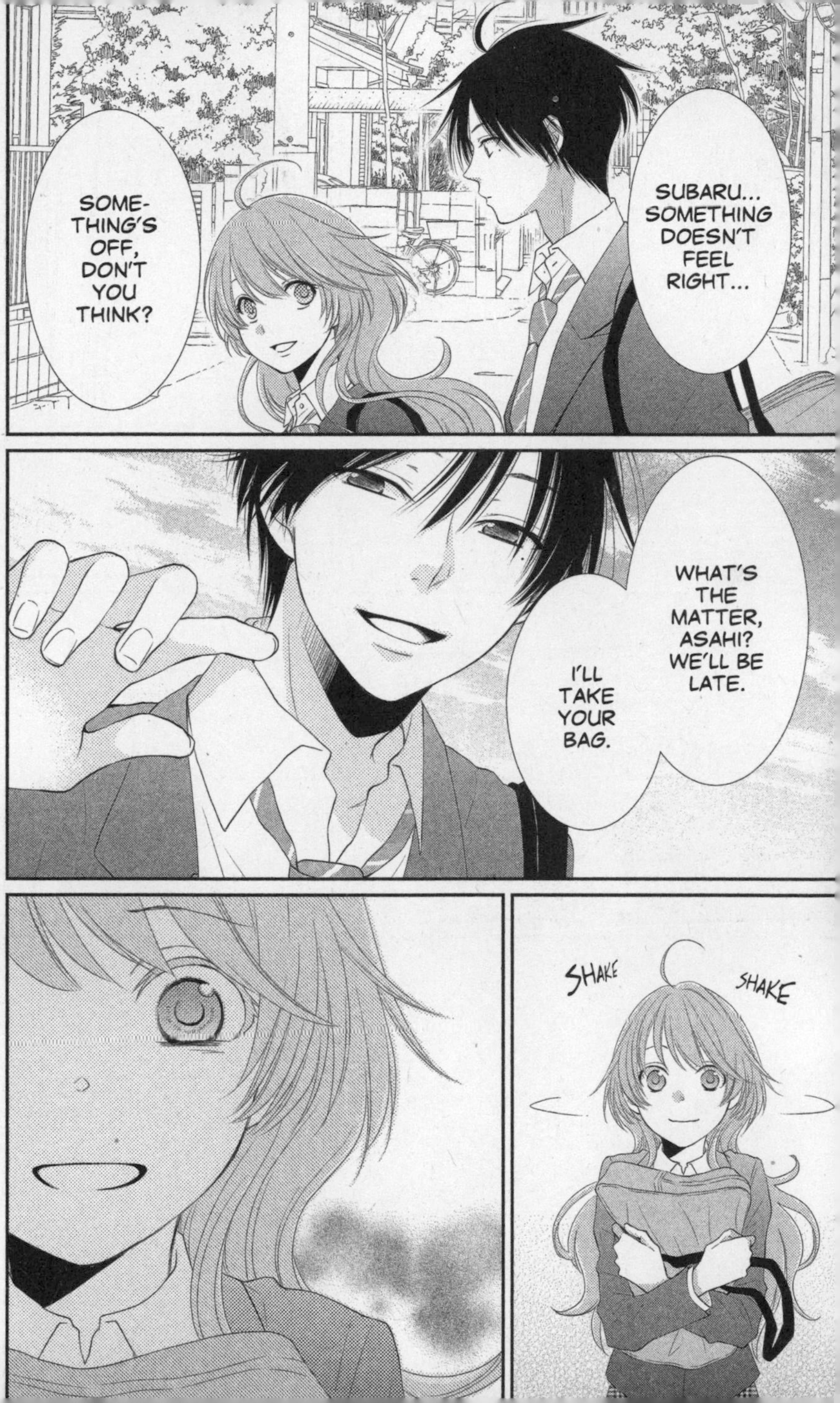
SUBARU... SOMETHING DOESN'T FEEL RIGHT...
SOME-THING'S OFF, DON'T YOU THINK?
WHAT'S THE MATTER, ASAHI? WE'LL BE LATE.
I'LL TAKE YOUR BAG.
SHAKE
SHAKE

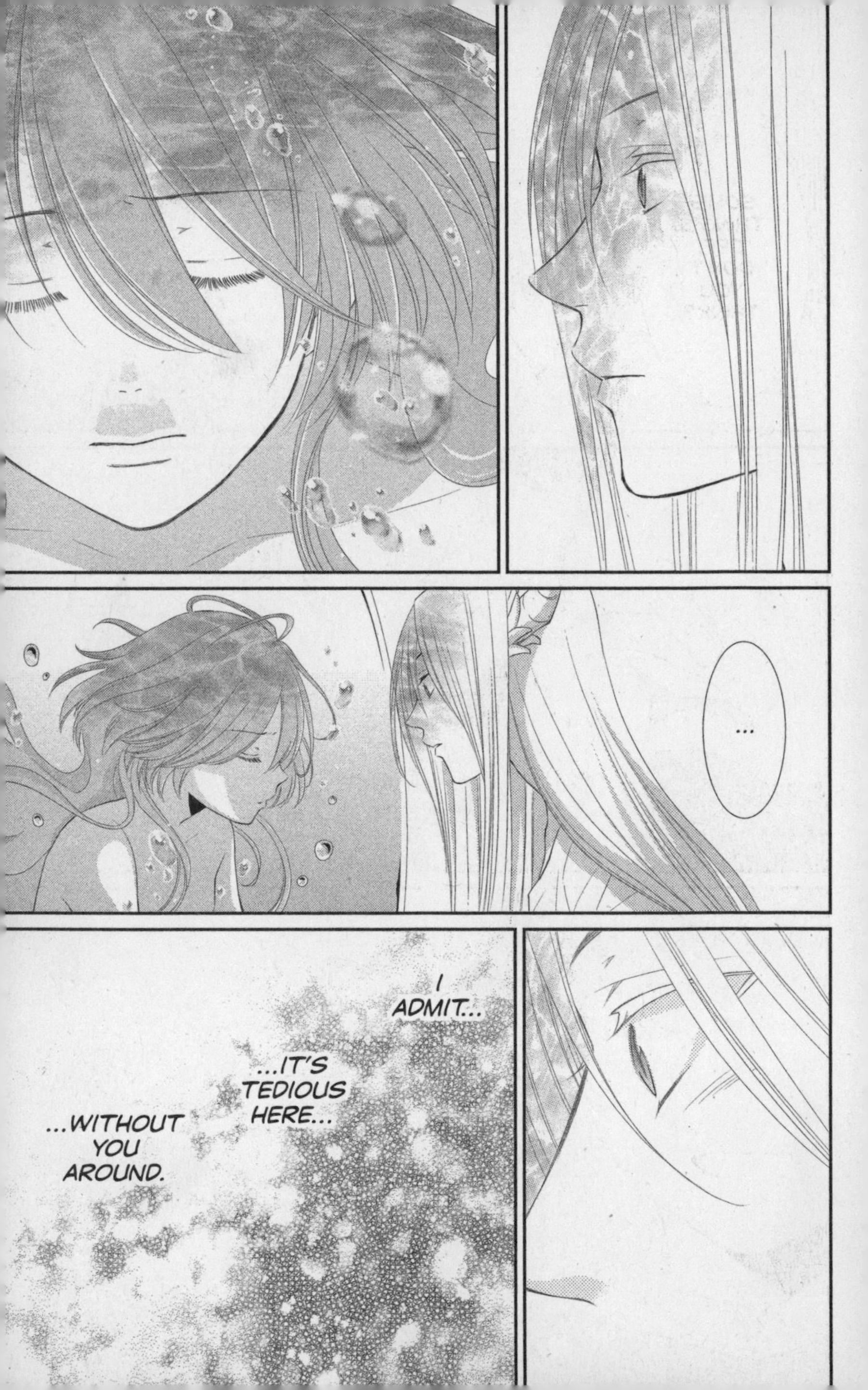
...
I ADMIT...
...IT'S TEDIOUS HERE...
...WITHOUT YOU AROUND.

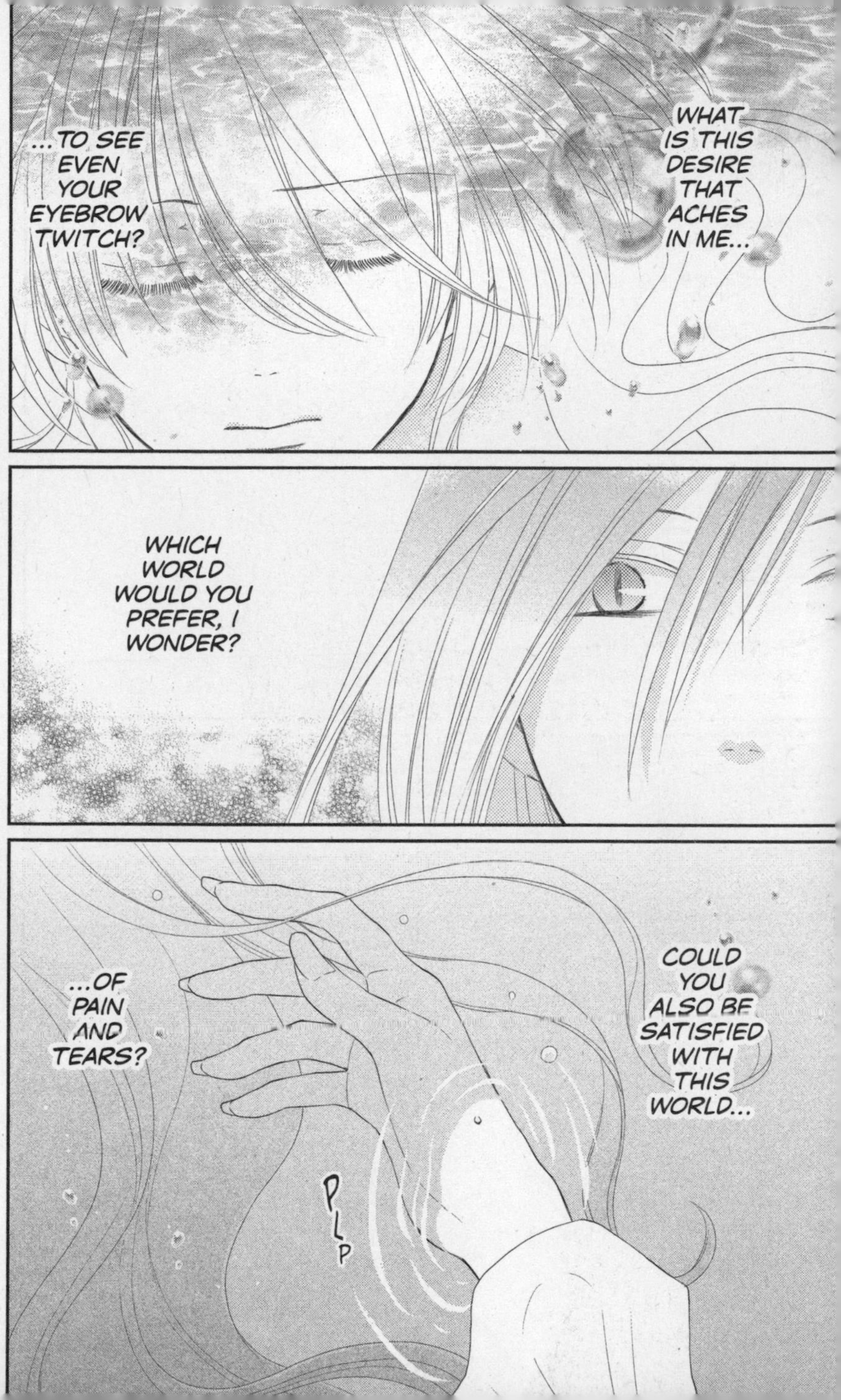
WHAT IS THIS DESIRE THAT ACHES IN ME...
...TO SEE EVEN YOUR EYEBROW TWITCH?
WHICH WORLD WOULD YOU PREFER, I WONDER?
COULD YOU ALSO BE SATISFIED WITH THIS WORLD...
...OF PAIN AND TEARS?
PLP

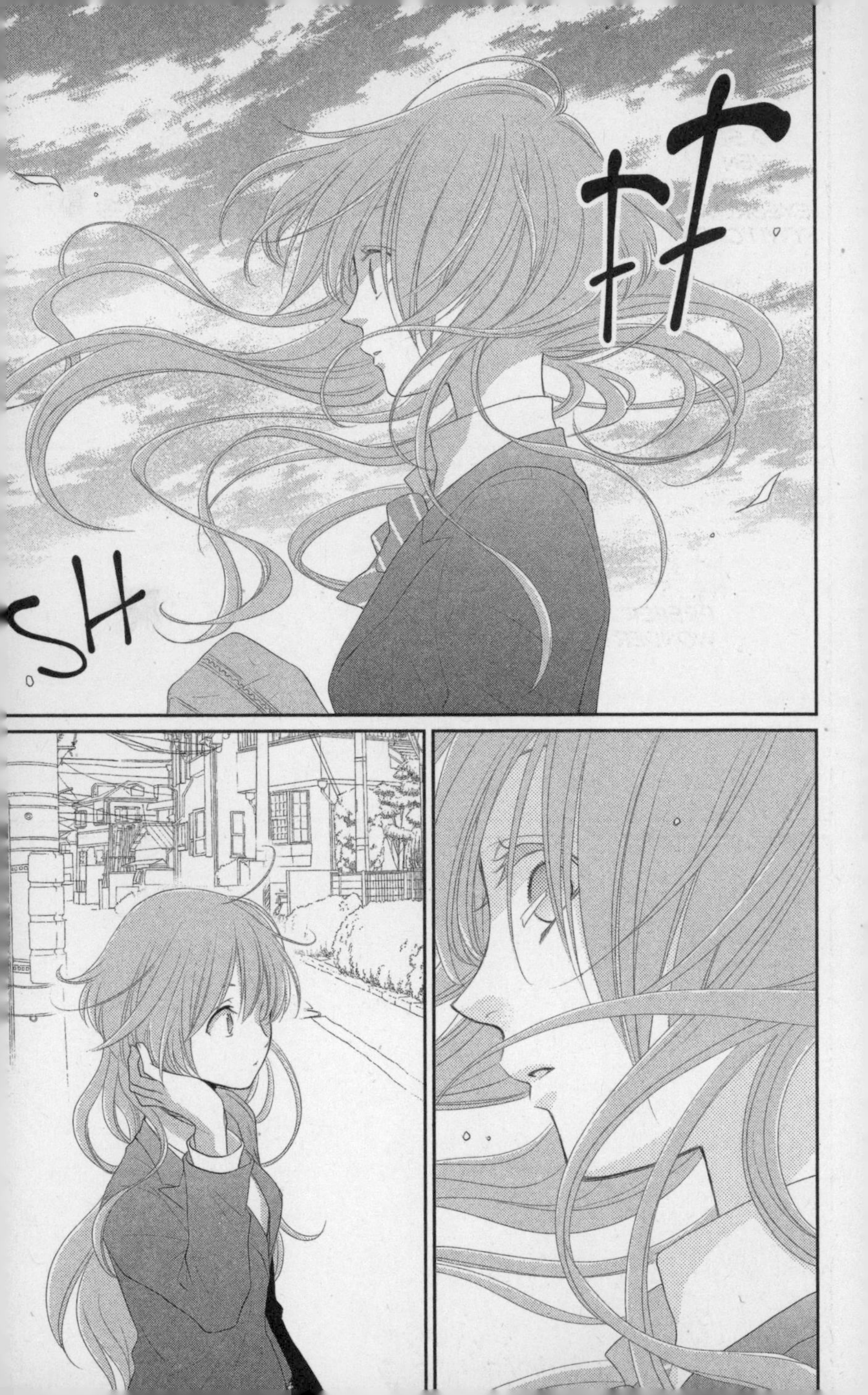
SH

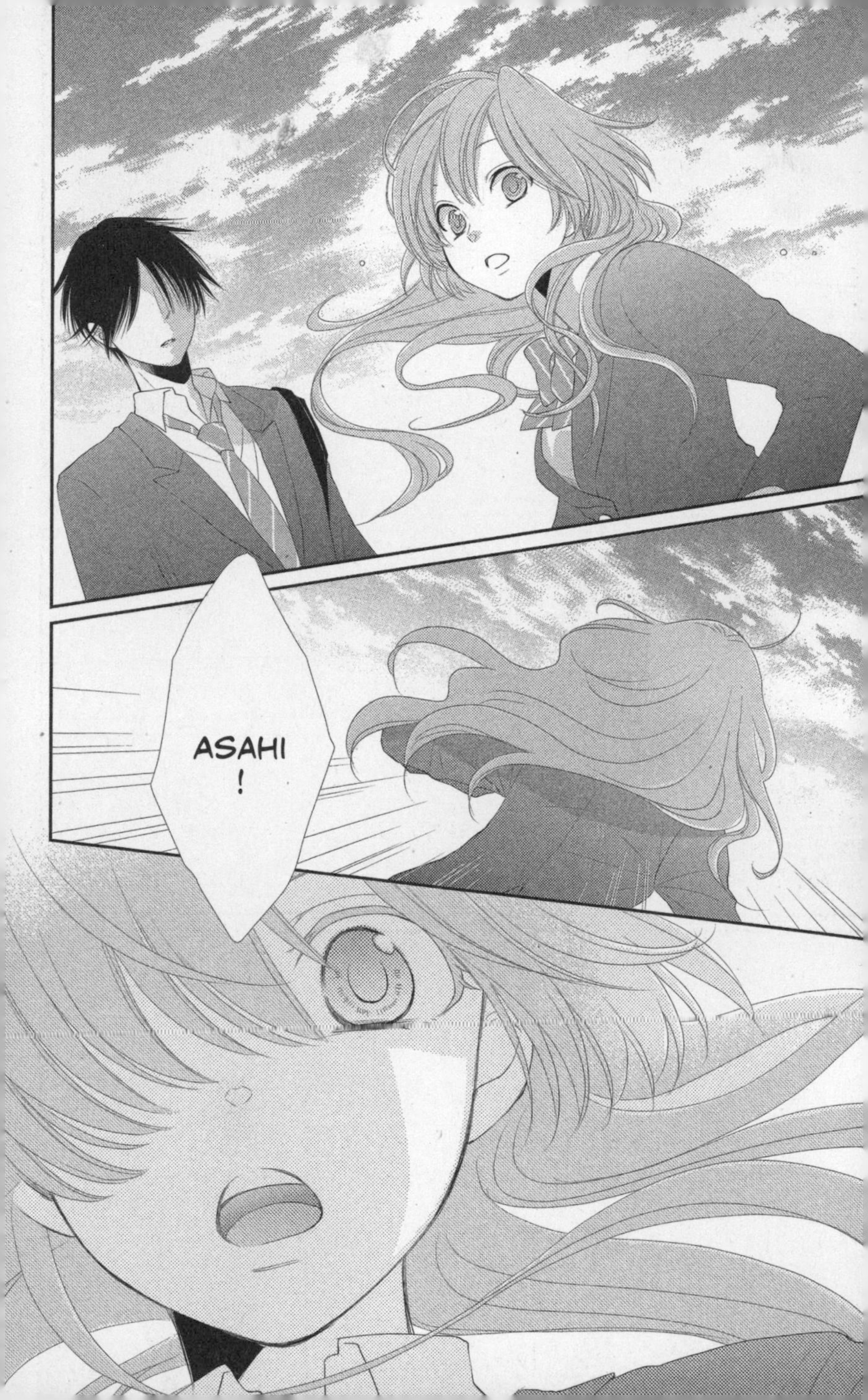
ASAHI
!

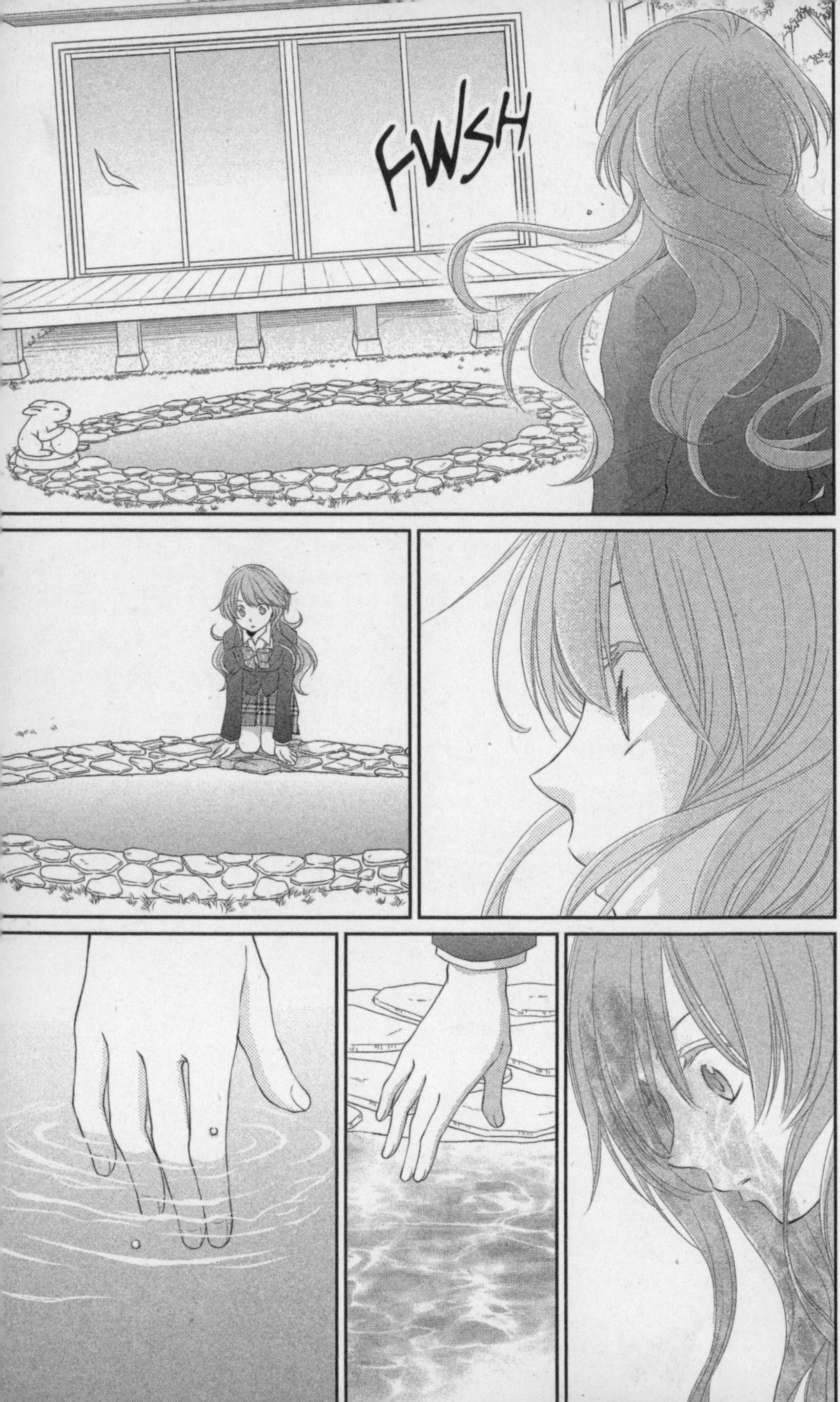
FWSH

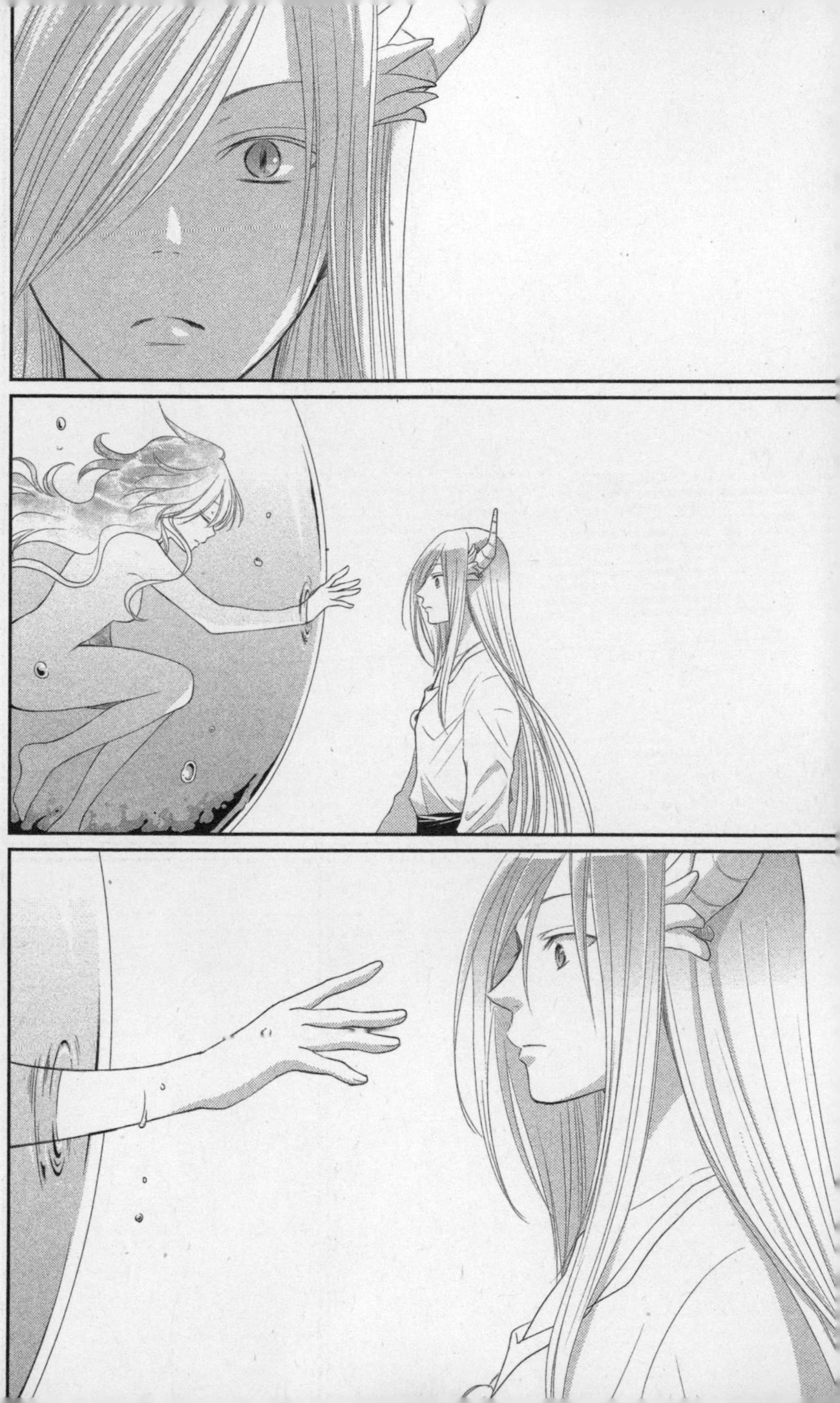

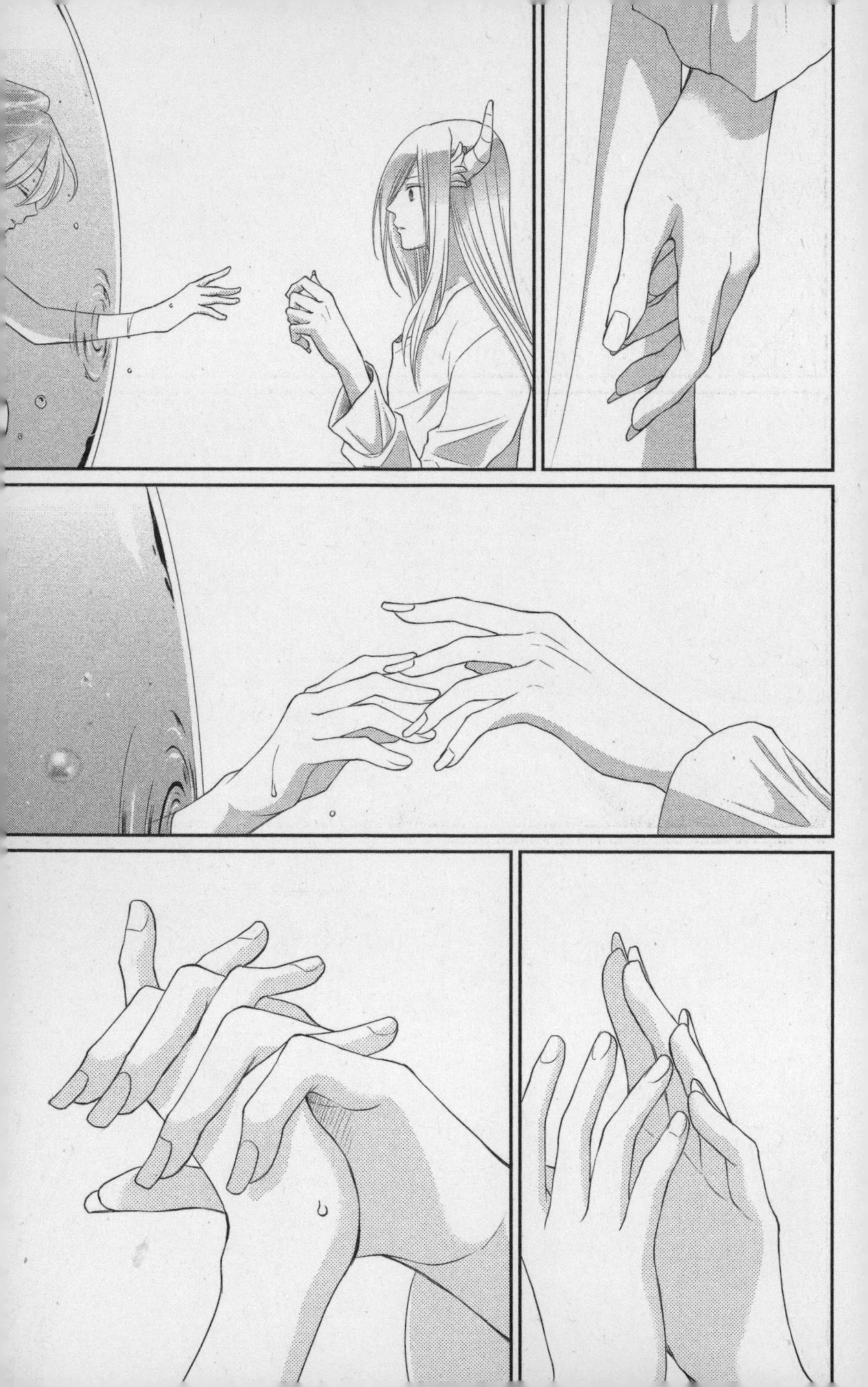

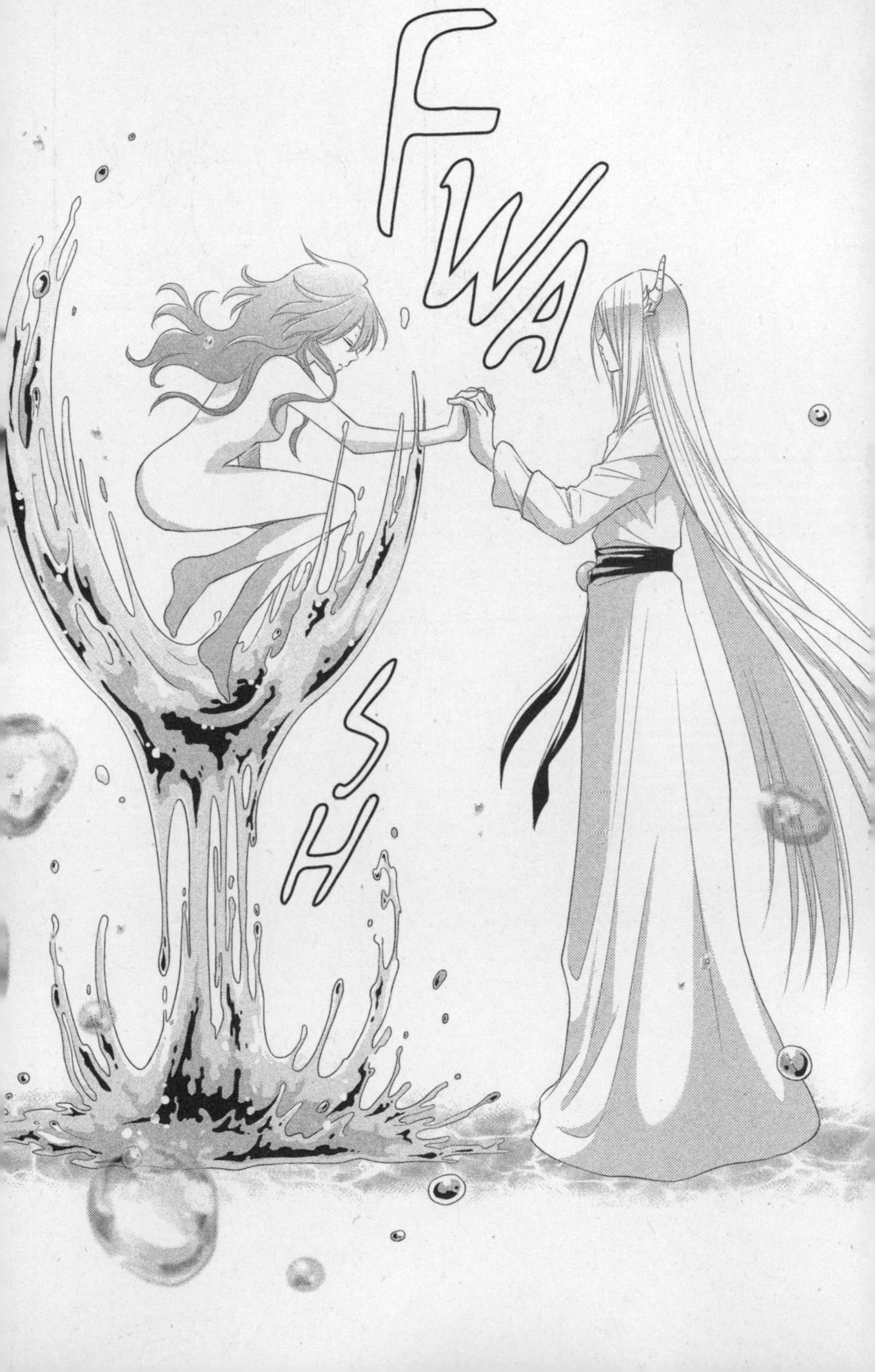
FWASH

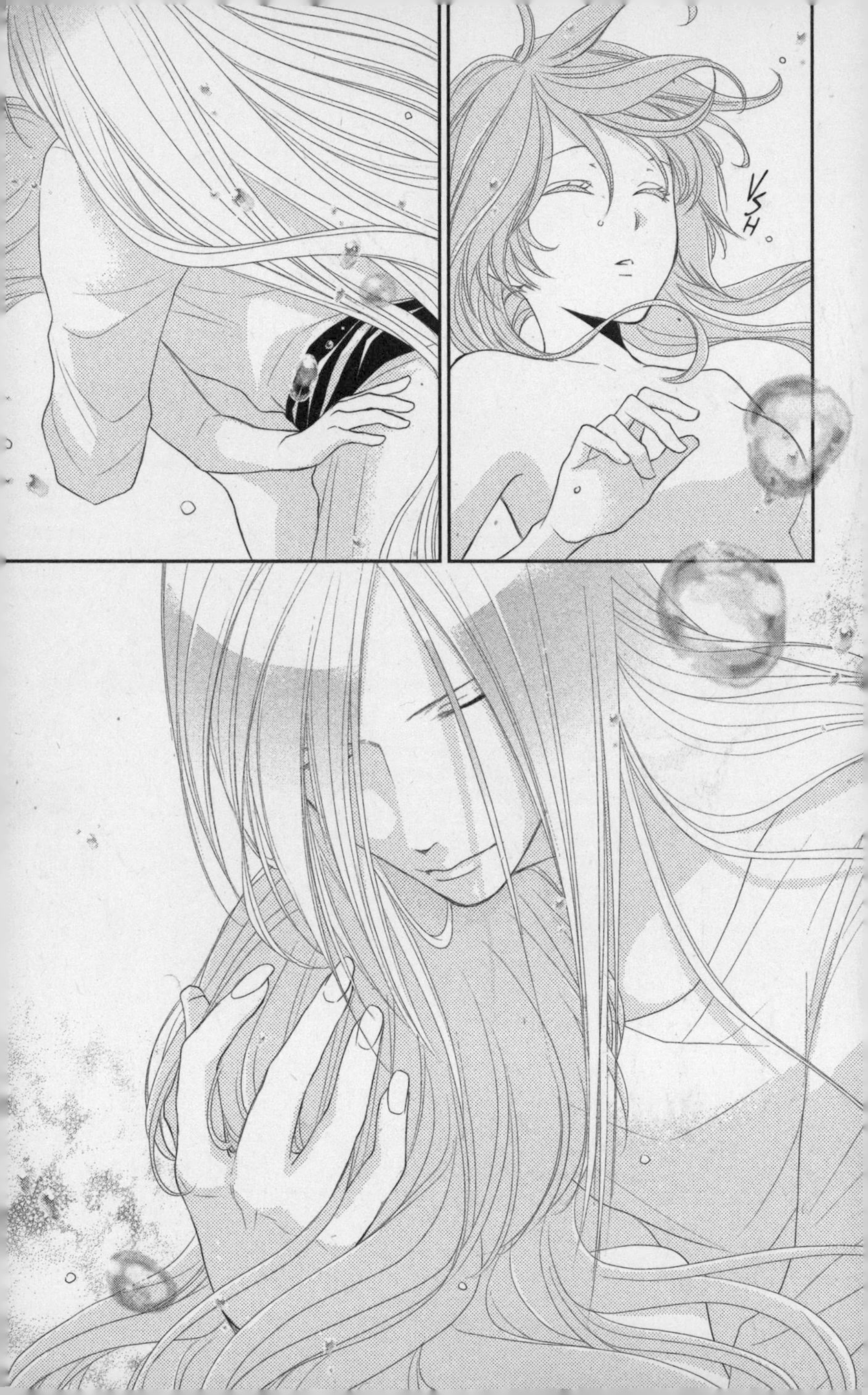
VSSH

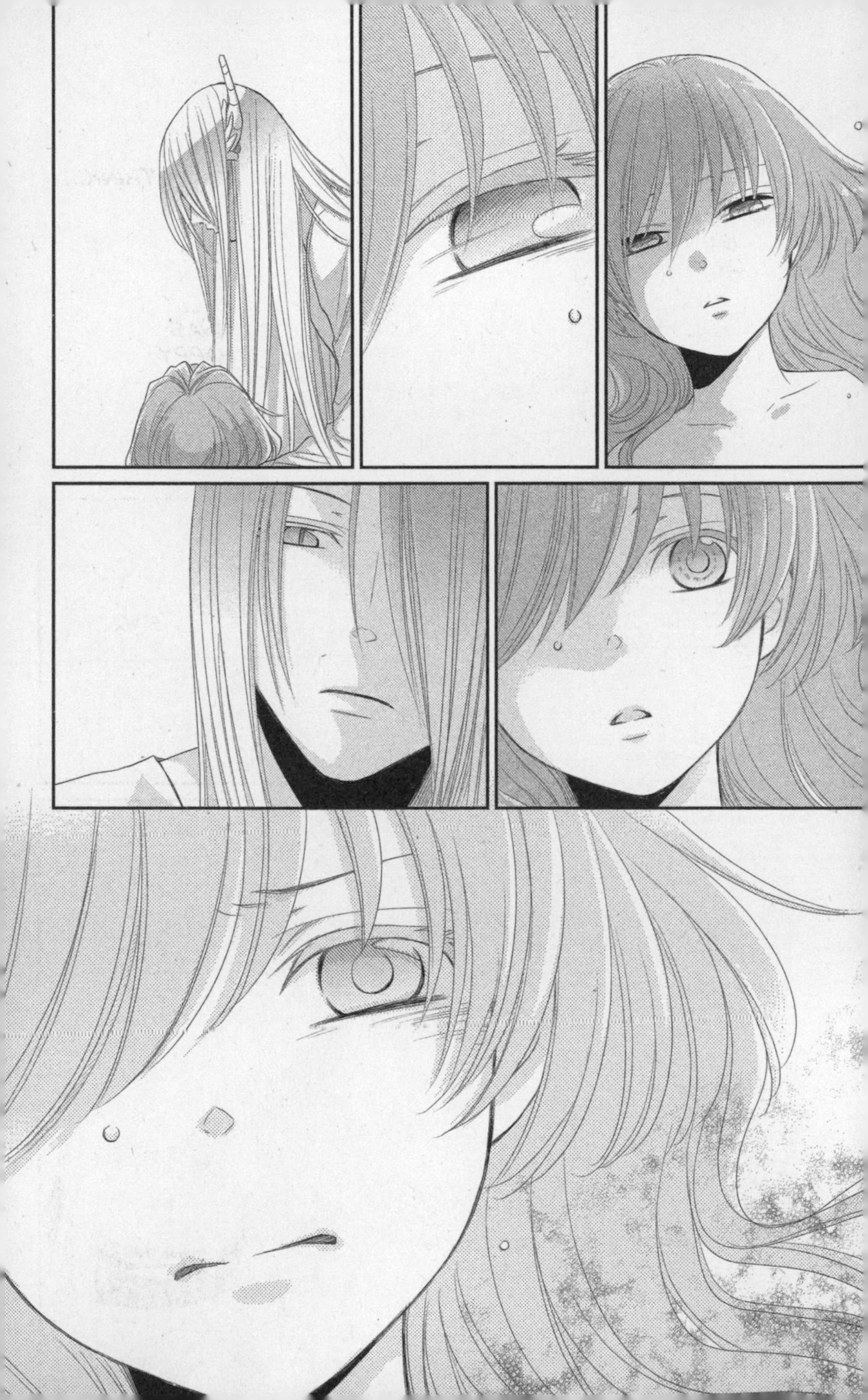

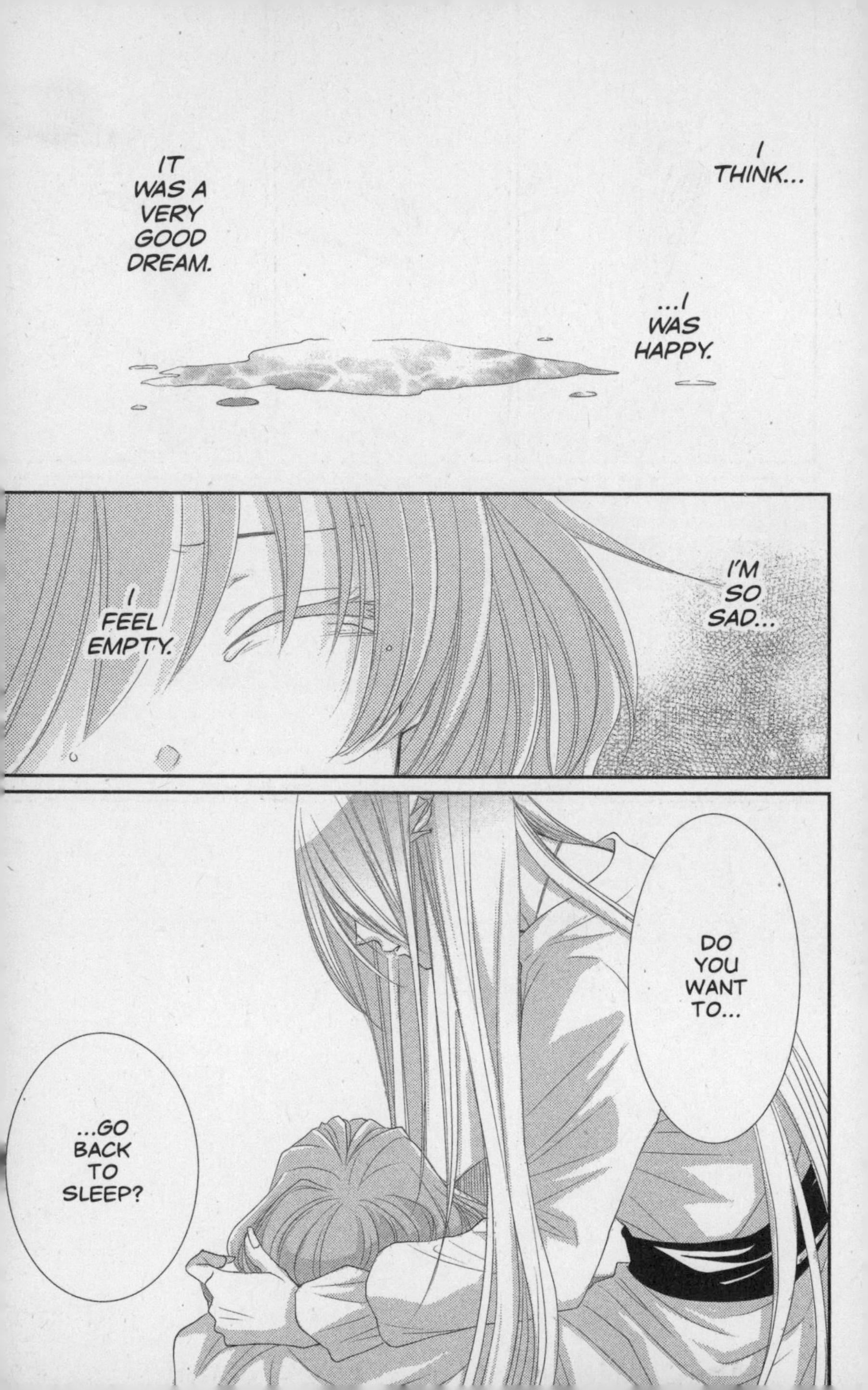
I THINK...
...I WAS HAPPY.
IT WAS A VERY GOOD DREAM.
I'M SO SAD...
I FEEL EMPTY.
DO YOU WANT TO...
...GO BACK TO SLEEP?

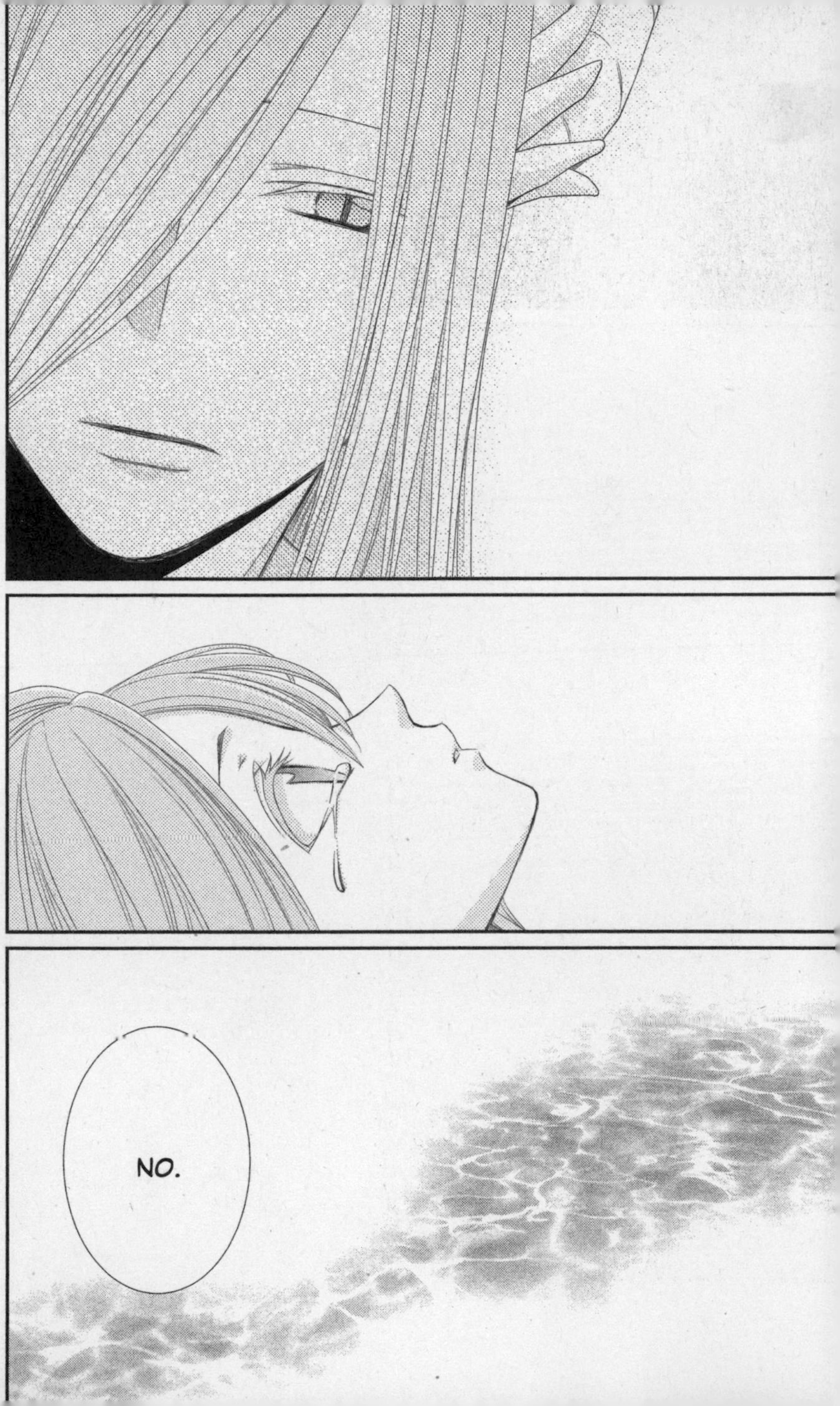
NO.

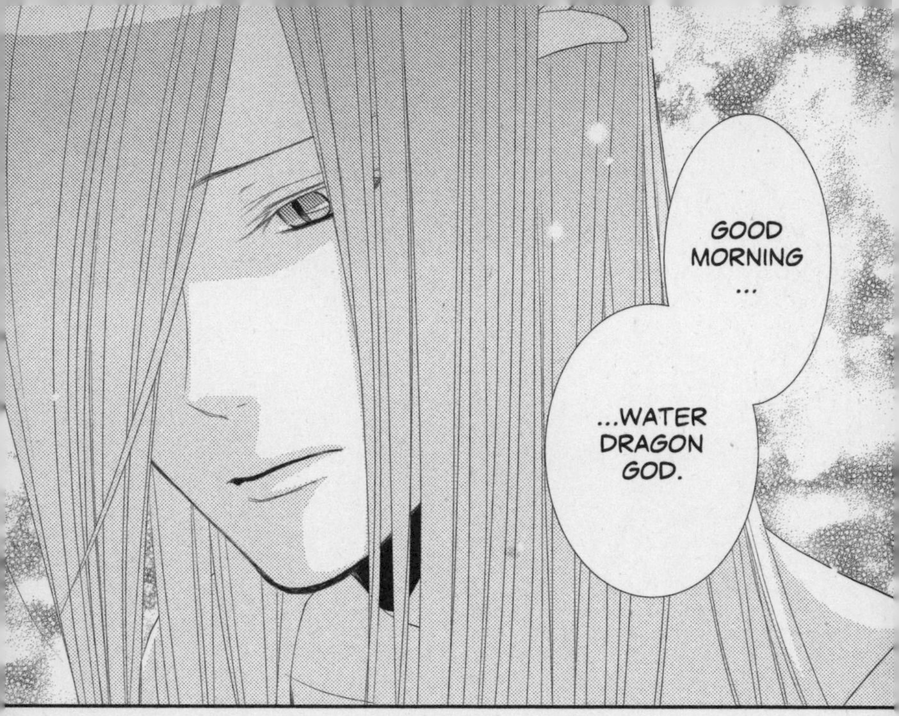
GOOD MORNING ...
...WATER DRAGON GOD.
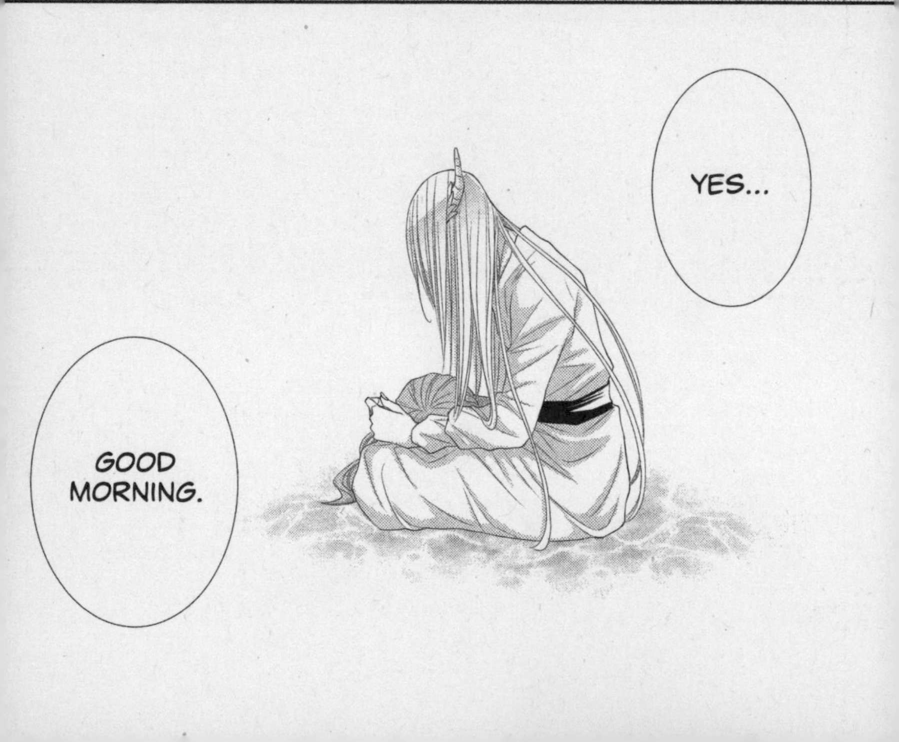
YES...
GOOD MORNING.

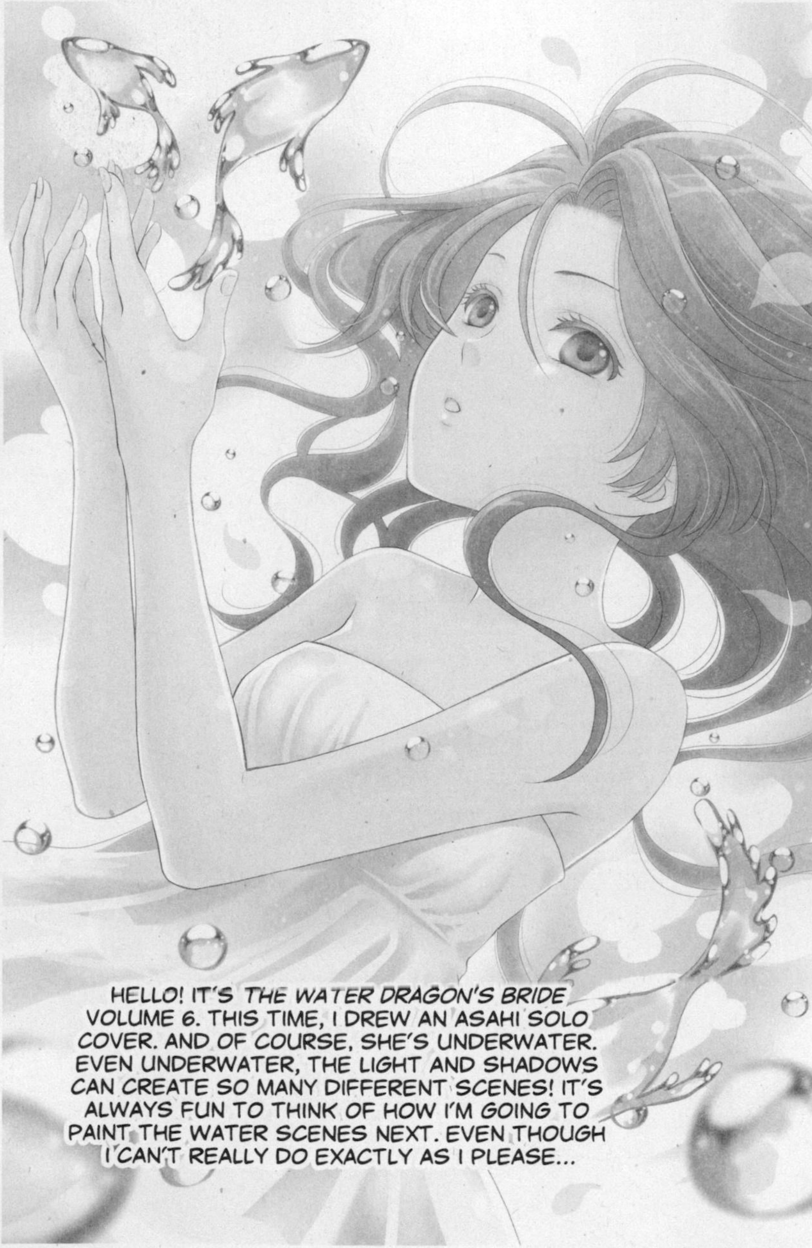
HELLO! IT'S *THE WATER DRAGON'S BRIDE* VOLUME 6. THIS TIME, I DREW AN ASAHI SOLO COVER. AND OF COURSE, SHE'S UNDERWATER. EVEN UNDERWATER, THE LIGHT AND SHADOWS CAN CREATE SO MANY DIFFERENT SCENES! IT'S ALWAYS FUN TO THINK OF HOW I'M GOING TO PAINT THE WATER SCENES NEXT. EVEN THOUGH I CAN'T REALLY DO EXACTLY AS I PLEASE...

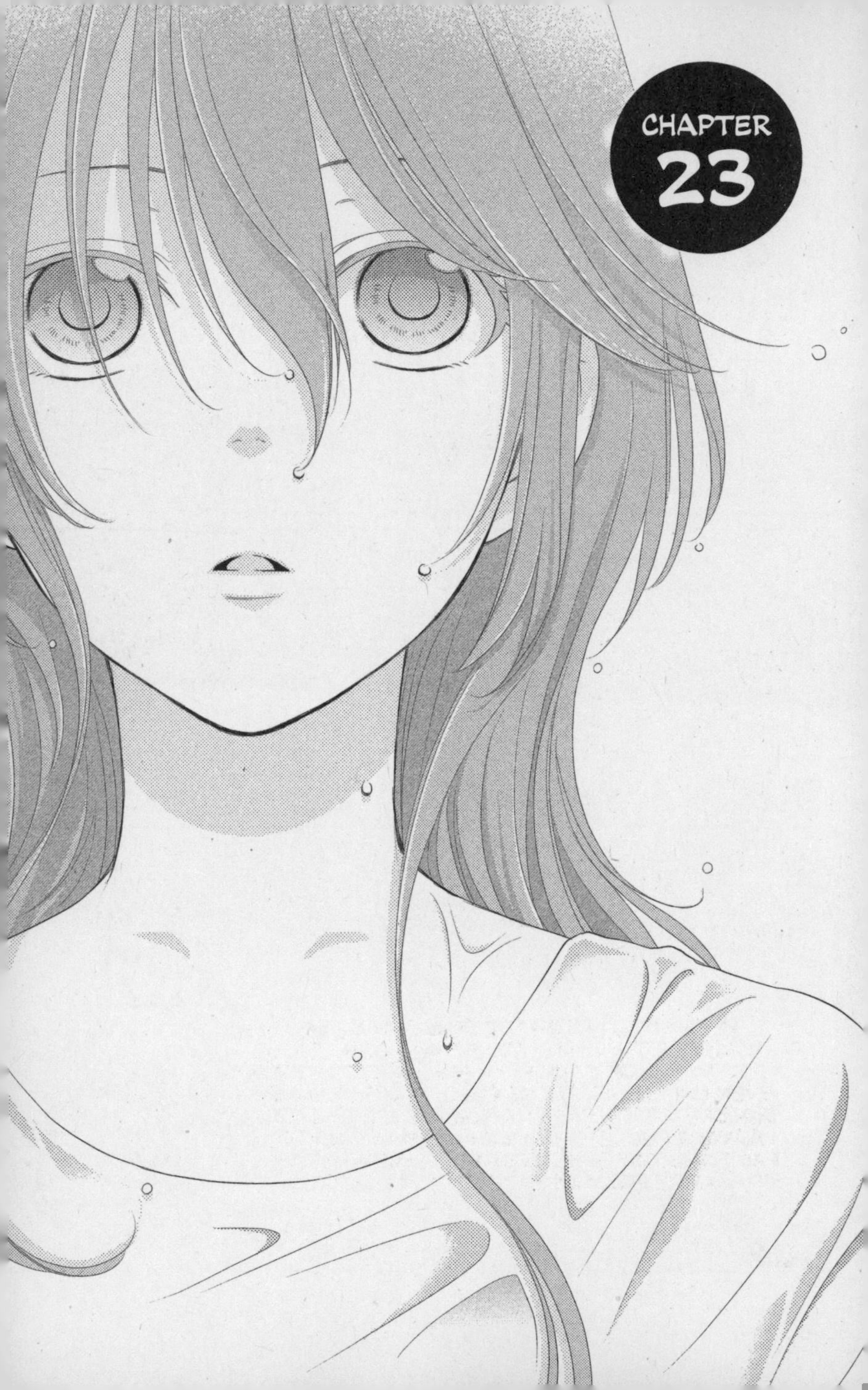
CHAPTER
23

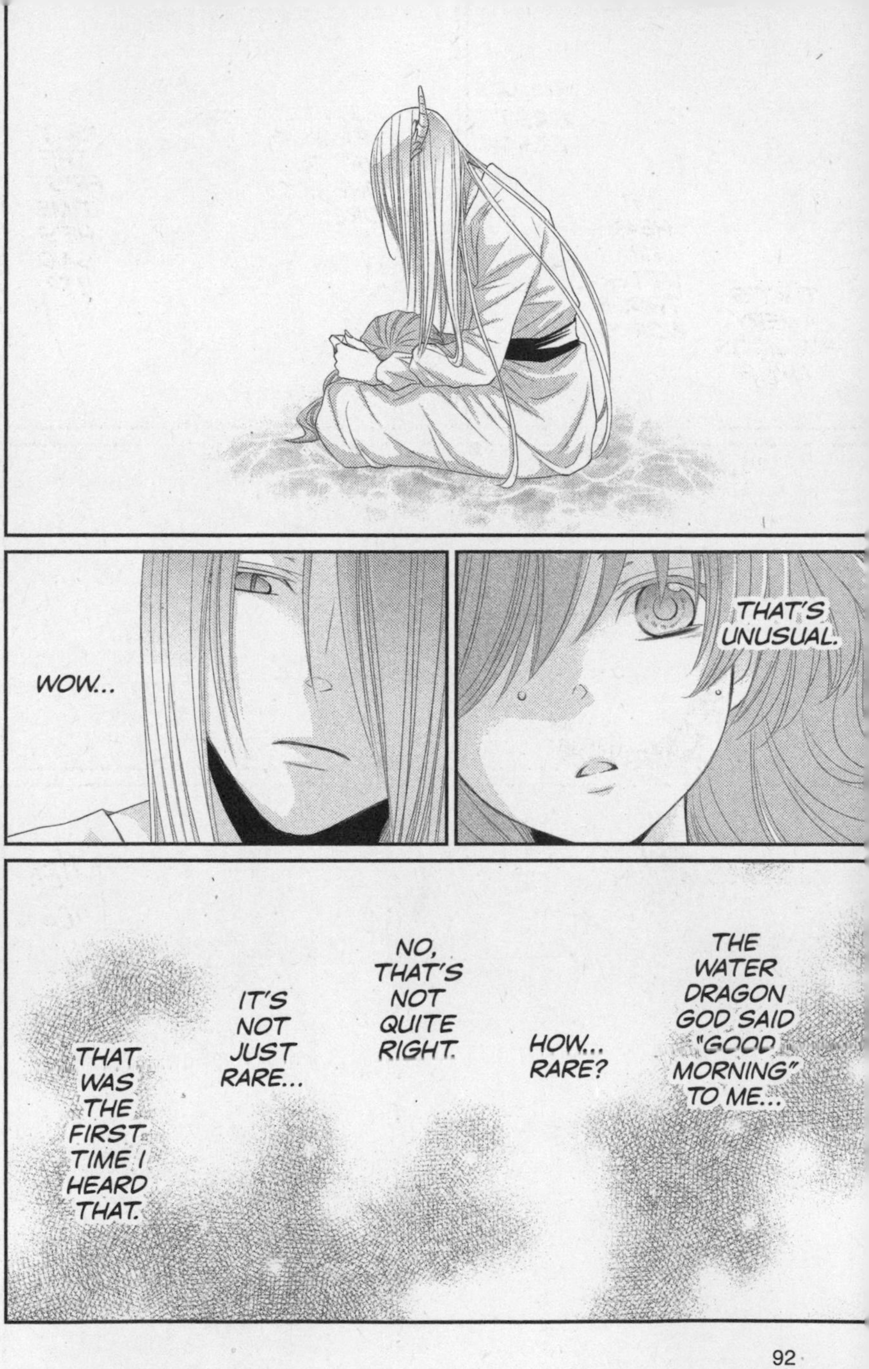
THAT'S UNUSUAL.
WOW...
THE WATER DRAGON GOD SAID "GOOD MORNING" TO ME...
HOW... RARE?
NO, THAT'S NOT QUITE RIGHT.
IT'S NOT JUST RARE...
THAT WAS THE FIRST TIME I HEARD THAT.

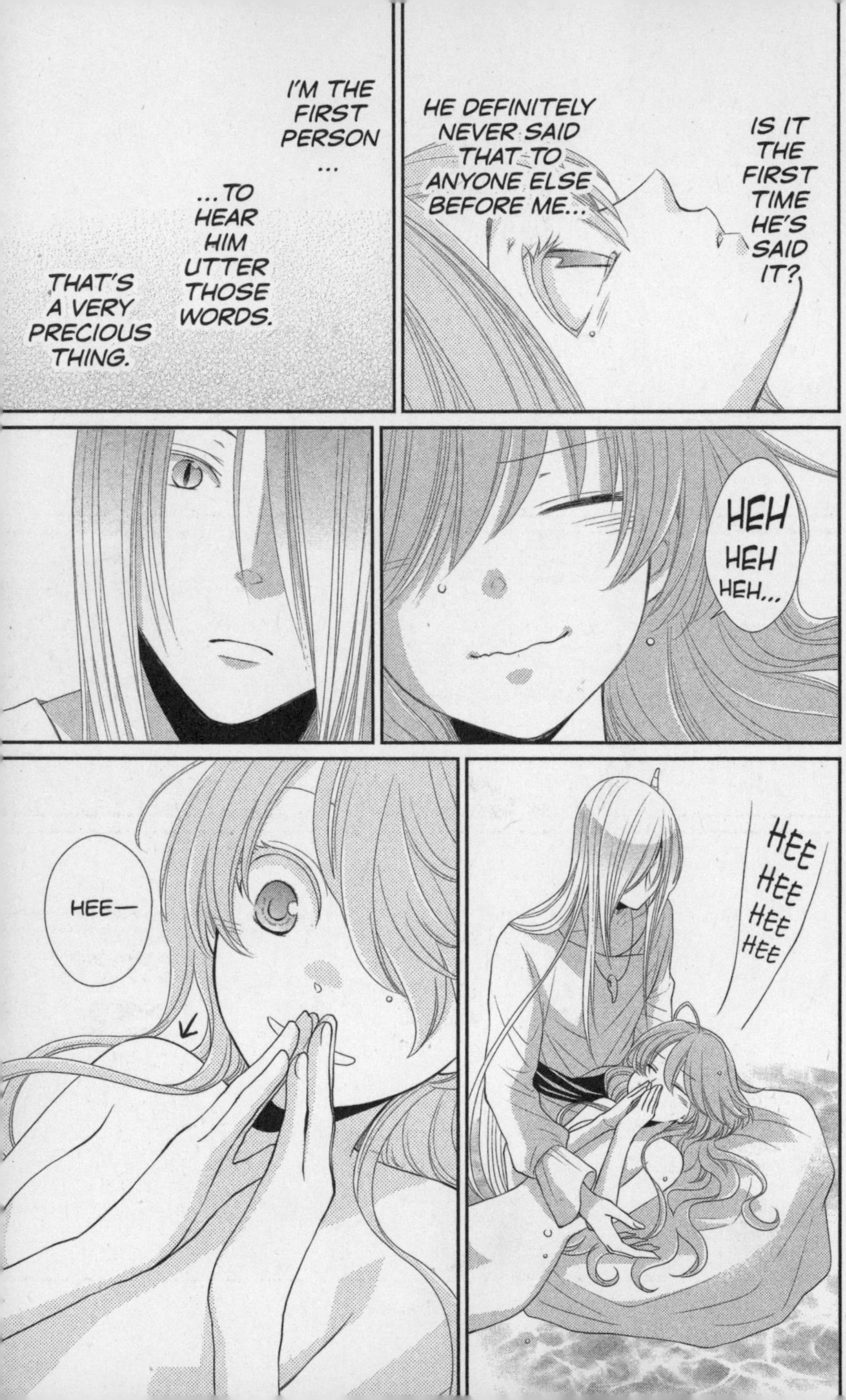
IS IT THE FIRST TIME HE'S SAID IT?
HE DEFINITELY NEVER SAID THAT TO ANYONE ELSE BEFORE ME...
I'M THE FIRST PERSON ...
...TO HEAR HIM UTTER THOSE WORDS.
THAT'S A VERY PRECIOUS THING.
HEH HEH HEH...
HEE HEE HEE HEE
HEE—

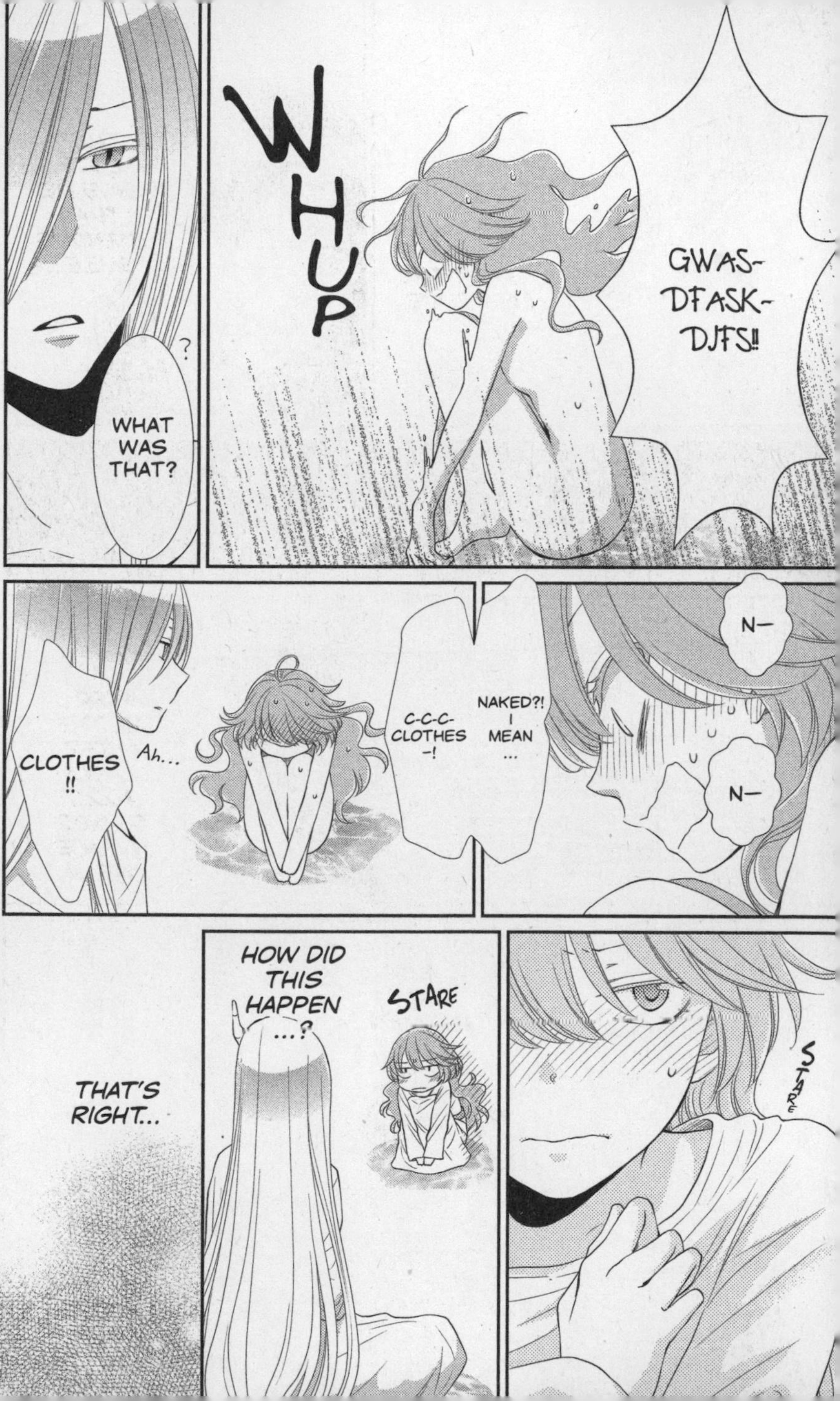
GWAS-DFASK-DJFS!!
WHUP
?
WHAT WAS THAT?
N—
N—
NAKED?! I MEAN...
C-C-C-CLOTHES—!
Ah...
CLOTHES!!
STARE
HOW DID THIS HAPPEN...?
STARE
THAT'S RIGHT...

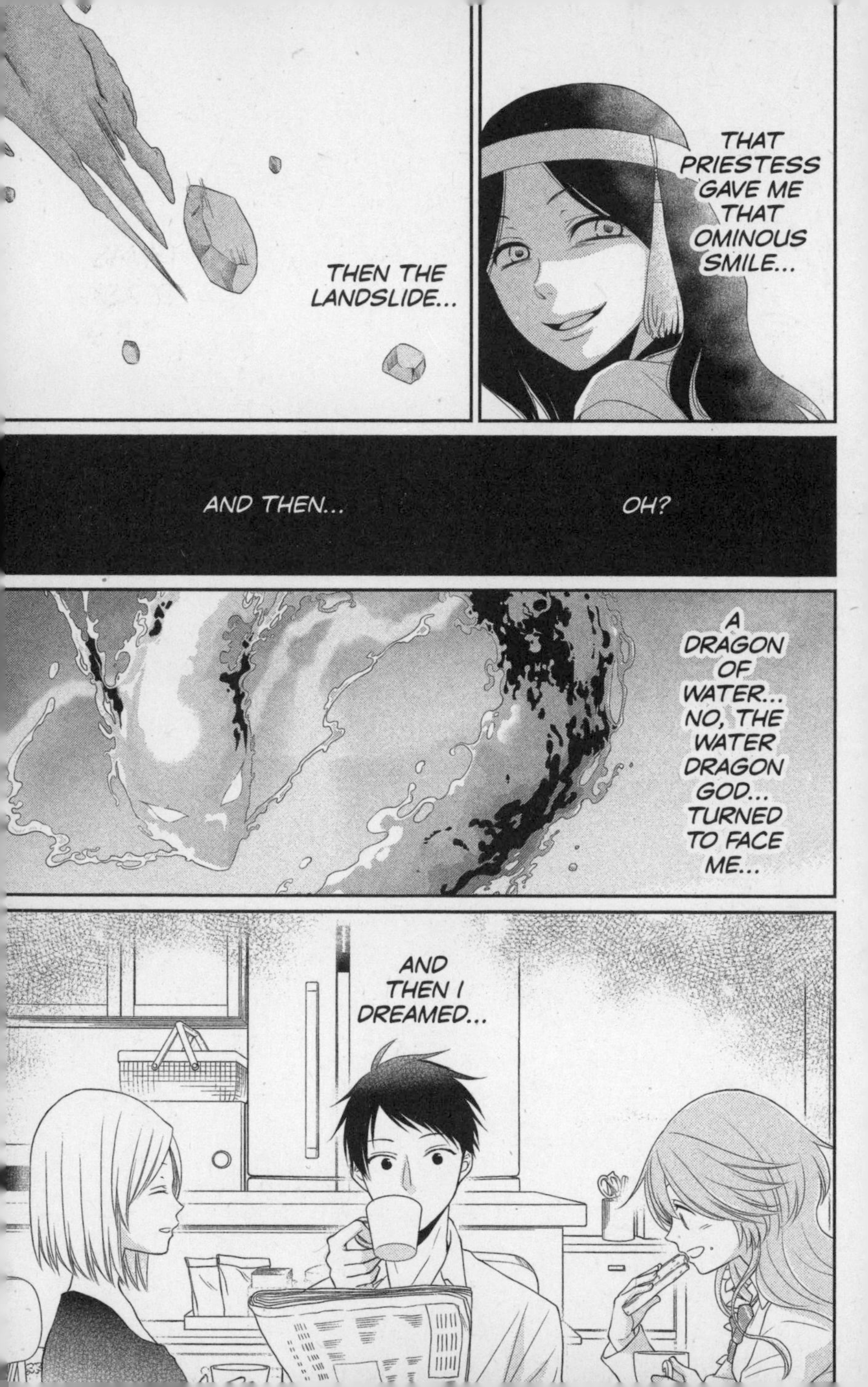
THAT PRIESTESS GAVE ME THAT OMINOUS SMILE...
THEN THE LANDSLIDE...
AND THEN...
OH?
A DRAGON OF WATER... NO, THE WATER DRAGON GOD... TURNED TO FACE ME...
AND THEN I DREAMED...

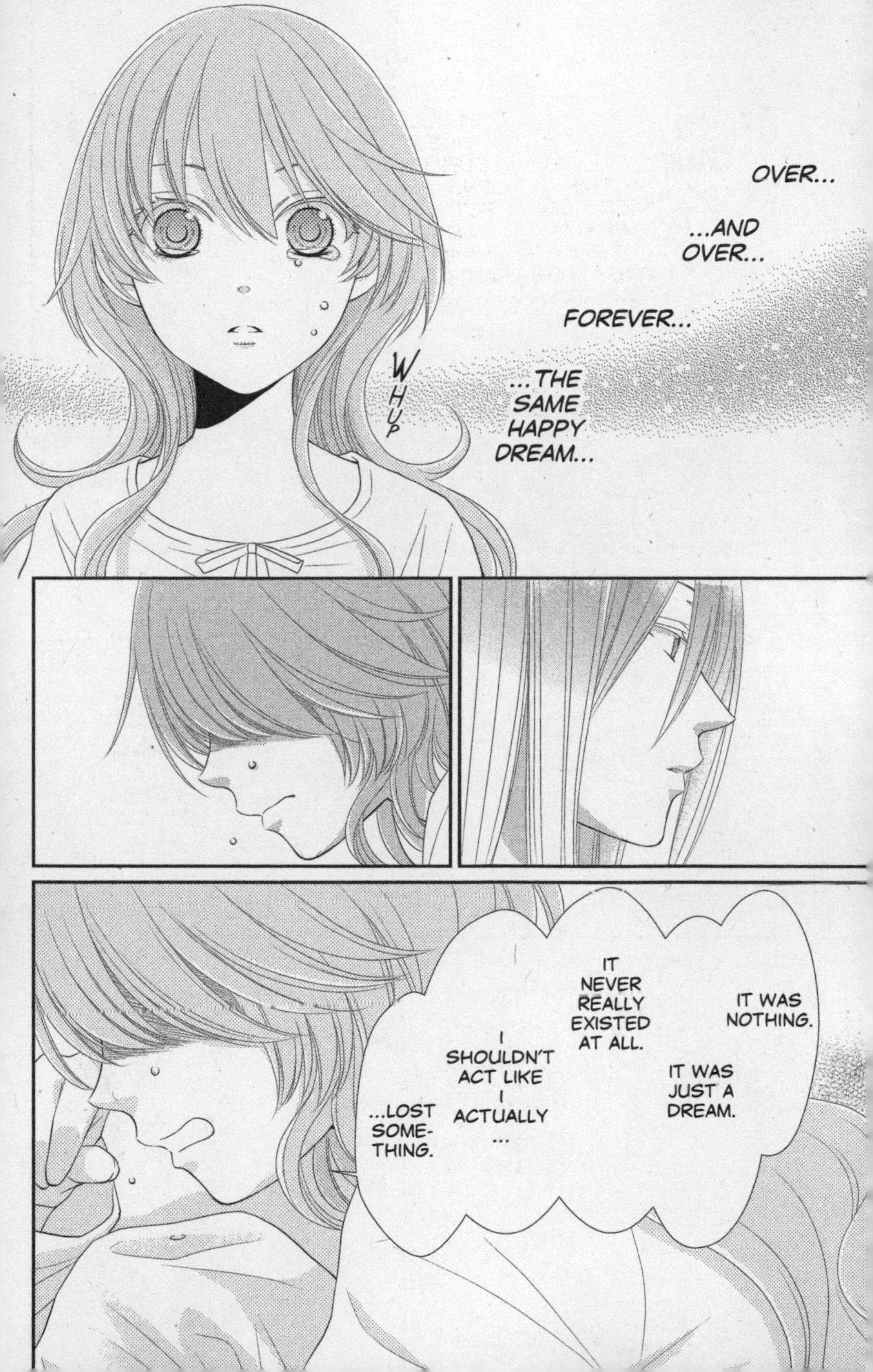
OVER...
...AND OVER...
FOREVER...
...THE SAME HAPPY DREAM...
WHUP
IT WAS NOTHING.
IT WAS JUST A DREAM.
IT NEVER REALLY EXISTED AT ALL.
I SHOULDN'T ACT LIKE I ACTUALLY...
...LOST SOME-THING.

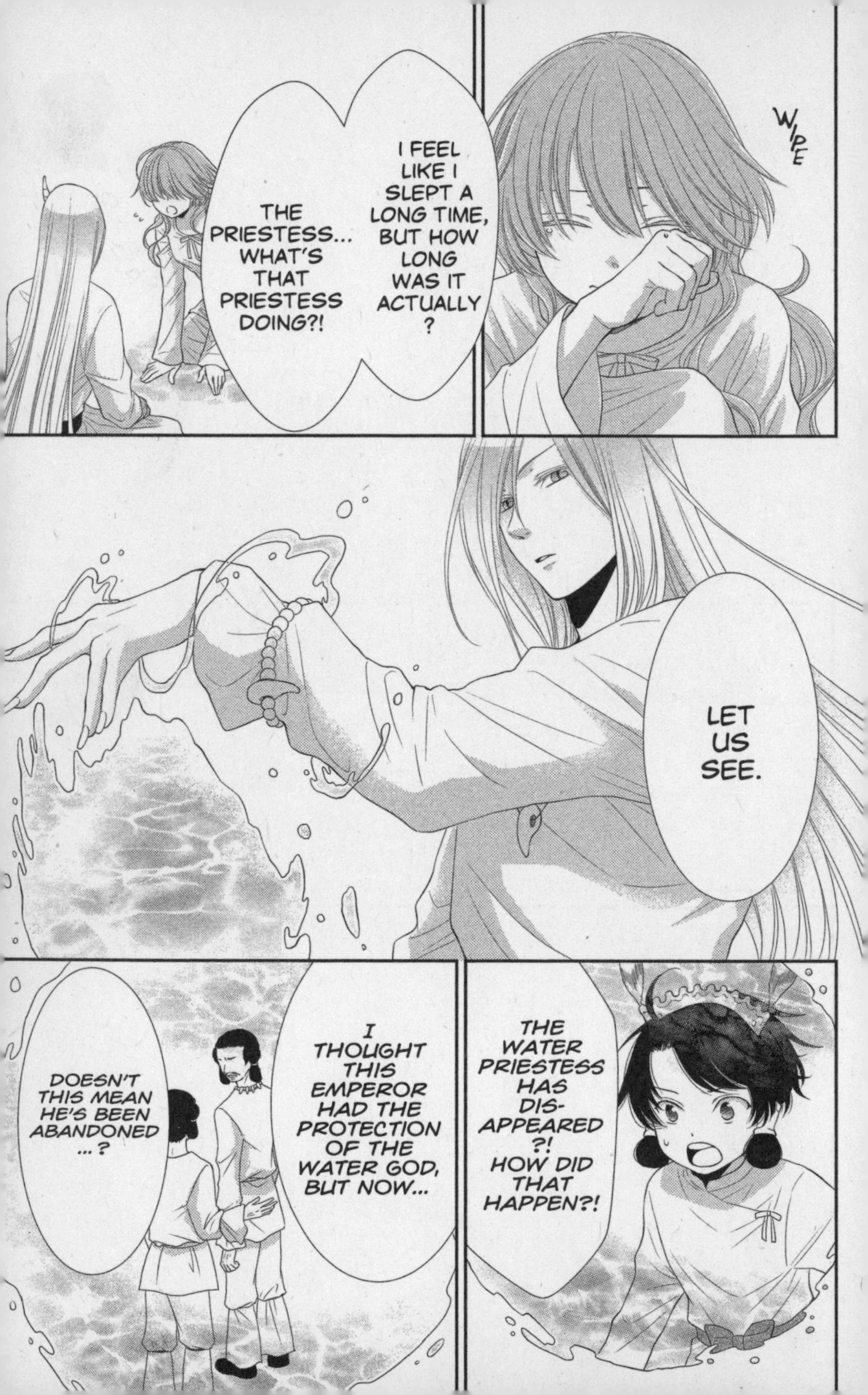
WIPE
I FEEL LIKE I SLEPT A LONG TIME, BUT HOW LONG WAS IT ACTUALLY?
THE PRIESTESS... WHAT'S THAT PRIESTESS DOING?!
LET US SEE.
THE WATER PRIESTESS HAS DIS-APPEARED?! HOW DID THAT HAPPEN?!
I THOUGHT THIS EMPEROR HAD THE PROTECTION OF THE WATER GOD, BUT NOW...
DOESN'T THIS MEAN HE'S BEEN ABANDONED...?

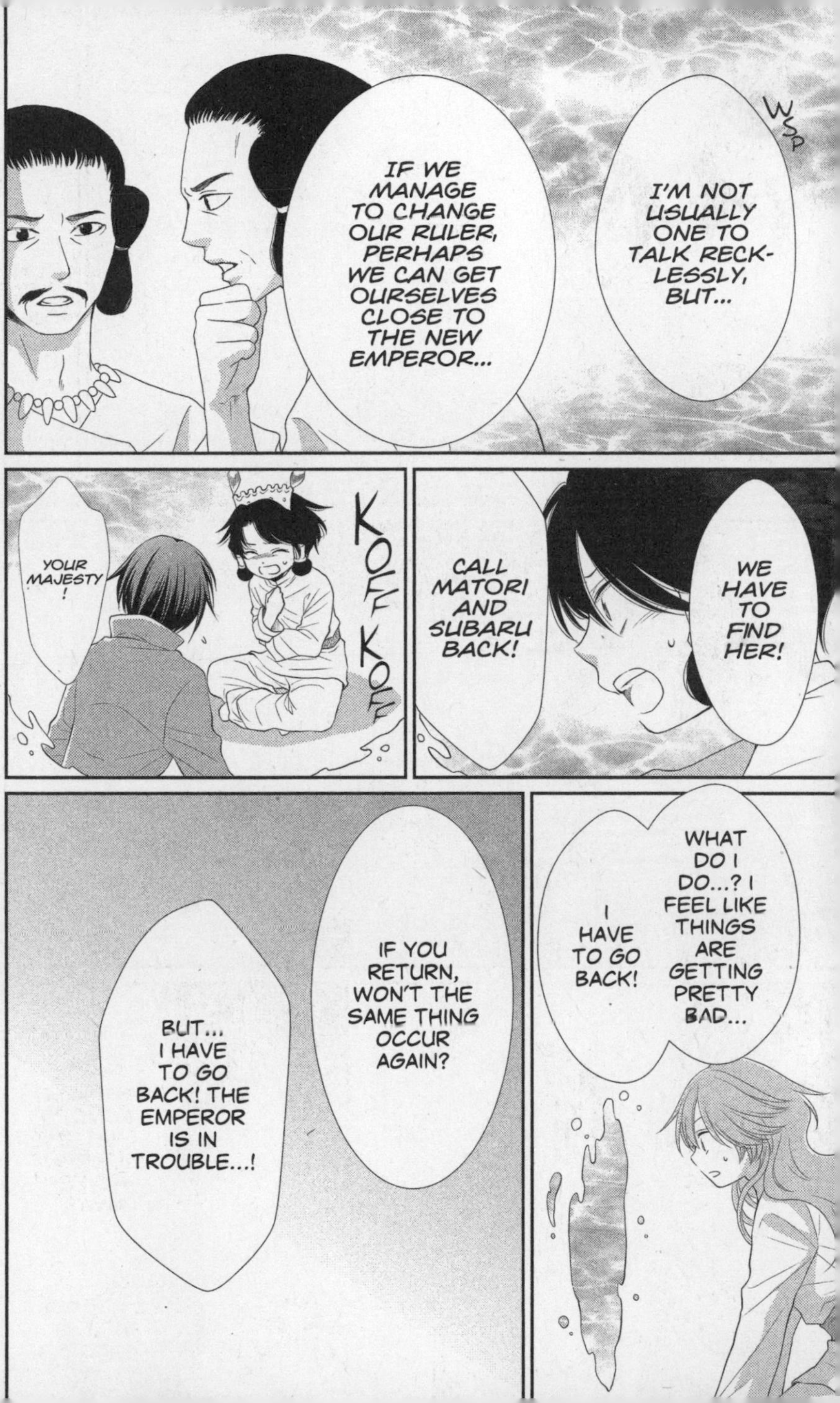
WSP
I'M NOT USUALLY ONE TO TALK RECK-LESSLY, BUT...
IF WE MANAGE TO CHANGE OUR RULER, PERHAPS WE CAN GET OURSELVES CLOSE TO THE NEW EMPEROR...
WE HAVE TO FIND HER!
CALL MATORI AND SUBARU BACK!
KOFF KOFF
YOUR MAJESTY!
WHAT DO I DO...? I FEEL LIKE THINGS ARE GETTING PRETTY BAD...
I HAVE TO GO BACK!
IF YOU RETURN, WON'T THE SAME THING OCCUR AGAIN?
BUT... I HAVE TO GO BACK! THE EMPEROR IS IN TROUBLE...!

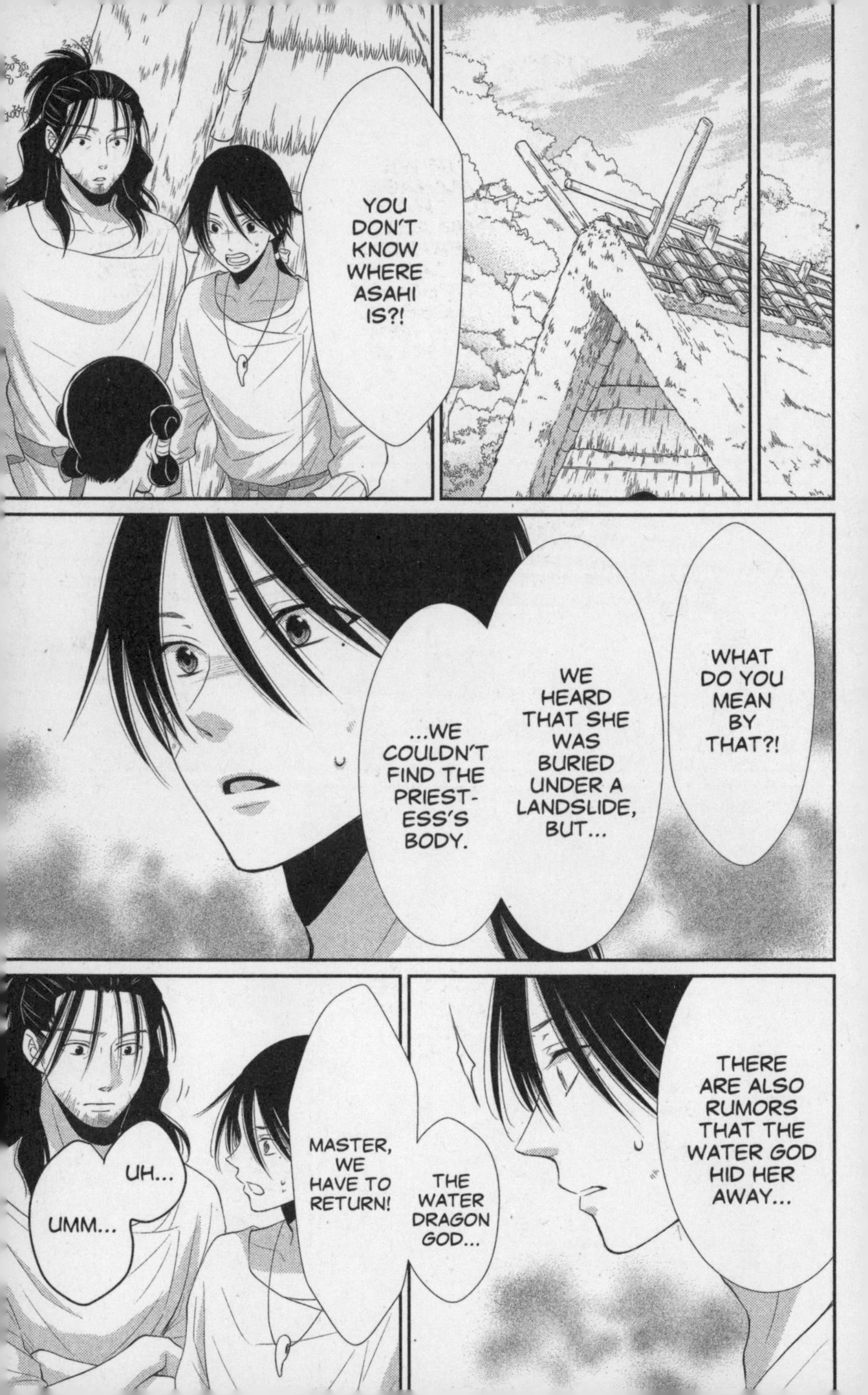
YOU DON'T KNOW WHERE ASAHI IS?!
WHAT DO YOU MEAN BY THAT?!
WE HEARD THAT SHE WAS BURIED UNDER A LANDSLIDE, BUT...
...WE COULDN'T FIND THE PRIEST-ESS'S BODY.
THERE ARE ALSO RUMORS THAT THE WATER GOD HID HER AWAY...
THE WATER DRAGON GOD...
MASTER, WE HAVE TO RETURN!
UH...
UMM...

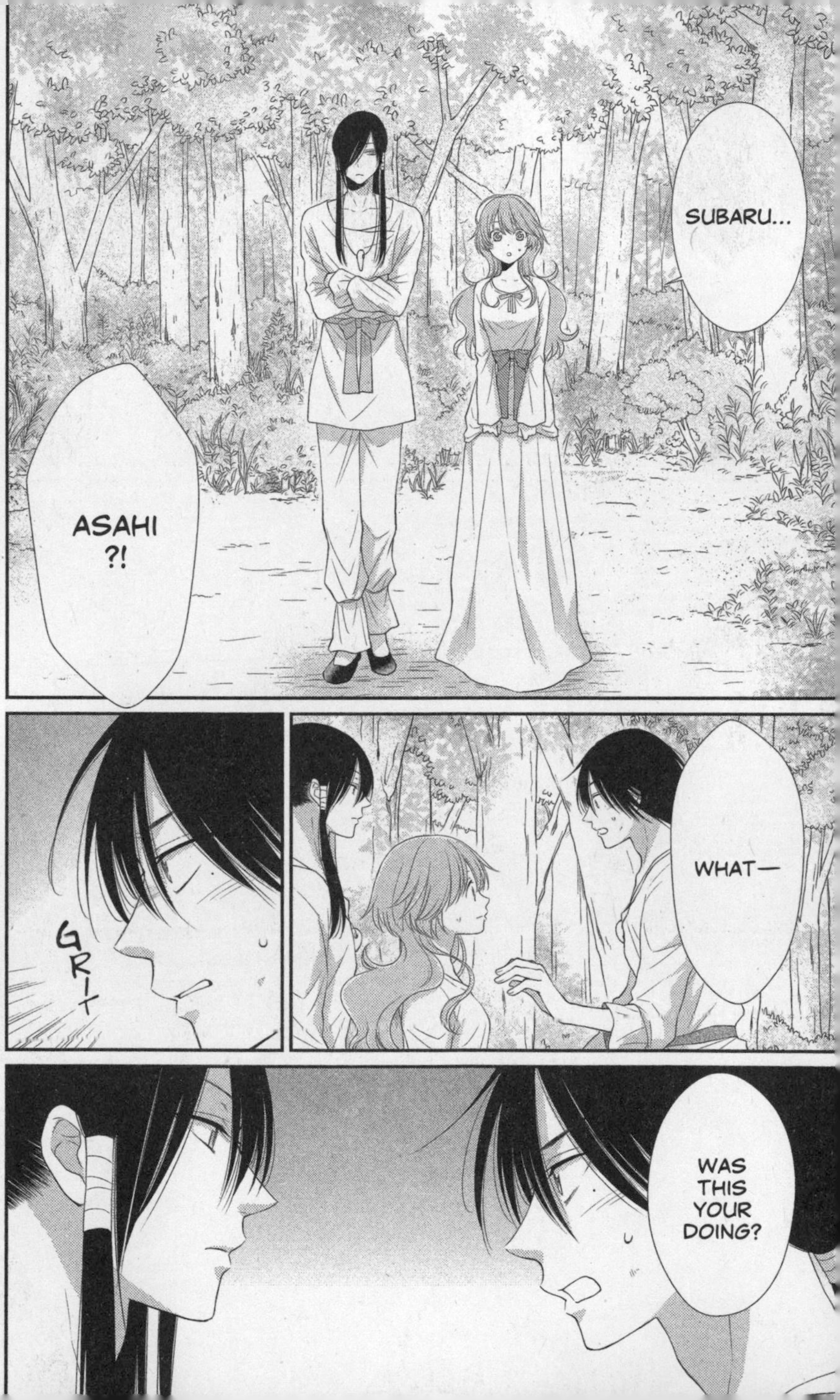
SUBARU...
ASAHI ?!
WHAT—
GRIT
WAS THIS YOUR DOING?

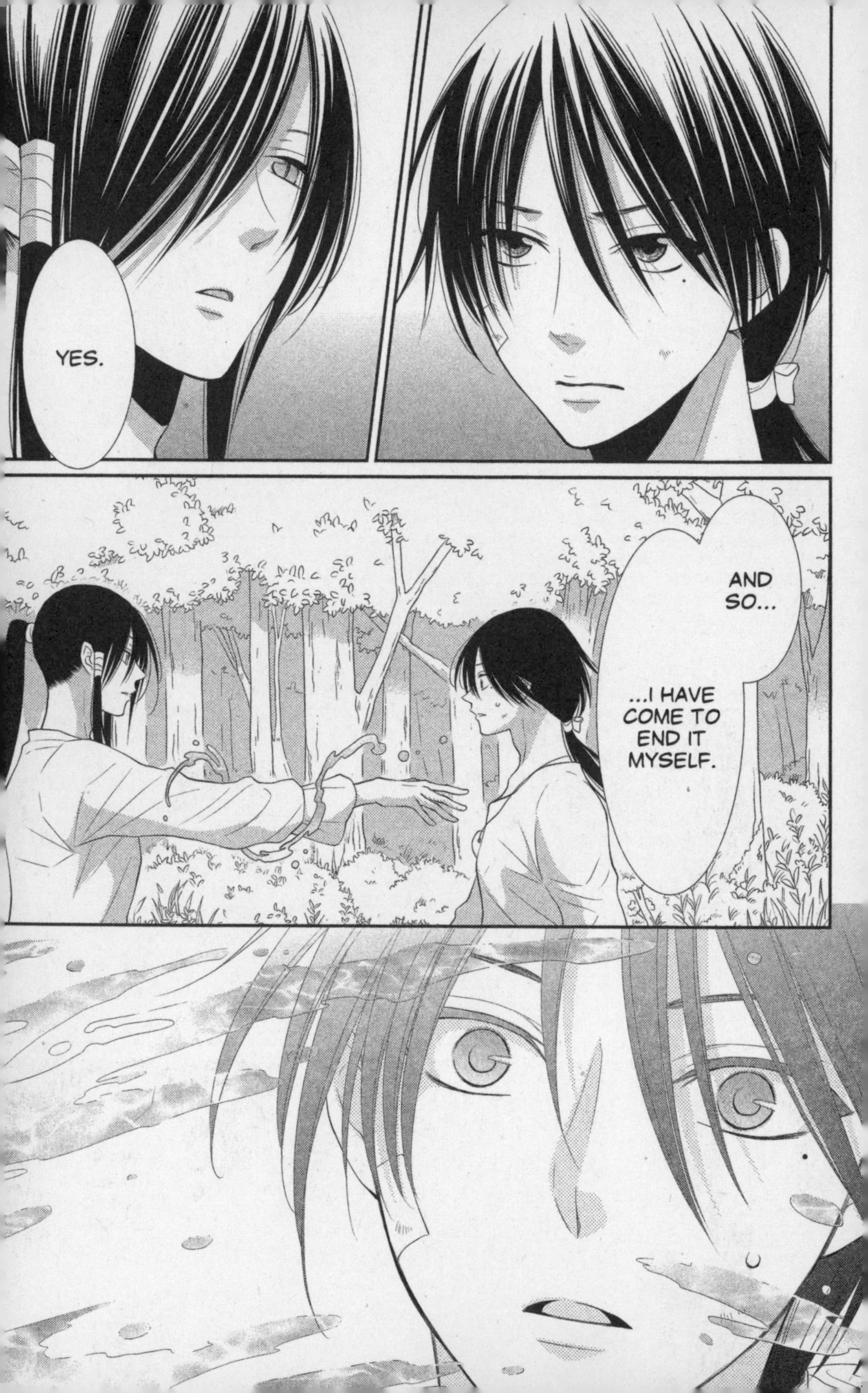
YES.
AND SO...
...I HAVE COME TO END IT MYSELF.

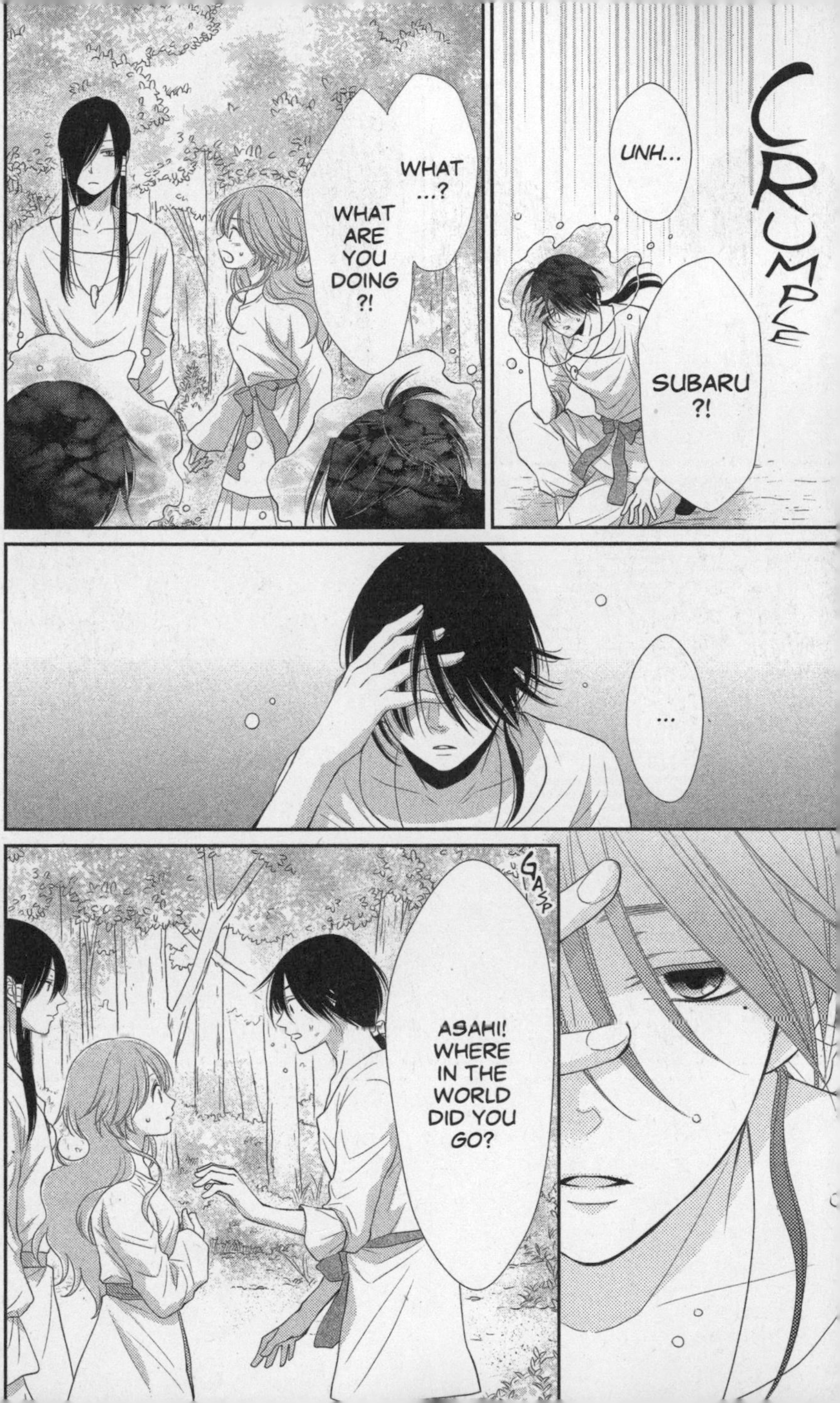
CRUMPLE
UNH...
SUBARU ?!
WHAT ...?
WHAT ARE YOU DOING ?!
...
GASP
ASAHI! WHERE IN THE WORLD DID YOU GO?

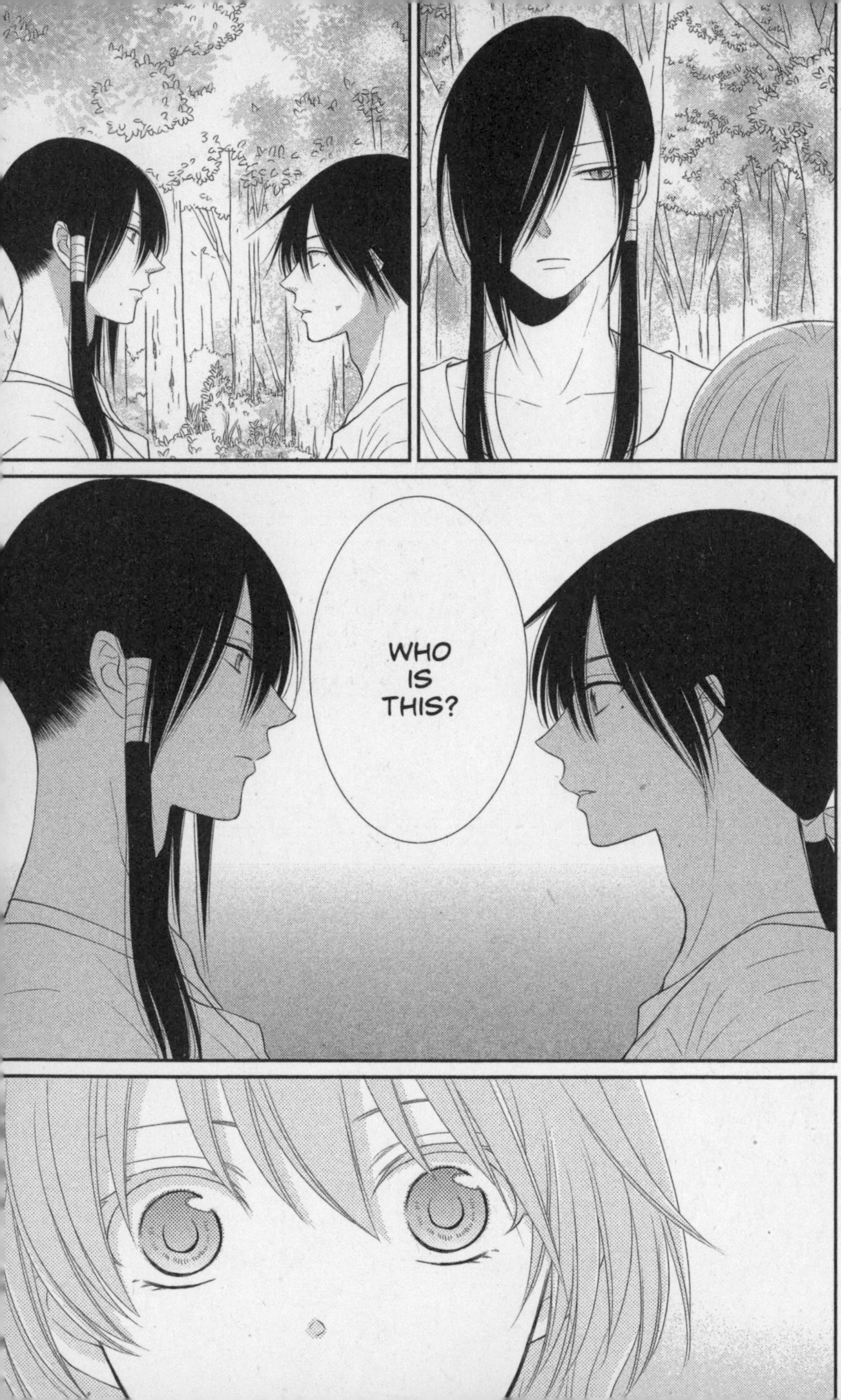
WHO IS THIS?

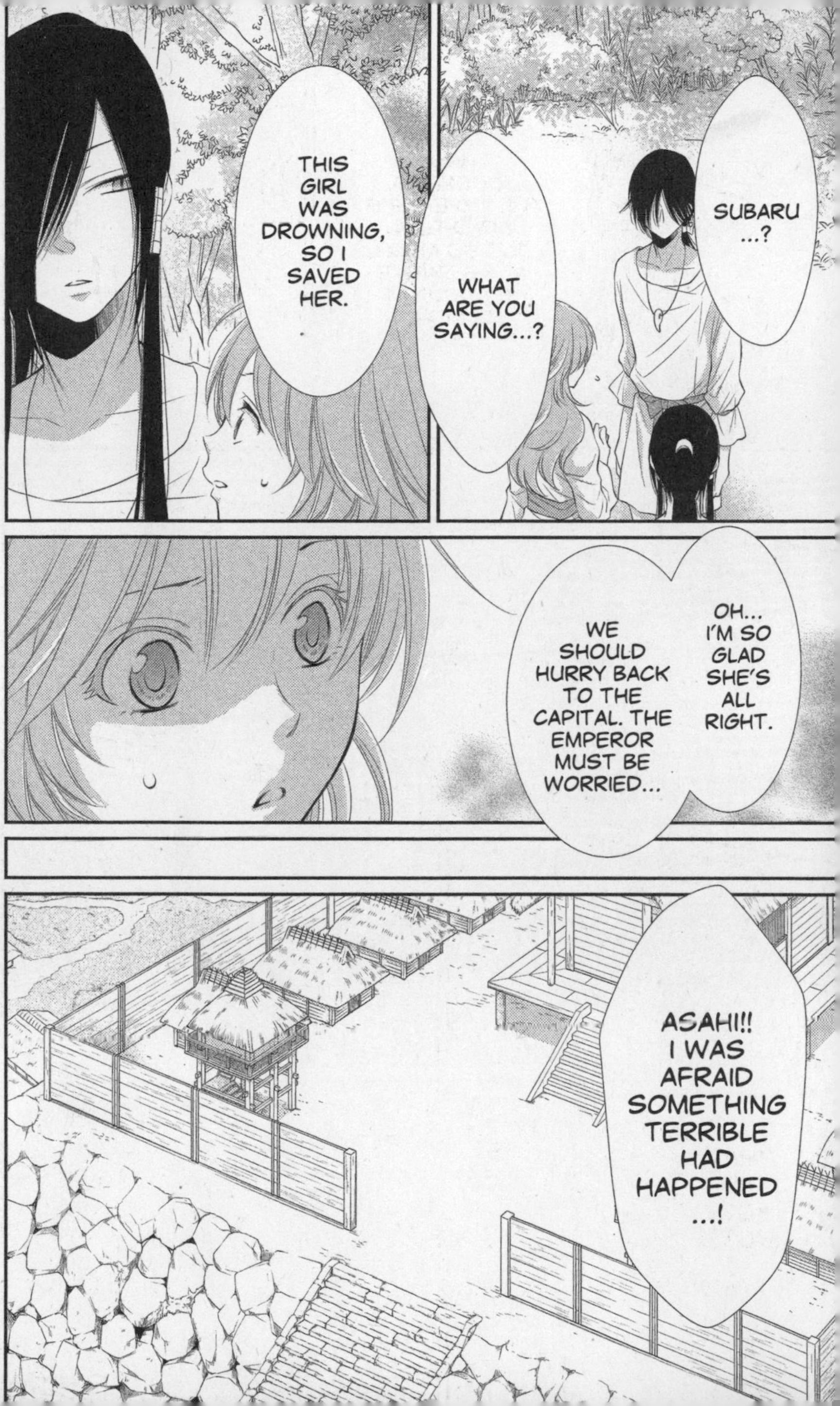
SUBARU ...?
WHAT ARE YOU SAYING...?
THIS GIRL WAS DROWNING, SO I SAVED HER.
OH... I'M SO GLAD SHE'S ALL RIGHT.
WE SHOULD HURRY BACK TO THE CAPITAL. THE EMPEROR MUST BE WORRIED...
ASAHI!! I WAS AFRAID SOMETHING TERRIBLE HAD HAPPENED ...!

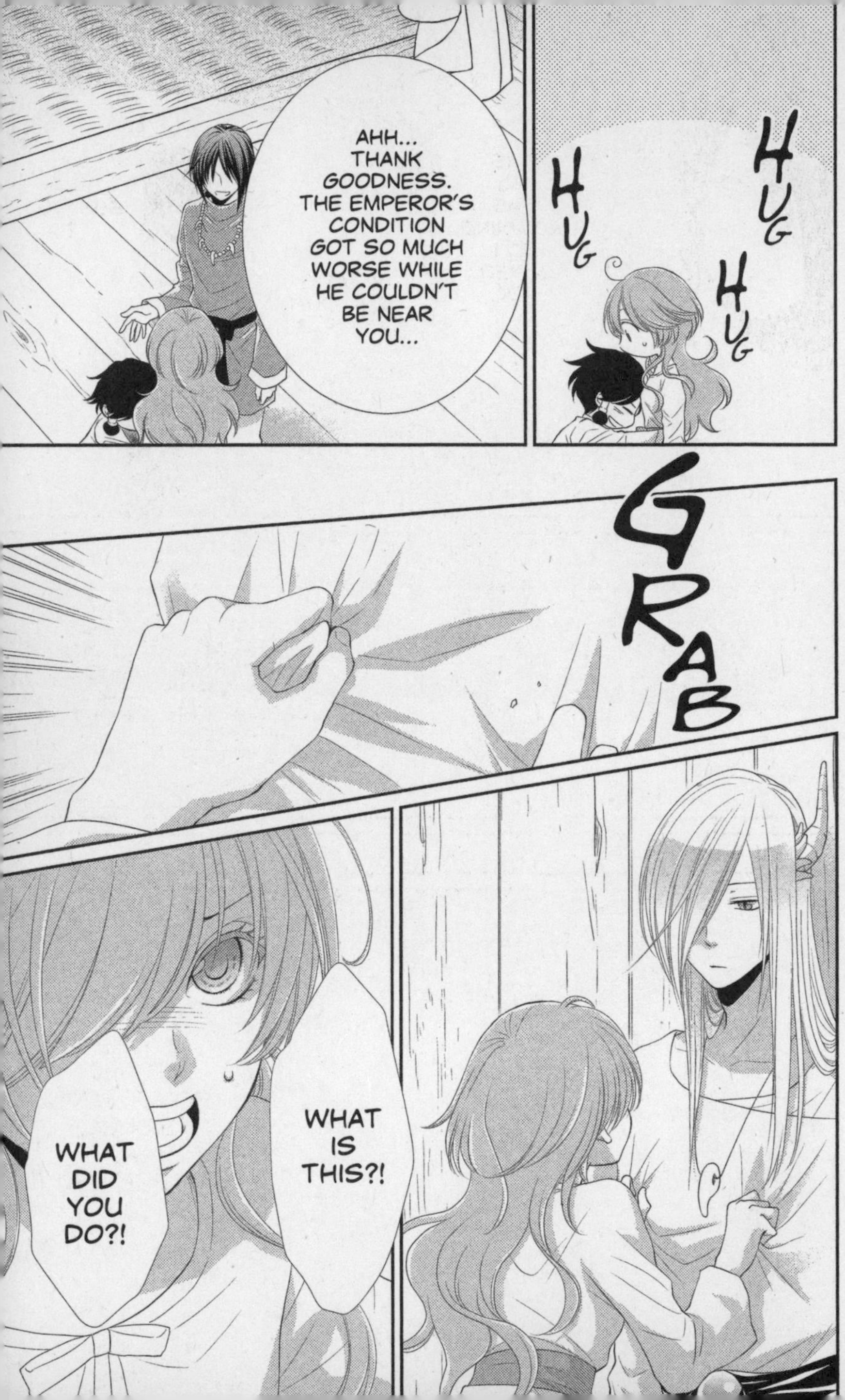
HUG HUG
HUG HUG
AHH... THANK GOODNESS. THE EMPEROR'S CONDITION GOT SO MUCH WORSE WHILE HE COULDN'T BE NEAR YOU...
GRAB
WHAT IS THIS?!
WHAT DID YOU DO?!

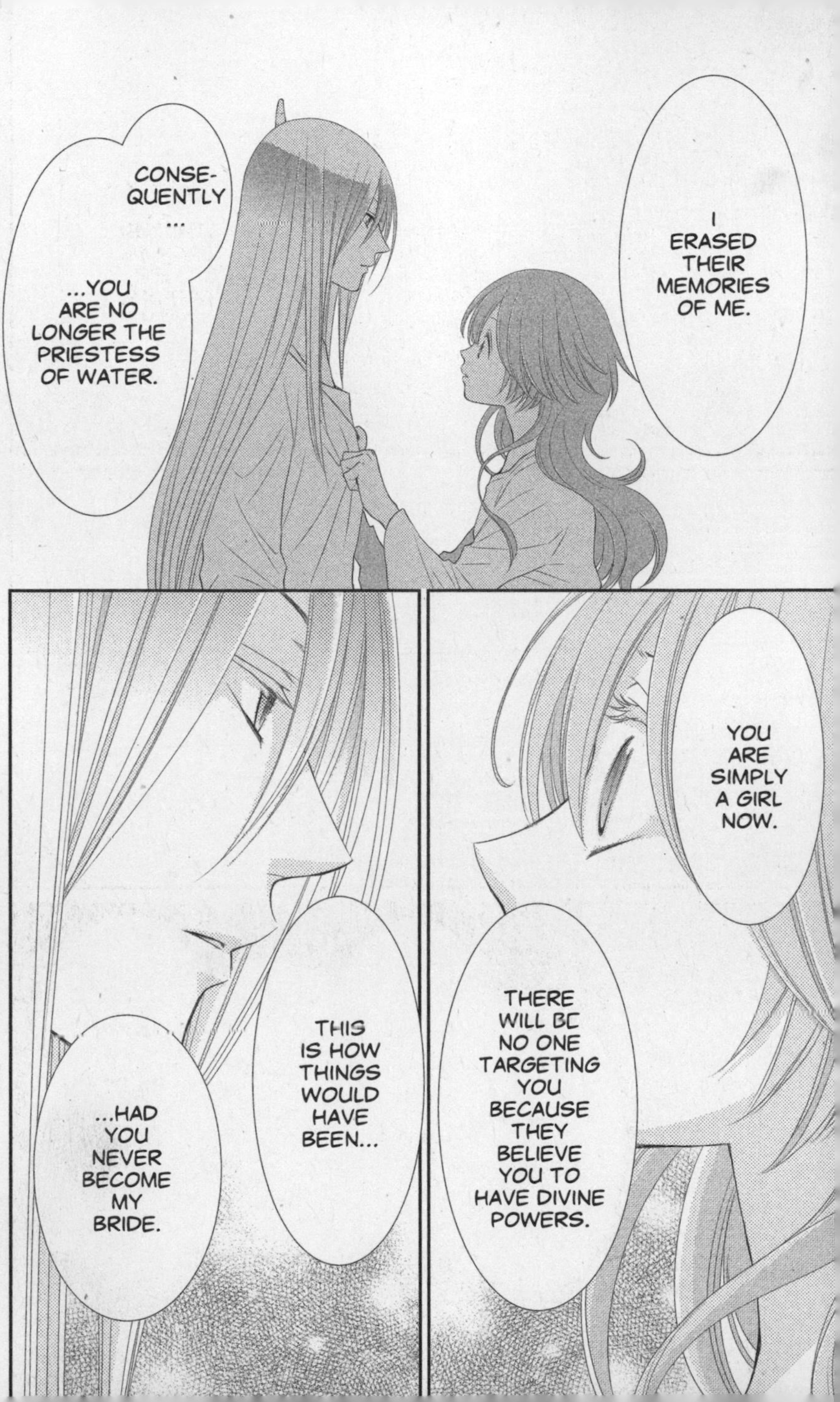
I ERASED THEIR MEMORIES OF ME.
CONSEQUENTLY...
...YOU ARE NO LONGER THE PRIESTESS OF WATER.
YOU ARE SIMPLY A GIRL NOW.
THERE WILL BE NO ONE TARGETING YOU BECAUSE THEY BELIEVE YOU TO HAVE DIVINE POWERS.
THIS IS HOW THINGS WOULD HAVE BEEN...
...HAD YOU NEVER BECOME MY BRIDE.

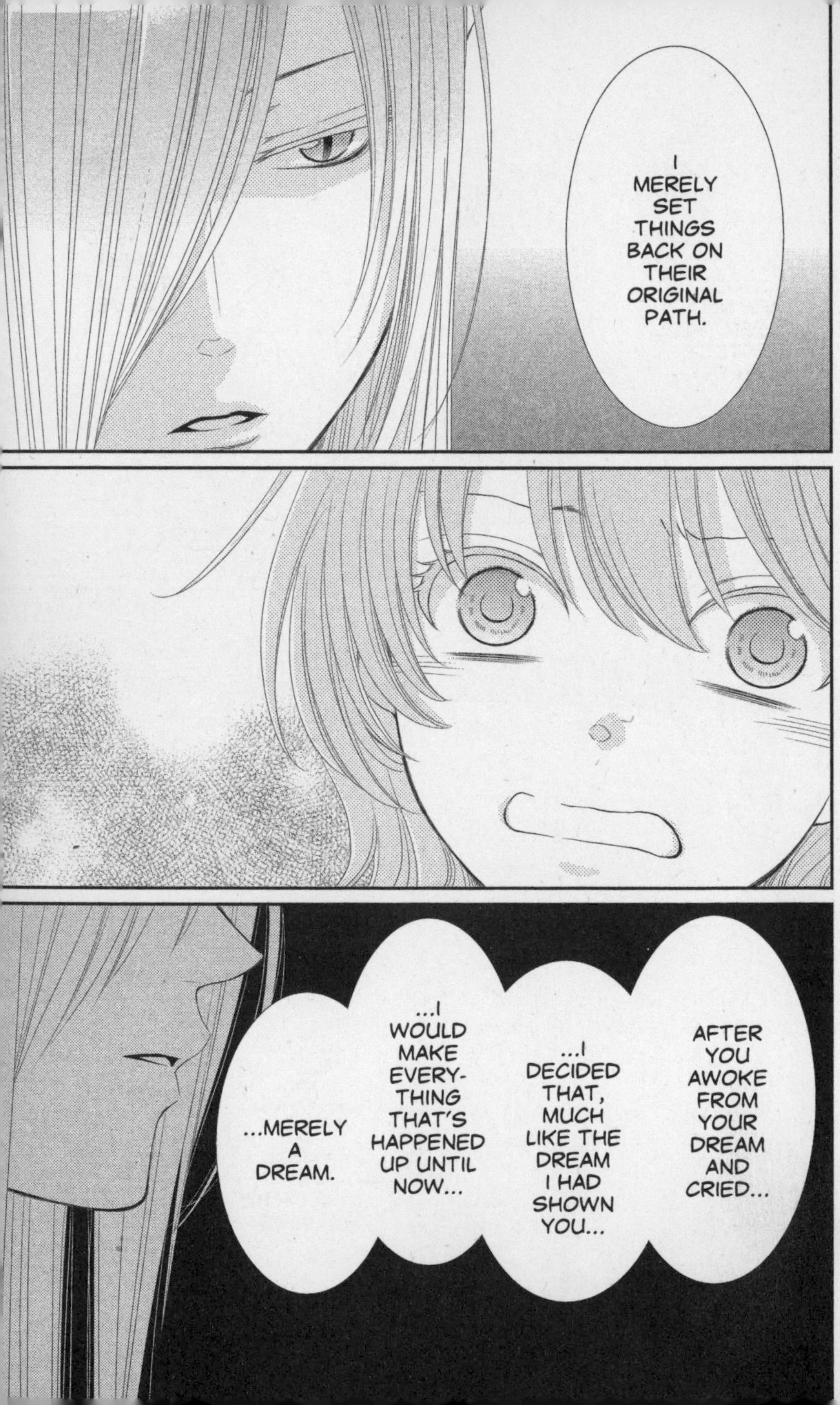
I MERELY SET THINGS BACK ON THEIR ORIGINAL PATH.
AFTER YOU AWOKE FROM YOUR DREAM AND CRIED...
...I DECIDED THAT, MUCH LIKE THE DREAM I HAD SHOWN YOU...
...I WOULD MAKE EVERY-THING THAT'S HAPPENED UP UNTIL NOW...
...MERELY A DREAM.

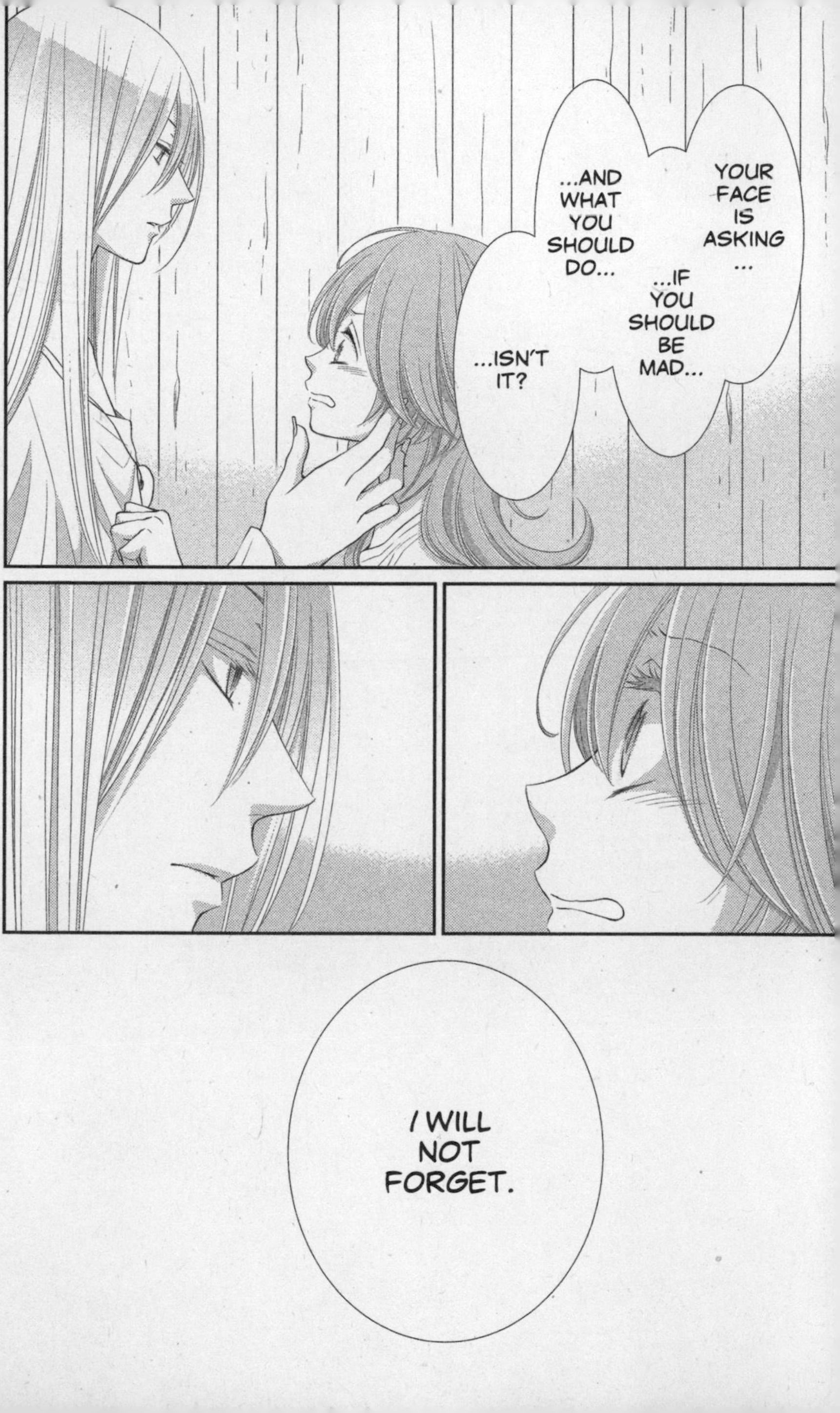
YOUR FACE IS ASKING ...
...IF YOU SHOULD BE MAD...
...AND WHAT YOU SHOULD DO...
...ISN'T IT?
I WILL NOT FORGET.

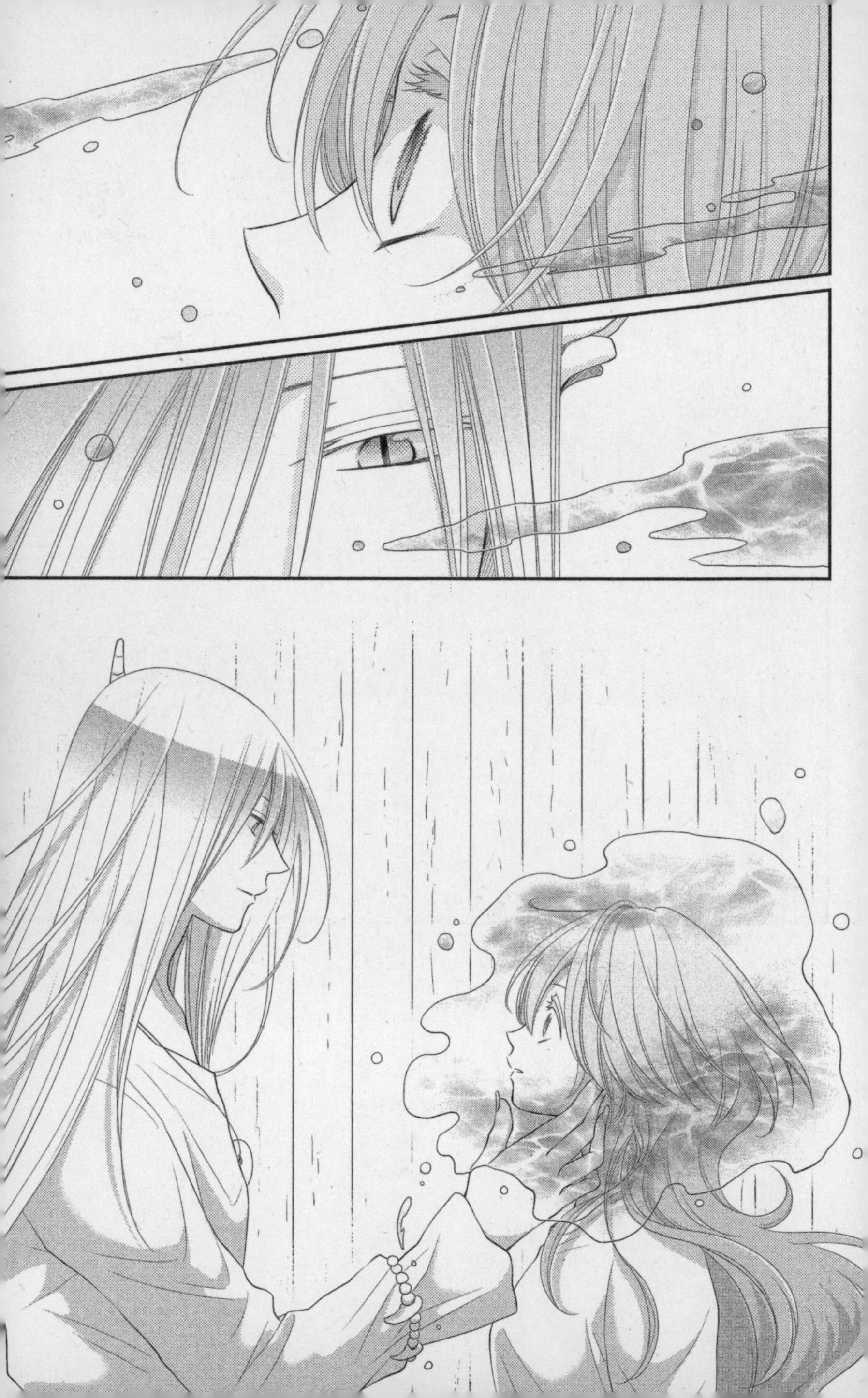

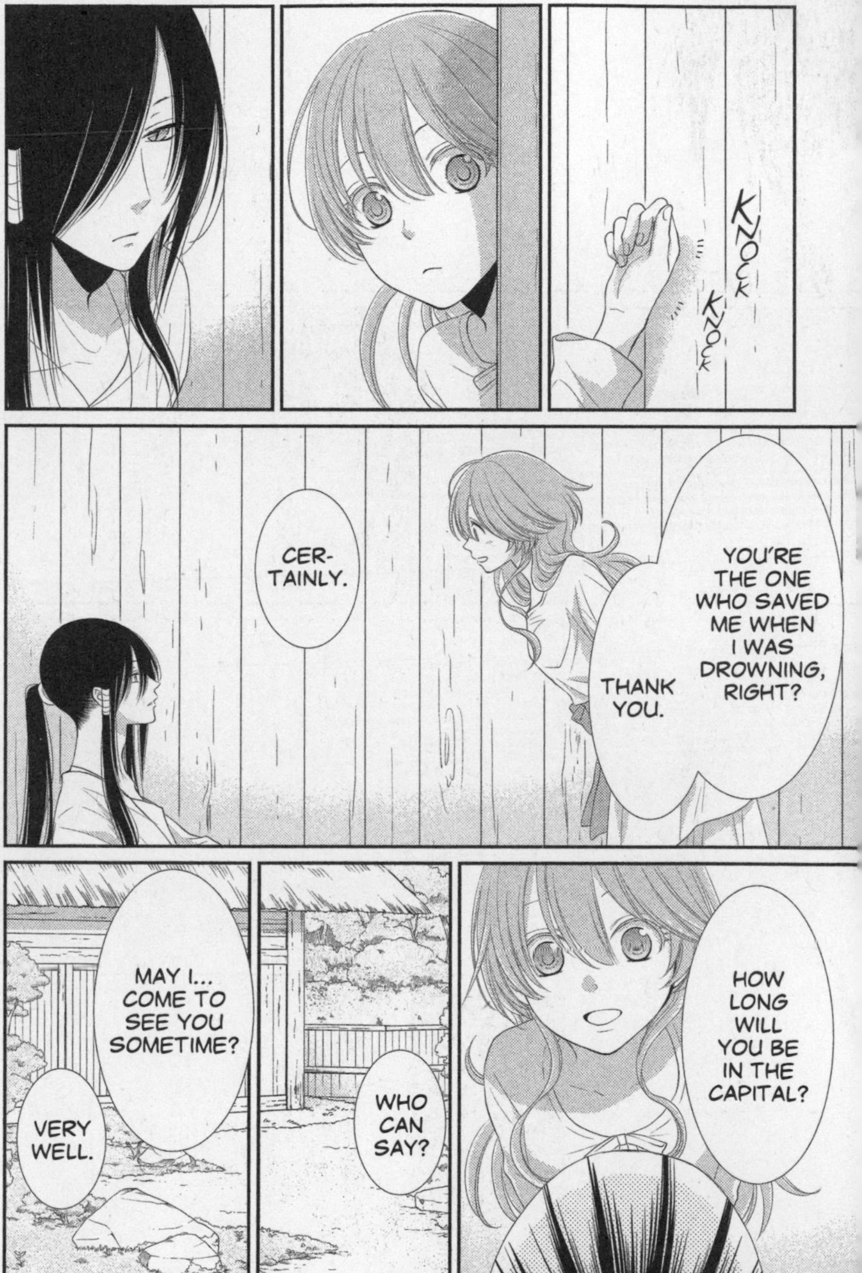
KNOCK
KNOCK
YOU'RE THE ONE WHO SAVED ME WHEN I WAS DROWNING, RIGHT?
THANK YOU.
CER-TAINLY.
HOW LONG WILL YOU BE IN THE CAPITAL?
WHO CAN SAY?
MAY I... COME TO SEE YOU SOMETIME?
VERY WELL.

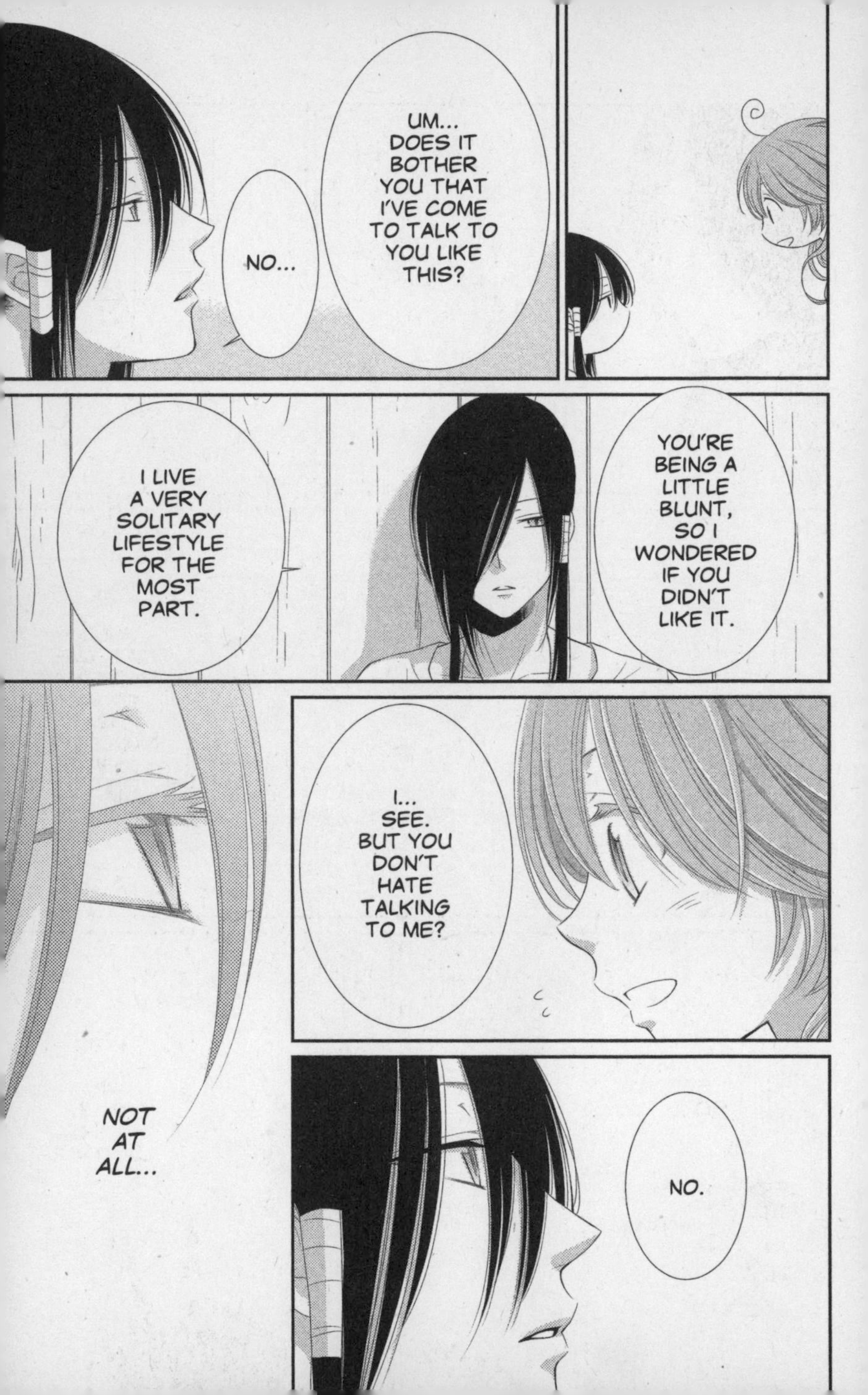
UM... DOES IT BOTHER YOU THAT I'VE COME TO TALK TO YOU LIKE THIS?
NO...
YOU'RE BEING A LITTLE BLUNT, SO I WONDERED IF YOU DIDN'T LIKE IT.
I LIVE A VERY SOLITARY LIFESTYLE FOR THE MOST PART.
I... SEE. BUT YOU DON'T HATE TALKING TO ME?
NO.
NOT AT ALL...

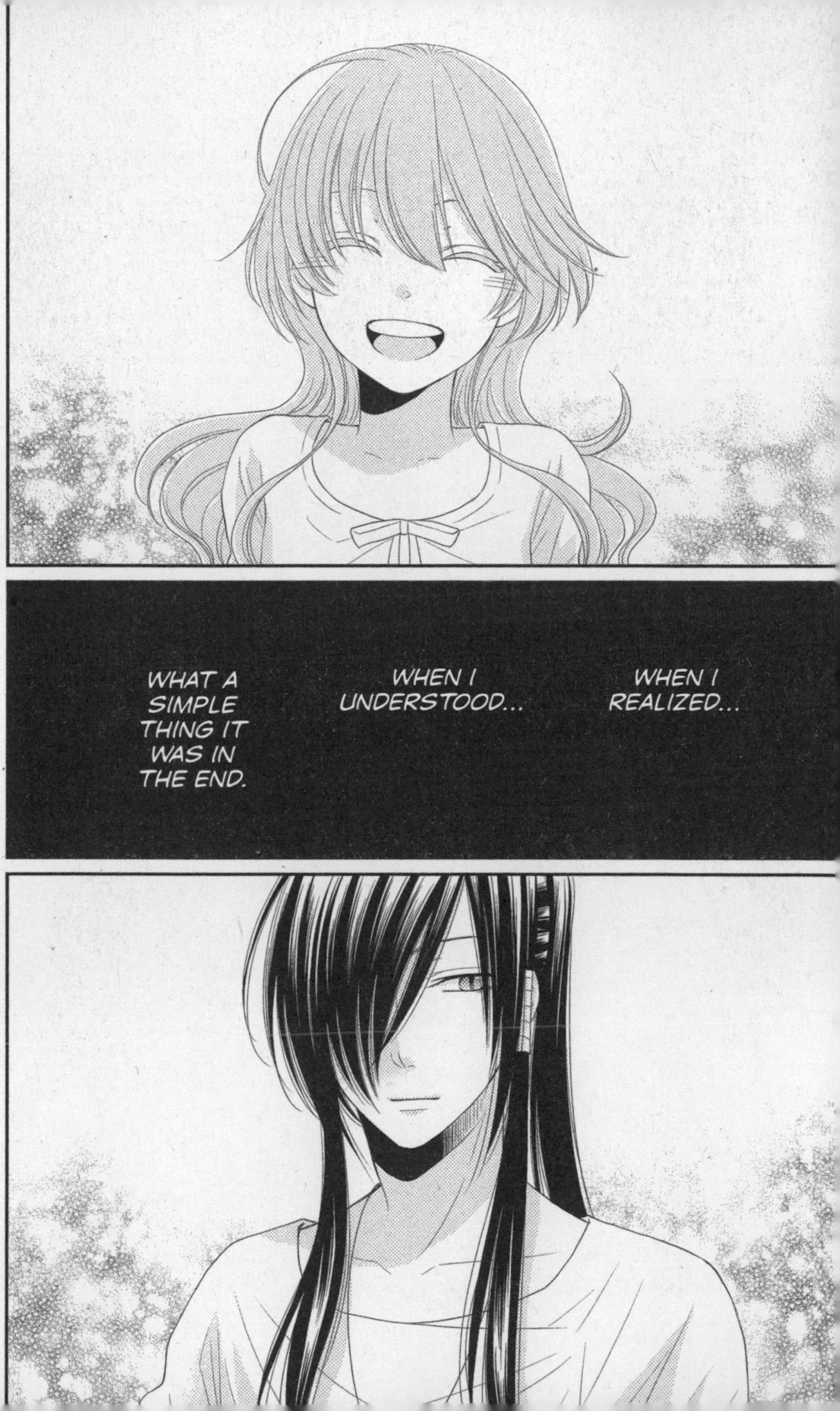
WHEN I REALIZED...
WHEN I UNDERSTOOD...
WHAT A SIMPLE THING IT WAS IN THE END.

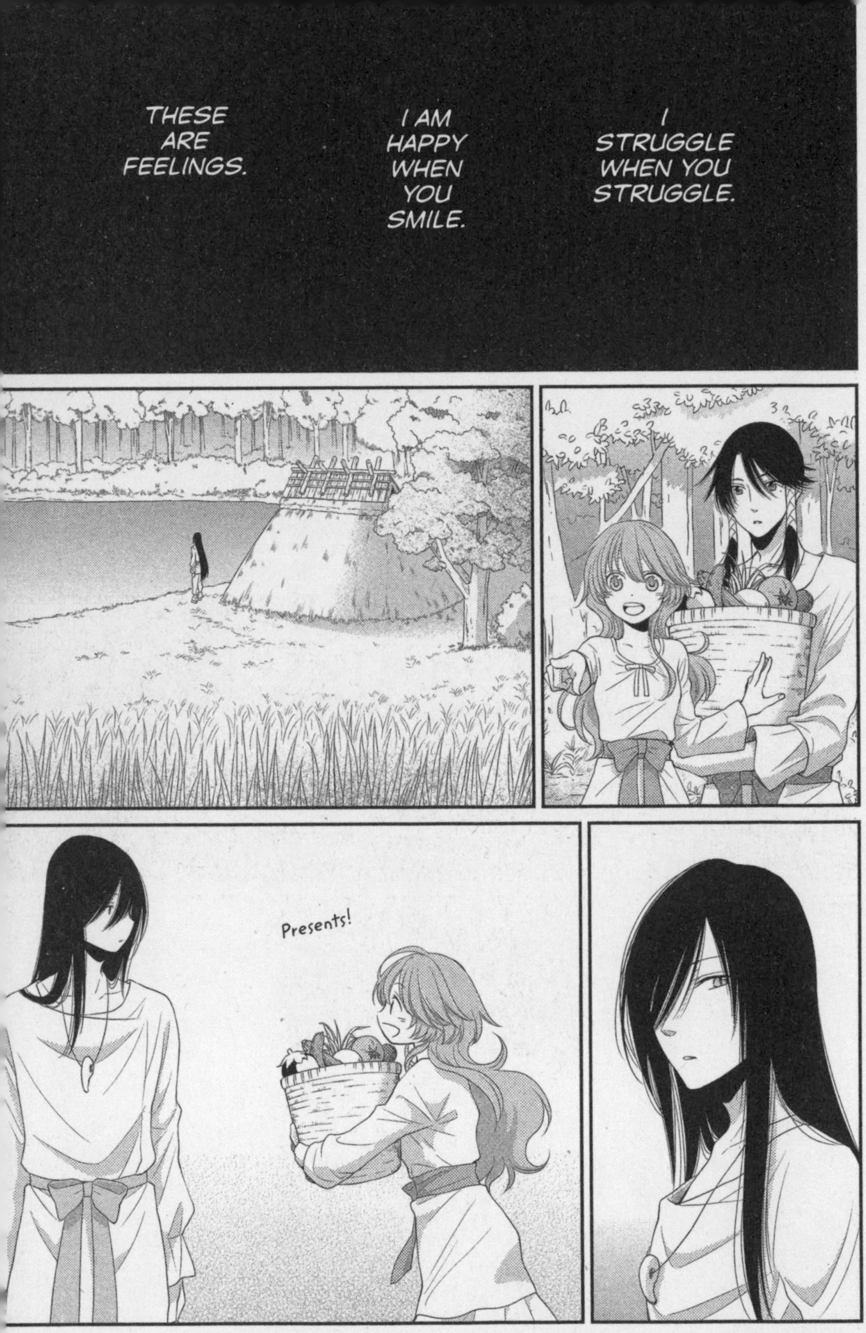
I STRUGGLE WHEN YOU STRUGGLE.
I AM HAPPY WHEN YOU SMILE.
THESE ARE FEELINGS.
Presents!

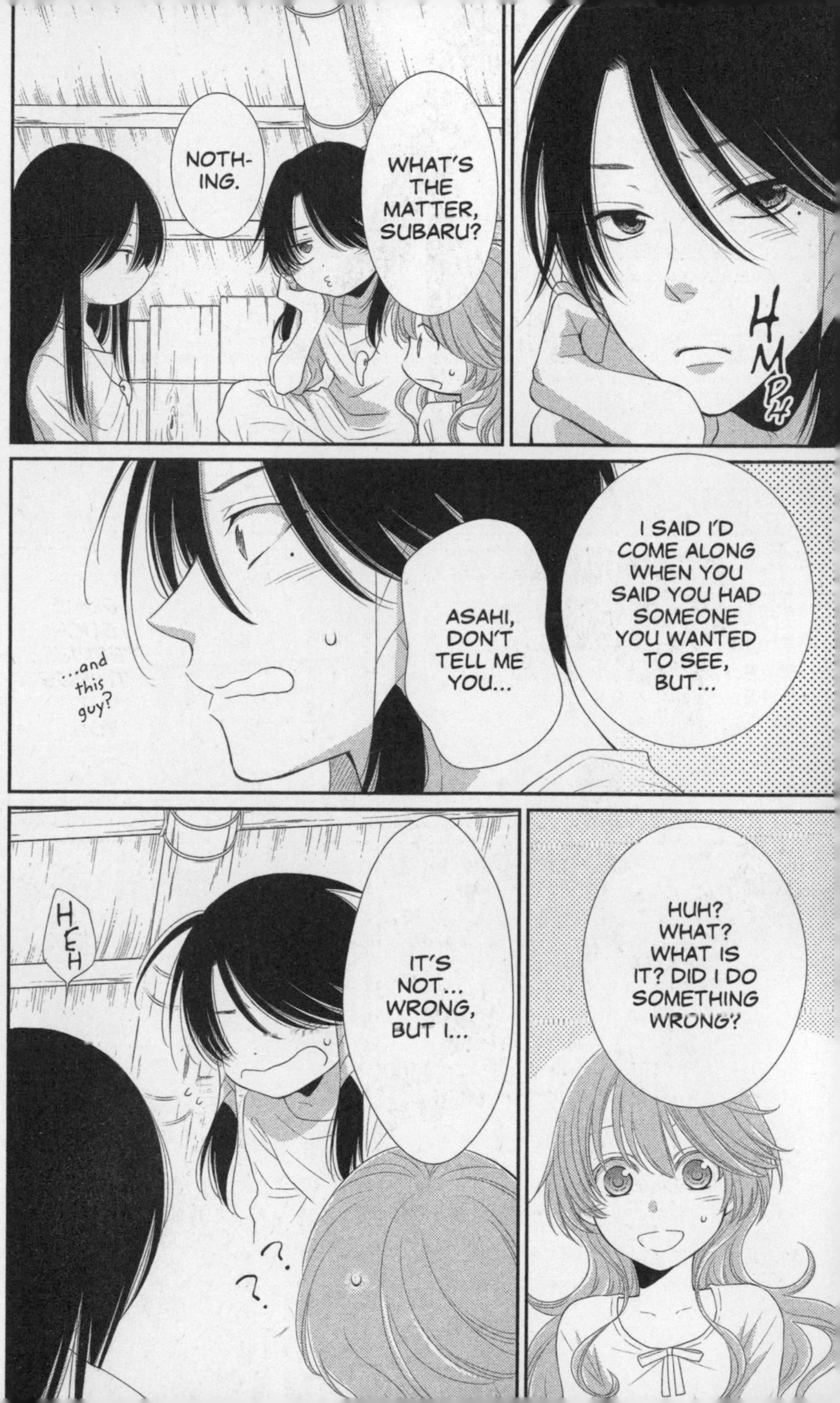
HMPH
WHAT'S THE MATTER, SUBARU?
NOTH-ING.
I SAID I'D COME ALONG WHEN YOU SAID YOU HAD SOMEONE YOU WANTED TO SEE, BUT...
ASAHI, DON'T TELL ME YOU...
...and this guy?
HUH? WHAT? WHAT IS IT? DID I DO SOMETHING WRONG?
IT'S NOT... WRONG, BUT I...
HEH

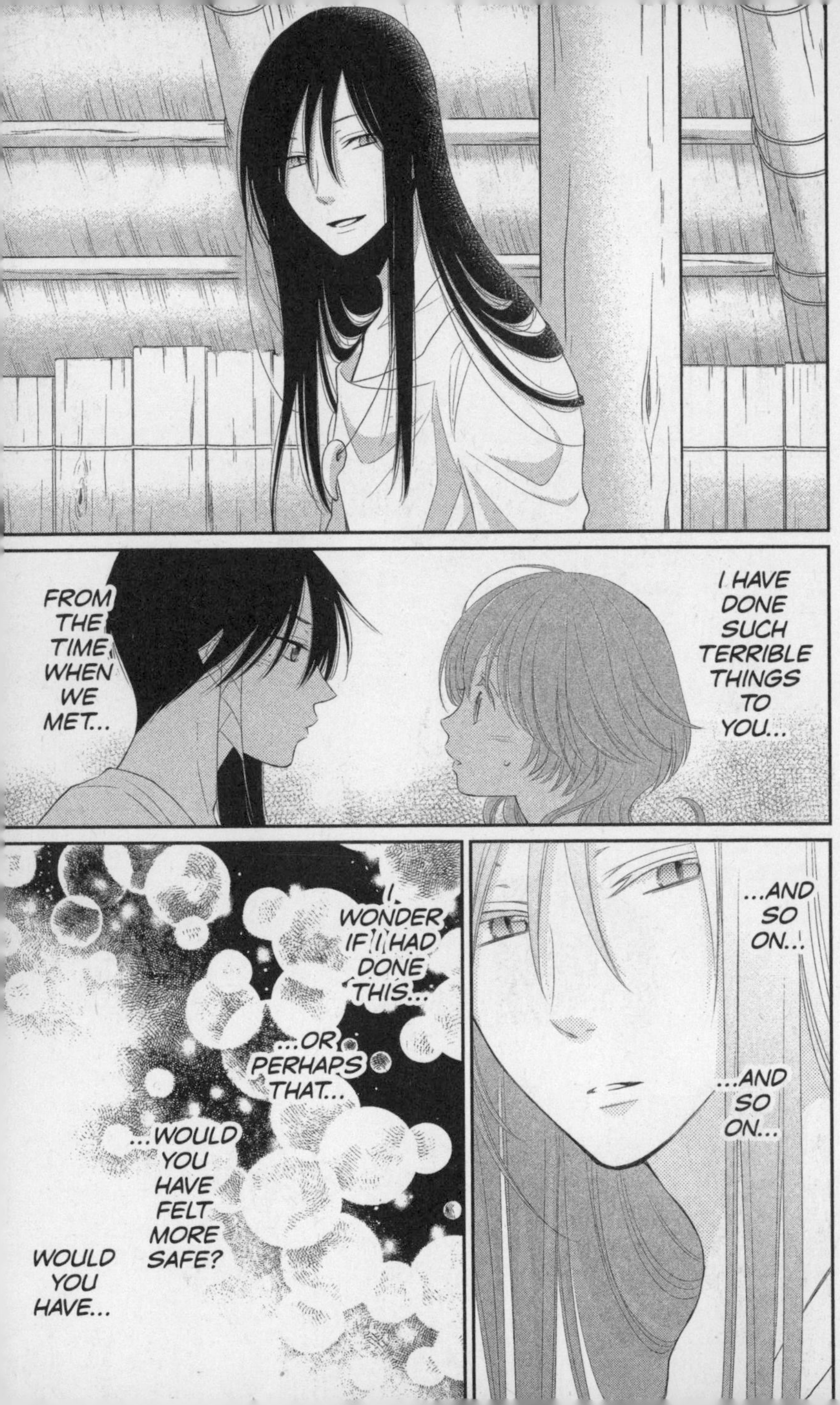
I HAVE DONE SUCH TERRIBLE THINGS TO YOU...
FROM THE TIME WHEN WE MET...
...AND SO ON...
...AND SO ON...
I WONDER IF I HAD DONE THIS...
...OR PERHAPS THAT...
...WOULD YOU HAVE FELT MORE SAFE?
WOULD YOU HAVE...

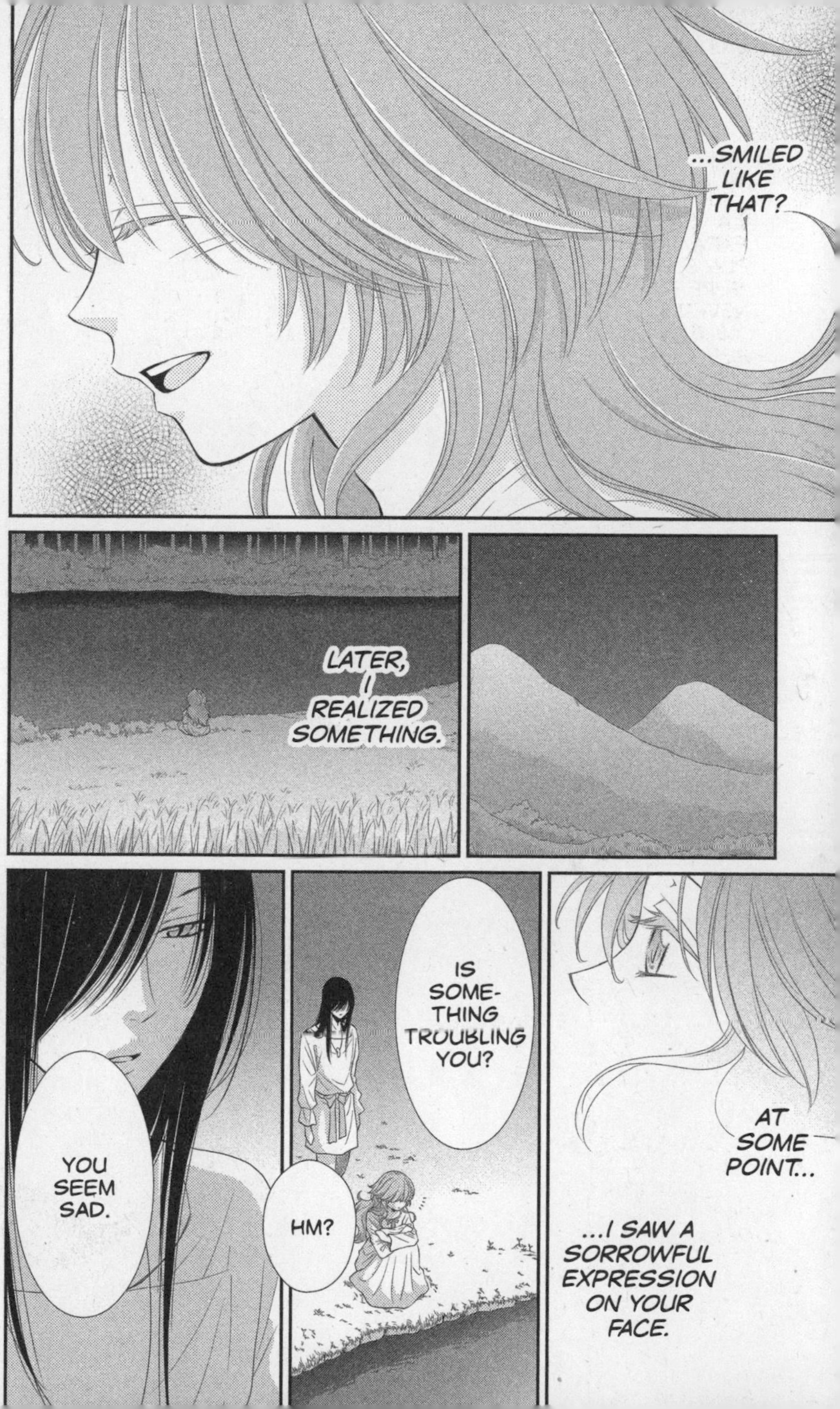
...SMILED LIKE THAT?
LATER, I REALIZED SOMETHING.
AT SOME POINT...
...I SAW A SORROWFUL EXPRESSION ON YOUR FACE.
IS SOME-THING TROUBLING YOU?
HM?
YOU SEEM SAD.

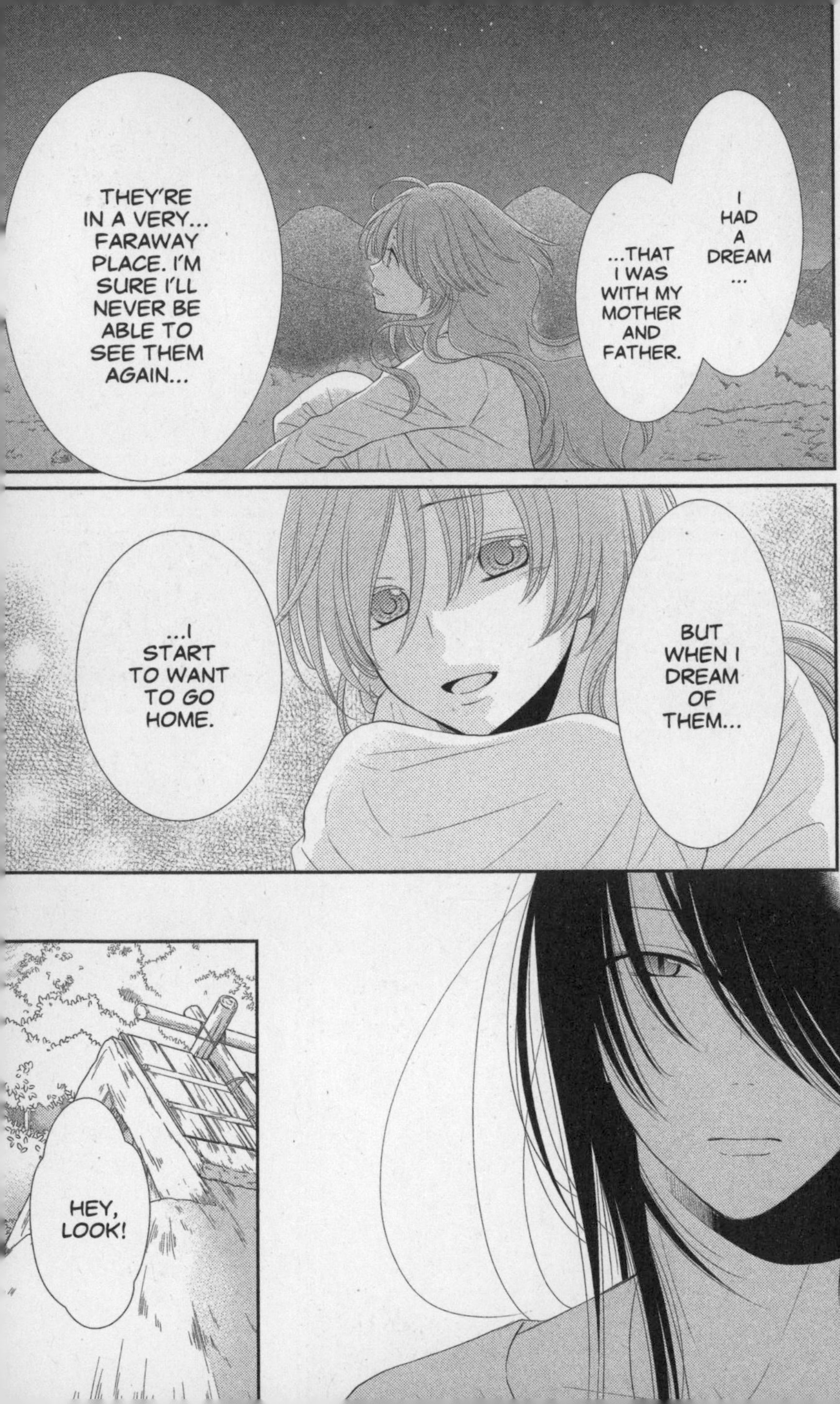
I HAD A DREAM...
...THAT I WAS WITH MY MOTHER AND FATHER.
THEY'RE IN A VERY... FARAWAY PLACE. I'M SURE I'LL NEVER BE ABLE TO SEE THEM AGAIN...
BUT WHEN I DREAM OF THEM...
...I START TO WANT TO GO HOME.
HEY, LOOK!

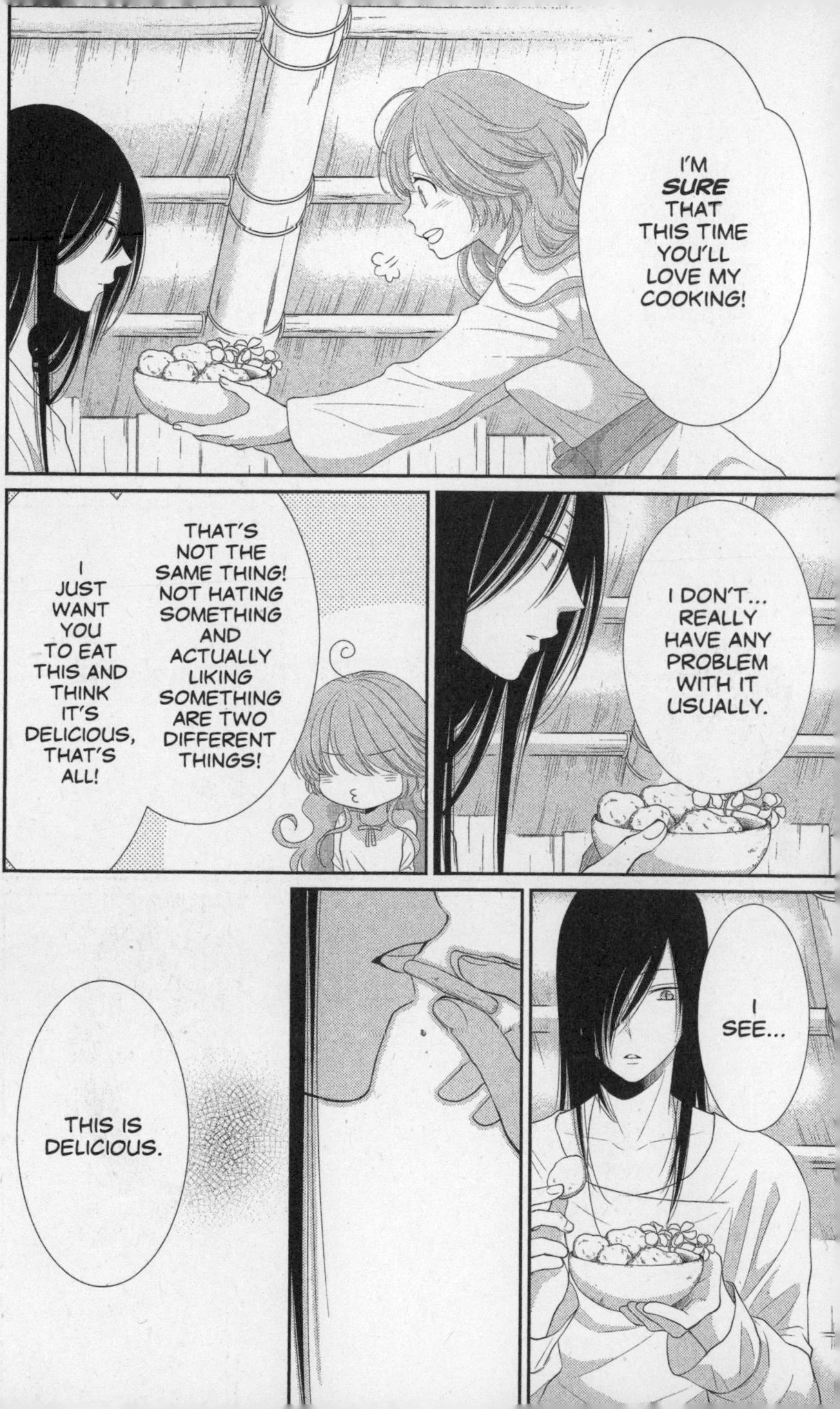
I'M SURE THAT THIS TIME YOU'LL LOVE MY COOKING!
I DON'T... REALLY HAVE ANY PROBLEM WITH IT USUALLY.
THAT'S NOT THE SAME THING! NOT HATING SOMETHING AND ACTUALLY LIKING SOMETHING ARE TWO DIFFERENT THINGS!
I JUST WANT YOU TO EAT THIS AND THINK IT'S DELICIOUS, THAT'S ALL!
I SEE...
THIS IS DELICIOUS.

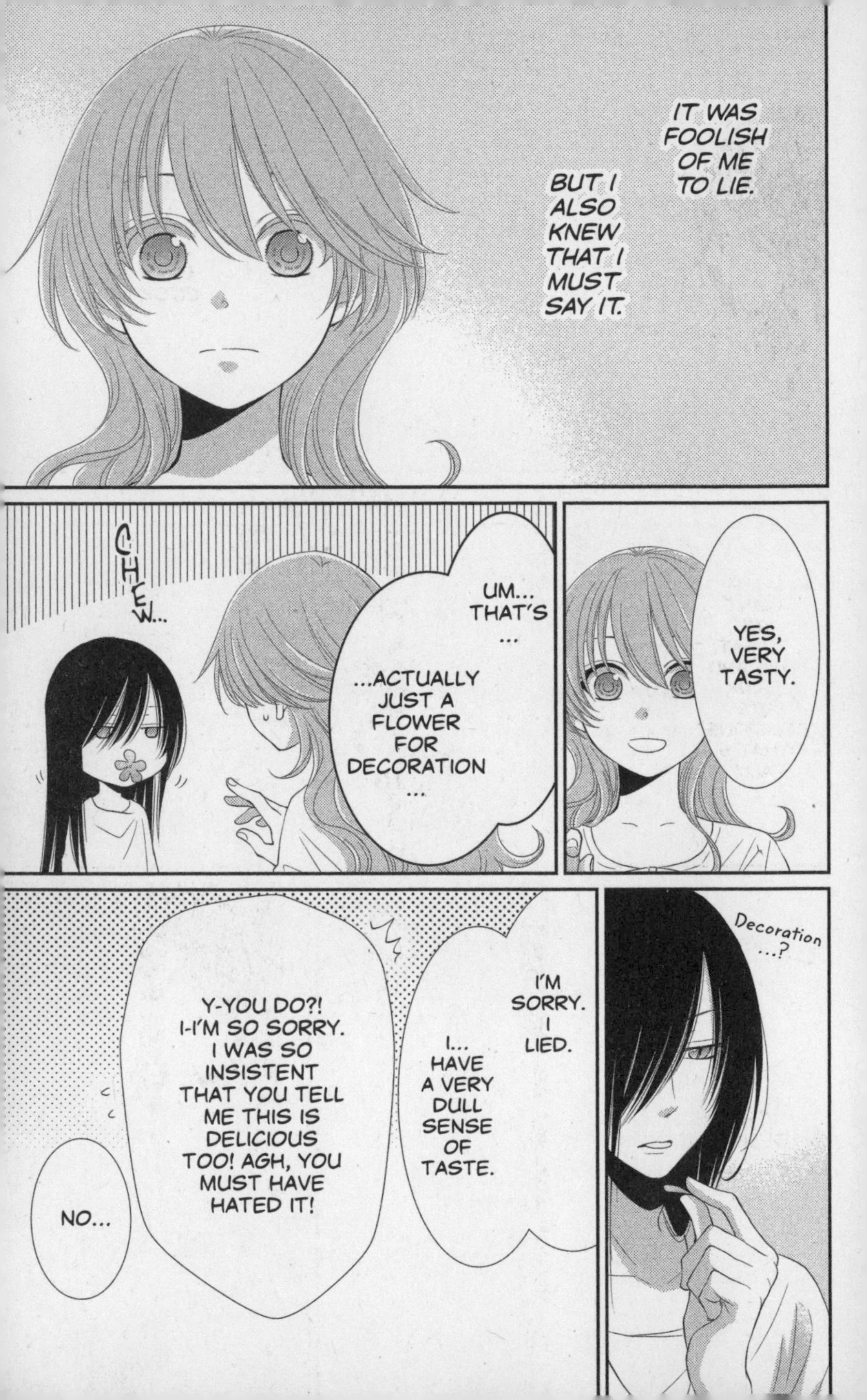
IT WAS FOOLISH OF ME TO LIE.
BUT I ALSO KNEW THAT I MUST SAY IT.
YES, VERY TASTY.
UM... THAT'S ...
...ACTUALLY JUST A FLOWER FOR DECORATION ...
CHEW...
Decoration ...?
I'M SORRY. I LIED.
I... HAVE A VERY DULL SENSE OF TASTE.
Y-YOU DO?! I-I'M SO SORRY. I WAS SO INSISTENT THAT YOU TELL ME THIS IS DELICIOUS TOO! AGH, YOU MUST HAVE HATED IT!
NO...

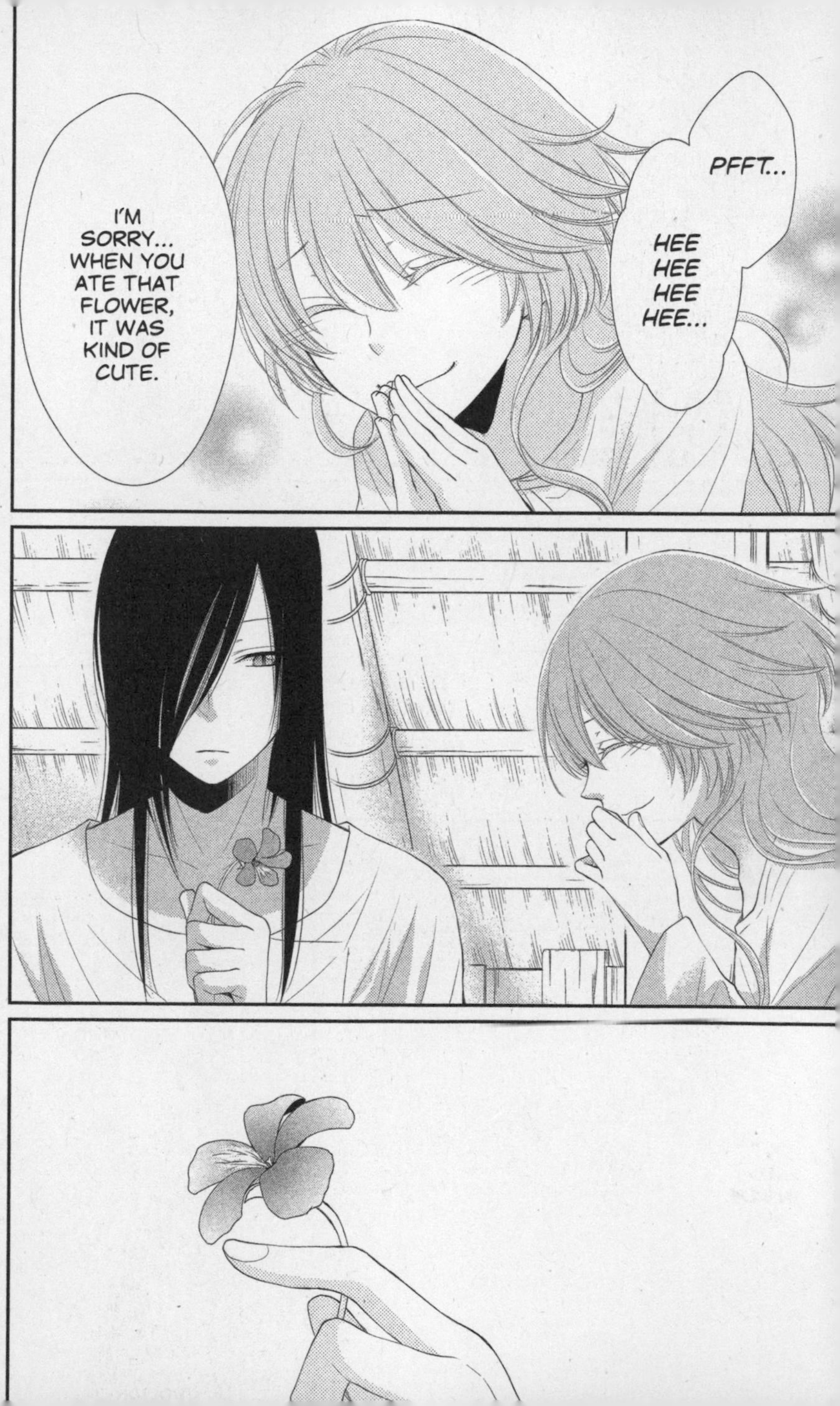
PFFT...
HEE HEE HEE HEE...
I'M SORRY... WHEN YOU ATE THAT FLOWER, IT WAS KIND OF CUTE.

WHAT IS THIS...

...STIRRING INSIDE ME?

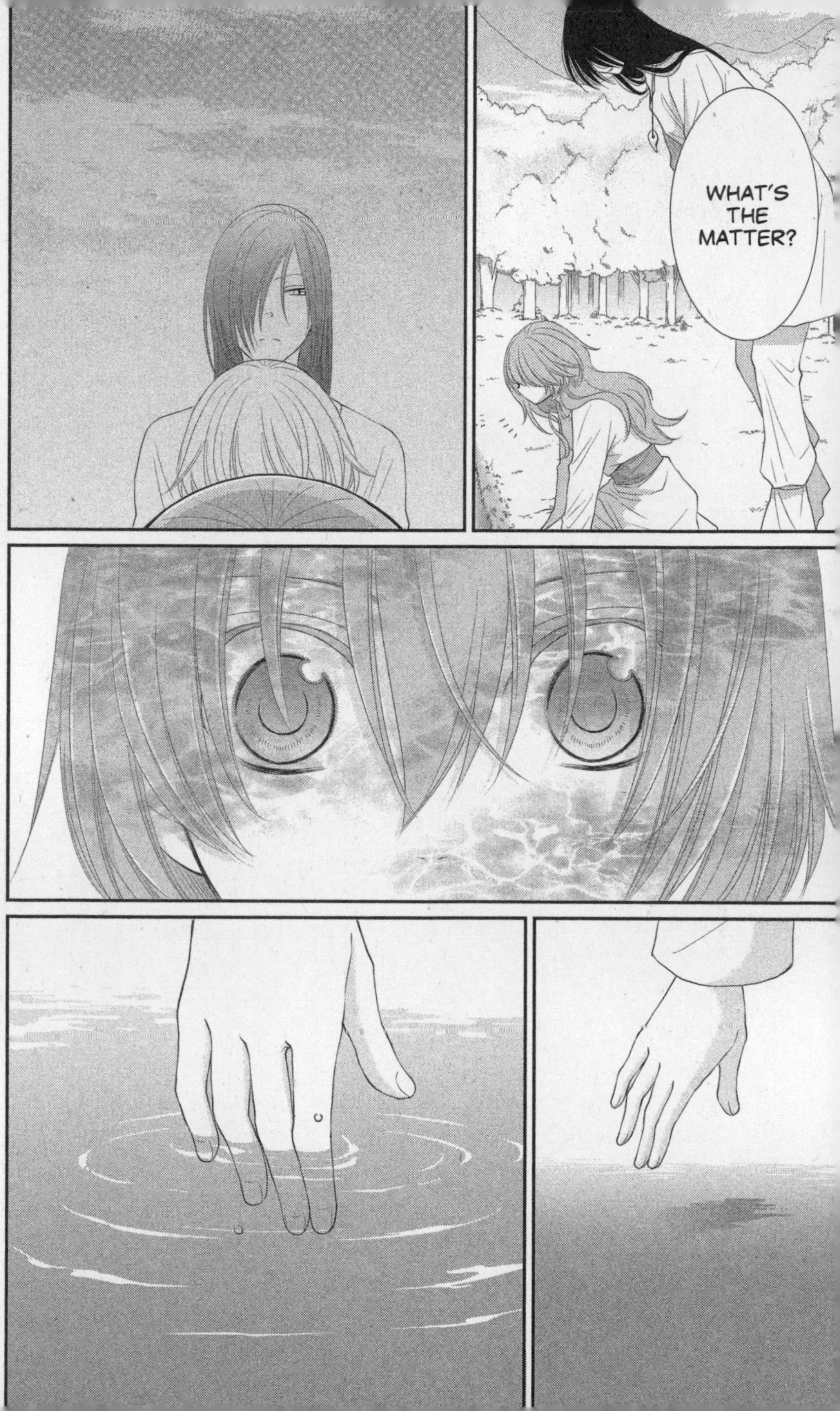
WHAT'S THE MATTER?

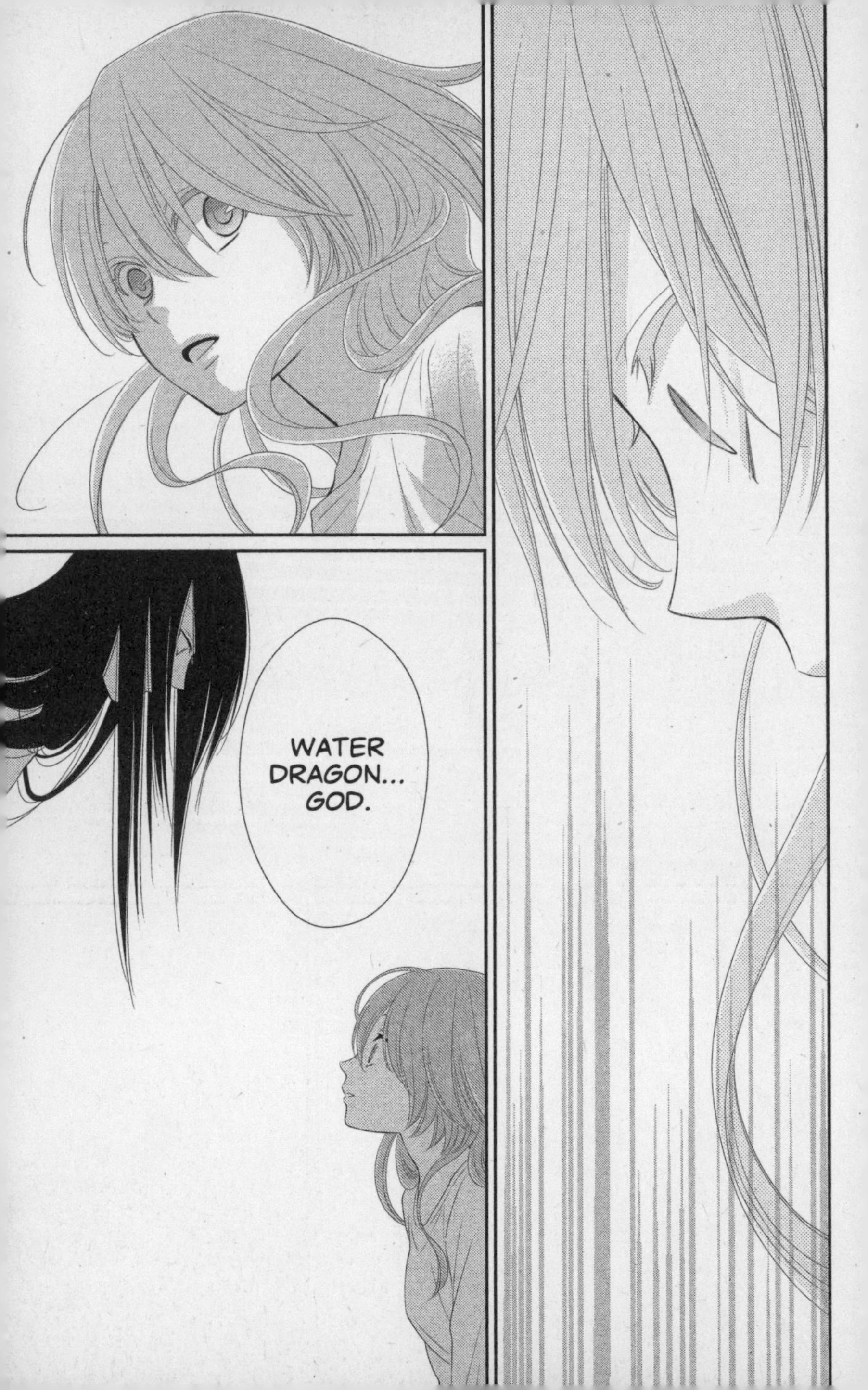
WATER DRAGON... GOD.

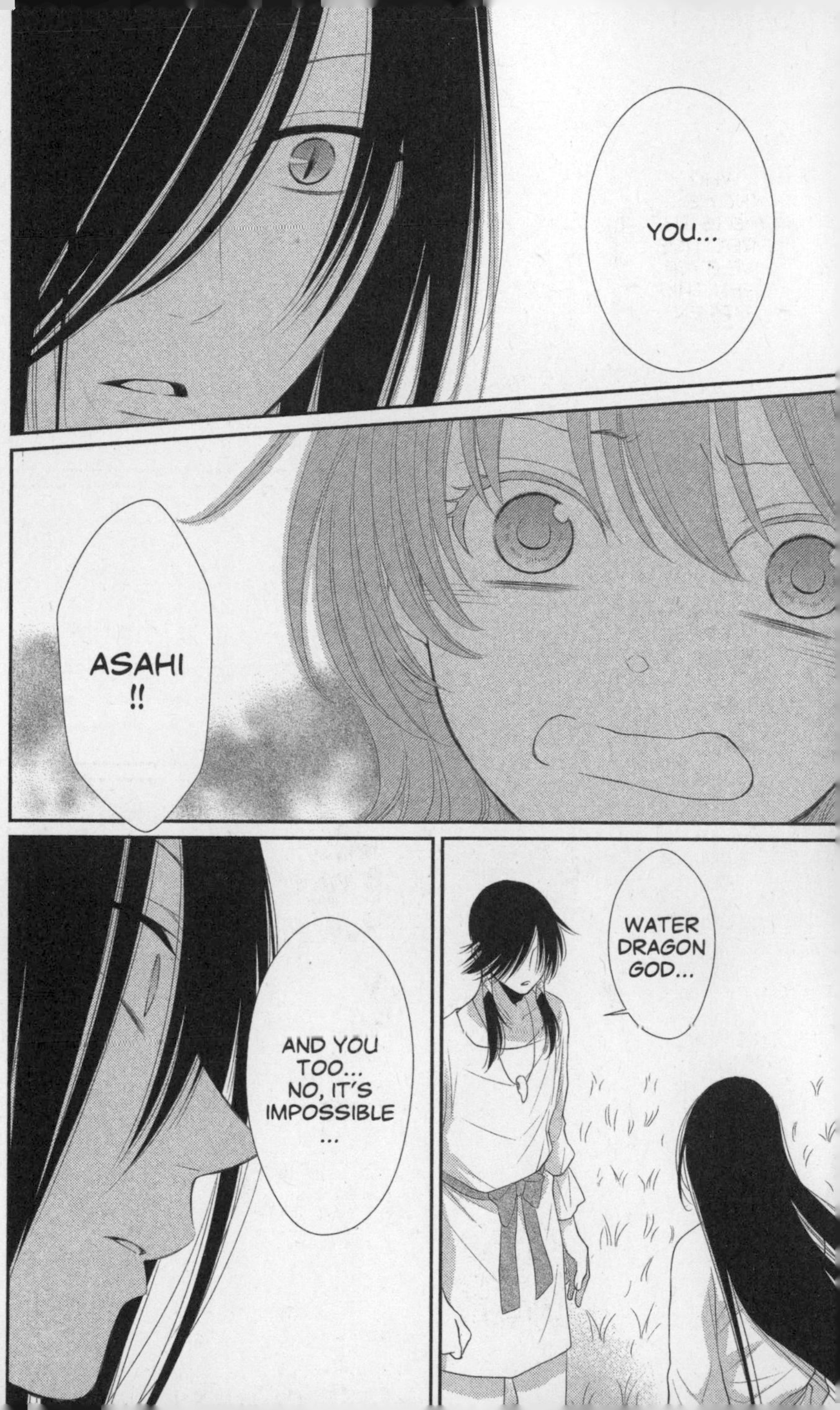
YOU...
ASAHI !!
WATER DRAGON GOD...
AND YOU TOO... NO, IT'S IMPOSSIBLE ...

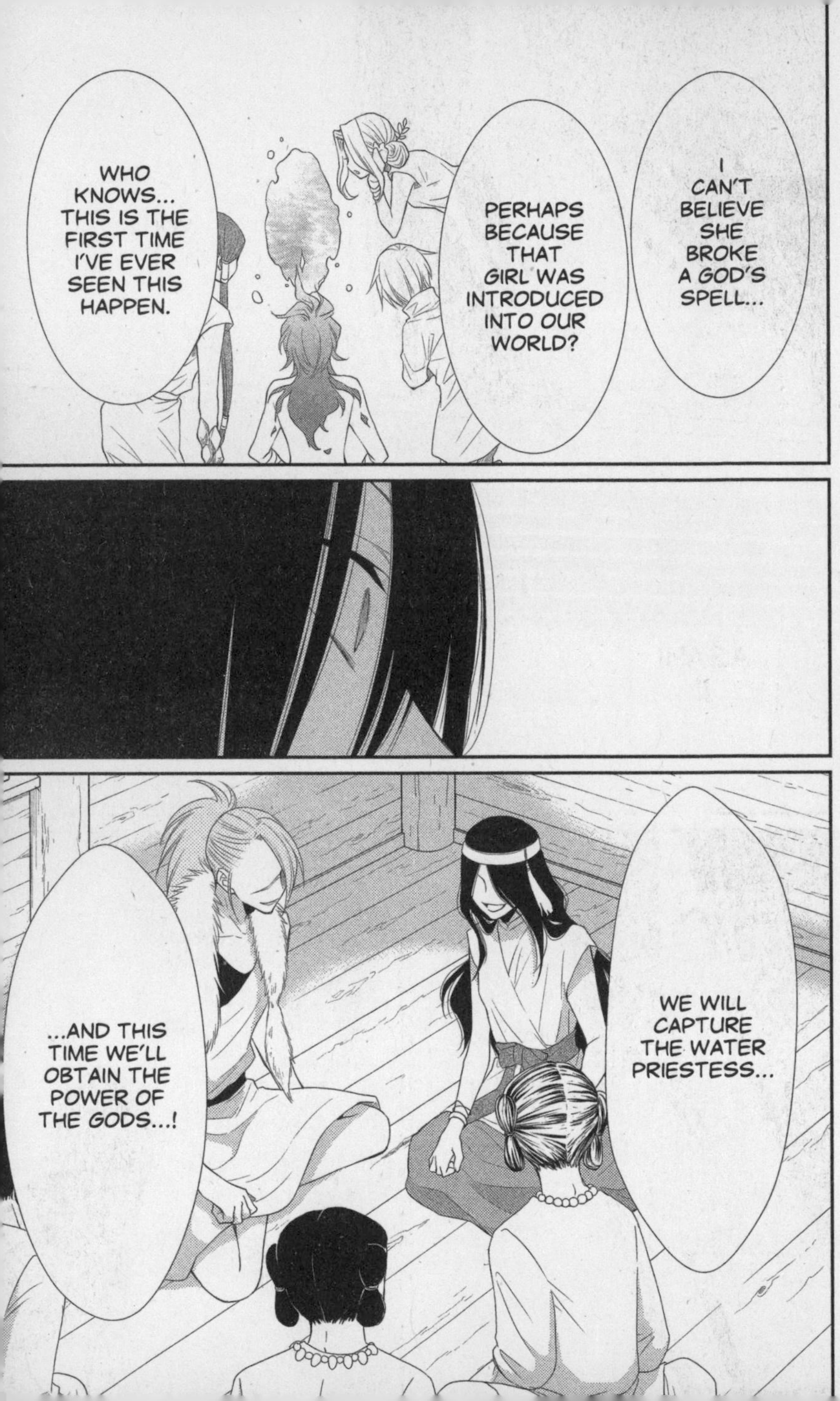
I CAN'T BELIEVE SHE BROKE A GOD'S SPELL...
PERHAPS BECAUSE THAT GIRL WAS INTRODUCED INTO OUR WORLD?
WHO KNOWS... THIS IS THE FIRST TIME I'VE EVER SEEN THIS HAPPEN.
WE WILL CAPTURE THE WATER PRIESTESS...
...AND THIS TIME WE'LL OBTAIN THE POWER OF THE GODS...!

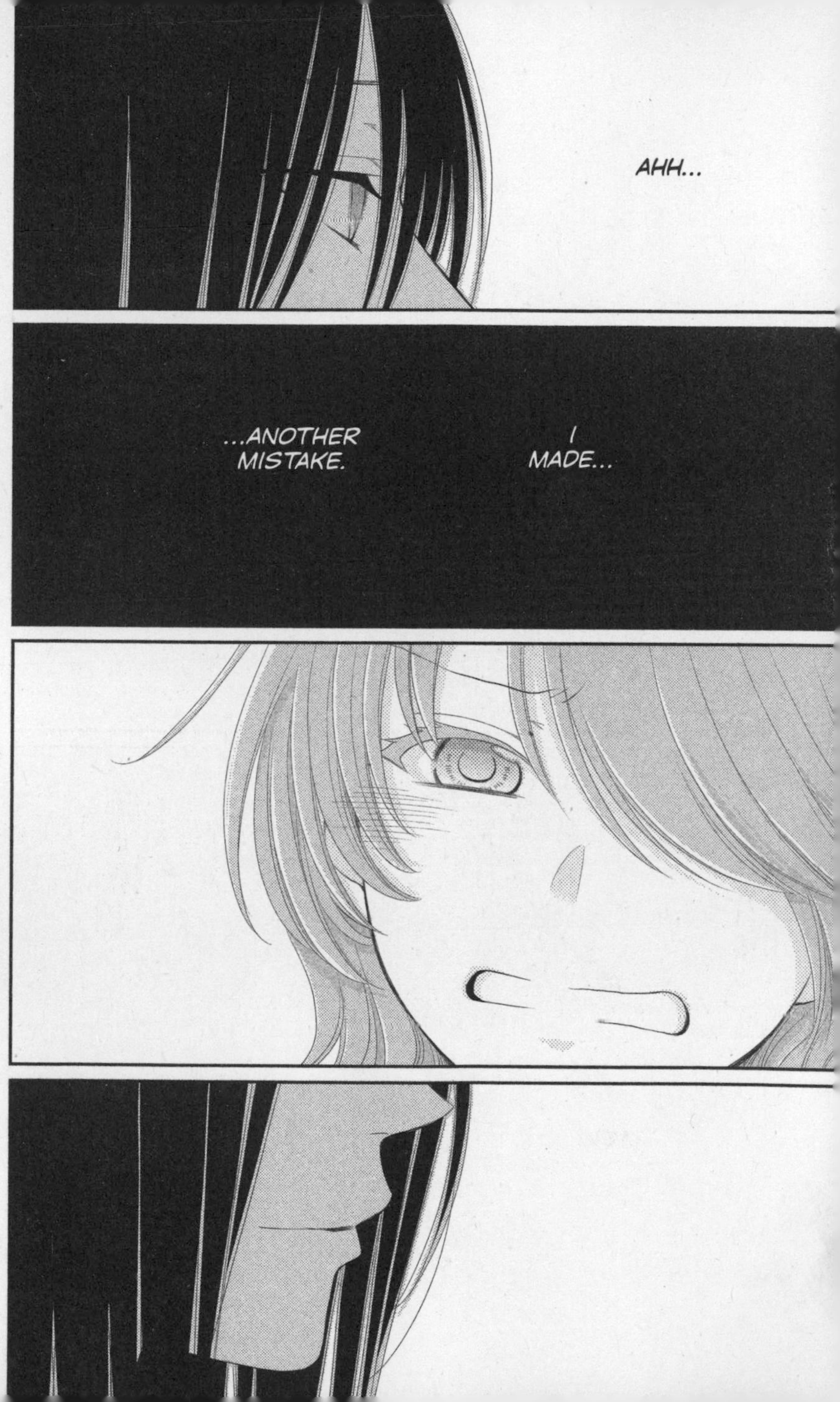
AHH...
I MADE...
...ANOTHER MISTAKE.

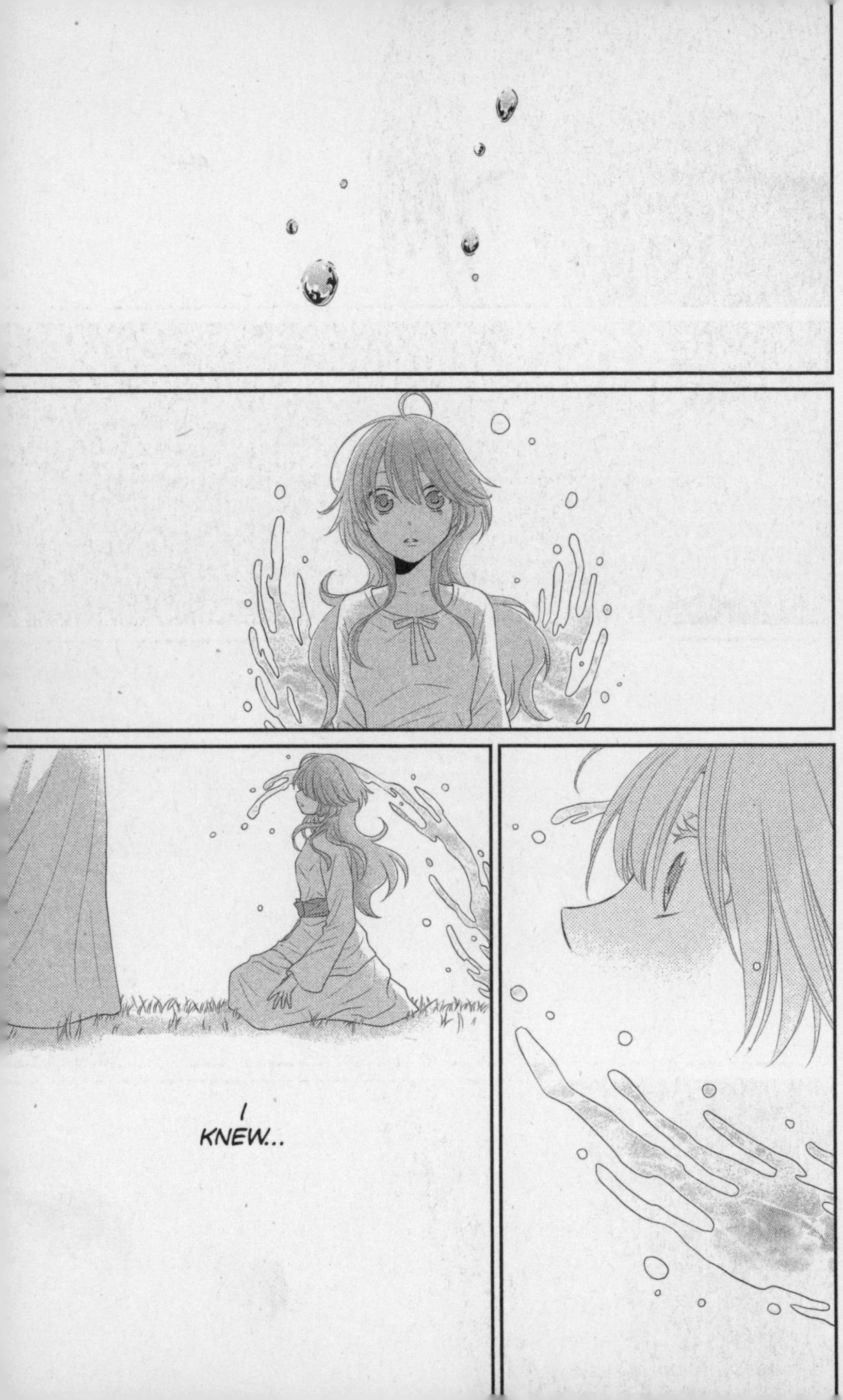
I KNEW...

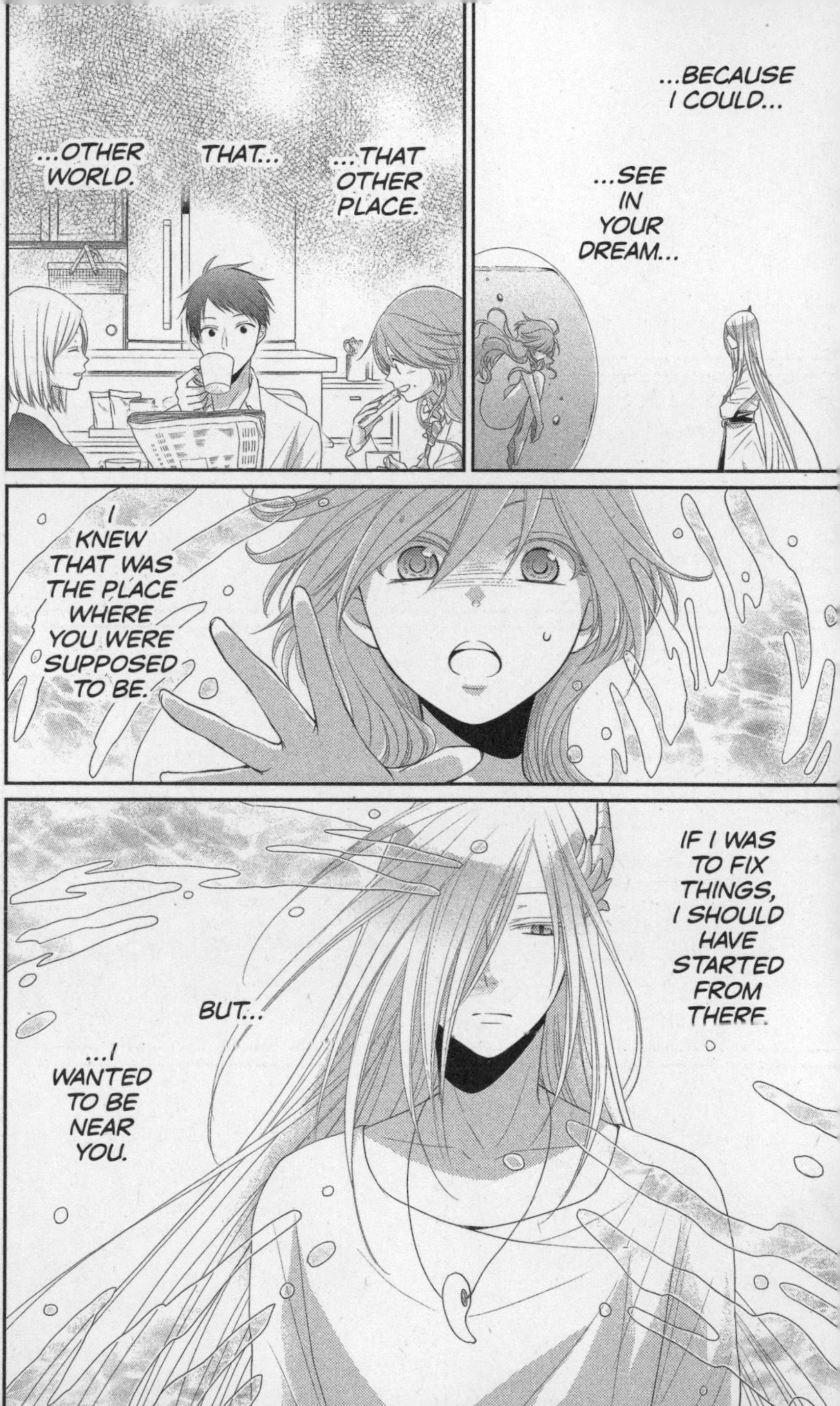
...BECAUSE I COULD...
...SEE IN YOUR DREAM...
...THAT OTHER PLACE.
THAT...
...OTHER WORLD.
I KNEW THAT WAS THE PLACE WHERE YOU WERE SUPPOSED TO BE.
IF I WAS TO FIX THINGS, I SHOULD HAVE STARTED FROM THERE.
BUT...
...I WANTED TO BE NEAR YOU.

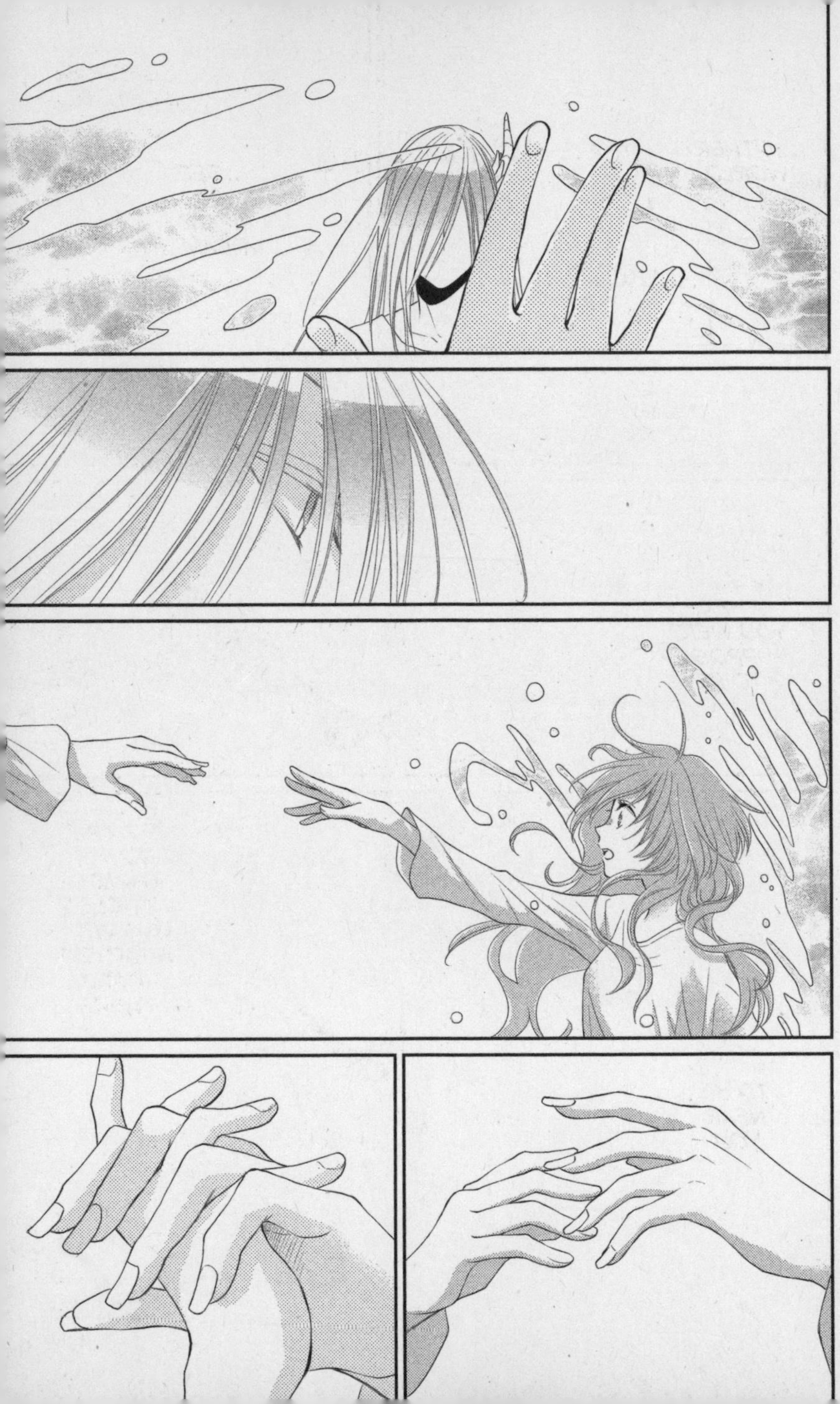

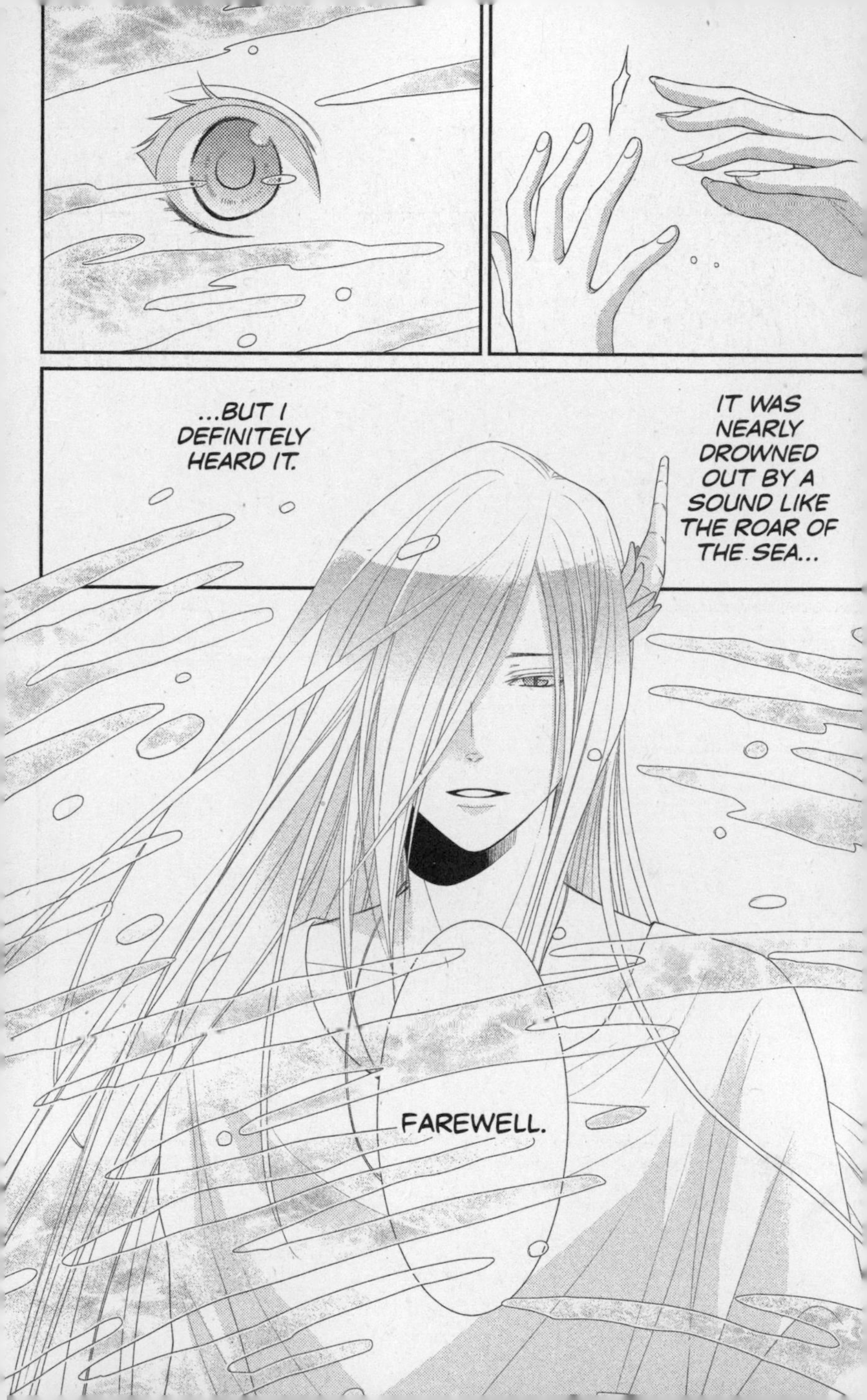
IT WAS NEARLY DROWNED OUT BY A SOUND LIKE THE ROAR OF THE SEA...
...BUT I DEFINITELY HEARD IT.
FAREWELL.

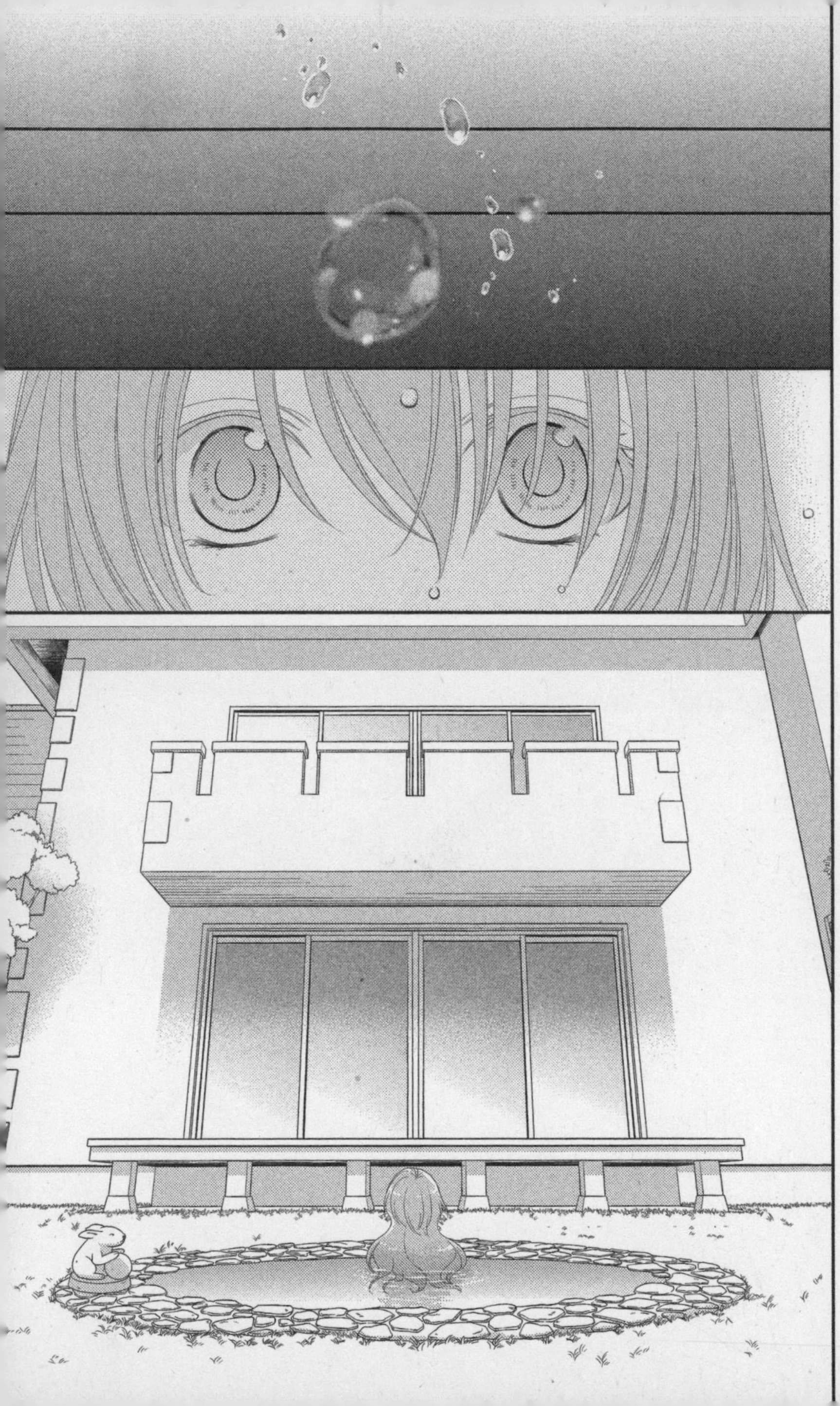

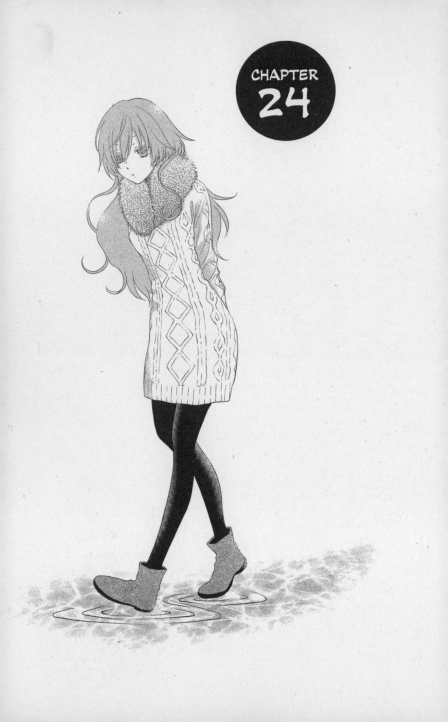

# CHAPTER 24

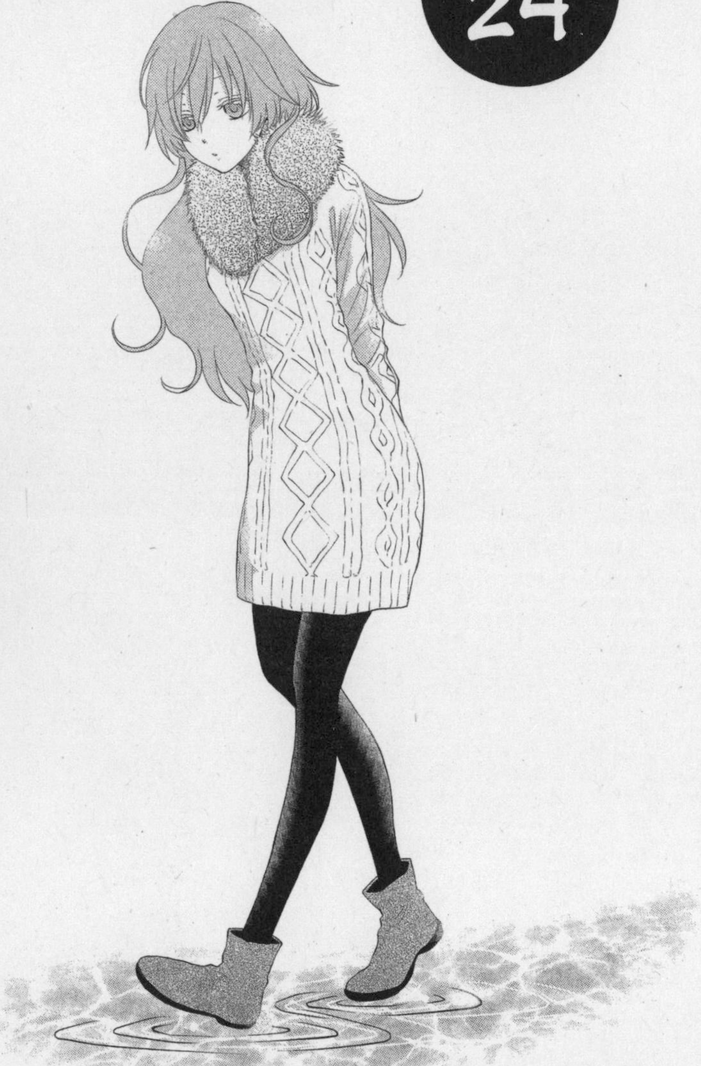

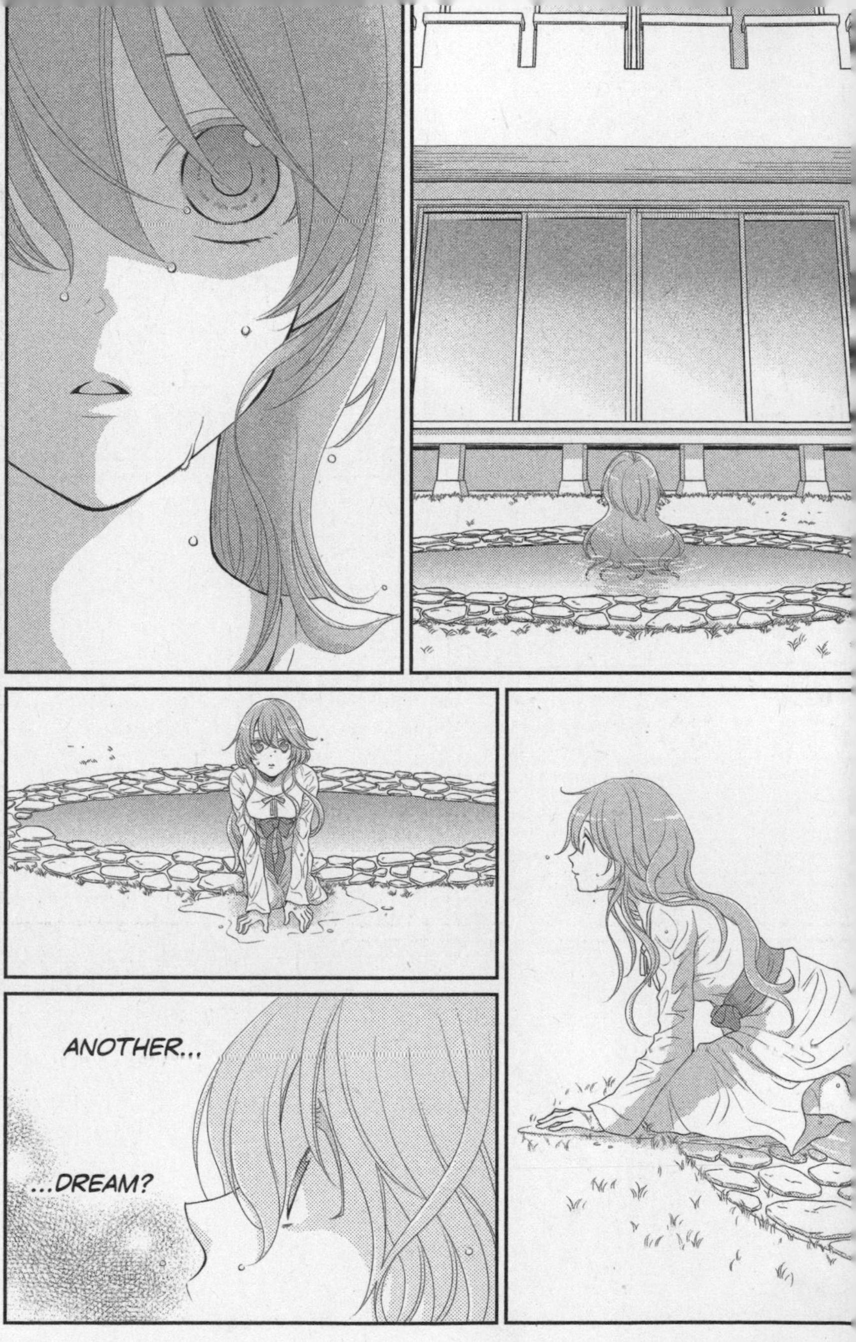
ANOTHER...
...DREAM?

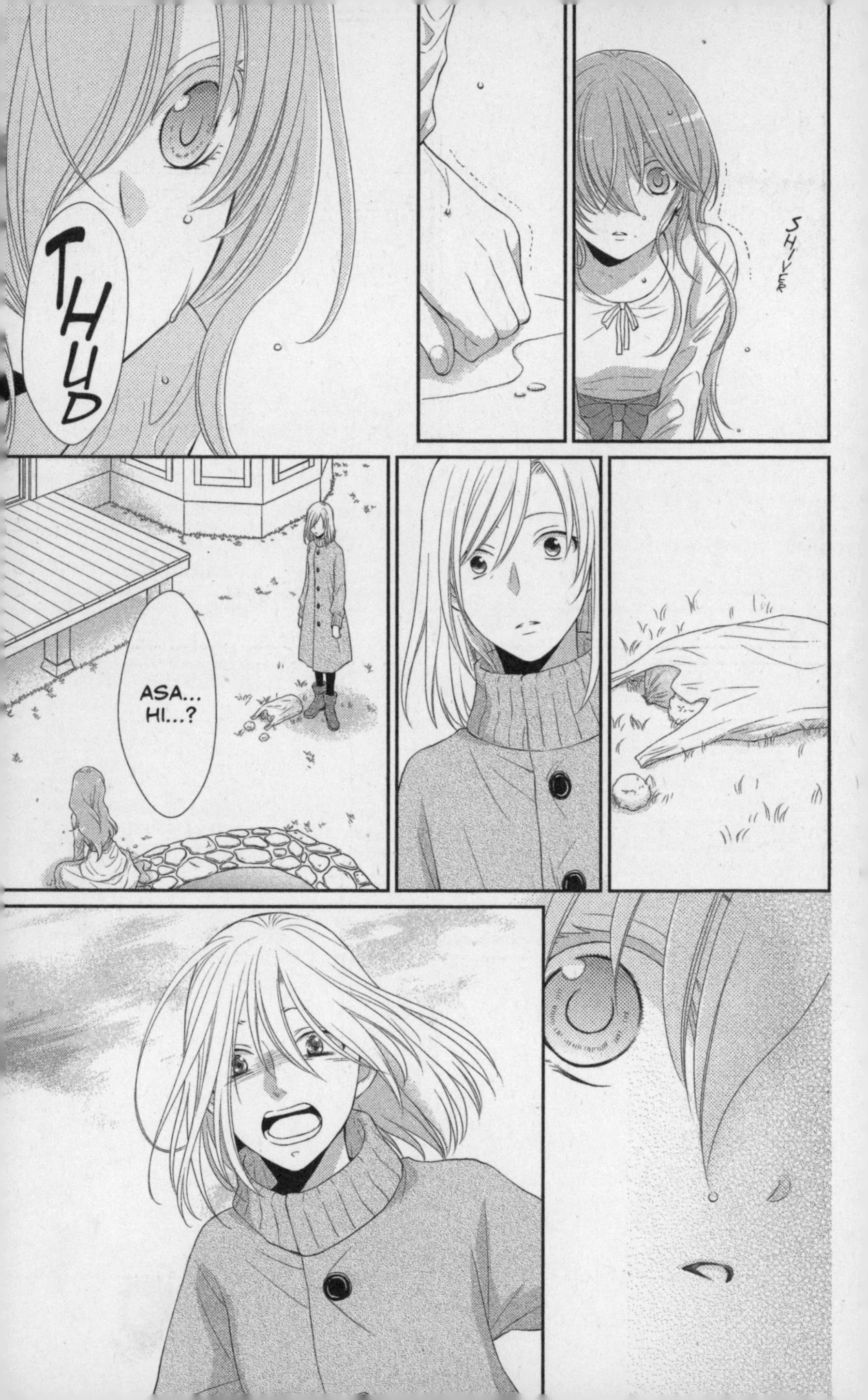
SHIVER
THUD
ASA... HI...?

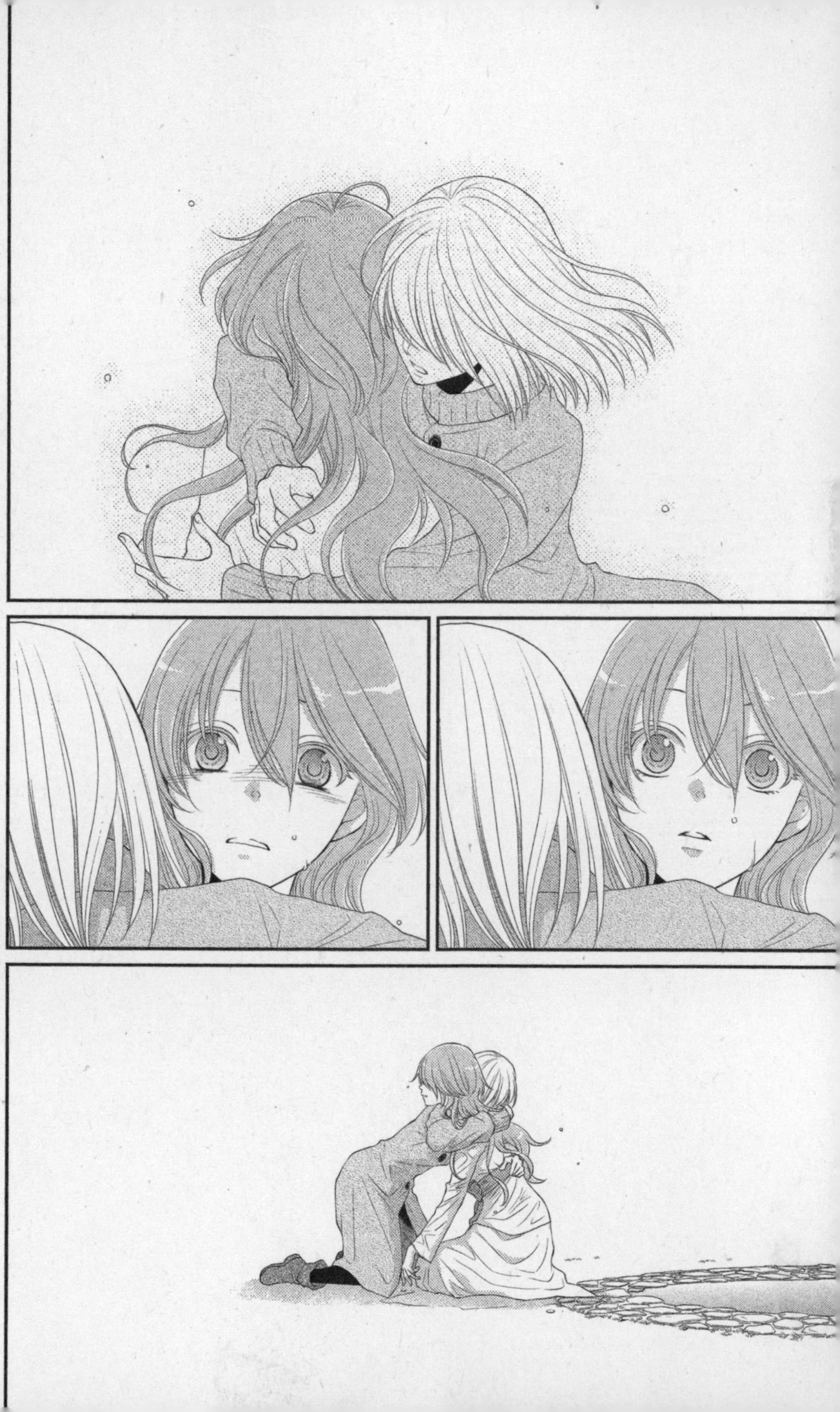

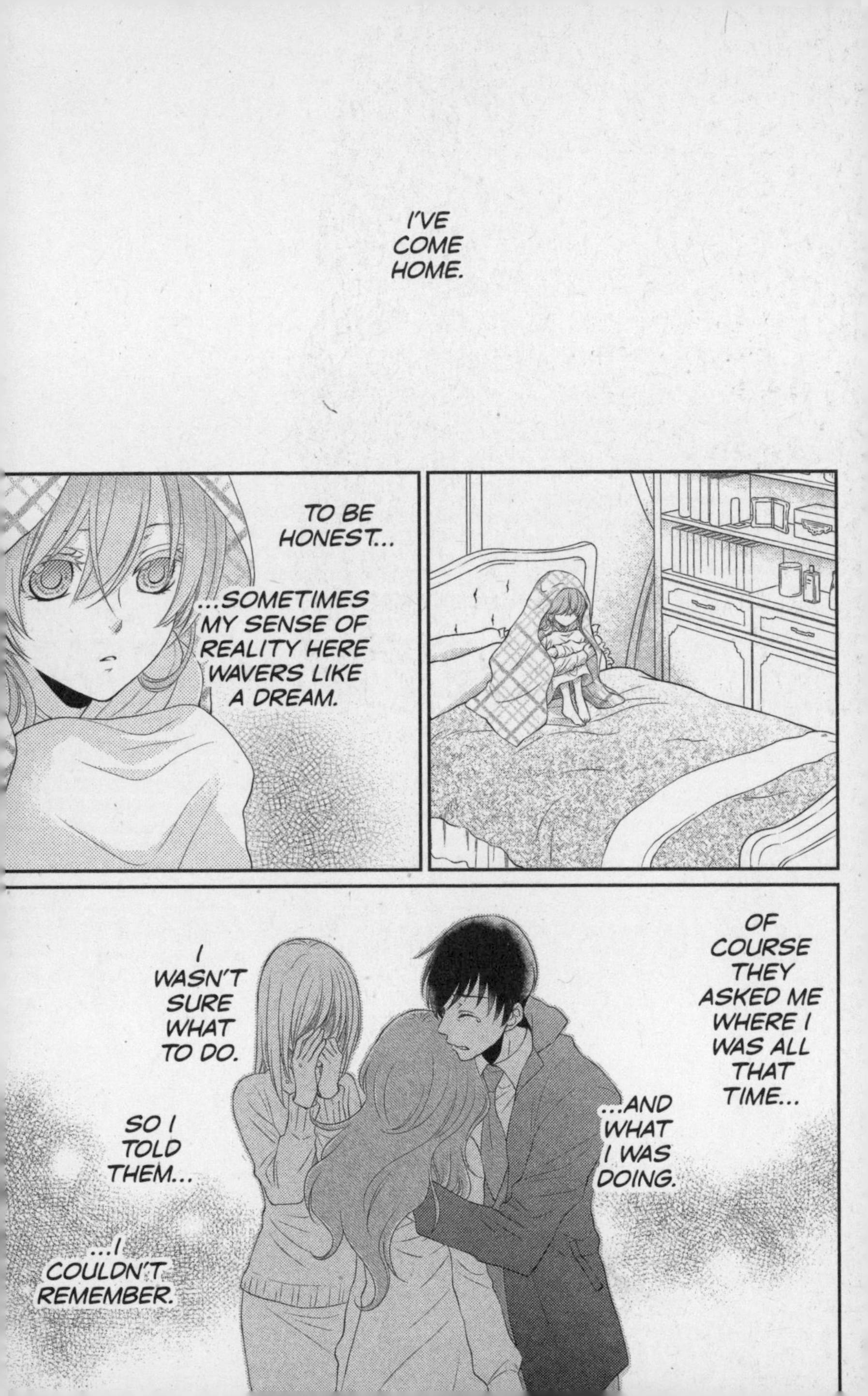
I'VE COME HOME.
TO BE HONEST...
...SOMETIMES MY SENSE OF REALITY HERE WAVERS LIKE A DREAM.
OF COURSE THEY ASKED ME WHERE I WAS ALL THAT TIME...
...AND WHAT I WAS DOING.
I WASN'T SURE WHAT TO DO.
SO I TOLD THEM...
...I COULDN'T REMEMBER.

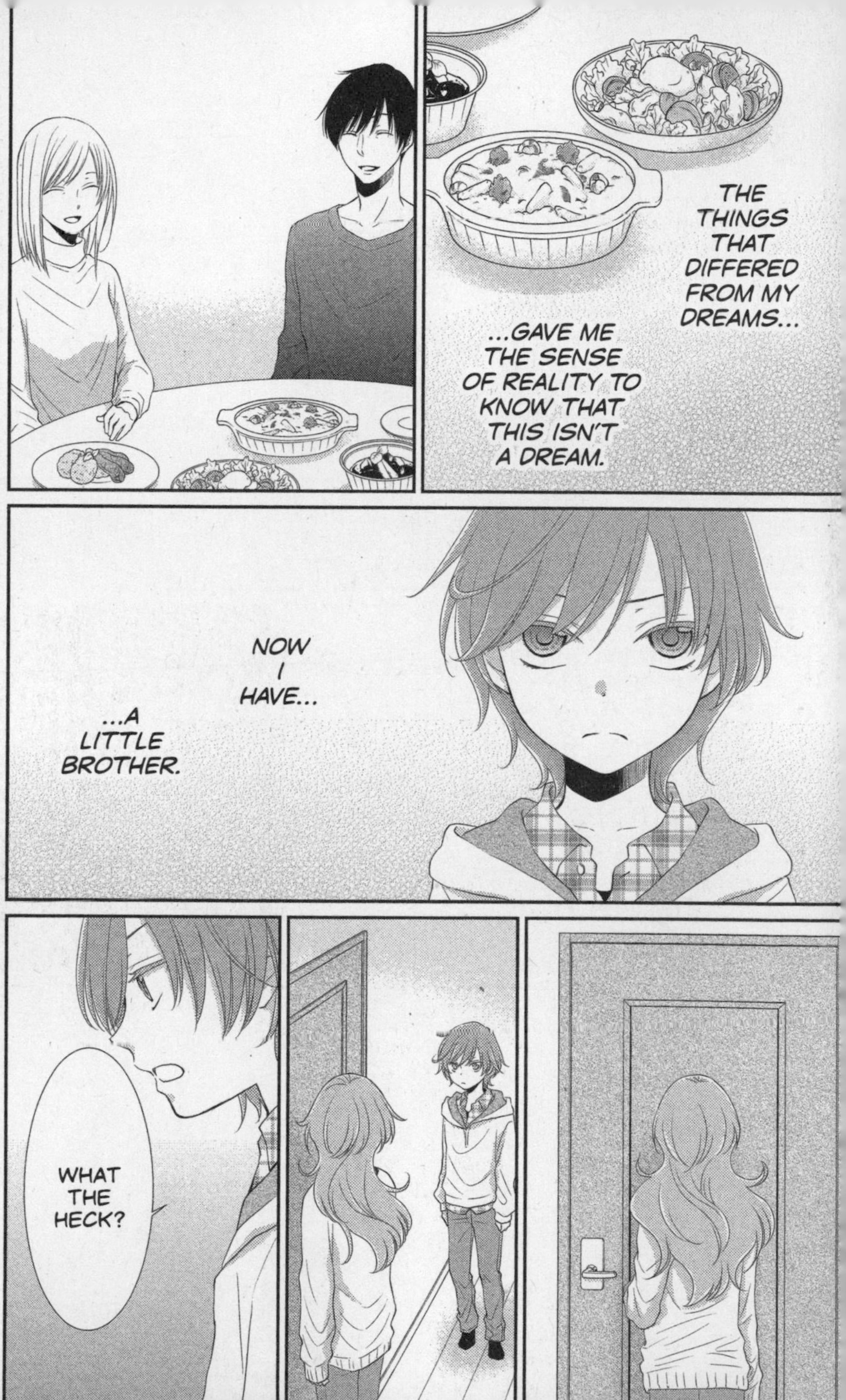
THE THINGS THAT DIFFERED FROM MY DREAMS...
...GAVE ME THE SENSE OF REALITY TO KNOW THAT THIS ISN'T A DREAM.
NOW I HAVE...
...A LITTLE BROTHER.
WHAT THE HECK?

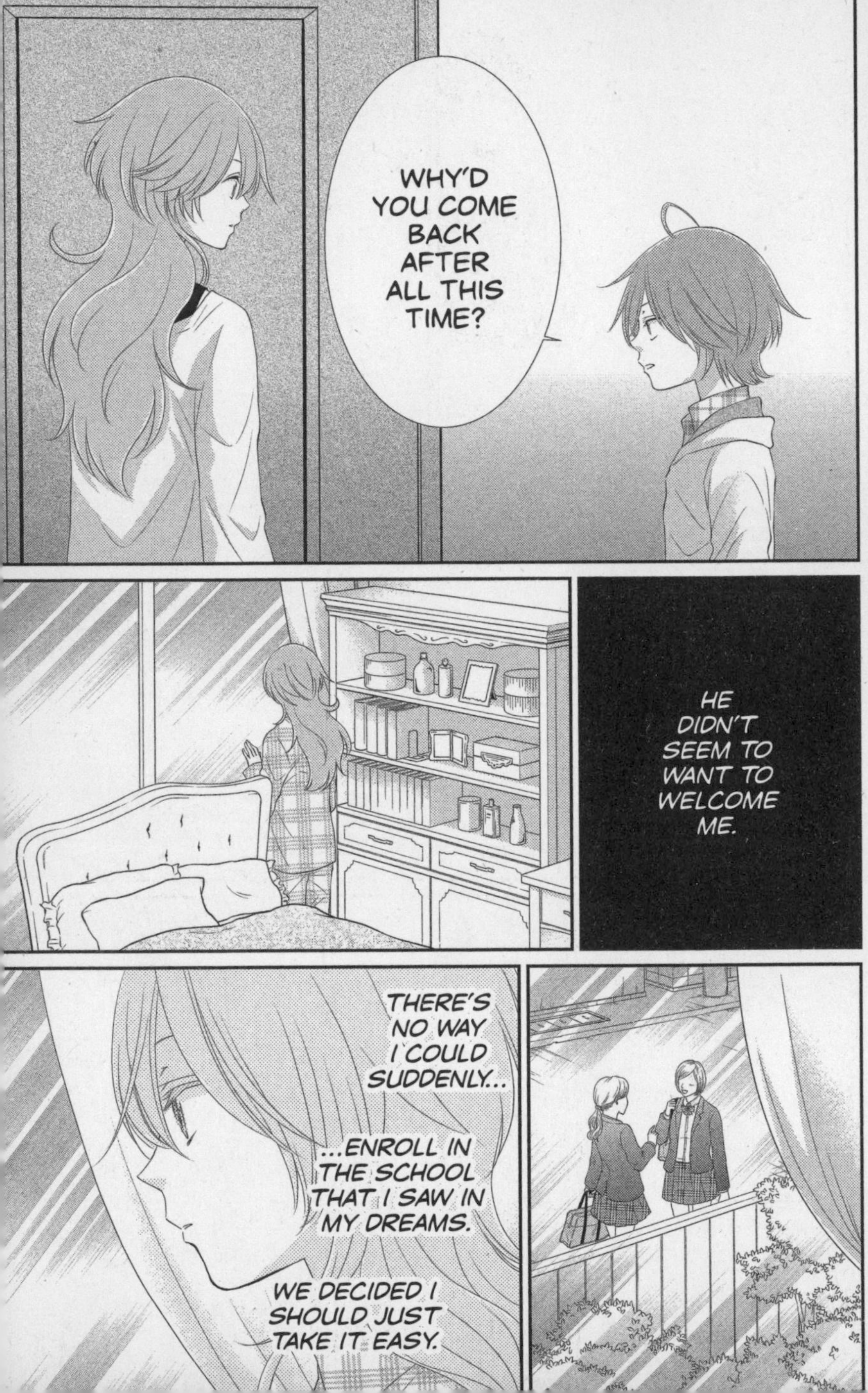
WHY'D YOU COME BACK AFTER ALL THIS TIME?
HE DIDN'T SEEM TO WANT TO WELCOME ME.
THERE'S NO WAY I COULD SUDDENLY...
...ENROLL IN THE SCHOOL THAT I SAW IN MY DREAMS.
WE DECIDED I SHOULD JUST TAKE IT EASY.

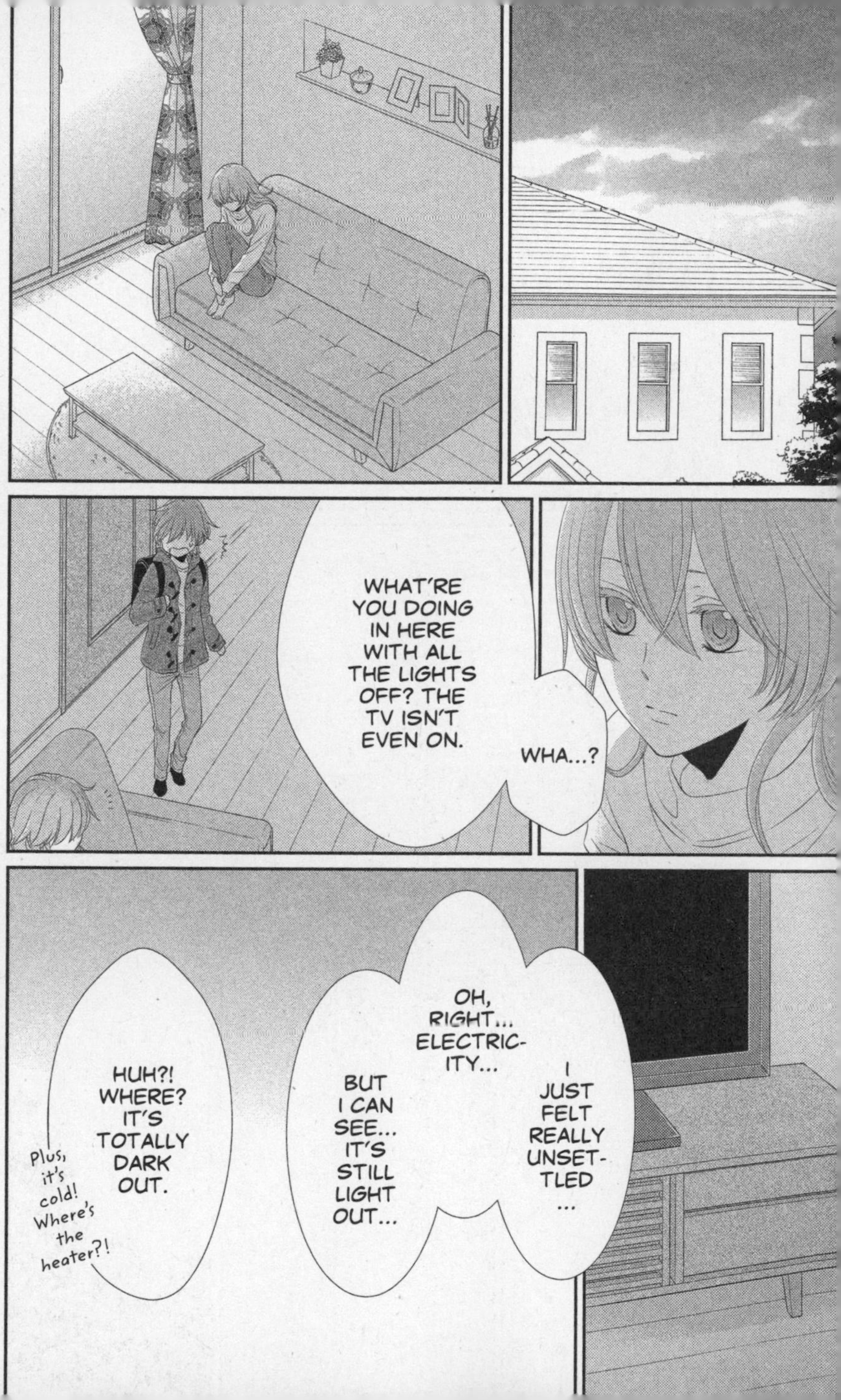
WHA...?
WHAT'RE YOU DOING IN HERE WITH ALL THE LIGHTS OFF? THE TV ISN'T EVEN ON.
I JUST FELT REALLY UNSET-TLED ...
OH, RIGHT... ELECTRIC-ITY...
BUT I CAN SEE... IT'S STILL LIGHT OUT...
HUH?! WHERE? IT'S TOTALLY DARK OUT.
Plus, it's cold! Where's the heater?!

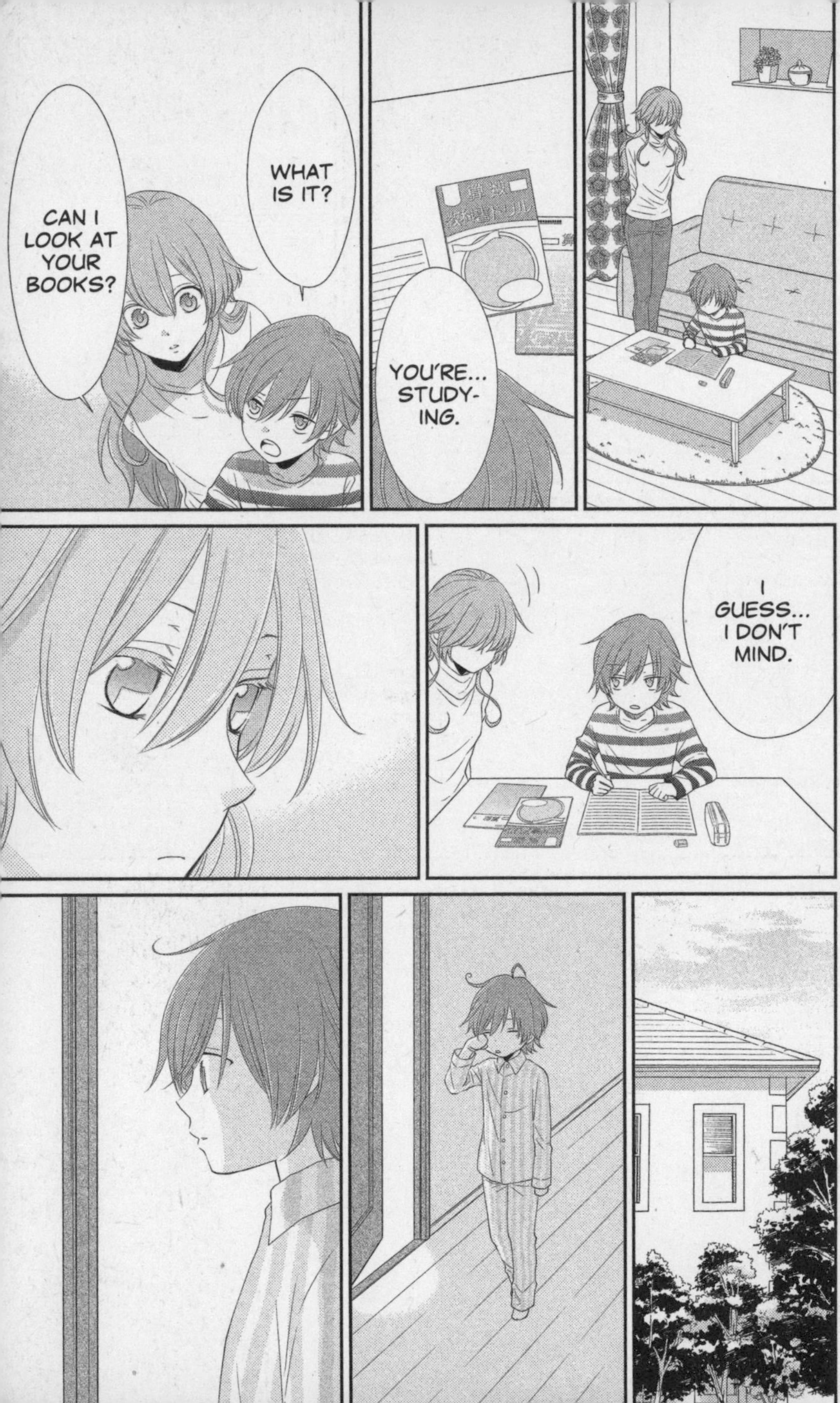
YOU'RE... STUDY-ING.
WHAT IS IT?
CAN I LOOK AT YOUR BOOKS?
I GUESS... I DON'T MIND.

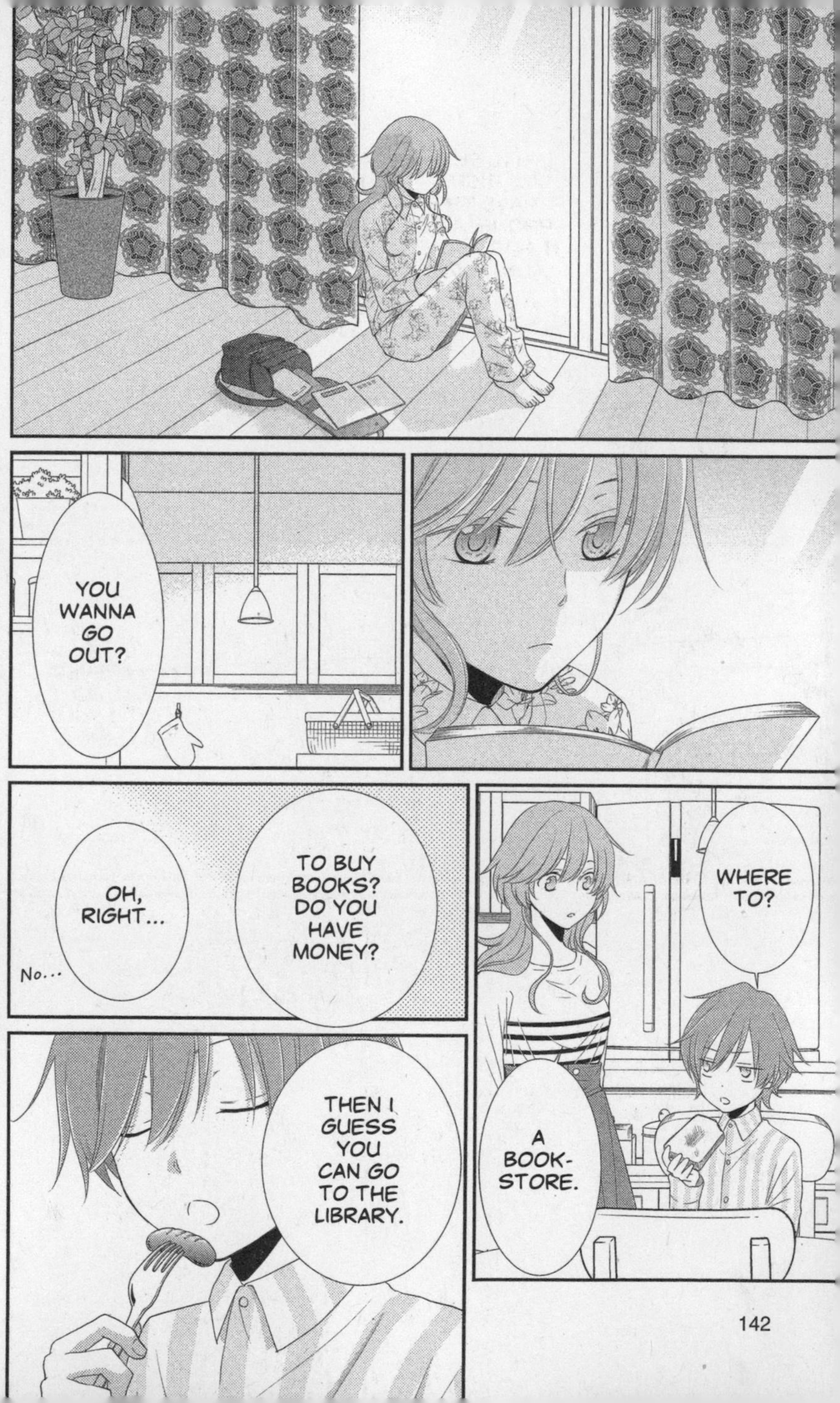
YOU WANNA GO OUT?
WHERE TO?
A BOOK-STORE.
TO BUY BOOKS? DO YOU HAVE MONEY?
OH, RIGHT...
No...
THEN I GUESS YOU CAN GO TO THE LIBRARY.

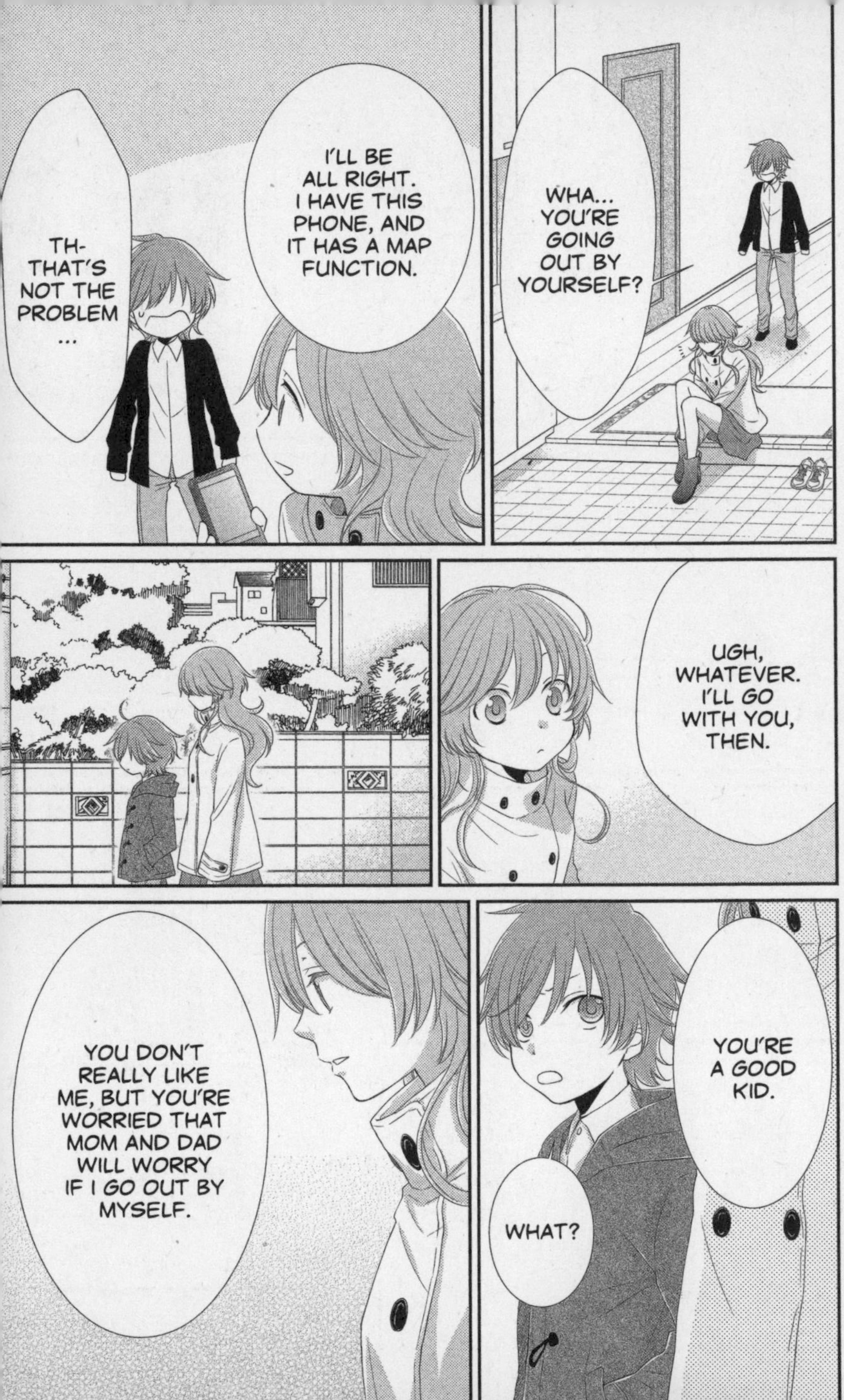
WHA... YOU'RE GOING OUT BY YOURSELF?
I'LL BE ALL RIGHT. I HAVE THIS PHONE, AND IT HAS A MAP FUNCTION.
TH- THAT'S NOT THE PROBLEM ...
UGH, WHATEVER. I'LL GO WITH YOU, THEN.
YOU'RE A GOOD KID.
WHAT?
YOU DON'T REALLY LIKE ME, BUT YOU'RE WORRIED THAT MOM AND DAD WILL WORRY IF I GO OUT BY MYSELF.

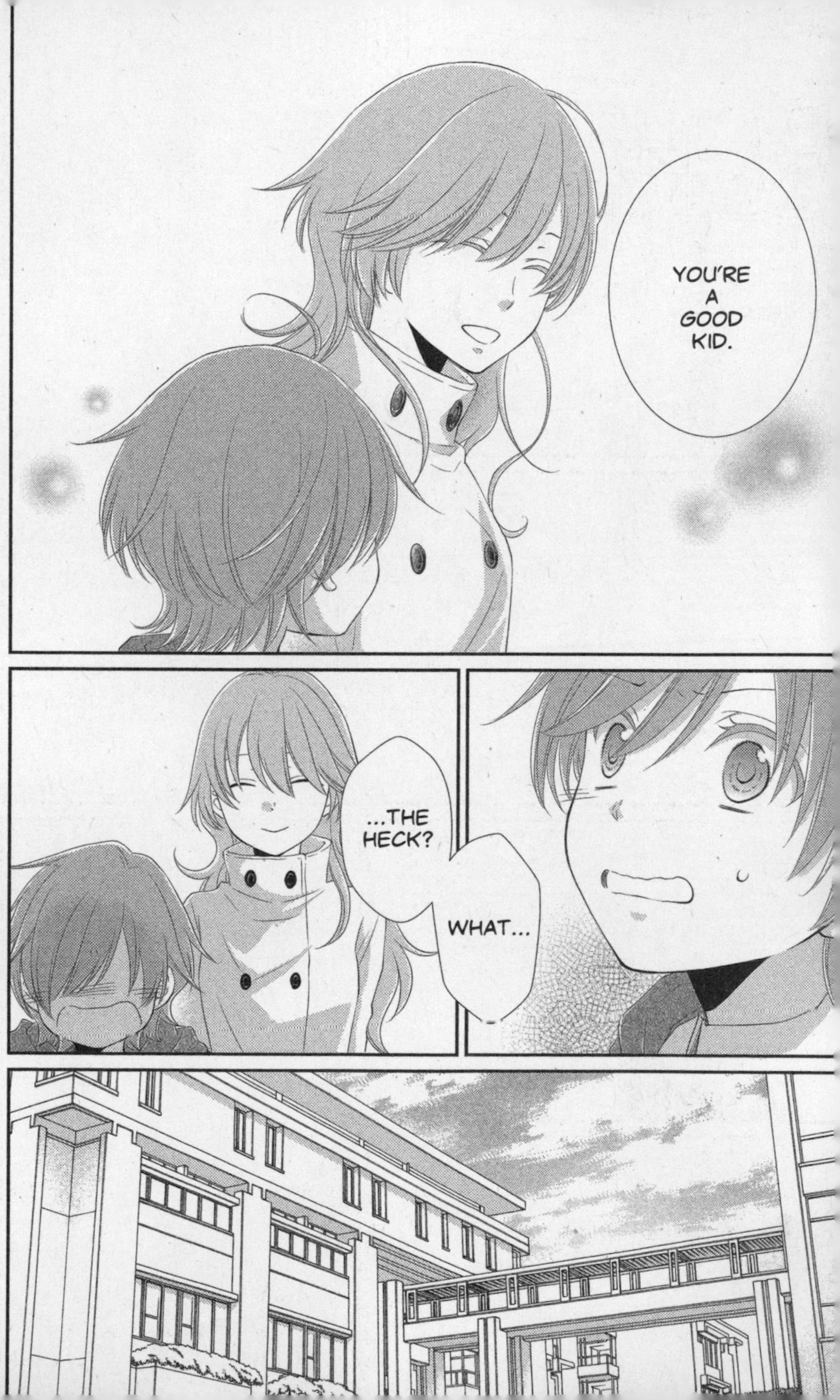
YOU'RE A GOOD KID.
WHAT...
...THE HECK?

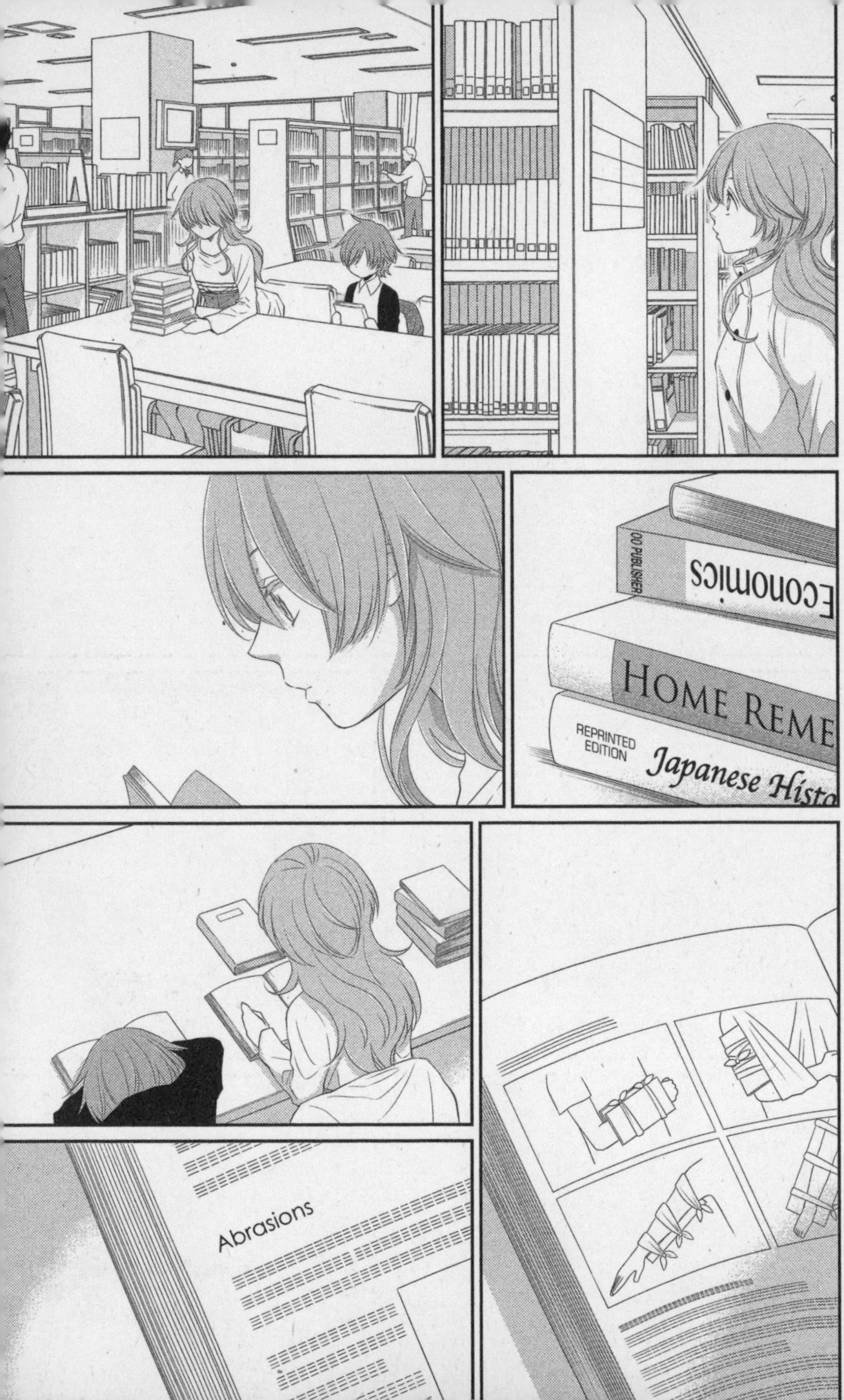
OO PUBLISHER
Economics
HOME REME
REPRINTED EDITION
Japanese Histo
Abrasions

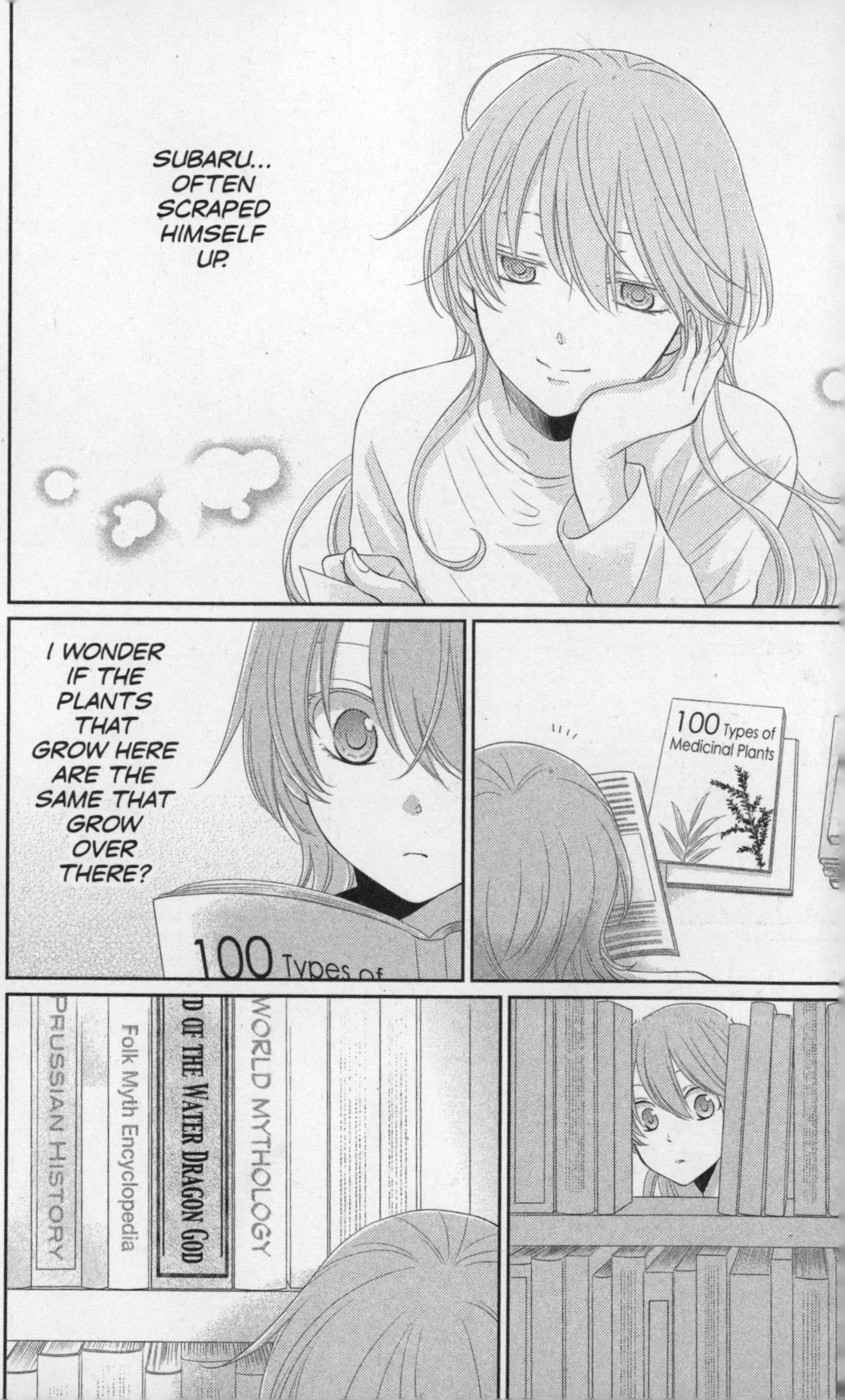
SUBARU... OFTEN SCRAPED HIMSELF UP.
100 Types of Medicinal Plants
I WONDER IF THE PLANTS THAT GROW HERE ARE THE SAME THAT GROW OVER THERE?
100 Types of
WORLD MYTHOLOGY
OF THE WATER DRAGON GOD
Folk Myth Encyclopedia
PRUSSIAN HISTORY

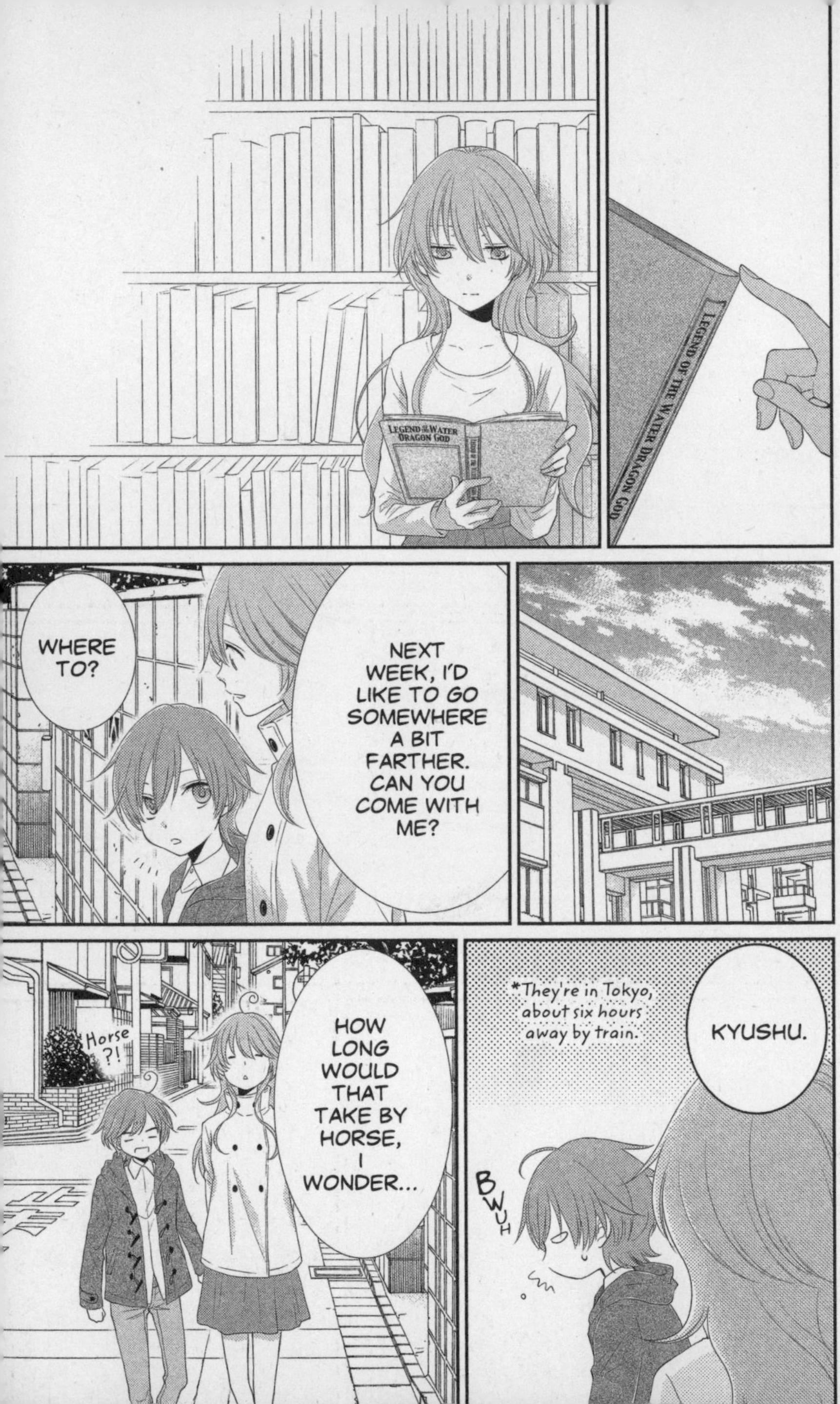
LEGEND OF THE WATER DRAGON GOD
LEGEND OF THE WATER DRAGON GOD
NEXT WEEK, I'D LIKE TO GO SOMEWHERE A BIT FARTHER. CAN YOU COME WITH ME?
WHERE TO?
KYUSHU.
*They're in Tokyo, about six hours away by train.
BWUH
HOW LONG WOULD THAT TAKE BY HORSE, I WONDER...
Horse?!

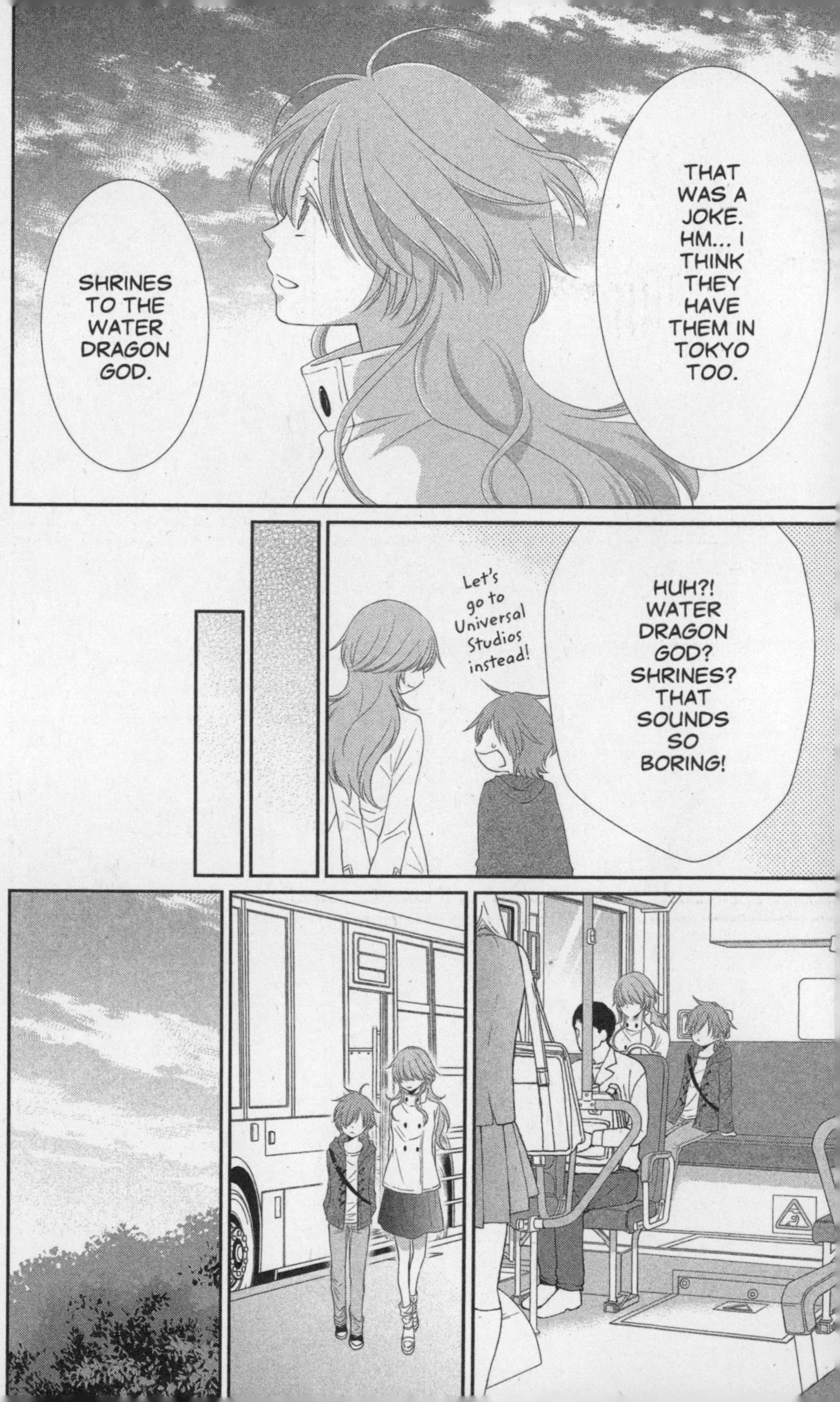
THAT WAS A JOKE. HM... I THINK THEY HAVE THEM IN TOKYO TOO.
SHRINES TO THE WATER DRAGON GOD.
HUH?! WATER DRAGON GOD? SHRINES? THAT SOUNDS SO BORING!
Let's go to Universal Studios instead!

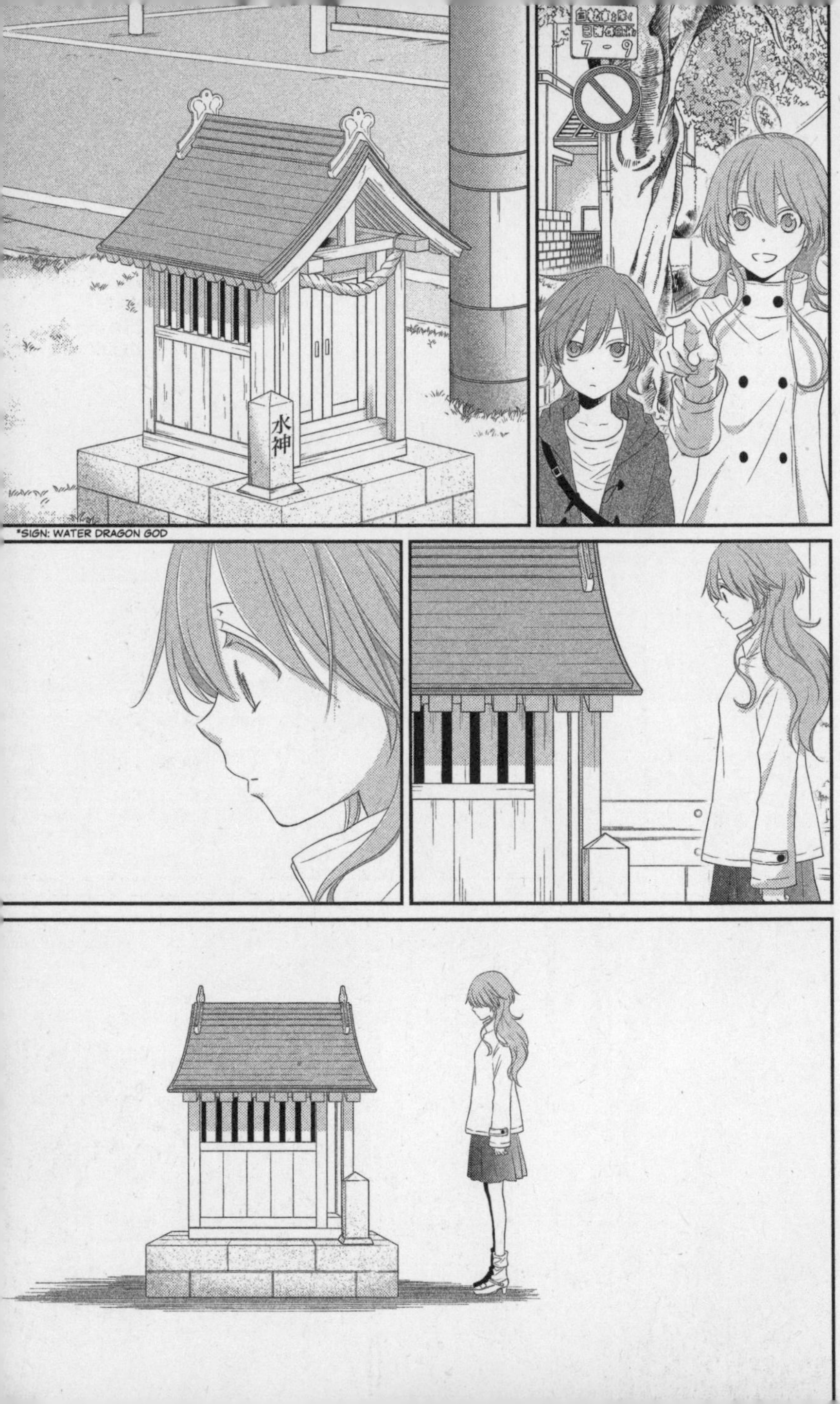
7 - 9
水神
*SIGN: WATER DRAGON GOD

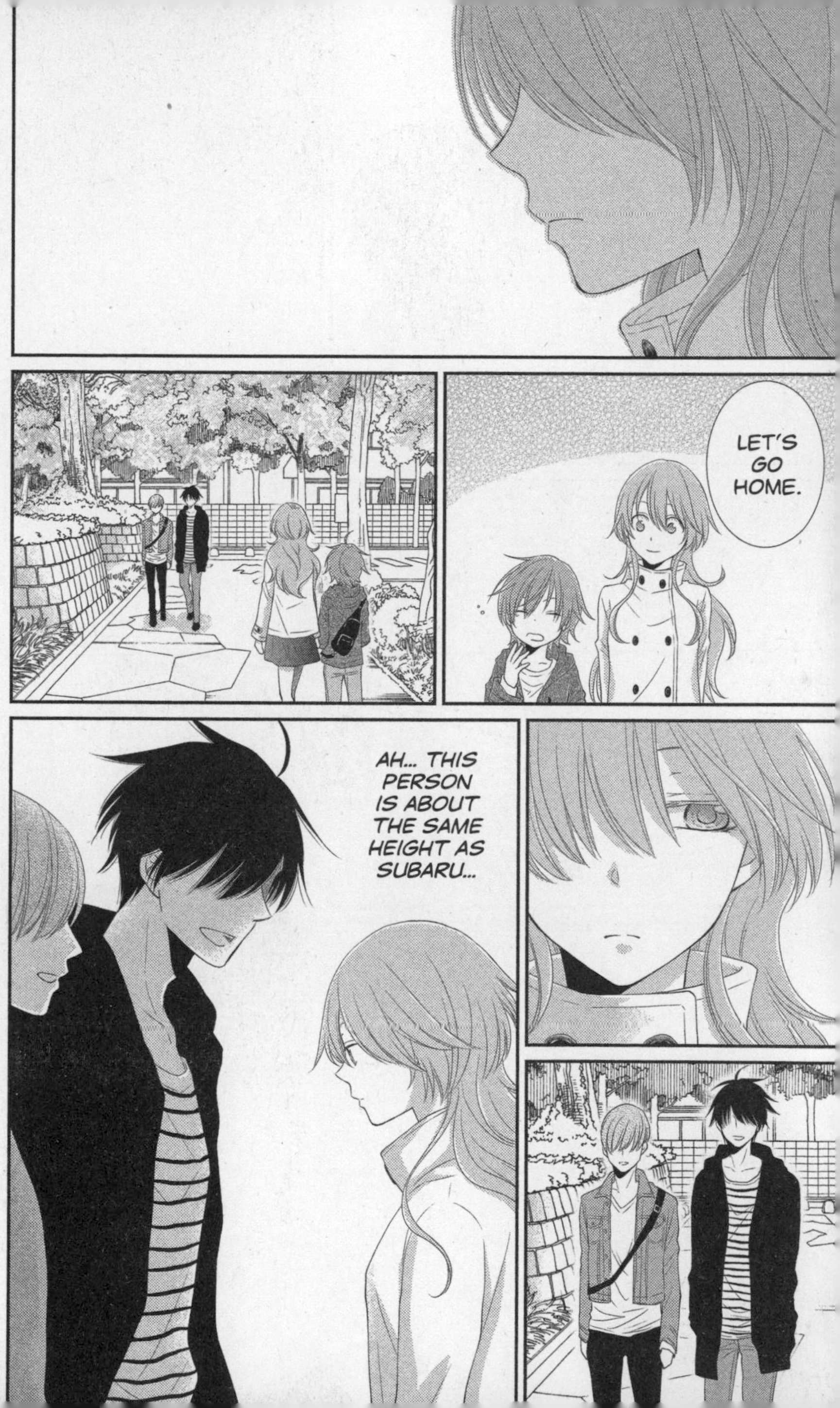
LET'S GO HOME.
AH... THIS PERSON IS ABOUT THE SAME HEIGHT AS SUBARU...

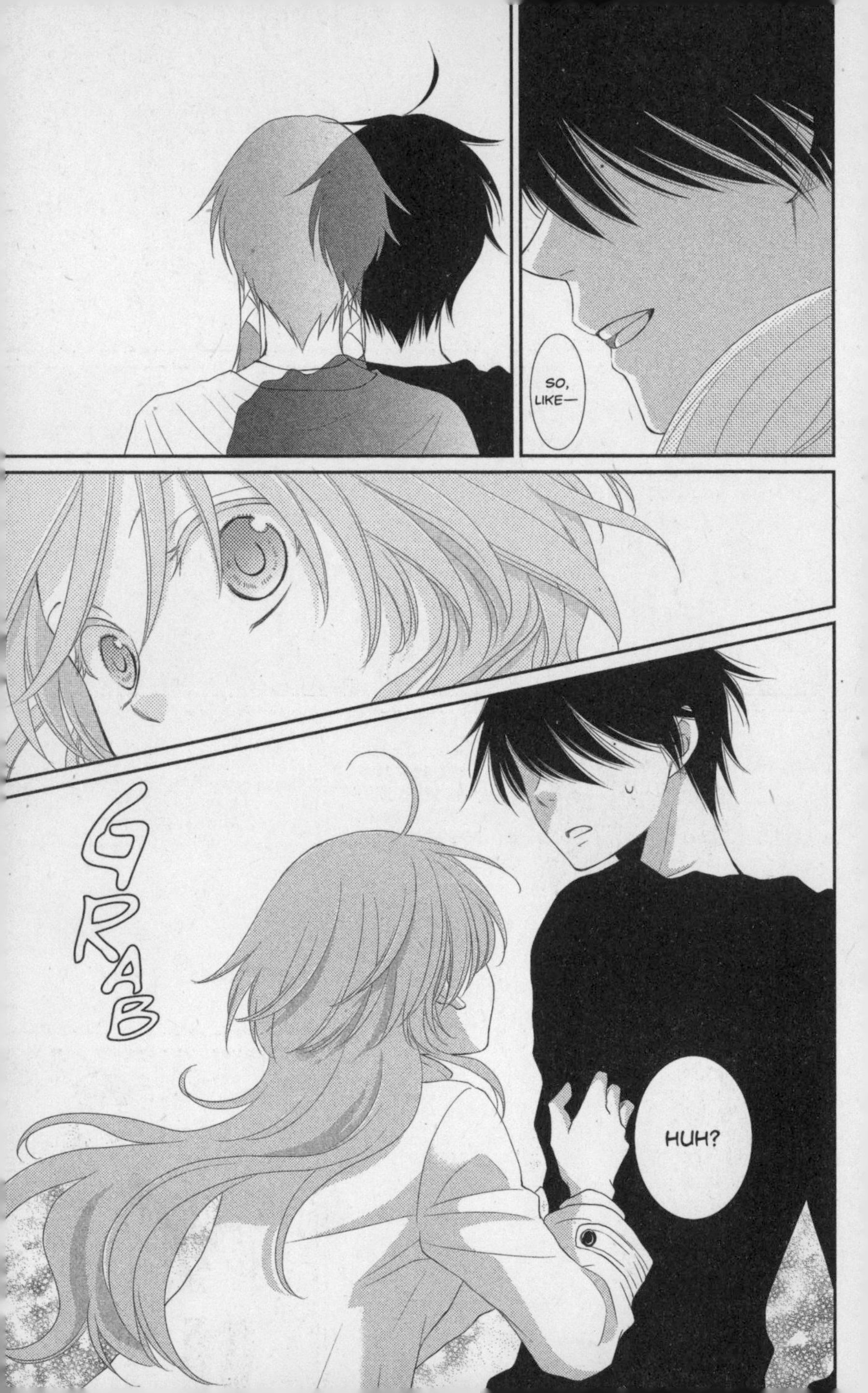
SO, LIKE—
GRAB
HUH?

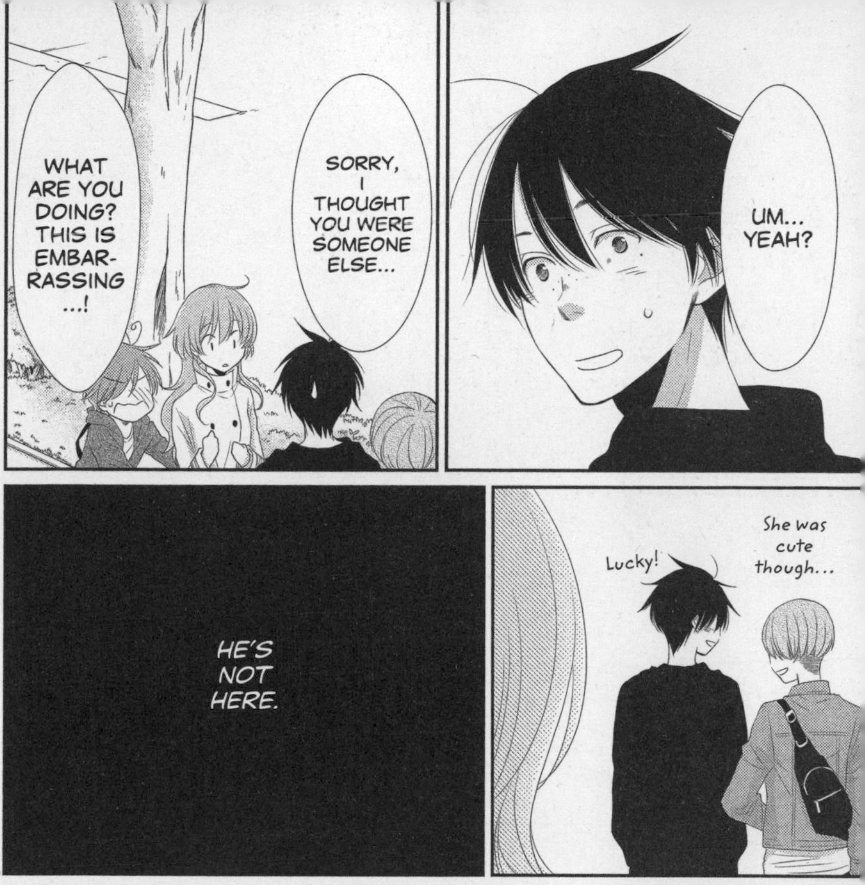
UM... YEAH?
SORRY, I THOUGHT YOU WERE SOMEONE ELSE...
WHAT ARE YOU DOING? THIS IS EMBARRASSING...!
She was cute though...
Lucky!
HE'S NOT HERE.

HE'S NOT...

...IN THIS WORLD.

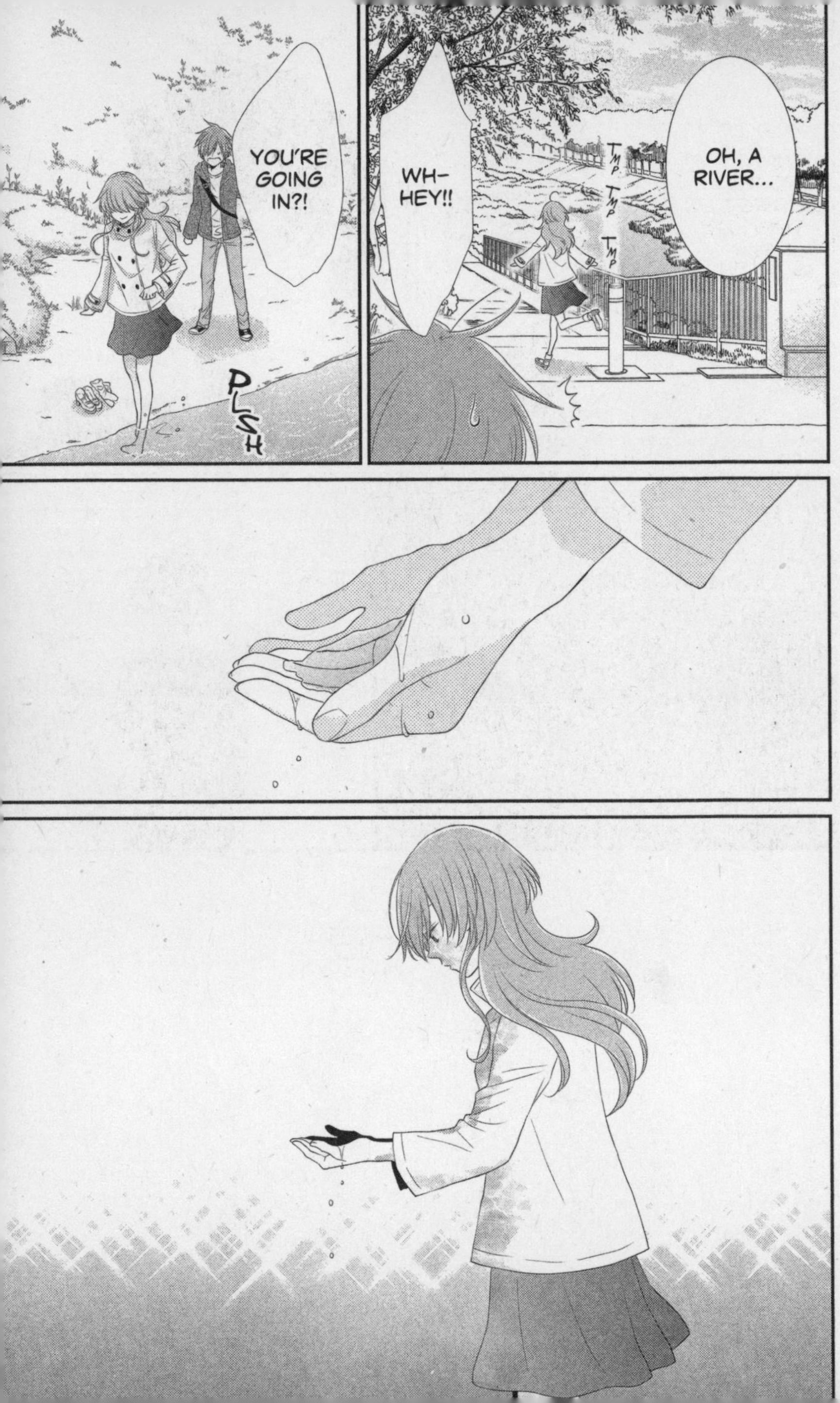
OH, A RIVER...
TMP TMP TMP
WH- HEY!!
YOU'RE GOING IN?!
PLSH

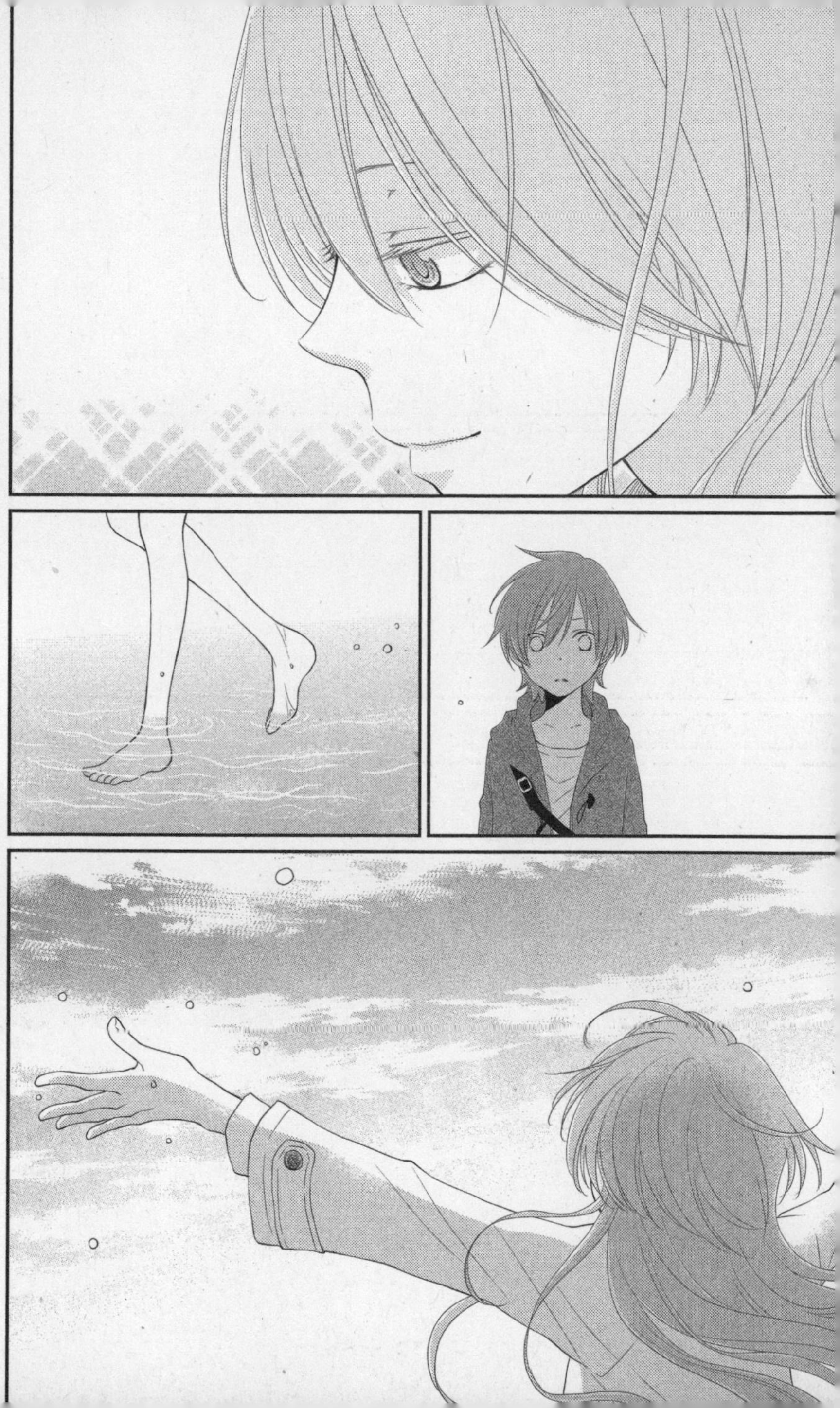

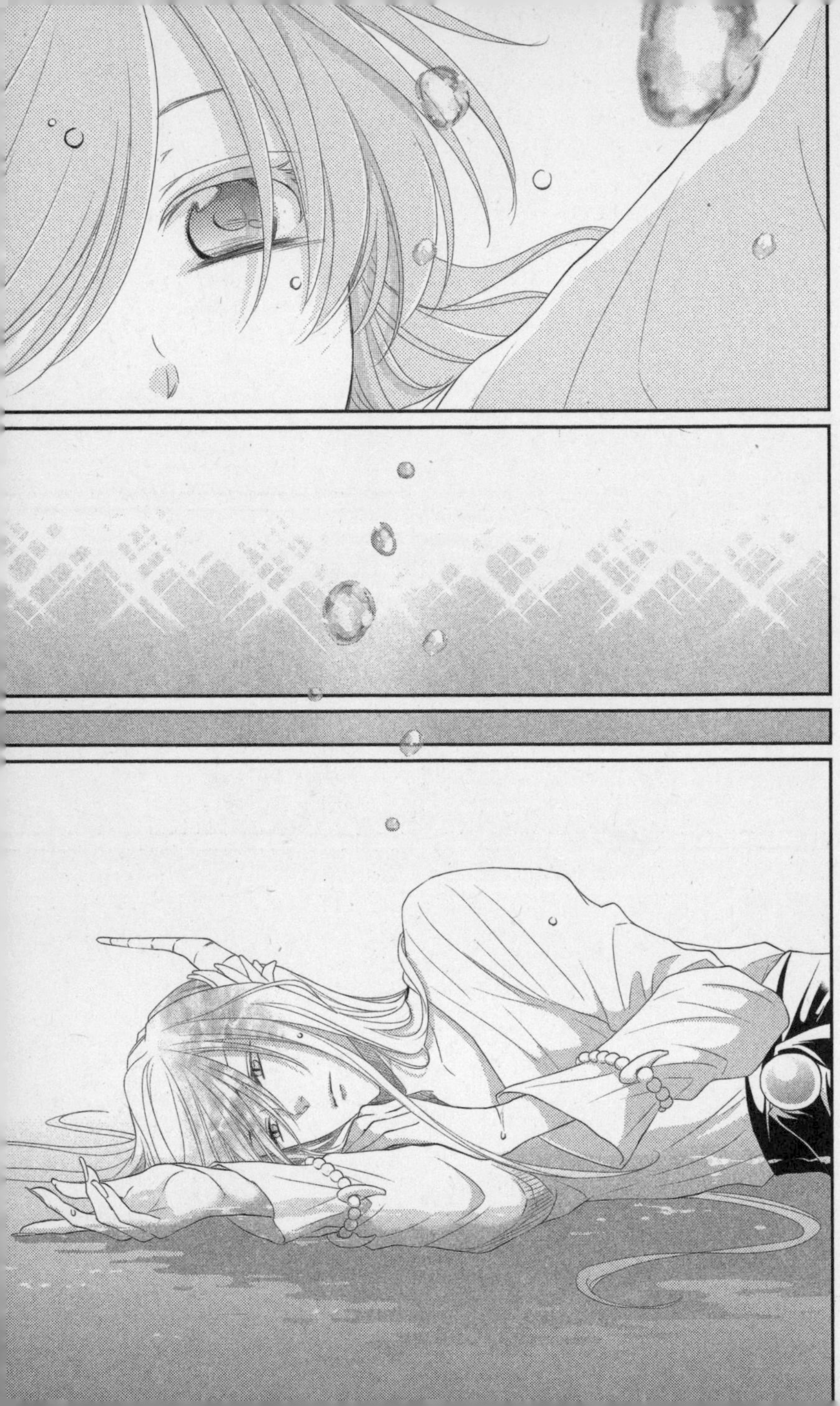

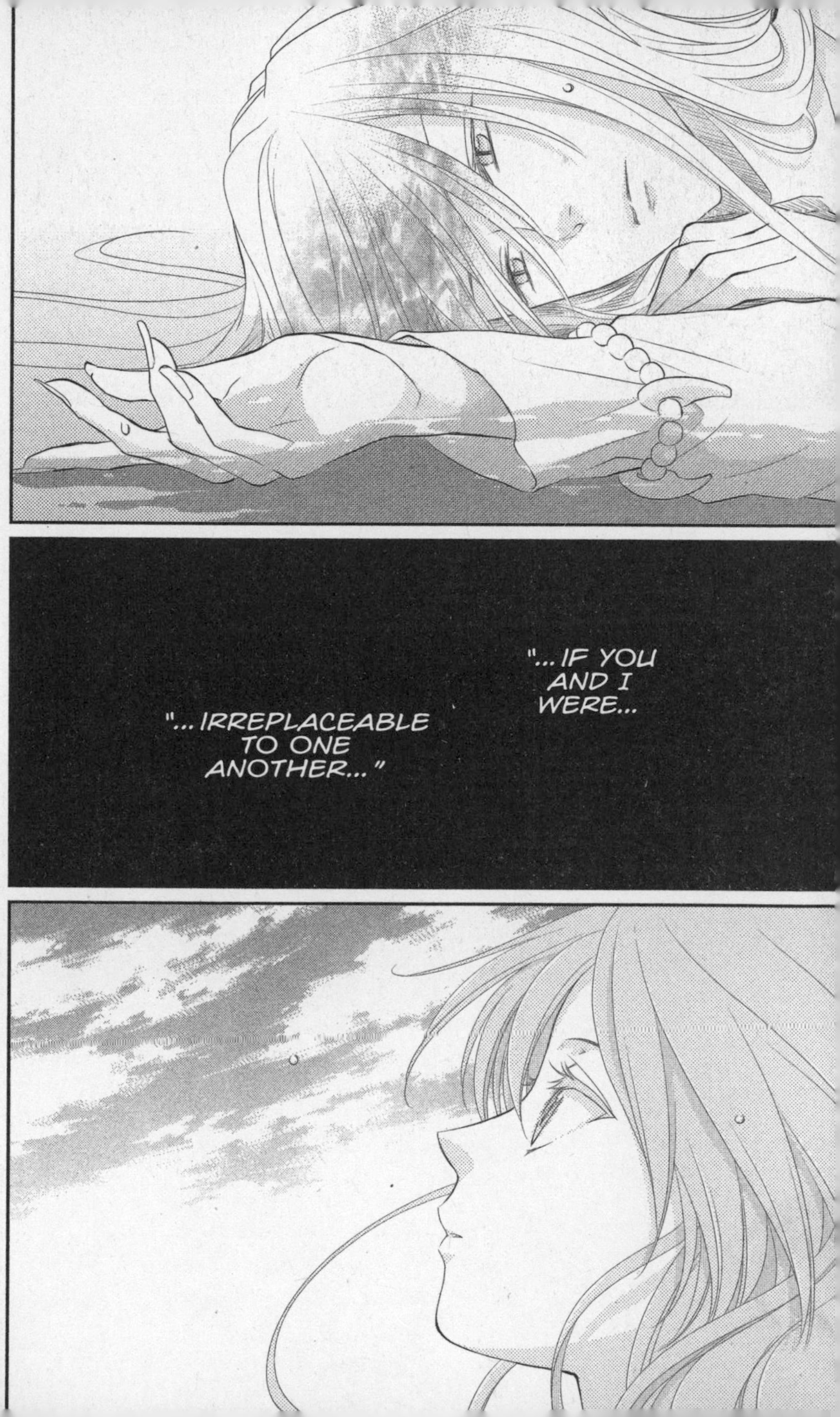
"...IF YOU AND I WERE...
"...IRREPLACEABLE TO ONE ANOTHER..."

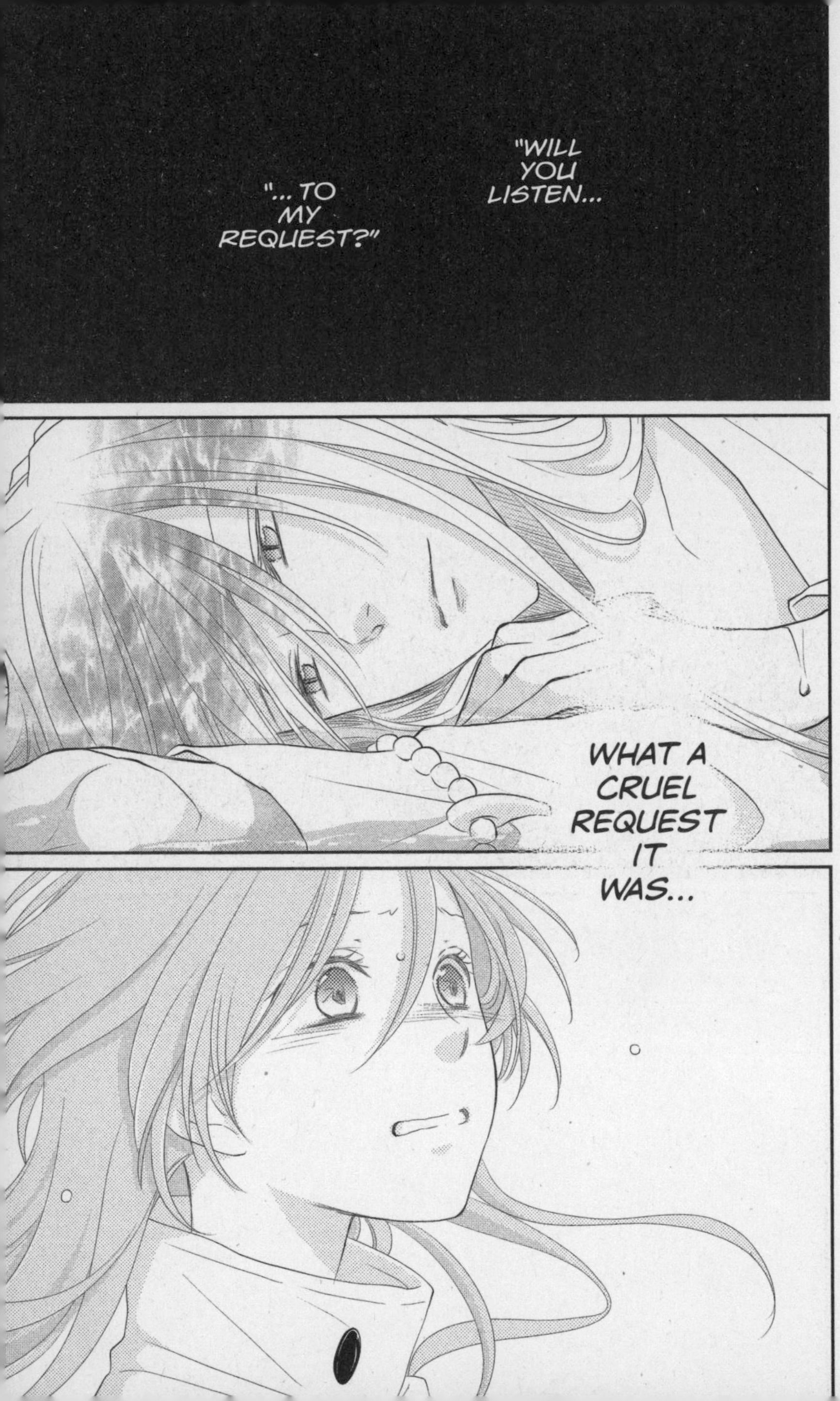
"WILL YOU LISTEN...
"...TO MY REQUEST?"
WHAT A CRUEL REQUEST IT WAS...

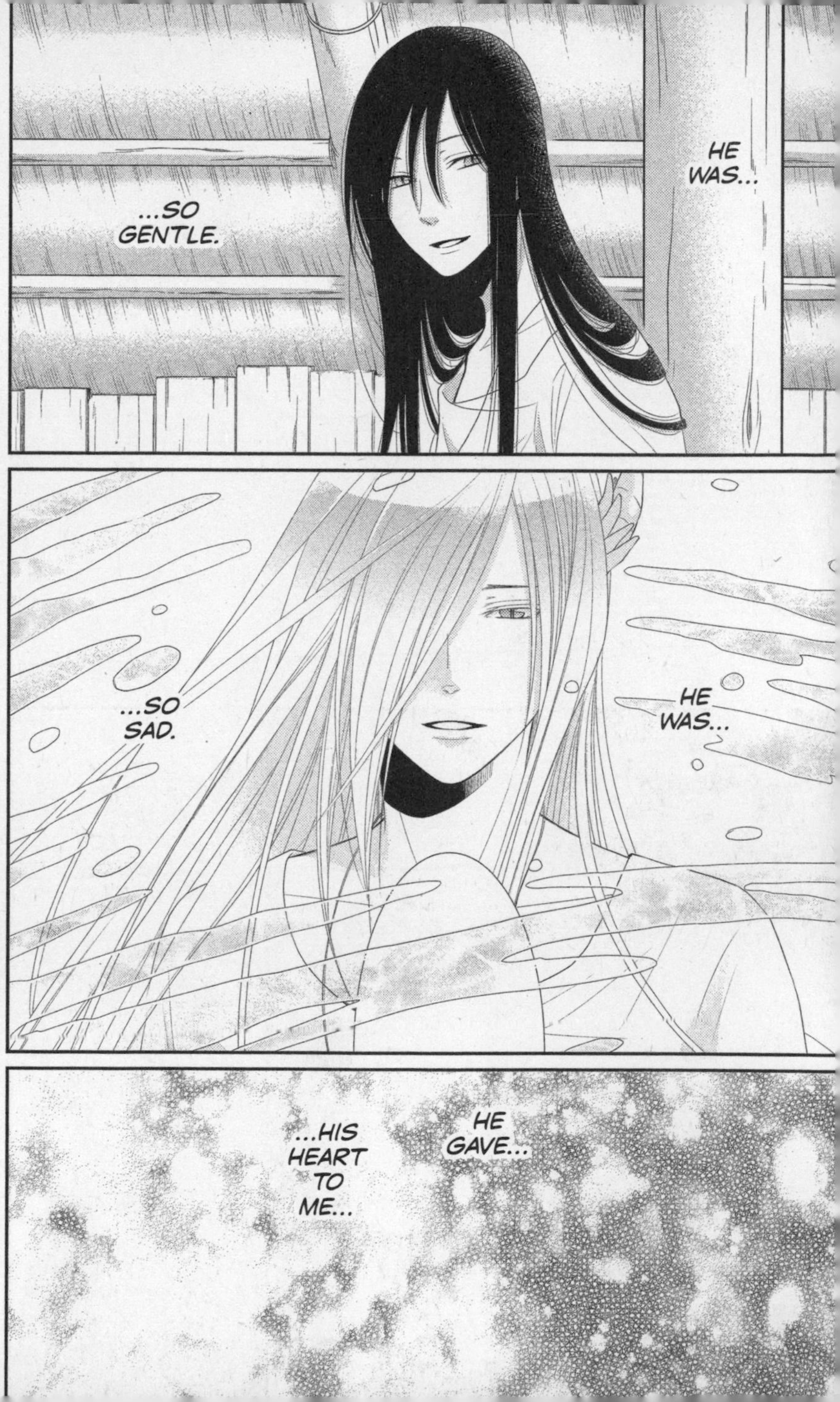
HE WAS...
...SO GENTLE.
HE WAS...
...SO SAD.
HE GAVE...
...HIS HEART TO ME...

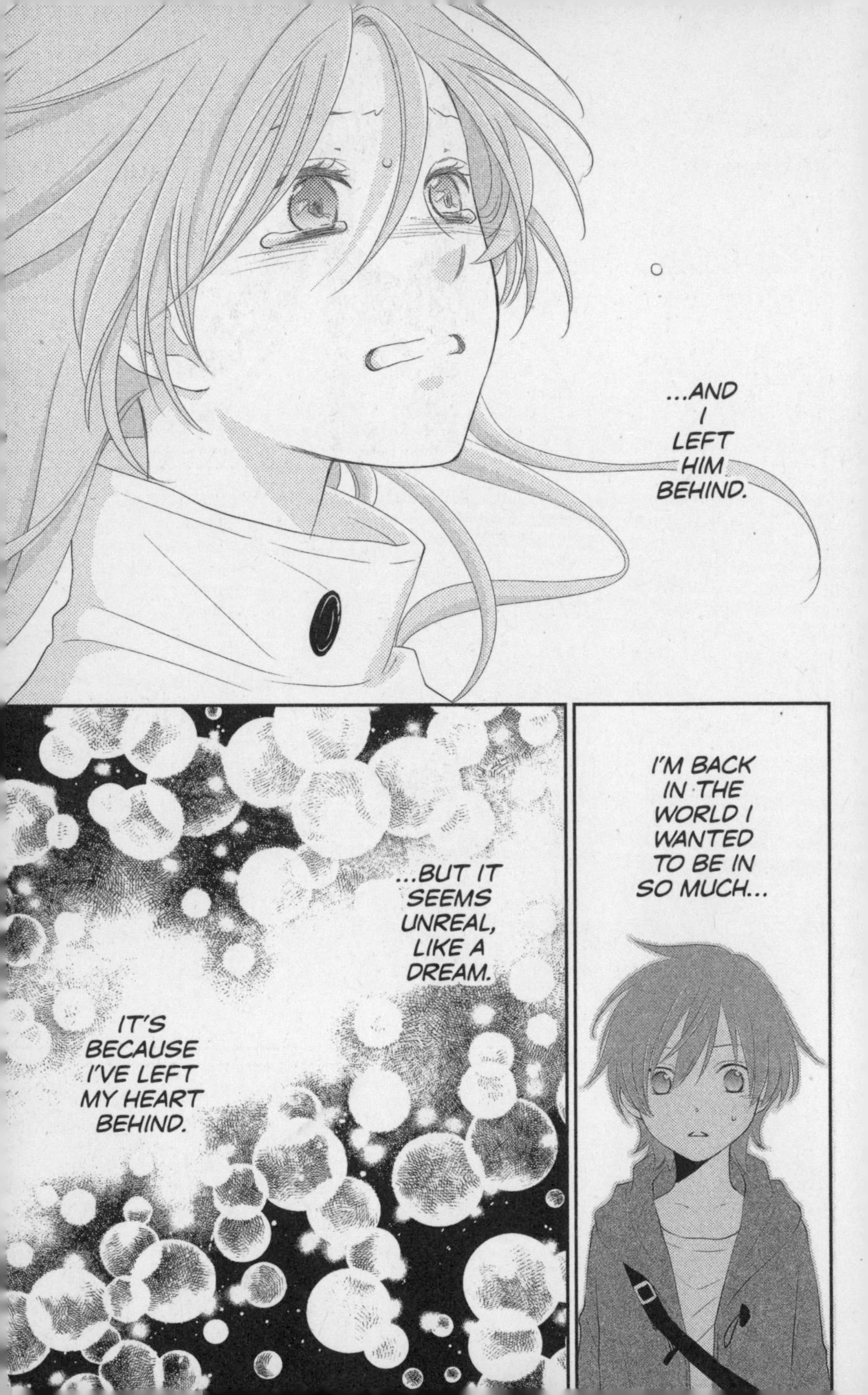
...AND I LEFT HIM BEHIND.
I'M BACK IN THE WORLD I WANTED TO BE IN SO MUCH...
...BUT IT SEEMS UNREAL, LIKE A DREAM.
IT'S BECAUSE I'VE LEFT MY HEART BEHIND.

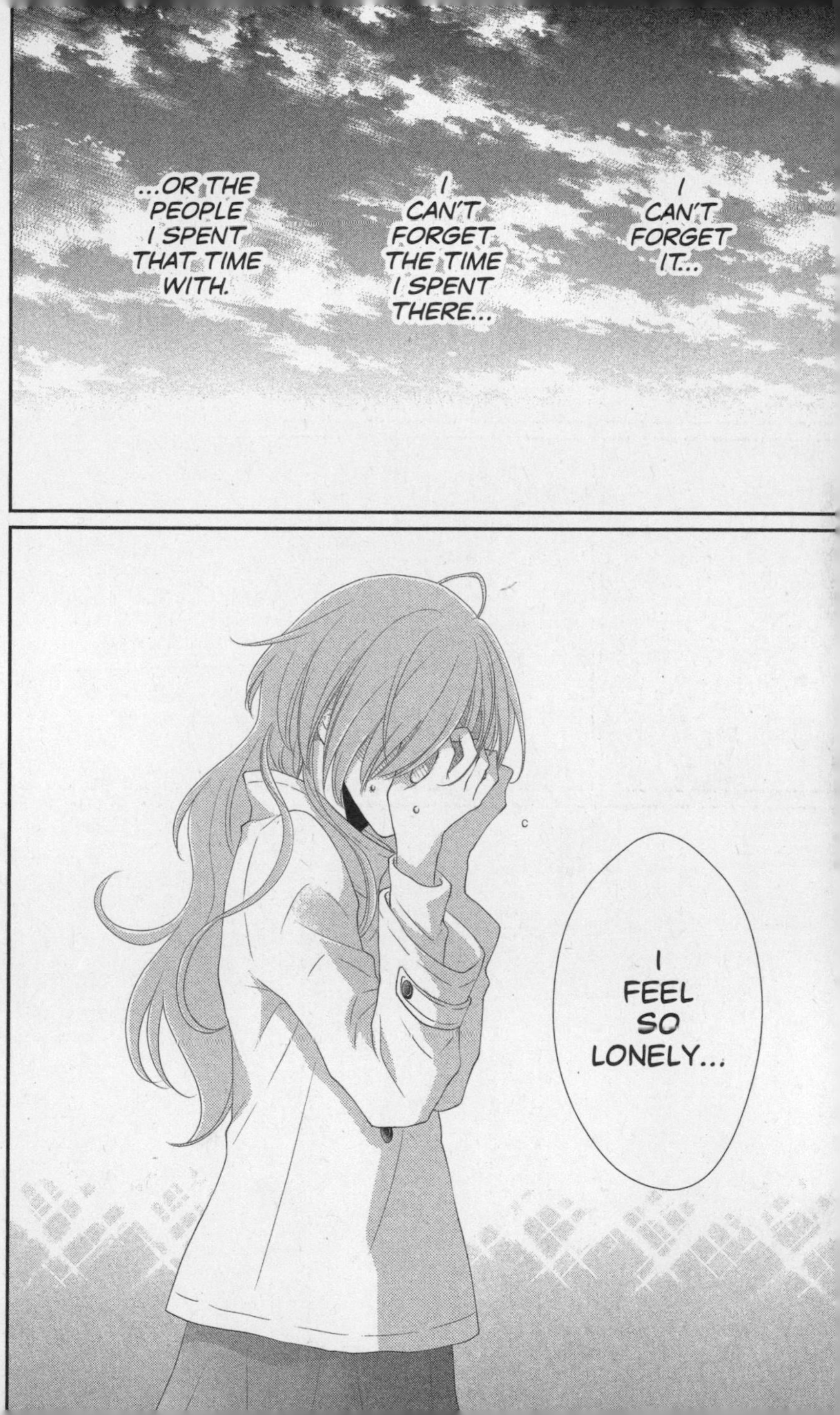
I CAN'T FORGET IT...
I CAN'T FORGET THE TIME I SPENT THERE...
...OR THE PEOPLE I SPENT THAT TIME WITH.
I FEEL SO LONELY...

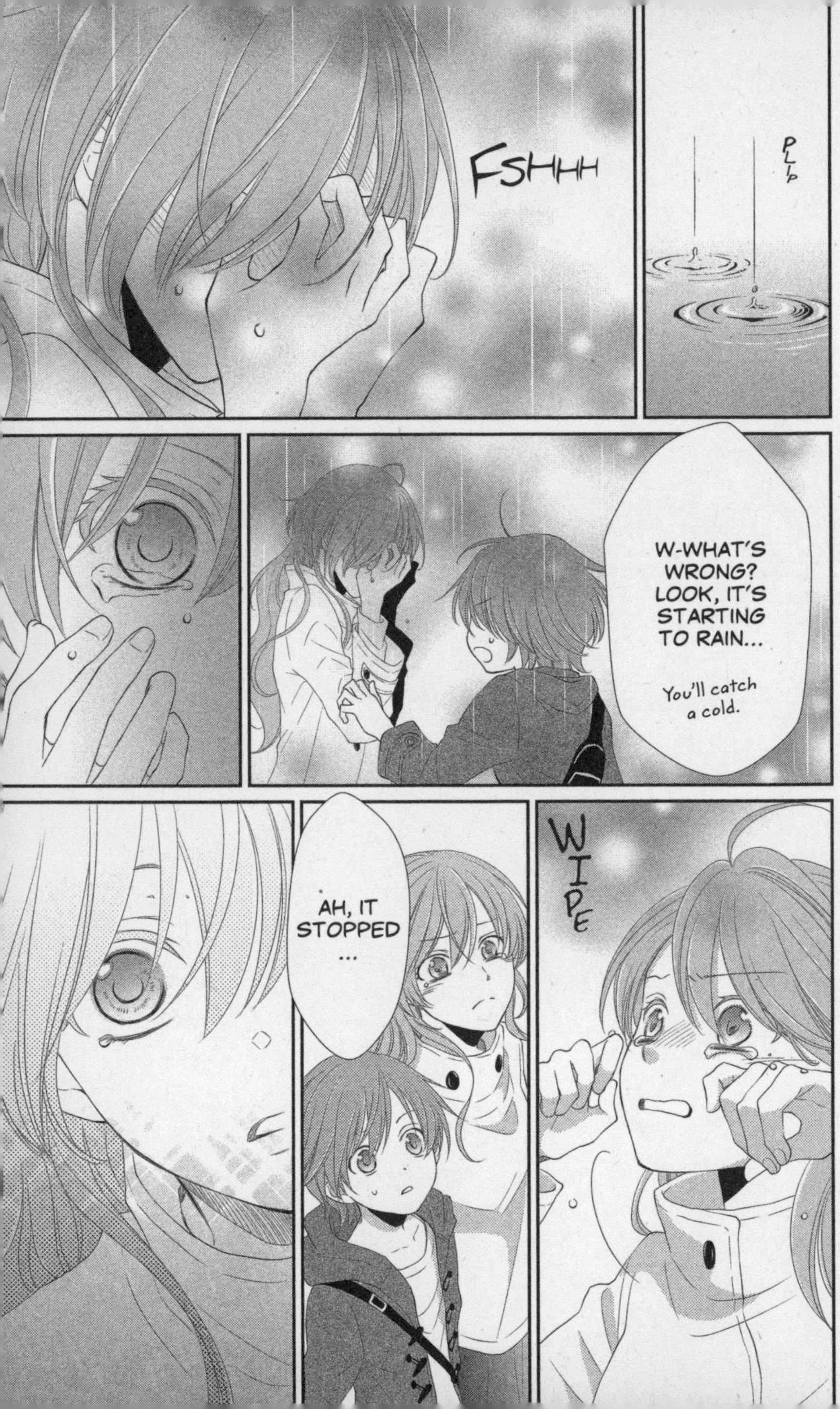
PLIP
FSHHH
W-WHAT'S WRONG? LOOK, IT'S STARTING TO RAIN...
You'll catch a cold.
WIPE
AH, IT STOPPED ...

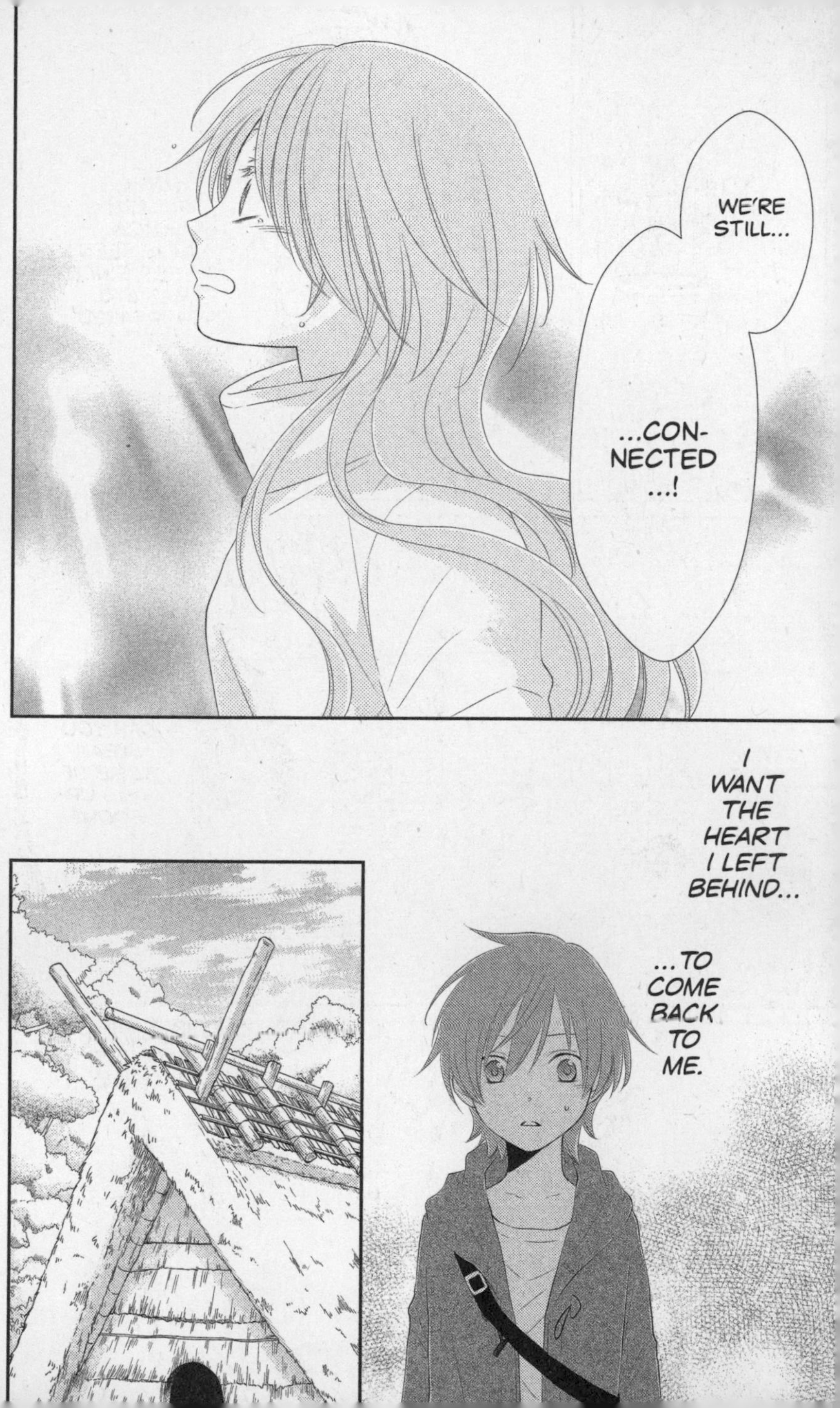
WE'RE STILL...
...CON-NECTED ...!
I WANT THE HEART I LEFT BEHIND...
...TO COME BACK TO ME.

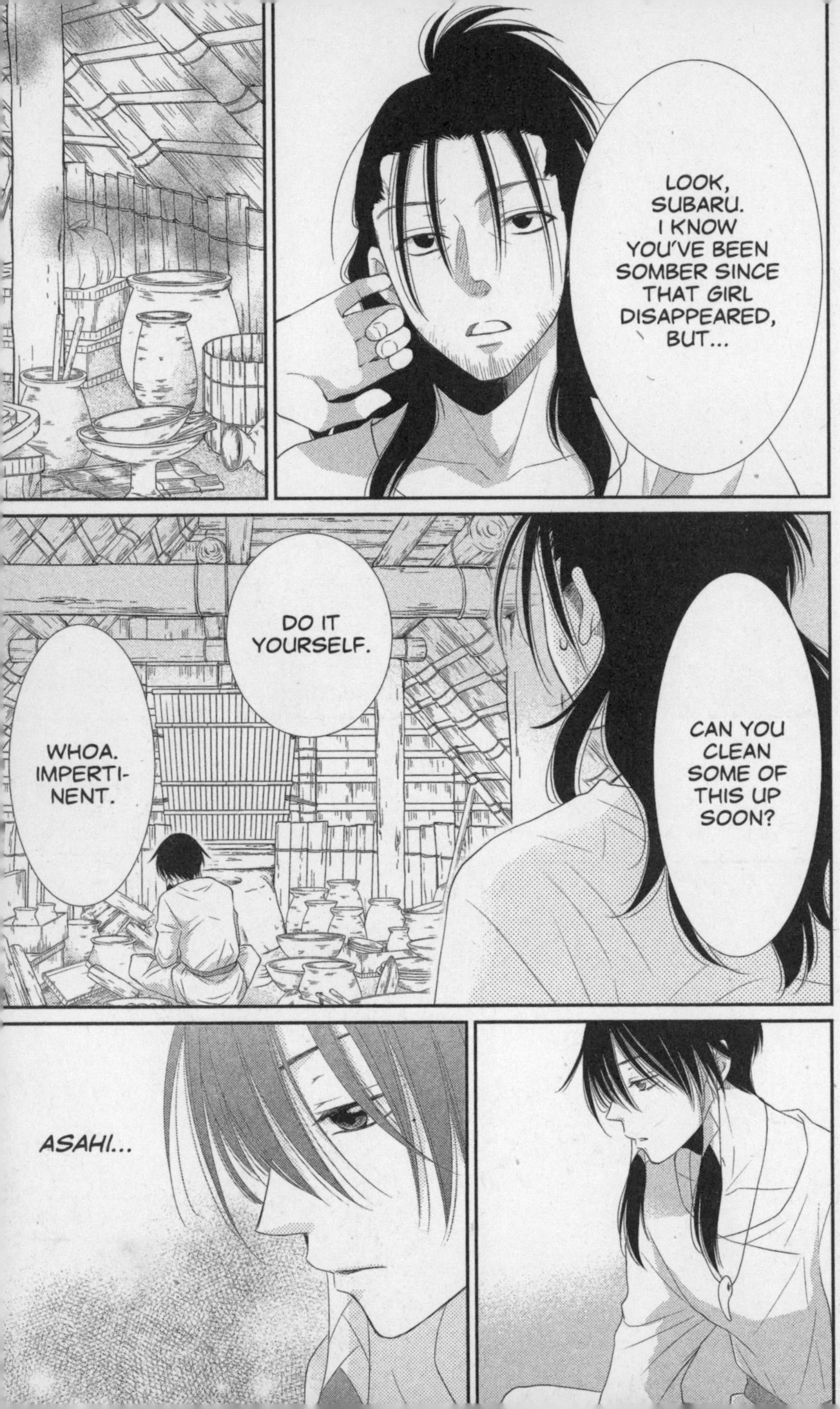
LOOK, SUBARU. I KNOW YOU'VE BEEN SOMBER SINCE THAT GIRL DISAPPEARED, BUT...
CAN YOU CLEAN SOME OF THIS UP SOON?
DO IT YOURSELF.
WHOA. IMPERTI-NENT.
ASAHI...

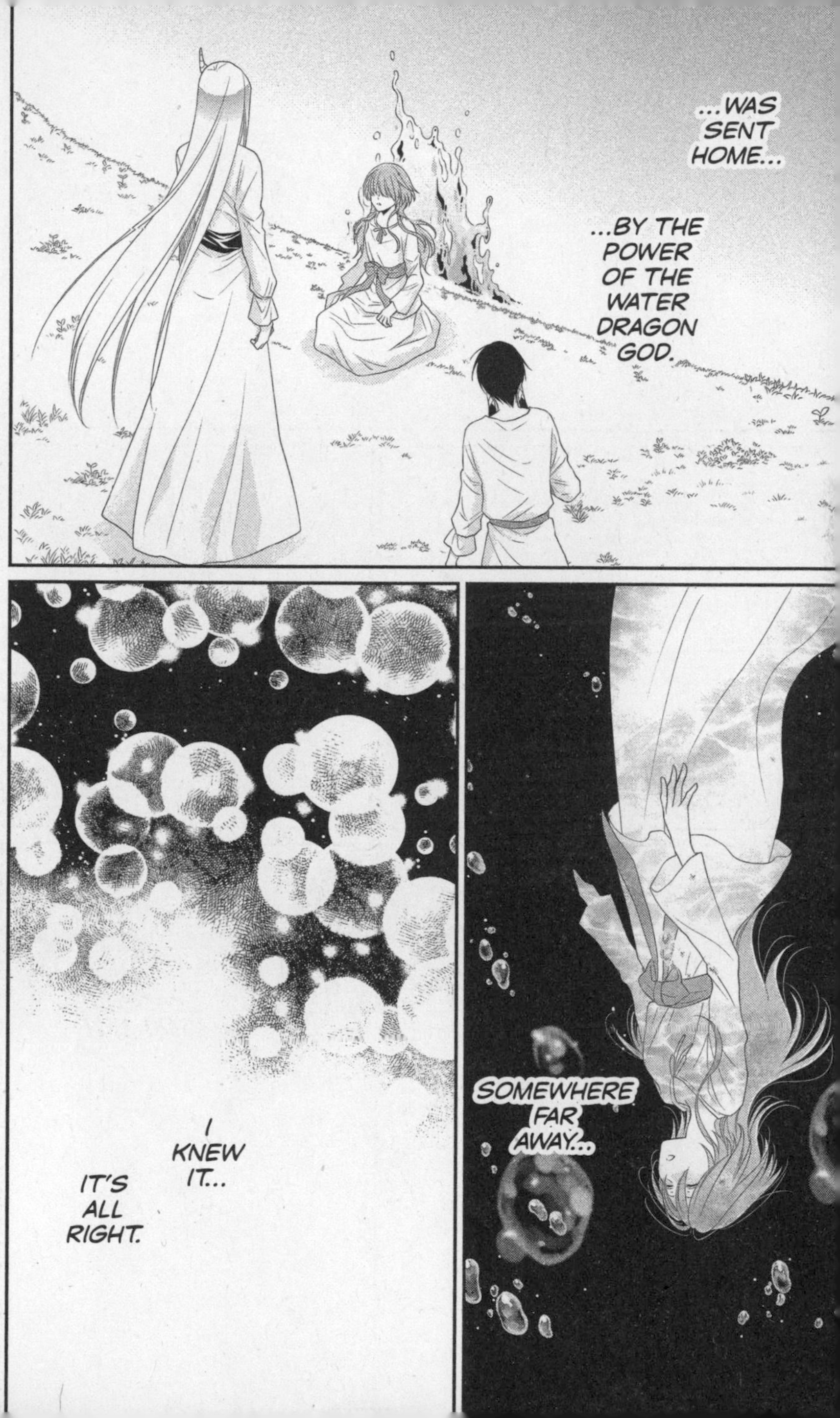
...WAS SENT HOME...
...BY THE POWER OF THE WATER DRAGON GOD.
SOMEWHERE FAR AWAY...
I KNEW IT...
IT'S ALL RIGHT.

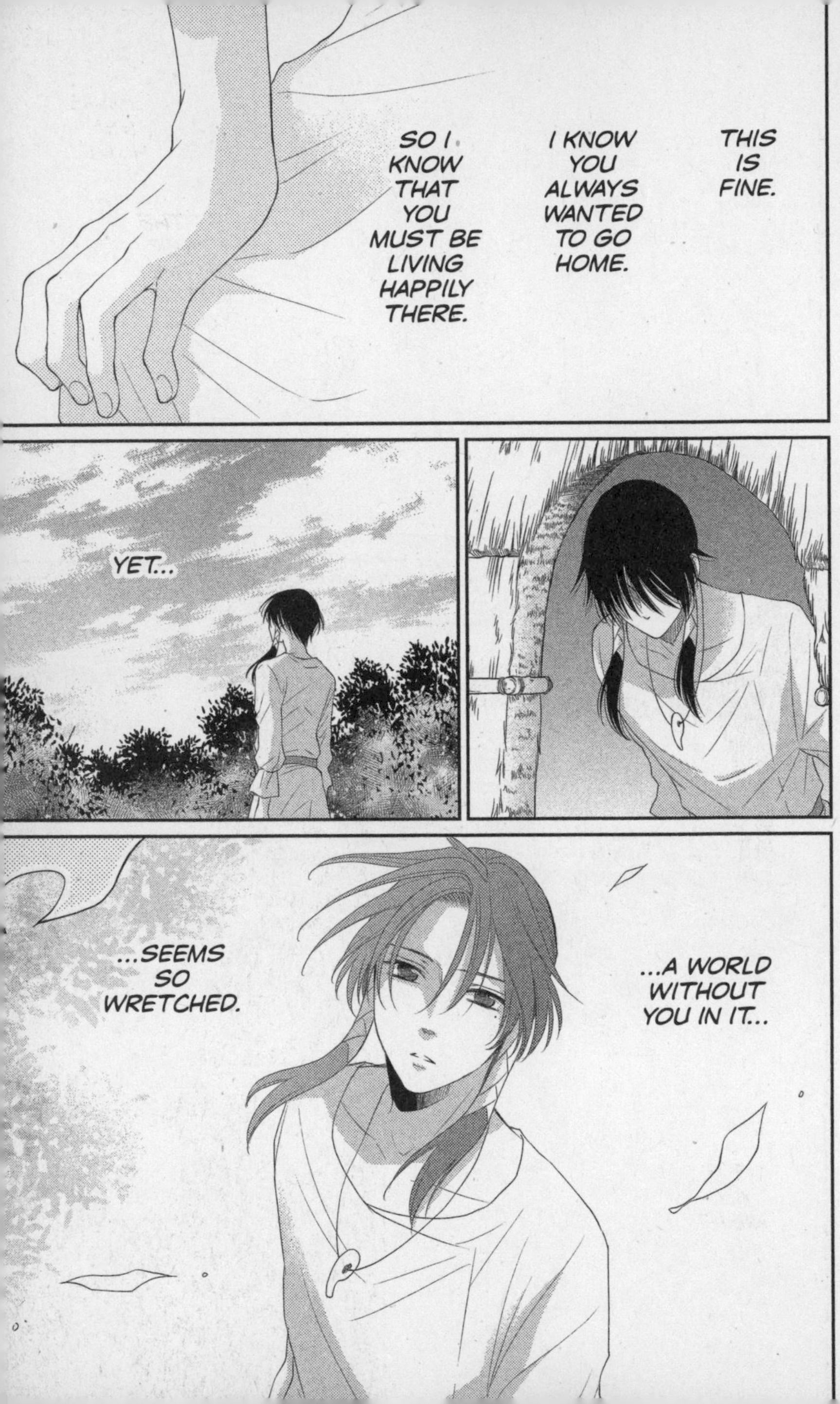
THIS IS FINE.
I KNOW YOU ALWAYS WANTED TO GO HOME.
SO I KNOW THAT YOU MUST BE LIVING HAPPILY THERE.
YET...
...A WORLD WITHOUT YOU IN IT...
...SEEMS SO WRETCHED.

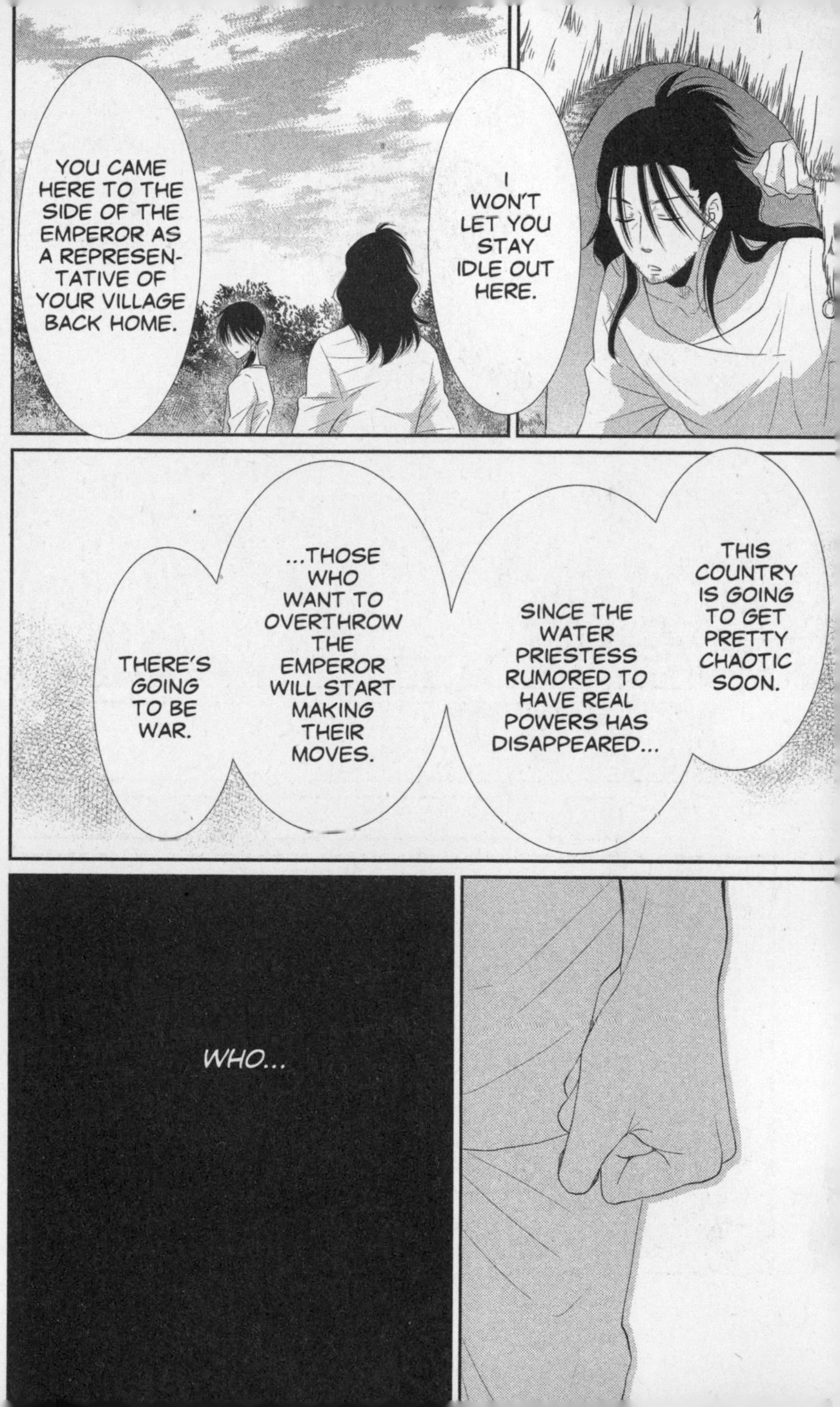
I WON'T LET YOU STAY IDLE OUT HERE.
YOU CAME HERE TO THE SIDE OF THE EMPEROR AS A REPRESEN-TATIVE OF YOUR VILLAGE BACK HOME.
THIS COUNTRY IS GOING TO GET PRETTY CHAOTIC SOON.
SINCE THE WATER PRIESTESS RUMORED TO HAVE REAL POWERS HAS DISAPPEARED...
...THOSE WHO WANT TO OVERTHROW THE EMPEROR WILL START MAKING THEIR MOVES.
THERE'S GOING TO BE WAR.
WHO...

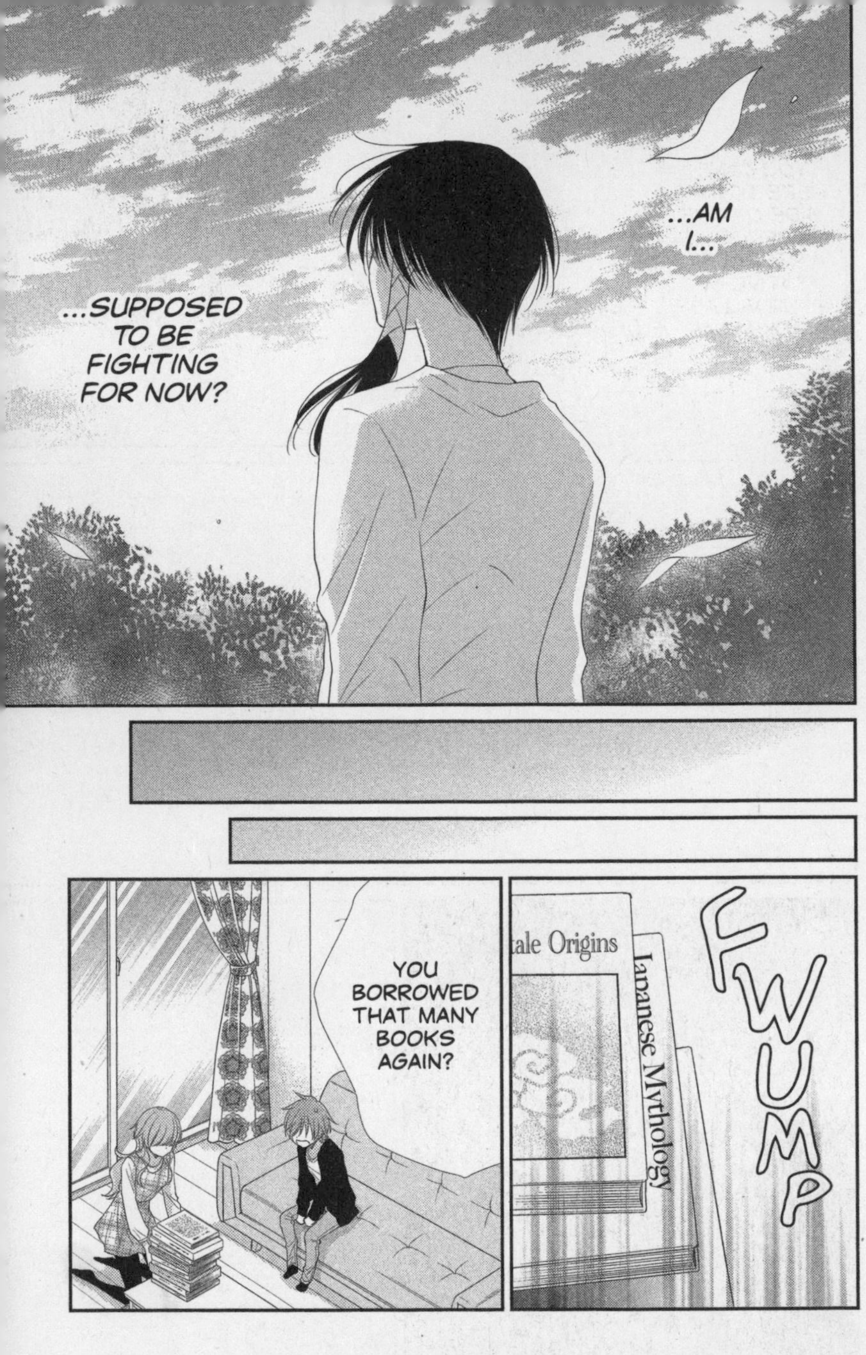
...AM I...
...SUPPOSED TO BE FIGHTING FOR NOW?
FWUMP
tale Origins
Japanese Mythology
YOU BORROWED THAT MANY BOOKS AGAIN?

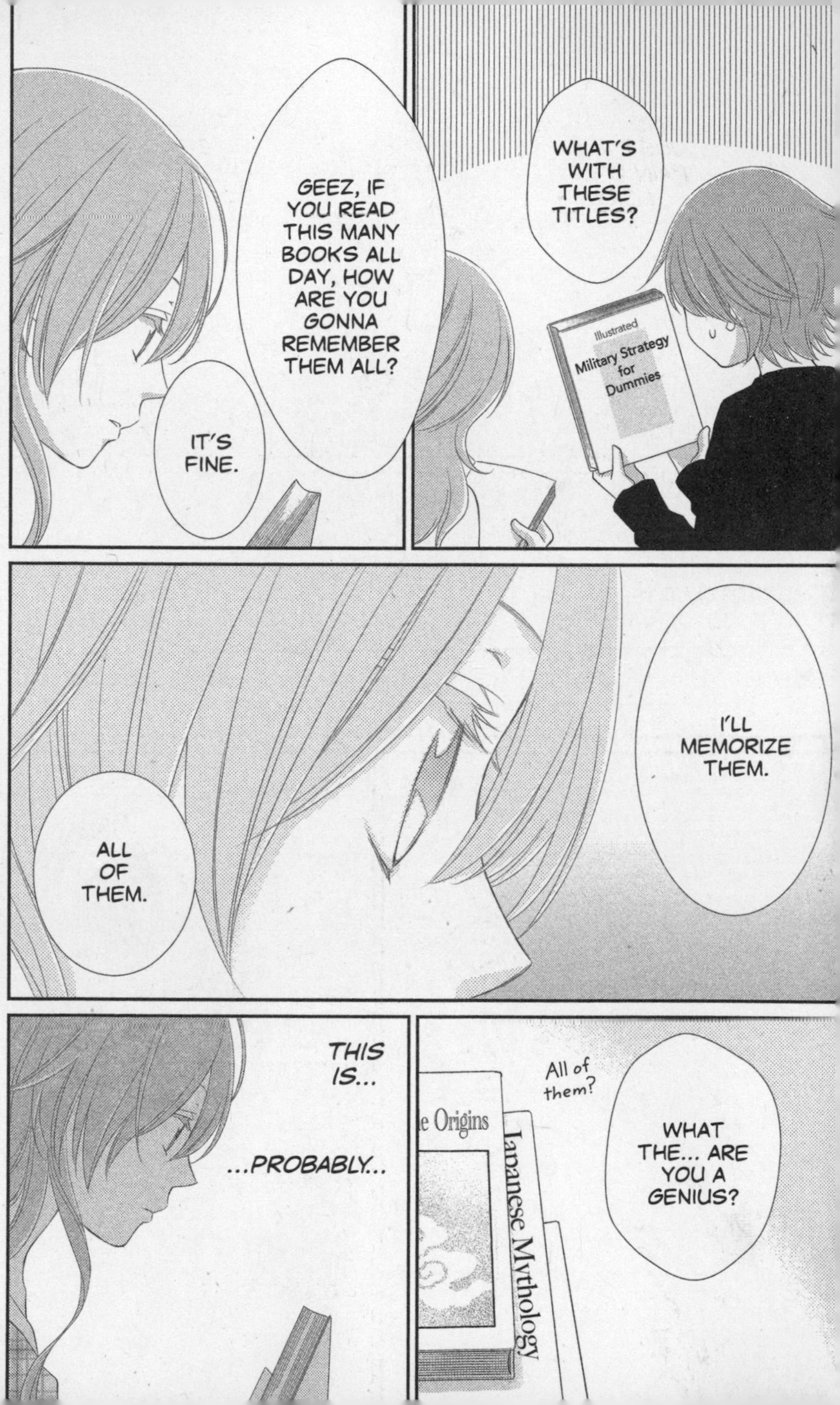
WHAT'S WITH THESE TITLES?
Illustrated
Military Strategy for Dummies
GEEZ, IF YOU READ THIS MANY BOOKS ALL DAY, HOW ARE YOU GONNA REMEMBER THEM ALL?
IT'S FINE.
I'LL MEMORIZE THEM.
ALL OF THEM.
All of them?
WHAT THE... ARE YOU A GENIUS?
e Origins
Japanese Mythology
THIS IS...
...PROBABLY...

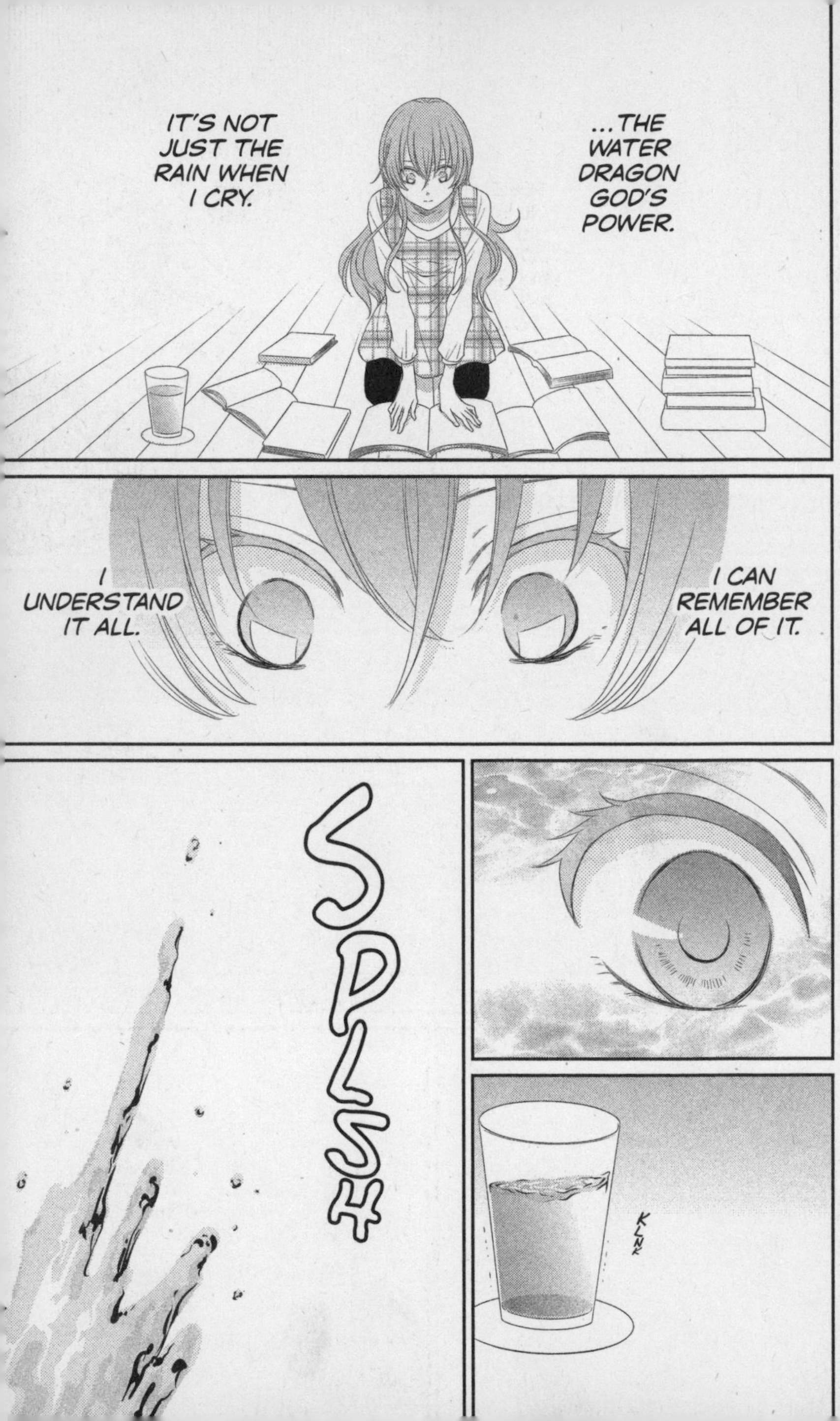
...THE WATER DRAGON GOD'S POWER.
IT'S NOT JUST THE RAIN WHEN I CRY.
I CAN REMEMBER ALL OF IT.
I UNDERSTAND IT ALL.
KLNK
SPLSH

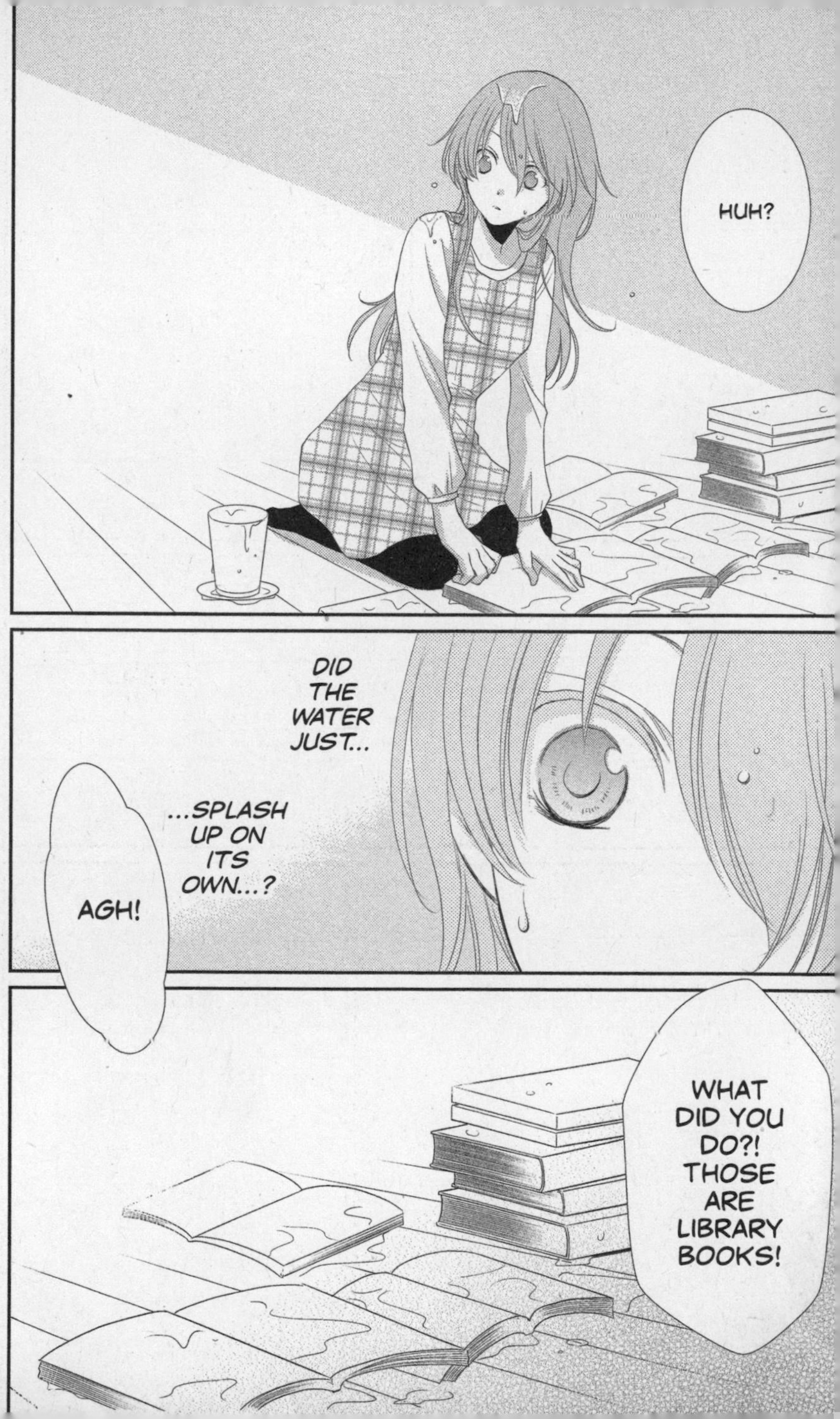
HUH?
DID THE WATER JUST...
...SPLASH UP ON ITS OWN...?
AGH!
WHAT DID YOU DO?! THOSE ARE LIBRARY BOOKS!

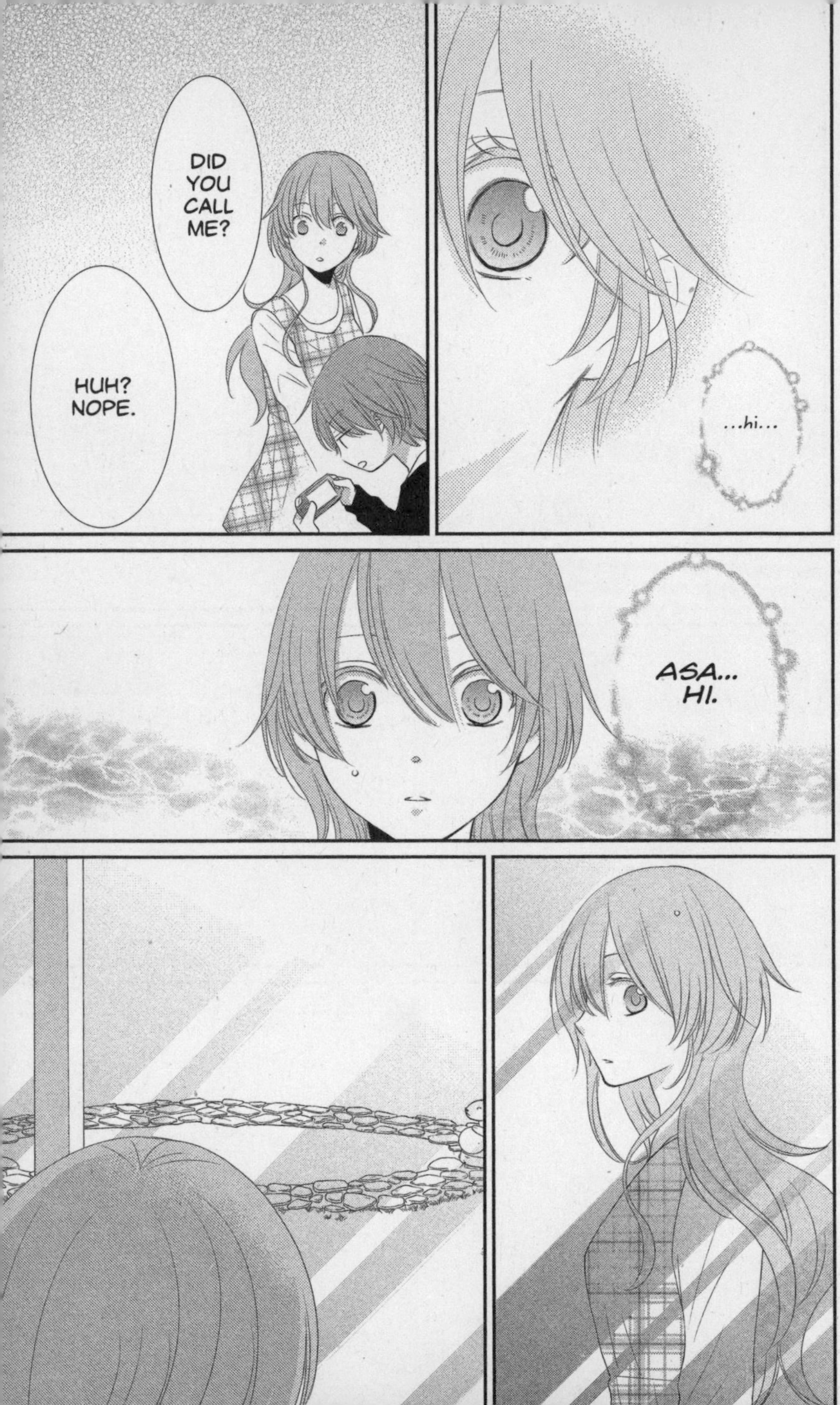
...hi...
DID YOU CALL ME?
HUH? NOPE.
ASA... HI.

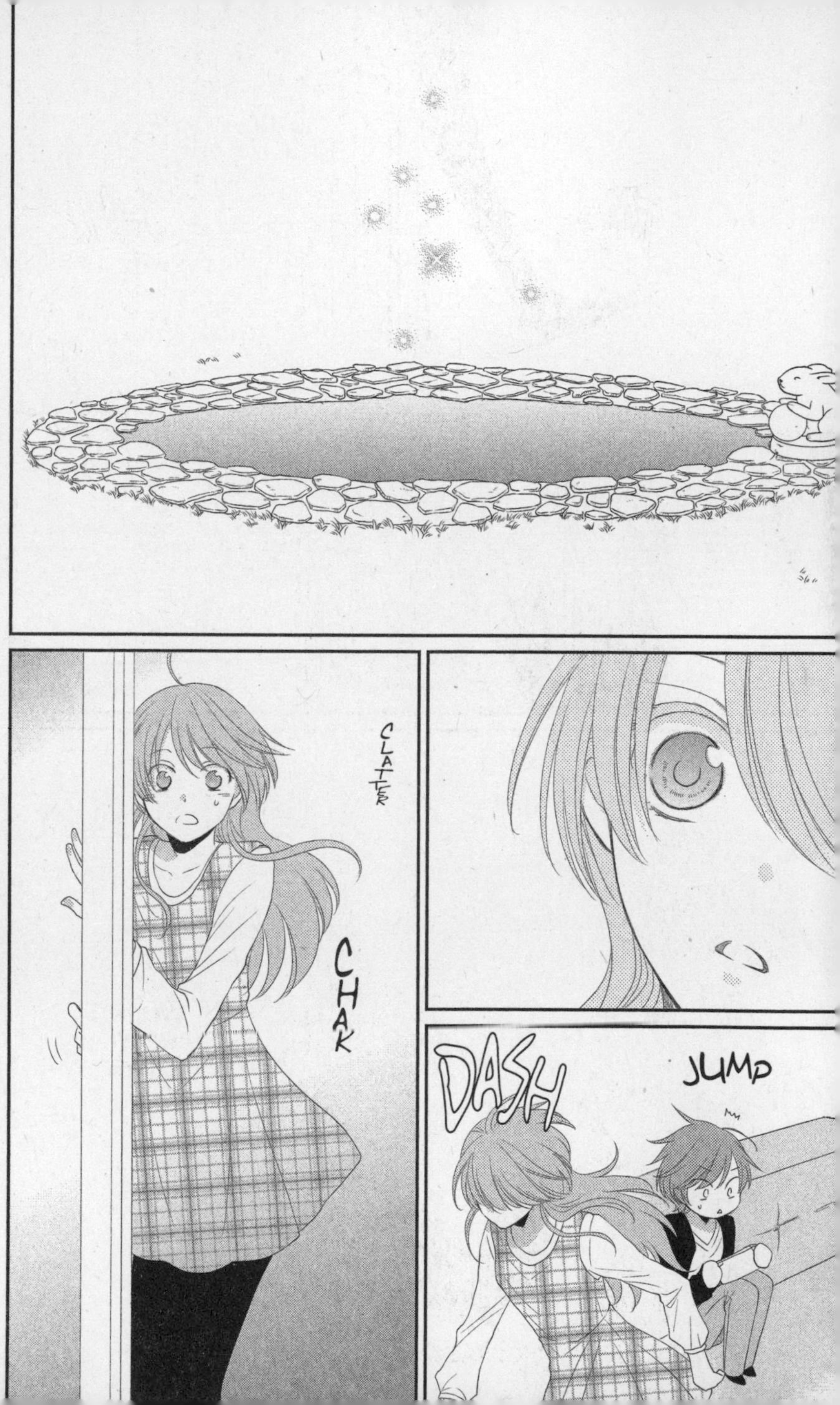
JUMP
DASH
CLATTER
CHAK

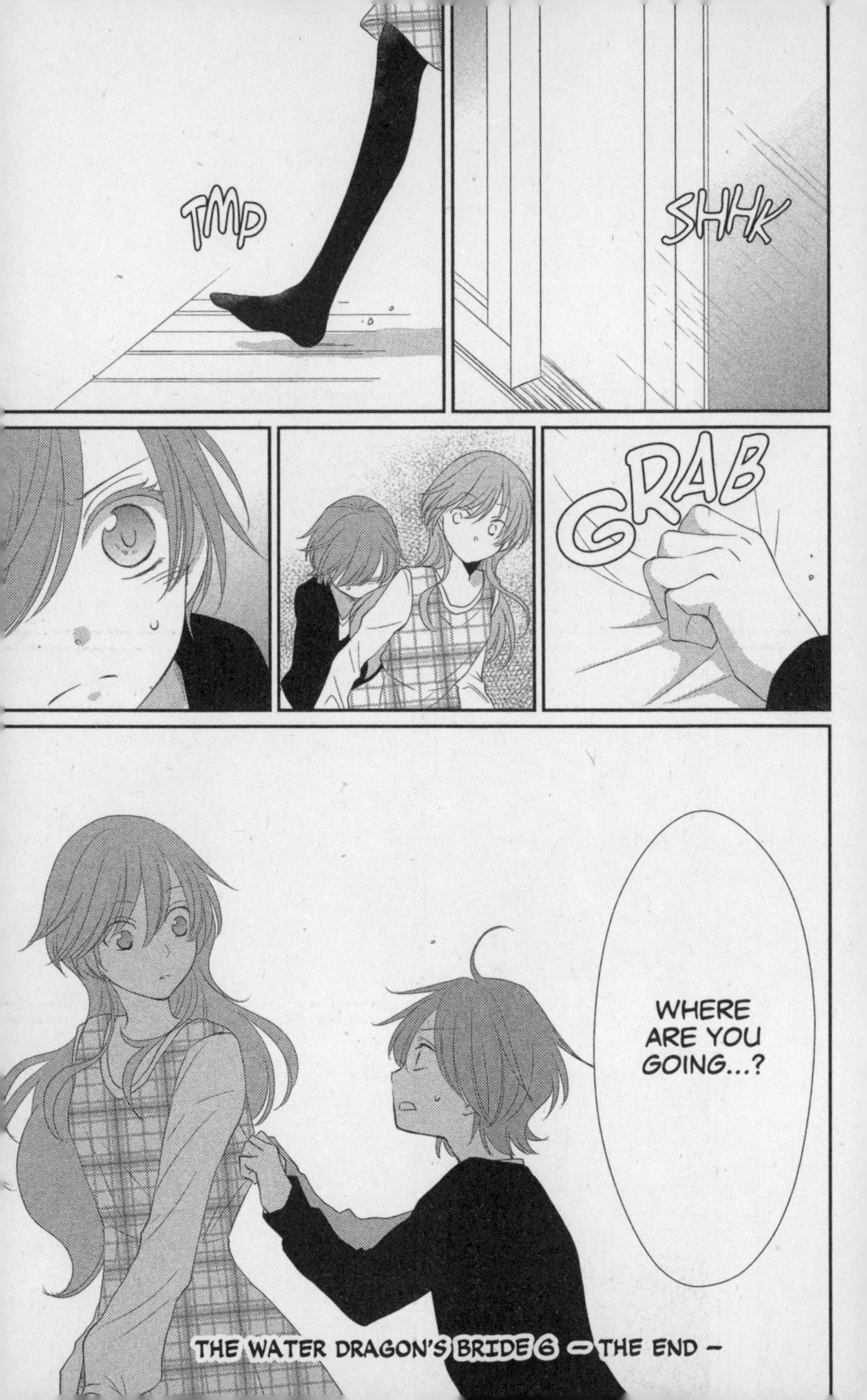
SHHK
TMP
GRAB
WHERE ARE YOU GOING...?
THE WATER DRAGON'S BRIDE 6 — THE END —

# I'VE GOT NO IDEAS, SO HERE'S SOME RANDOM STUFF.

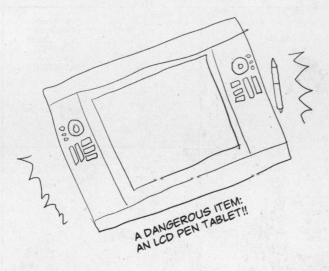

A DANGEROUS ITEM:
AN LCD PEN TABLET!!

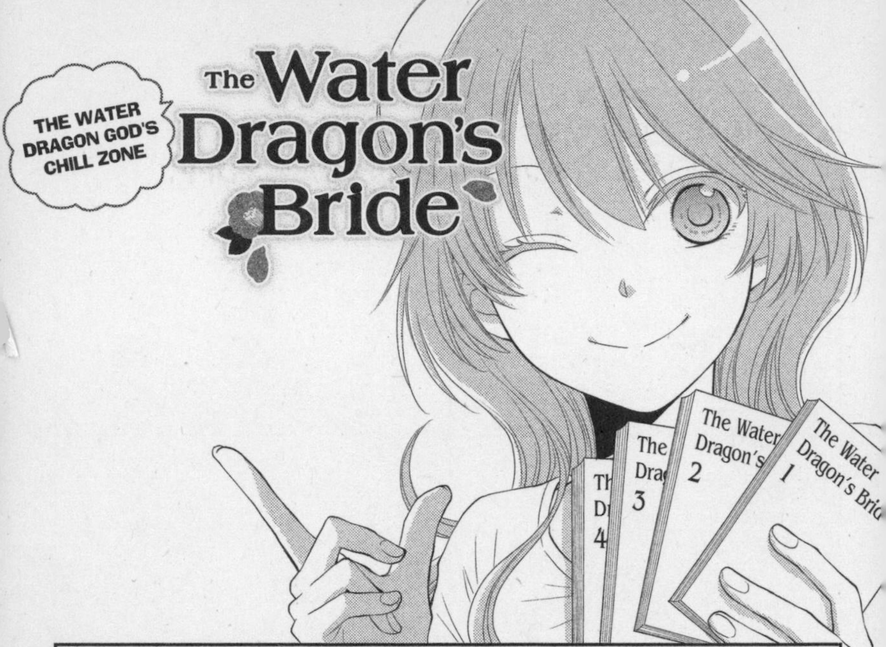
The Water Dragon's Bride
THE WATER DRAGON GOD'S CHILL ZONE
The Water Dragon's Bride 1
The Water Dragon's 2
The Drag 3
Th Dr 4

## Things You Shouldn't Say

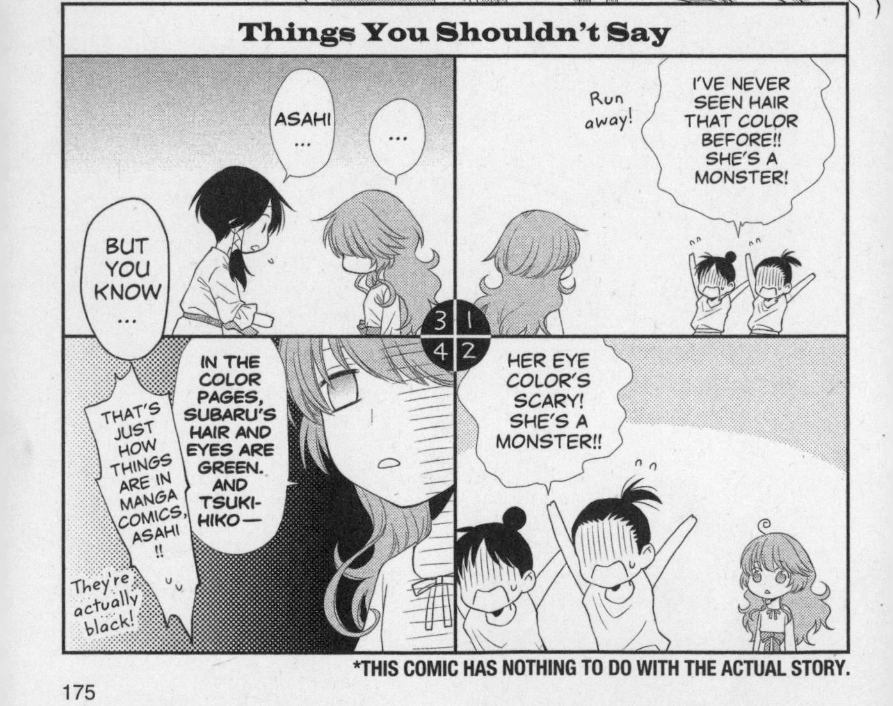
I'VE NEVER SEEN HAIR THAT COLOR BEFORE!! SHE'S A MONSTER!
Run away!
HER EYE COLOR'S SCARY! SHE'S A MONSTER!!
...
ASAHI ...
BUT YOU KNOW ...
IN THE COLOR PAGES, SUBARU'S HAIR AND EYES ARE GREEN. AND TSUKI-HIKO—
THAT'S JUST HOW THINGS ARE IN MANGA COMICS, ASAHI !!
They're actually black!

*THIS COMIC HAS NOTHING TO DO WITH THE ACTUAL STORY.

## Asahi's Comic

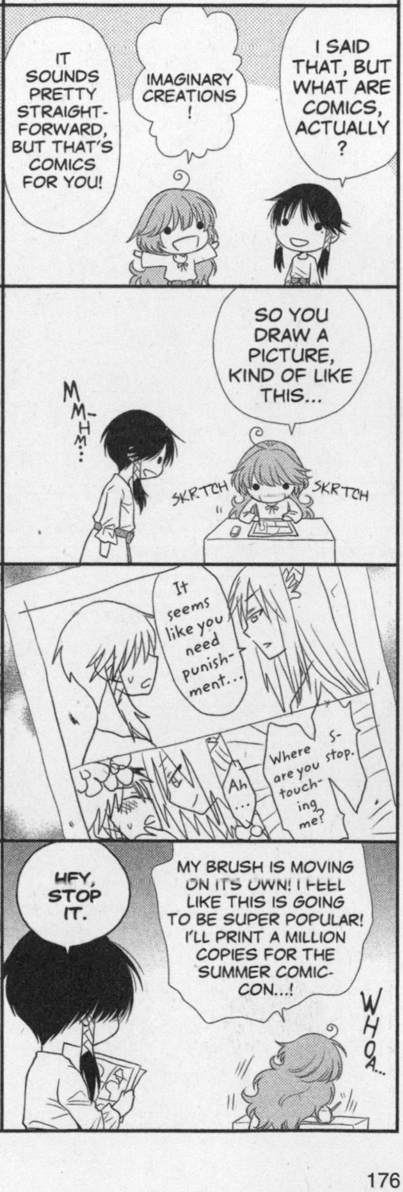
I SAID THAT, BUT WHAT ARE COMICS, ACTUALLY?
IMAGINARY CREATIONS!
IT SOUNDS PRETTY STRAIGHT-FORWARD, BUT THAT'S COMICS FOR YOU!
SO YOU DRAW A PICTURE, KIND OF LIKE THIS...
SKRTCH
SKRTCH
MMHM...
S-stop.
Where are you touching me?
Ah...
It seems like you need punish-ment...
MY BRUSH IS MOVING ON ITS OWN! I FEEL LIKE THIS IS GOING TO BE SUPER POPULAR! I'LL PRINT A MILLION COPIES FOR THE SUMMER COMIC-CON...!
HEY, STOP IT.
WHOA...

## Subaru's Comic

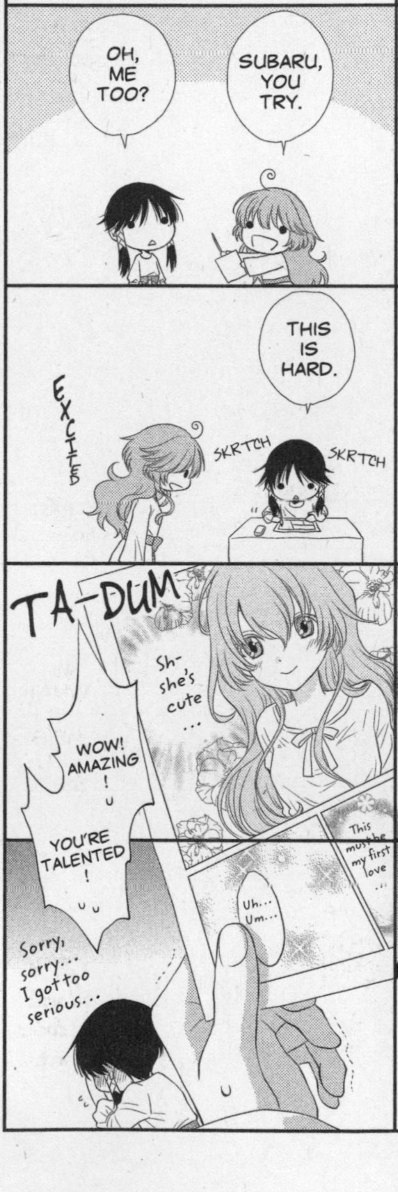
SUBARU, YOU TRY.
OH, ME TOO?
THIS IS HARD.
SKRTCH
SKRTCH
EXCITED
TA-DUM
Sh-she's cute...
WOW! AMAZING! YOU'RE TALENTED!
This must be my first love...
Uh... Um...
Sorry, sorry... I got too serious...

# The Water Dragon God's Comic

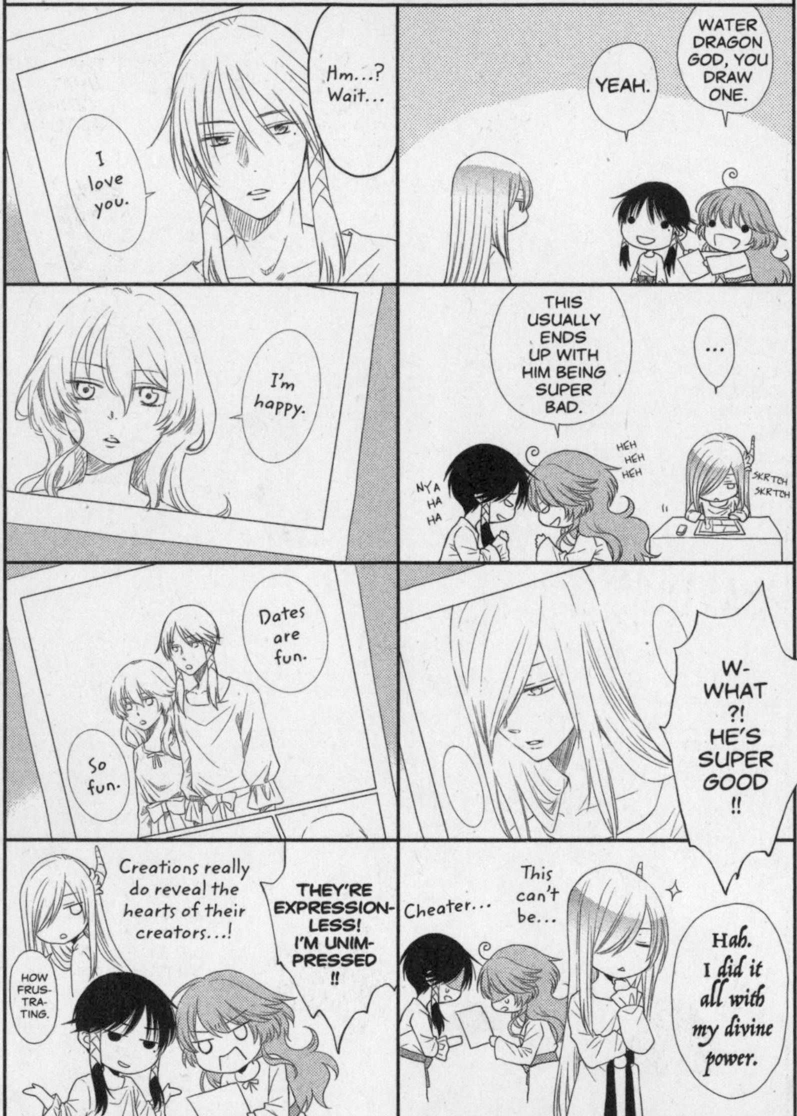
WATER DRAGON GOD, YOU DRAW ONE.
YEAH.
Hm...? Wait...
I love you.
...
THIS USUALLY ENDS UP WITH HIM BEING SUPER BAD.
HEH HEH HEH
SKRTCH SKRTCH
NYA HA HA
I'm happy.
W-WHAT?! HE'S SUPER GOOD!!
Dates are fun.
So fun.
Hah. I did it all with my divine power.
This can't be...
Cheater...
THEY'RE EXPRESSIONLESS! I'M UNIMPRESSED!!
Creations really do reveal the hearts of their creators...!
HOW FRUSTRATING.

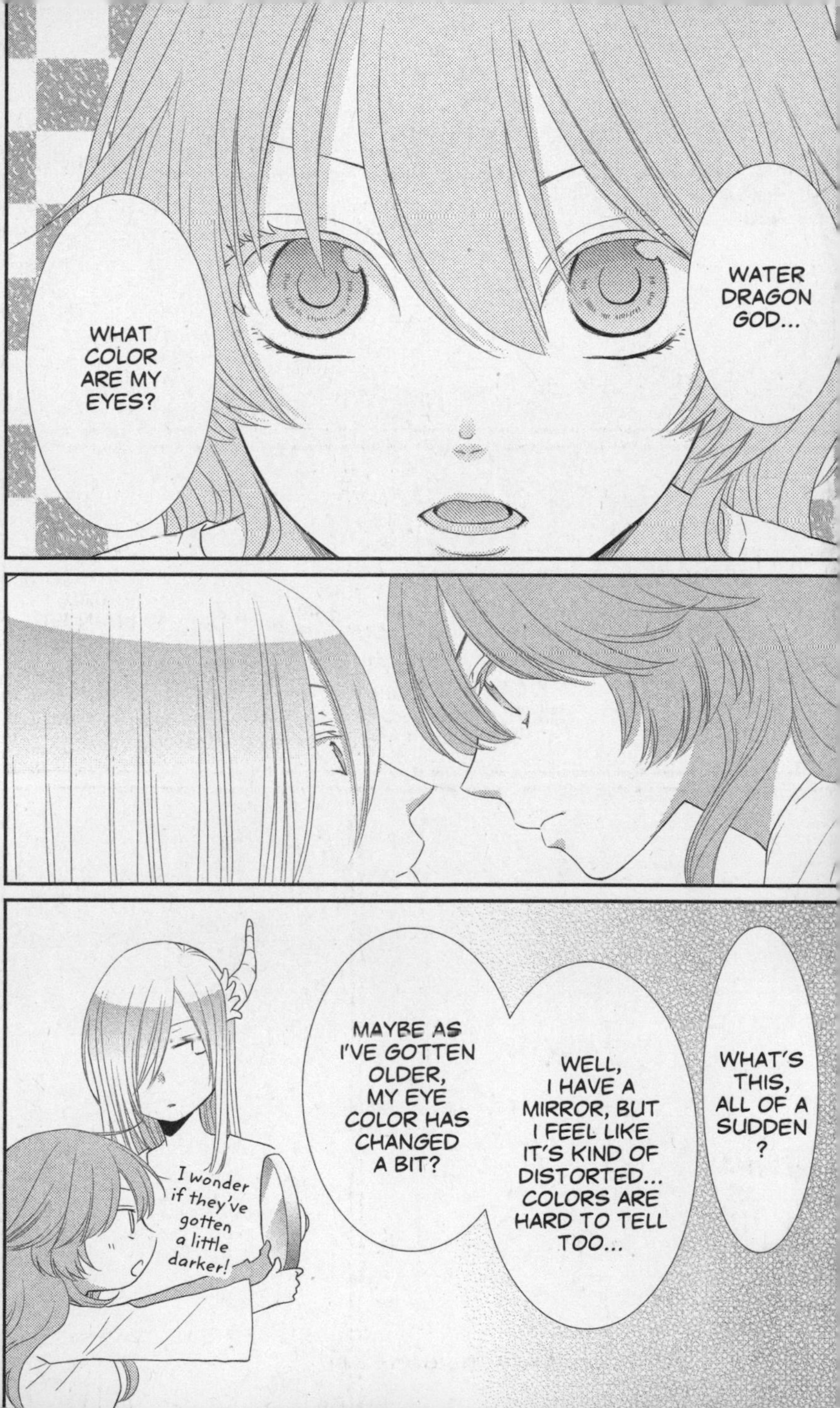
WATER DRAGON GOD...
WHAT COLOR ARE MY EYES?
WHAT'S THIS, ALL OF A SUDDEN?
WELL, I HAVE A MIRROR, BUT I FEEL LIKE IT'S KIND OF DISTORTED... COLORS ARE HARD TO TELL TOO...
MAYBE AS I'VE GOTTEN OLDER, MY EYE COLOR HAS CHANGED A BIT?
I wonder if they've gotten a little darker!

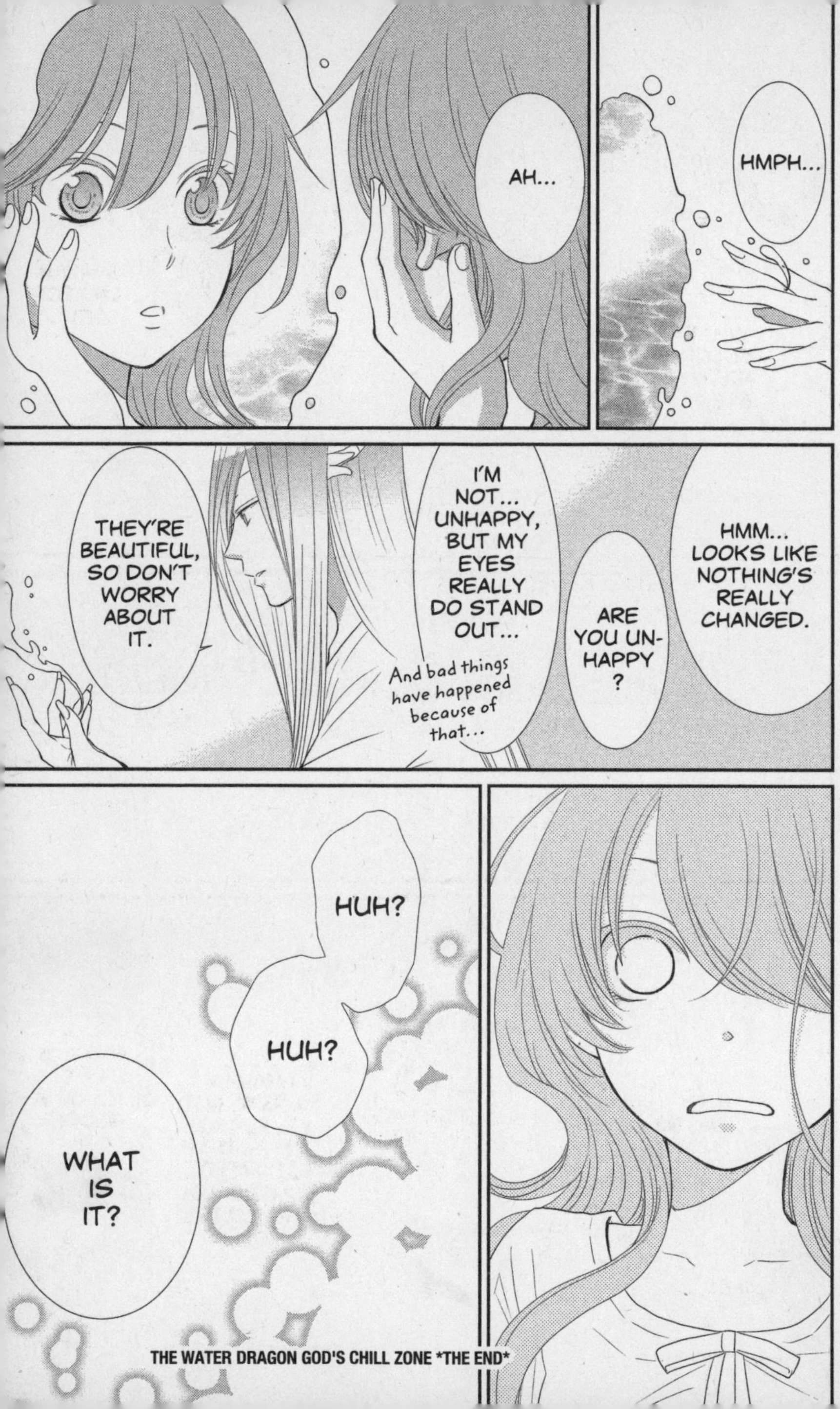
HMPH...
AH...
HMM... LOOKS LIKE NOTHING'S REALLY CHANGED.
ARE YOU UN-HAPPY?
I'M NOT... UNHAPPY, BUT MY EYES REALLY DO STAND OUT...
And bad things have happened because of that...
THEY'RE BEAUTIFUL, SO DON'T WORRY ABOUT IT.
HUH?
HUH?
WHAT IS IT?
THE WATER DRAGON GOD'S CHILL ZONE *THE END*

Thank you so much for all of your letters. I'm always so happy when I read them. Among the letters I've gotten was a letter from the first person I ever sent a fan letter to. I can't believe someone like me could get a letter from them... I thought, "You were my first...!" and other super-ridiculous things, but I was very happy. Earlier, someone else sent me a really beautiful illustration of Subaru on colored paper, and he looked so cool. I'm always so thrilled when I receive beautiful colored art in the mail. I get a lot of other great drawings too, so thank you very much!!

Please send your letters here!
Rei Toma
c/o The Water Dragon's Bride Editor
VIZ Media
P.O. Box 77010
San Francisco, CA 94107

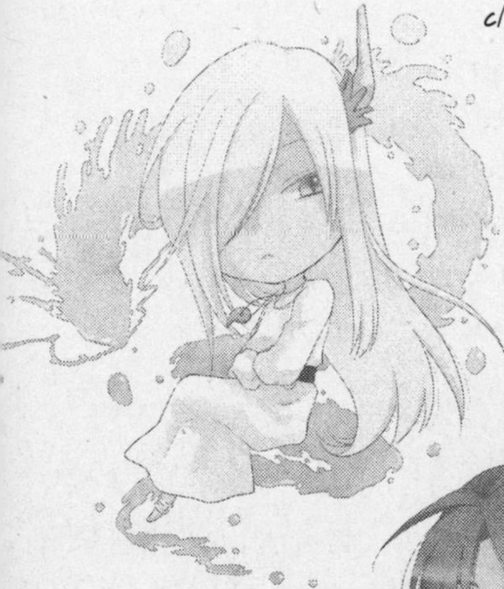

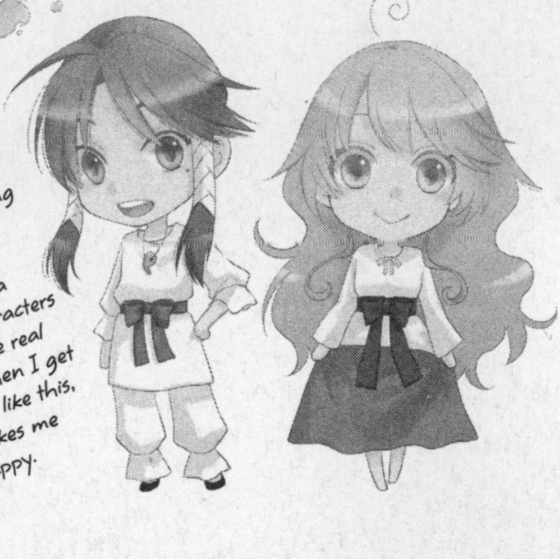

I drew these little caricatures for advertising in bookshops.

I haven't gotten a chance to draw characters in this style in the real comic much, so when I get requests for work like this, it always makes me really happy.